D0882632

THE I TATTI
RENAISSANCE LIBRARY

James Hankins, General Editor

MANETTI
BIOGRAPHICAL WRITINGS

ITRL 9

GIANNOZZO MANETTI

BIOGRAPHICAL WRITINGS

EDITED AND TRANSLATED BY

STEFANO U. BALDASSARRI

AND

ROLF BAGEMIHL

THE I TATTI RENAISSANCE LIBRARY

HARVARD UNIVERSITY PRESS

CAMBRIDGE, MASSACHUSETTS

LONDON, ENGLAND

2003

Printed in the United States of America

Series design by Dean Bornstein

Library of Congress Cataloging-in-Publication Data

Manetti, Giannozzo, 1396–1459.
[Selections. English & Latin. 2003]
Biographical writings / Giannozzo Manetti ; edited and translated
by Stefano U. Baldassarri and Rolf Bagemihl.
p. cm — (The I Tatti Renaissance library ; 9)
Includes bibliographical references and index.
ISBN 0-674 01134-1 (alk. paper)
1. Biography/ I. Baldassarri, Stefano Ugo.
II. Bagemihl, Rolf. III. Title. IV. Series.
CT102 .M26 2003
920—dc21 20020192239

Contents

Introduction

When the Byzantine scholar Manuel Chrysoloras arrived in Florence in February 1397 to teach Greek at the city's university, he brought with him two books that would play a particularly important role in his seminars: Aelius Aristides' *Panegyric of Athens* and Plutarch's *Parallel Lives*. Both great examples of epideictic rhetoric, the former was to show Florentine humanists how to extol a city, the latter how to pen exemplary sketches of remarkable men. In short, these ancient writers provided models for literary representation, just as surviving specimens of ancient art were in that same period providing the inspiration for the contemporary development of portraiture in Renaissance art. The influence of Chrysoloras's teaching proved wide and durable, soon passing beyond the borders of Florentine culture and lasting well into the sixteenth century. Among his disciples, in fact, were some of the leading scholars of the early Quattrocento, in particular the orator, historian and translator Leonardo Bruni — chancellor of the Republic of Florence from 1427 until his death in 1444 — who soon came to be regarded as the model humanist *par excellence*.

The power of Bruni's example did not mean, however, that later humanists passively absorbed the linguistic style, political leanings and cultural ideals of the group centered around Chrysoloras at the close of the fourteenth century. Quite the contrary, the fruitfulness of those seeds planted by the Byzantine teacher — to adopt a common metaphor in Quattrocento literature — is shown by the diverse uses to which those teachings were put. The life and works of Giannozzo Manetti (Florence, 1396–Naples, 1459) bear witness to this. Though a student and an admirer of Bruni, Manetti is far from sharing his innovative and bold stances either with respect to political ideology or literary production. While

rejecting the technicalities and the jargon of scholastic philosophy, he does not hesitate to resort to the tools (above all dictionaries, encyclopaedias, and chronicles) produced by the much condemned "Dark Ages," as many other humanists were to do after him. But let us first take a closer look at his life before introducing the writings collected in this volume.

Born into a wealthy merchant family (according to tax records, in 1427 his father Bernardo was the tenth richest man in Florence), Giannozzo soon entered the business world.[1] Working full time in Bernardo's company, however, did not quench his keen interest in the humanities. As his friend Vespasiano da Bisticci writes in a highly informative biography, at twenty-five Manetti started studying the humanities with great enthusiasm and zeal while keeping his position as head clerk in his father's bank. Within a few years, he managed to master Latin and Greek, thus making a name for himself as a gifted orator and writer. Furthermore, in 1437 he turned to the study of Hebrew, a language which was, at the time, utterly neglected by humanists.[2]

His mastery of Latin, his thriving business, and the support of the Medici faction paved the way for a successful political career. From 1440 to 1453, Manetti was elected to several important posts in the Florentine territory. He was vicar of Pescia and Scarperia (in 1440 and 1452–1453 respectively) and captain of Pistoia in 1446–1447. He also held a number of prestigious offices in the Florentine government. To name only the most important ones, he sat in the following councils: Twelve Good Men (1429, 1438, 1444–1445, 1451), University Trustees (1435, 1445), Sea Consuls (1436–1437 and 1447–1448), Eight on Security (1440–1441 and 1449), and Ten of War (1453). He also served as Standard-Bearer of a militia company (and thus as a de facto member of the town council) no less than three times (1436, 1444, and 1449–1450). Furthermore, the Republic of Florence often sent him as ambassador to important Italian cities and to the papal curia. Among his

main diplomatic missions are the ones to Genoa (1437), Siena (1448), Venice (1448 and 1450), to popes Eugenius IV and Nicholas V (various times between 1441 and 1453), Alfonso of Aragon (repeatedly from 1443 to 1451), and Sigismondo Pandolfo Malatesta, Lord of Rimini (1448). Finally, he led the Florentine embassy in Rome for the imperial coronation of Frederick III in March 1452.

Manetti's career as writer and orator went hand in hand with his political involvement. First, each diplomatic mission demanded at least one lengthy and polished speech (mostly in Latin) to the local authorities. Many such orations soon became veritable bestsellers, as modern studies of his speeches have shown.[3] Secondly, Manetti's earliest texts date from the same years when he entered politics. Between the late 1430s and the early 1440s he authored—to name just his principal works—two *Elogia Ianuensium* (1436–1442), the *Dialogus de Antonini filii sui morte consolatorius* (1438, which he translated into the vernacular the following year), the long collection of biographies *De illustribus longaevis* (1439), the *Vita Socratis and Senecae* (1440) and, in the same year, the lives of Dante, Petrarca, and Boccaccio.

Such remarkable accomplishments inevitably aroused envy and suspicion in some fellow-citizens. After Cosimo's unexpected diplomatic *volte-face* in 1450—which broke the old alliance with Venice in favor of one with the new Duke of Milan, Francesco Sforza—Manetti was repeatedly accused of maintaining excessively strong ties with the Venetian republic. Such charges were not completely without reason. Though a staunch patriot, Manetti had considerable economic interests in Venice. Besides, he had not refrained from criticizing the new course Cosimo had given to Florentine foreign policy. Suspected of being a spy in the service of Venice and burdened with heavy taxes, in February 1453 he finally resolved to leave Florence for Rome. Five months later, Nicholas V made him papal secretary. For the yearly salary of six hundred

ducats, the pope commissioned Manetti to translate the Bible anew and author texts in support of the Christian faith. Though the plan of a complete new translation of the Scriptures fell through, between July 1451 and Nicholas V's death in March 1455 Manetti edited a translation of the Psalms from Hebrew into Latin, accompanied by a defense of this epoch-making version (the *Apologeticus*).[4] Furthermore, he started work on the voluminous *Contra Iudaeos et Gentes*, whose atmosphere of spiritual renewal also marks Manetti's best-known work today: the treatise *De dignitate et excellentia hominis*, dedicated to King Alfonso of Aragon in 1452.[5]

Manetti's stay in Rome did not bring about a complete break with the Florentine authorities. Evidence of this is offered by his election to the Ten of War in June 1453. During this six-month term of office he also delivered a famous speech to Sigismondo Pandolfo Malatesta upon the latter's election as Captain of the Florentine army. However, a permanent return to his native city had become impossible owing to the opposition of such influential citizens as Luca Pitti and Niccolò Soderini.[6] Soon after Nicholas V's death, therefore, Manetti left Rome for Naples to serve as counsellor at the court of his wealthiest dedicatee, Alfonso of Aragon.[7] Despite the handsome yearly salary (nine hundred ducats) paid by the new patron, the humanist's first work in Naples was a celebratory life of the late Nicholas V, completed in 1455.[8] Soon afterwards, he turned to praise the Aragonese ruler by writing the first draft of a *Vita Alfonsi regis*, now lost. He then dedicated the following texts to Alfonso: the *De terrae motu* (a treatise on earthquakes based on a careful reading of the main classical sources) and a translation of two works by Aristotle (the *Magna Moralia* and the *Nicomachean Ethics*). Around 1456 Manetti also entrusted his son Agnolo with the third and last redaction of the *Vita Socratis et Senecae*.[9] Soon after the king's death in June 1458, Manetti's post as counsellor and his salary were confirmed by

Ferdinand, who had succeeded his father to the Aragonese throne. In December of that same year the new pontiff Pius II elected him papal secretary. These, however, were the last honors of his successful career. Nursed by his son Agnolo, who had assisted him on several embassies and in the transcription of most of his books, Manetti died in Naples on 26 October 1459.[10]

In his biography of Manetti, Vespasiano celebrates his late friend as an unparalleled exemplar of civic virtue and scholarship, as the one who, more than any other humanist, had shed luster on the city of Florence.[11] Significantly, his lengthy life of Manetti is placed between (much shorter) lives of Bruni and Poggio Bracciolini. The famous bookseller reiterates these praises in the *Commentary on the Life of Giannozzo Manetti,* a text separate from his collection of lives of illustrious men. All such laudatory statements, to be sure, have to be taken with due caution. Yet there can be no doubt as to Manetti's remarkably vast knowledge. His erudition, his eagerness for learning and desire for fame stand out in all his texts. His literary output is impressive both in its volume and in the variety of its topics, moving as it does from treatises on the dignity of man and translation theory to biographies and works of historiography. At the same time, the flaws of his encyclopaedic knowledge are also clear. Above all, his lack of methodological rigor (particularly his uncritical use of sources) marks a regression if compared with the works of not only Bruni and Bracciolini, but even Salutati. Though fascinated by the rhetoric of his older fellow-humanists and the republicanism they fostered, Manetti's lack of originality makes him a rather conservative figure, both culturally and politically.

The biographies in this volume (including the sketches from *On Famous Men of Great Age* and *Against the Jews and the Gentiles*) bear witness to these features of Manetti's personality.[12] As pointed out above, between the end of the Trecento and the beginning of the

following century this genre enjoyed great popularity in Florence thanks to the rediscovery of classical Greek literature fostered by the teaching of Chrysoloras. In his courses, students read and imitated, above all, Plutarch's lives as well as panegyrics such as Aelius Aristides' praise of Athens, the *Panathenaicus*. This practice, given contemporary relevance by the requirements of personal promotion and political propaganda, gave rise to a flurry of epideictic texts—including, of course, biographies. In a city like early Quattrocento Florence, constantly at war with Viscontean Milan, the celebration of illustrious citizens could prove a useful political tool. Such was the case with Bruni's *Lives of Dante and Petrarca*, which the Florentine authorities commissioned from the chancellor in 1436.

The novelty of this booklet is twofold. On the one hand, Bruni adopts Plutarch's classical pattern to unite for the first time the biographies of the two best-known Florentine men of letters. On the other hand, true to his civic ideology, the chancellor upholds Dante as a model citizen by virtue of his honorable political career, the courage he showed at the battle of Campaldino and his intense cultural activity amidst great hardships. In so doing, Bruni offers a portrait of the distinguished poet in sharp contrast with his main predecessor, Giovanni Boccaccio and his *Treatise in Praise of Dante* (*c*. 1350). There Boccaccio celebrated the author of the *Commedia* as a contemplative spirit, a philosopher forced to enter politics by the corrupt society of his time. According to Boccaccio, Dante's exile and the failure of his marriage to Gemma Donati are proof of his unfitness for social life.

Such, then, were the two main models Manetti could rely on when composing his biography of Dante: Boccaccio's portrait of Dante as a scholastic philosopher and Bruni's celebration of him as a politically engaged intellectual. In light of Manetti's admiration of Bruni, one would expect him to solve this dichotomy by following his mentor's model. He chooses, instead, to mix the two

portraits by reporting as many anecdotes as possible, regardless of their reliability and consistency. In defiance of Bruni's critically-informed skepticism, Manetti revives all the fanciful accounts that in the course of the Trecento had created a legendary aura around the Florentine poet, starting with the dream of Dante's pregnant mother.[13] Such a portrait could only be extremely eclectic, not to say inconsistent; Dante appears at the same time as a solitary philosopher and as a patriot. He is an experienced politician and a moral exemplar who nevertheless abandons his family before being exiled.

As already pointed out, the main reasons for this incoherent sketch are Manetti's undiscriminating use of his sources and his tendency to accumulate information regardless of its reliability or provenance. In essence, he copied down all the information he found on a certain topic. He then rearranged the sources thus collected, often without making significant changes in the language and the syntax of the original. This procedure also accounts, at least in part, for his redundant style and the shortcomings of his prose (repetitions, slips, mistakes in the use of tenses and moods, especially the subjunctive). More important still, Manetti's style, with its lavish use of rhetorical figures, is a clear sign of his personality, including his political attitudes.[14] His ideology can be summed up as follows: power should be celebrated, regardless of its form, as long as law and order are preserved in defense of the Christian faith and in the interests of the mercantile class. A fairly simplistic view, to be sure, though sufficient perhaps to support his main moral tenets: religious orthodoxy and civic virtue.

In this light, his long career as a businessman, writer and ambassador in three cities as different as Florence, Rome and Naples ceases to appear contradictory. As we have seen, after serving as rhetorician for a republic, he became secretary to pope Nicholas V, the humanist and bibliophile, before ending as a handsomely paid counsellor to a king as authoritarian as Alfonso of Aragon. Most

likely, the desire to protect his economic interests played a role in these decisions. He was, first and foremost, a merchant, and it must be kept in mind that the Aragonese king granted him and his family extraordinary commercial privileges.[15] Despite his modern image as a republican thinker, his rhetoric was in many ways more fitted to celebrate the glorious triumphs of a kingdom than the wayward aggrandizement of a republic. In a sense, Manetti can be said to anticipate the spirit and the language of the Italian academies of the late Renaissance, when the lack of political freedom forced intellectuals to limit their erudition to exercizes in epideictic literature.[16]

What has just been said of Manetti's life of Dante also applies to the other biographies in this volume. With respect to the biographies of Petrarca and Boccaccio, it is important to note that Manetti is the first to bring together the lives of the so-called "Three Crowns of Florence." His laudatory aim is evident throughout. In the case of Petrarca, the portrait is particularly idealized owing both to the poet's self-celebration in his epistles (Manetti's main source) and to the pseudo-hagiographic cult which his Augustinian friends had developed about him. Petrarca is thus presented as a kind of humanist Father of the Church, a new Saint Jerome who alternates intense study with mystical raptures. Yet the importance of Manetti's biographies collected here does not simply lie in their indebtedness to late medieval sources. More importantly, all of them, from the lives of the "Three Crowns" to the excerpts in *On Famous Men of Great Age* and *Against the Jews and the Gentiles* (including, to a lesser extent, the *Lives of Socrates and Seneca*), show the Florentine humanists' great self-awareness concerning the rediscovery of classical culture they were promoting. This is particularly clear in two texts: Manetti's lives of Petrarca and Boccaccio and his sketches of famous humanists collected at the end of Book VI of *Against the Jews and the*

Gentiles.[17] Above all, it is in Boccaccio's biography that Manetti—for once true to Bruni's teaching—traces the history of the rediscovery of Greek culture between the end of the Trecento and the beginning of the following century. There he also comments with remarkable keenness on the gradual development of Latin prose from Petrarca's epistles to the polished style of contemporary humanists. Manetti's patriotism thus culminates in the praise of Petrarca and Boccaccio as the harbingers of a long-lasting cultural renewal centered in Florence.

Finally, specific attention should be paid to the *Lives of Socrates and Seneca*. First of all, it is noteworthy that these two biographies, clearly patterned after Plutarch's model, originally circulated together with those of the "Three Crowns of Florence." This is attested to not only by a number of manuscripts containing all five of these works but also by Manetti's own words as preserved in a letter to Vespasiano.[18] The present edition thus recreates the original unity of these five biographies. In this light, an interpretation of the *Lives of Socrates and Seneca* becomes easier. The portraits of the two classical philosophers and those of the three Florentine men of letters emerge as complementary. In Manetti's opinion, the hero-martyr Socrates, being a kind of prototype of Christ, shows the compatibility of the classical heritage with the Christian faith—a typically humanist belief.[19] On the other hand, making good use of Tacitus' rediscovered *Annales*, he presents Seneca as a philosopher who taught how to steer a middle course between the cynicism of politics and an intense spiritual life. Manetti, in fact, believes in the authenticity of Seneca's relationship with Saint Paul and defends him from the charge of hypocrisy for his attitude towards Claudius and Nero.[20] In Manetti's eyes, the way Seneca faced death after being charged with plotting against the much-hated emperor is the ultimate proof of his moral dignity.

The "Three Crowns of Florence" are thus upheld by Manetti as the modern response to classical antiquity. By virtue of their moral

worth and unparalleled scholarship, they are deemed fit to be compared with their great classical predecessors. Indeed, their Christian faith, when combined with the greatness of their literary achievement — all the more remarkable for having followed a long period of cultural decadence — makes Manetti regard them as superior to the ancients. As such, the lives collected here constitute an important chapter in the long history of the *querelle des anciens et des modernes*.

Stefano U. Baldassarri
Florence, June 2002

NOTES

1. For information on Manetti's family and his business and political career see L. Martines, *The Social World of the Florentine Humanists 1390–1460* (Princeton: Princeton University Press, 1963), esp. pp. 131–138 and 176–191; and N. A. Eckstein, *The District of the Green Dragon: Neighbourhood Life and Social Change in Renaissance Florence* (Florence: Olschki, 1995), esp. pp. 23–24 and 165–167.

2. On Manetti's study of Hebrew see C. Trinkaus, *'In Our Image and Likeness': Humanity and Divinity in Italian Humanist Thought* (London: Constable, 1970), vol. II, pp. 571–601, and C. Dröge, *Giannozzo Manetti als Denker und Hebraist* (Frankfurt am Main: Lang, 1987).

3. H. W. Wittschier, *Giannozzo Manetti: Das Korpus der Orationes* (Köln-Graz: Böhlau, 1968).

4. See A. De Petris's introduction to his critical edition of the *Apologeticus* (Rome: Edizioni di storia e letteratura, 1981) and Dröge, *Giannozzo Manetti*.

5. On this treatise see O. Glaap, *Untersuchungen zu Giannozzo Manetti, 'De dignitate et excellentia hominis': Ein Renaissance-Humanist und sein Menschenbild* (Stuttgart-Leipzig: Teubner, 1994). On Manetti's theory of the dignity of man see also Trinkaus, *Image and Likeness*, vol. I, pp. 230–270, and C. Dröge, "Zur Idee der Menschenwürde in Giannozzo Manetti's *Protesti di giustizia*," *Wolfenbüttler Renaissance-Mitteilungen*, 14 (1990), pp. 109–123.

6. On Manetti's later political career and his opponents, see W. J. Connell, "The Humanist Citizen as Provincial Governor," in *Florentine Tuscany: Structures and Practices of Power*, ed. W. J. Connell and A. Zorzi (Cambridge: Cambridge University Press, 2000), pp. 144–164, esp. pp. 161–163.

7. On Manetti's sojourn in Naples and his role at the Aragonese court see J. H. Bentley, *Politics and Culture in Renaissance Naples* (Princeton: Princeton University Press, 1987), pp. 60–61, 122–127, and 209–212.

8. See the informative essays by Anna Modigliani and Massimo Miglio in Modigliani's Italian translation of the *Vita Nicolai V* (Rome: Roma nel Rinascimento, 1999), pp. 9–67. Modigliani is preparing a critical edition of this work.

9. On the three redactions of the *Vita Socratis et Senecae*, originally dedicated to the Spanish nobleman Nuño de Guzmán then to Alfonso of Aragon in 1450, see A. De Petris's critical edition (Florence: Olschki, 1979), pp. 42–44. For Manetti's relationship with the Guzmán family see J. N. H. Lawrance, *Un episodio del proto-humanismo español: Tres opúscolos de Nuño de Guzmán y Giannozzo Manetti* (Salamanca: Biblioteca Española del Siglo XV, 1989).

10. On Giannozzo's son Agnolo see G. M. Cagni, "Agnolo Manetti e Vespasiano da Bisticci," *Italia medioevale e umanistica*, 14 (1971), pp. 293–312.

11. The best study on Vespasiano's lives of Manetti remains H. W. Wittschier, "Vespasiano da Bisticci und Giannozzo Manetti," *Romanische Forschungen*, 79.3 (1967), pp. 271–287. See also A. Greco, "Giannozzo Manetti nella biografia di un contemporaneo," *Studi umanistici piceni*, 3 (1983), pp. 155–170, reprinted in idem, *La memoria delle lettere* (Rome: Bonacci, 1985), pp. 59–84.

12. See my article, "Clichés and Myth-Making in Giannozzo Manetti's Biographies," *Italian History and Culture*, 8 (2002), pp. 15–33.

13. On the contrast between Bruni's boldness of conception and Manetti's traditionalism, see R. Fubini, "Leonardo Bruni e la discussa recezione dell'opera: Giannozzo Manetti e il *Dialogus* di Benedetto

Accolti," in idem, *L'umanesimo italiano e i suoi storici* (Milan: Franco Angeli, 2001), pp. 104–129, esp. pp. 118–122.

14. See the excellent essay by M. Martelli, "Profilo ideologico di Giannozzo Manetti," *Studi italiani*, 1.1 (1989), pp. 5–41.

15. See Bentley, *Politics and Culture*, pp. 60–61, and M. Del Treppo, *I mercanti catalani e l'espansione della corona d'Aragona nel secolo XV* (Naples: L'Arte Tipografica, 1967), pp. 272–275. See also the document published by P. Fanfani in Vespasiano da Bisticci, *Commentario della vita di Messer Giannozzo Manetti* (Turin: Unione Tipografico-Editrice, 1862), pp. 159–161.

16. As pointed out by C. A. Madrignani, "Di alcune biografie umanistiche di Dante e Petrarca," *Belfagor*, 18 (1963), pp. 42–48.

17. Much work still needs to be done on the *De illustribus longaevis* and the *Contra Iudaeos et Gentes*, both still unpublished. As for the former, in 1436 Lapo da Castiglionchio dedicated to Manetti a Latin translation of a work by Lucian on the same topic. Lucian's *Octogenarians*, however, is very different from the *De illustribus longaevis*. It is more likely that Manetti derived the idea for this collection of lives from a letter by Petrarca; see *Familiares* 6.3 ("de optimis atque lectissimis senibus"). As for the *Contra Iudaeos et Gentes*, an unfinished apologetic text in defense of the Christian faith, see Trinkaus, *Image and Likeness*, vol. II, pp. 726–734 and Dröge, *Giannozzo Manetti*, pp. 65–85. See also the following articles: N. Badaloni, "Filosofia della mente e filosofia delle arti in Giannozzo Manetti," *Critica storica*, 2.4 (1963), pp. 418–434; A. De Petris, "L'*Adversus Iudaeos et Gentes* di Giannozzo Manetti," *Rinascimento*, ser. 2, 16 (1976), pp. 193–205, and G. Fioravanti, "L'apologetica anti-giudaica di Giannozzo Manetti," *Rinascimento*, ser. 2, 23 (1983), pp. 3–32.

18. See Manetti's letter dated Rome, 23 November 1454, in G. M. Cagni, *Vespasiano da Bisticci e il suo epistolario* (Rome: Edizioni di storia e letteratura, 1969), p. 132.

19. On the importance of Manetti's sketch of Socrates see M. Montuori, *Socrates: Physiology of a Myth* (Amsterdam: Gieben, 1981), pp. 3–18. On p. 11 Montuori writes: "The fundamental aspects which Manetti had specially stressed when sketching the humanity of Socrates, such as his

exemplary moral and civil virtues and the serenity and nobility with which he faced an unjust death, acquired a permanent place in modern Socratic mythology. From whatever angle the Socratic message is understood, it is an unquestionable fact that from Manetti onwards Socrates has symbolized the just man unjustly accused." A third edition of this work was published in Italian under the title *Socrate: Fisiologia di un mito* (Milan: Vita e pensiero, 1998).

20. See esp. par. 29 in the present edition of the *Vita Senecae*.

BIOGRAPHICAL WRITINGS

TRIUM ILLUSTRIUM POETARUM FLORENTINORUM VITA

Praefatio

1 Non alienum fore putavimus si post laboriosum ac prolixum *Longaevorum* opus quod nuper in sex libris conscripsimus, singulas trium illustrium nostrorum poetarum vitas, recreandi animi gratia, latinis litteris mandaremus. Nam cum in memorato *Longaevorum* nostrorum volumine cuncta prope maiora omnium virorum facta, qui vel sanctitate morum vel excellentia doctrinae vel rerum gestarum gloria penes unamquamque gentem diutius floruerunt, ab origine orbis supra quinque annorum milia breviter repetita simul collegerimus atque ex his omnibus velut unum florum undique decerptorum corpusculum effecerimus, quis sanae mentis descriptionem rerum vel domesticarum vel civilium nostrorum poetarum nobis alienam, seu non potius propriam et peculiarem fore censebit, qui tot et tantas non modo nostrorum et Latinorum sed etiam Graecorum et externorum vitas — partim penuria scriptorum, partim negligentia temporum apud nos obscuratas et paene deletas, partim etiam per multiplices et varios codices passim hinc inde dispersas — nuper e tenebris in lucem revocavimus atque nimirum prostratas humi iacentesque in terra in unum ereximus atque extulimus?

2 Nisi si quis forte dixerit haec ipsa quae nos in praesentiarum scribere instituimus a pluribus doctissimis simul atque eloquentissimis viris iampridem fuisse descripta. Quod equidem non nego, sed me primum Dantis vitam ab Ioanne Boccacio, viro eruditissimo, materno sermone editam, et a Leonardo postea Arretino, omnium nostri temporis eloquentissimo, eiusdem poetae simul atque Petrarchae gesta florentino idiomate elegantius conscripta le-

LIVES OF THREE ILLUSTRIOUS FLORENTINE POETS

Preface

We thought it not unsuitable, having recently completed a long and laborious work in six books *On Famous Men of Great Age*, to write in Latin for the sake of relaxation the lives of our three illustrious poets. In fact, having summarized, collected and inserted in the aforementioned work on men of great age a nosegay, as it were, containing nearly every important deed of all men from every country who in the over five thousand years since the creation of the world have distinguished themselves for the piety of their habits, the excellence of their doctrine and their military glory, what sensible person would think it unfit for us to describe the private and public lives of our poets? It is rather highly appropriate and fitting, given that we have recently rediscovered, collected and published not only the lives of many important fellow citizens and representatives of the Latin-speaking world, but also those of Greeks and foreigners. They had fallen into oblivion and neglect owing partly to the paucity of writers, partly to the indifference of the times, and partly because they had been dispersed here and there in many different manuscripts. 1

Yet some may argue that numerous learned and eloquent men have already discussed the topic I have chosen at the present time. Far from denying it, I admit that Giovanni Boccaccio, a most erudite author, first wrote a life of Dante in the vernacular, followed by Leonardo [Bruni] of Arezzo, the most eloquent man of our 2

gisse fateor; quamquam etiam Philippus Villanus, inter hos duos eruditissimos viros temporibus interiectus, nonnulla de florentinis illustribus viris latinis litteris in opusculum quoddam redegerit. Quocirca hunc scribendi laborem frustra assumpsisse videbor, quandoquidem de eisdem rebus a plurimis non indignis auctoribus scriptum constat, nisi paucis causas prius assignavero quae me ad scribendum compulerunt.

3 Dantem, Petrarcham et Boccacium, tres illos peregregios poetas nostros, quorum vitas in hoc codice nuper adumbravimus, usque adeo in vulgus consensu omnium claruisse constat, ut nulli alii hac vulgari opinione paene illustres poetae a conditione orbis fuisse videantur; quod ideo contigisse arbitror, quoniam illi cum carmine tum soluta oratione in hoc materno scribendi genere ceteris omnibus praestiterunt, cum in latina lingua multis non modo veteribus sed etiam novis nostri temporis scriptoribus inferiores appareant. Itaque quemadmodum apud vulgares homines litterarum ignaros et omnis doctrinae imperitos praeclari viri in maxima et ingenii et eruditionis admiratione habentur, ita apud eruditos et doctos cuncta passim vulgaria scripta, in quibus illi excelluisse perhibentur, floccipendentes et pro nihilo habentes parvi existimantur et fiunt. Ita evenit ut plerumque ab ignaris et indoctis hominibus laudentur, eruditorum vero nullus vel poemata vel fabulas aliave eorum scripta, nisi forte vel ridendi vel iocandi gratia, aliquando in manus sumit.

4 Quod longe aliter evenire intelligimus quam meritis tantorum virorum laudibus convenire videatur, ac etiam secus sibi accidisse arbitramur quam vel viventes concupissent vel nunc mortui cuperent, si quis illis rerum nostrarum sensus esset. Omnes enim eruditi viri quicumque ullo umquam tempore fuerunt illustrium ac laudatorum hominum laudes, frivolis ceterorum commendationibus posthabitis, etiam atque etiam adamaverunt, ut Hector ille naevianus agebat, qui nonnisi a laudato viro laudari cupiebat; quod non ab Hectore, cuius fortassis illa sententia non erat, sed a Nae-

time, who composed another, more elegant life of Dante in the Florentine dialect, paired with a life of Petrarca.[1] Finally, Filippo Villani, too, who happened to live in between these two most erudite men, wrote a booklet in Latin on renowned Florentines.[2] The work I am about to start may thus seem useless, since numerous worthy authors have already treated the subject. So let me put forth briefly my reasons for writing it.

Dante, Petrarca, and Boccaccio, our three extraordinary poets 3
whose lives I have sketched in this latest work of mine, seem to have received so much praise from the many that no other poets since the beginning of the world can boast of such fame among the common people. In my opinion, the reason for this lies in their superiority to all other vernacular writers both in verse and prose, whereas in Latin they are clearly inferior not only to many ancient writers but also to more recent writers of our own times. Consequently, while the common people, who are illiterate and uneducated, hold these famous men in the highest esteem for their intellect and erudition, the erudite and the learned, on the other hand, despise and dismiss the vernacular writings at which they excelled as if they were worth little or nothing. So it happens that they are praised to the skies by illiterate and uneducated people, whereas learned men take up their poems or their stories, if ever, only to amuse themselves.

This outcome, in our opinion, is not at all in keeping with 4
either the merits of these great men or with what they would have desired were they alive (or perhaps still hope for after their death, supposing they have any consciousness of the things of this world). In all ages, the learned have always adored receiving praise from illustrious and praiseworthy men, despising all other commendation as worthless, just like Hector, the character in Naevius, who longed only for the praises of praiseworthy men (which, we believe, reflects not so much the opinion of Hector, who probably never said that, but of Naevius, the great poet).[3] Now, if the

vio peregregio poeta dictum accepimus. Quod si docti homines eruditorum virorum laudes, ceterorum non ita exoptant et cupiunt, profecto poetas nostros vel parvifacere, si res humanas curant, has omnes imperiti et illaudati vulgi commendationes, vel parum excellentibus eorum laudationibus ex his vulgaribus gestorum suorum scriptis satisfactum fuisse existimandum est.

5 Ad haec etiam illud accedit, quod Boccacius Dantem dumtaxat expressit; Leonardus vero et Dantis et Petrarchae vitas, tertio penitus omisso, in unum coniunxit. Haec pauca ad duos illos eruditissimos viros dixisse sufficiat. Ad Villanum autem, qui, non ut illi singularissimi viri vulgares nostrorum poetarum vitas, sed latinas effecit, aliter respondendum esse censemus. Legimus enim eius eum librum qui *De florentinis illustribus viris* inscribitur, in quo omnes omnium nostrorum vitas — quicumque vel armis, vel scientia, vel arte, vel facultate quadam excelluerunt — in unum congessit. Unde et nonnullorum principum et medicorum et theologorum et iurisconsultorum et poetarum denique et pictorum laudes admiscuit, quod cum facere conatur, id profecto effecisse videtur, ut horum nostrorum poetarum laudationes ieiune et exiliter, quasi mendicans in angustiis nescio quibus compingeret atque in angulis quibusdam coartaret, et non ex rerum gestarum ubertate affluenter redundaret ac paulo latius explicaret.

6 Quapropter ego his singularissimis civibus nostris atque peregregiis etiam poetis pro virili mea succurrere aggressus, novas eorum vitas latinis litteris mandavi, idque praecipue ea causa adductus feci, ut maximas eorum laudes, quae in plebecula hactenus latere videbantur, ad eruditos et doctos viros tandem aliquando conferrem, qui vulgaria cunctorum hominum scripta, qualia pleraque nostrorum poetarum praecipua et habentur et sunt, semper contemnere atque floccipendere consueverunt.

learned desire and hope only for praise that comes from erudite men, and not from anybody else, we must conclude that these poets of ours, if they care at all for human affairs, either care little for the commendation of the ignorant and the unknown, or find unsatisfactory the lavish praise they have received from these vernacular biographers.

We must also add that Boccaccio only treated Dante, while Le- 5
onardo put together the lives of Dante and Petrarca, omitting the third. This may suffice as regards those two highly erudite men. Things are different, however, as regards Villani, who, unlike those extraordinary men, did not write the lives of our poets in the vernacular but in Latin. We have read that book of his entitled *Illustrious Florentines,* in which he collected the lives of all our fellow citizens who have excelled in the arms, the sciences, the arts or in any other field. He then appended the praise of various rulers, doctors, theologians, jurisconsults, poets and painters. In so doing, he touched on these praiseworthy poets of ours dryly and succinctly, as though starved of sufficient materials, almost cramming them into a corner of his book instead of writing effusively and at length about the wealth of their accomplishments.

Having thus decided to assist as best I can these outstanding 6
fellow citizens and extraordinary poets, I have written their lives in Latin. Above all, I was moved by the desire to have their great merits, hitherto hidden among the common people, spread to the erudite and the learned, who until now have despised and dismissed all works of vernacular literature, of which our poets are duly regarded as the chief ornaments.

7 Dantes, poeta clarissimus, ex urbe Roma, ut ipse quodam loco innuere videtur, originem traxit. Principium vero generis ab Helisaeo quodam—ex Frangipanorum, ut quidam ferunt, familia—inveterata opinione hominum referebat. Florentiam quippe a sullanis militibus diu antea conditam, seu ab Attila Hunnorum, seu potius a Totila Gothorum rege, confuso propter similitudinem utriusque vocabulo, vel funditus vel certe aliqua ex parte deletam utcumque fuisse constat; quam quidem Carolus, inclitus Francorum rex, trecentos, si ab Attila eversam, si vero a Totila ducentos post eversionem circiter annos egregie admodum recondiderat, cui profecto, ob rerum a se gestarum magnitudinem, Magno cognomen erat.

8 Per haec igitur ipsa reconditionis tempora, Helisaeus quidam romanus egregius praeter ceteros adulescens Florentiam accessisse perhibetur. Hic enim romanus adulescens sive multiplices ac propemodum infinitas clades Romanis primum a Gothis, deinde a Vandalis, postremo rursus saepius a Gothis inflictas fugiens, sive a Carolo illo Romanorum Augusto, veterem eorum ritum imitato, ad inhabitandum noviter urbem una cum multis aliis romanis colonis transmissus accesserit, incertum est; certe tamen, per ea quae scripta sunt, Florentiam applicuisse creditur. Romani namque ab illis barbaris gentibus, quas paulo ante commemoravi, varias et quasi infinitas omnium prope generum clades iam diutius pertulerant; ad inhabitandum quoque noviter urbes novos colonos iampridem mittere consueverant, quibus praedia colenda atque inhabitandas sedes tradebantur. Unde has civium deductiones consignationesque agrorum 'colonias' appellabant. Huius igitur accessionis suae sive hanc, sive illam causam, utramvis accipiendam equidem censeo; quamquam enim una verisimilior altera esse videatur, utra tamen seorsum esse potuit.

Dante, that most famous poet, was descended from ancestors 7
originally from Rome, as he himself seems to suggest in one of his writings.[4] According to an old belief, the first of his stock was a certain Eliseo, a member, as some say, of the Frangipani family. It is well known that Florence, which had been founded by some soldiers of Sulla, was destroyed—whether completely or in part is not certain—either by Attila, king of the Huns, or by Totila, king of the Goths, such uncertainty deriving from their similar names.[5] It was then admirably refounded by Charlemagne, the great Frankish king, either three hundred years later, if it had been destroyed by Attila, or about two hundred years later, if it was Totila who destroyed it. Understandably, Charles was given the title "The Great" for his mighty deeds.[6]

It was at the time of this refoundation, so it seems, that a cer- 8
tain Eliseo, a gifted young man from Rome, came to Florence. It is uncertain whether at the time this young Roman was trying to flee the innumerable and almost endless defeats that first the Goths, then the Vandals, and finally the Goths again, had inflicted on the Romans, or if he had been sent by the famous Charles, emperor of the Romans, following the old custom, to repopulate that city together with many other Roman settlers. It is certain, however, as written records attest, that he went to Florence. The Romans in fact had for a long time suffered various and almost endless defeats of all sorts from the above-mentioned barbarous peoples; they had thus started repopulating cities by sending settlers, to whom they gave land to cultivate and houses to inhabit. These transfers of citizens and allotments of land were called "colonies." I am not sure which one of these two causes made him move, or whether it was both causes acting together; although one might seem more plausible than the other, both causes could have operated separately.

9 Cum per longa deinde tempora huius Helisaei genus multum admodum propagaretur, in magnam demum sobolem evasit; proinde factum est ut vetusto patritiae familiae suae nomine abdicato, ab Helisaeo, primo eorum Florentiae habitatore, Helisaei omnes vocarentur. In hac itaque clarissima Helisaeorum familia, multo post tempore per ordinem successionis, quendam natum esse ferunt magni ingenii ac potentiae virum, nomine Cacciaguidam; qui, ob sua quaedam praeclara in re militari gesta sub Currado imperatore militans, egregia militiae insignia non immerito reportavit. Hic igitur nobilis Cacciaguida, Moronto et Helisaeo duobus fratribus suis omissis ceu ad propositum nostrum[1] minime pertinentibus, virginem quandam forma viribusque praestantem e clara quadam Aldigherorum Ferrariensium familia in matrimonium accepit, ex qua cum plures filios suscepisset, unum ex multis, ut uxori morem gereret, nomine familiae uxoris suae 'Aldigherum' cognominavit, quamquam 'd' littera, ut in plerisque fit, euphoniae causa e medio sublata, pro Aldighero 'Aligherum' appellaret. Huius profecto tanta ac tam clara virtutum opera extiterunt, ut eius posteri, quemadmodum olim maiores sui, pristino familiae nomine prorsus[2] extincto, pro Frangipanis Helisaei cognominati sunt, ita nunc pro Helisaeis Aligheri ab eo undique nominarentur. Ex hoc igitur primo praeclaroque Alighero, inter multos ab ipso per longa tempora oriundos, demum, Federico secundo imperante, alter Aligherus extitit, qui Dantis eius, de quo haec scribimus, parens fuit.

10 In tanta itaque et tam clara familia natum illum ferunt millesimo ac ducentesimo supra sexagesimum quintum christianae salutis anno, vacante ob mortem iam memorati Federici romano imperio, sedente autem Clemente quarto in summo pontificatu. At vero praegnanti matri, paulo ante quam pareret, mirabile quoddam in somniis phantasma apparuisse perhibent. Namque in viridi prato iuxta limpidum fontem sibi consistere videbatur, ibique sub procera admodum lauru apparebat filium parere; qui cum bac-

Eventually, the offspring of the said Eliseo multiplied until they grew into a large family. Thus it happened that, abandoning the old patrician family name, they named themselves the Elisei after Eliseo, their first ancestor to move to Florence. Into this distinguished family of the Elisei, at a much later time, a man of great intelligence and power was born, Cacciaguida by name, who, in recognition of his heroic military deeds while fighting under the Emperor Conrad, was duly rewarded with important distinctions. This noble Cacciaguida — leaving aside his two brothers, Moronto and Eliseo, as much less significant for our discourse — married a wealthy and beautiful girl from the distinguished Ferrarese family of the Aldighieri,[7] who bore him several children, one of whom, in compliance with his wife's wishes, he named Aldighiero after his wife's family. This child, however, was later called "Alighiero," instead of Aldighiero, omitting the "d," as often happens, to make it sound better. He performed so many famous and meritorious deeds that his descendants started to be called Alighieri instead of Elisei, just as earlier the family name had been changed by their ancestors from Frangipani to Elisei. From this first and illustrious Alighiero, after a long time in which many other descendants were born, came another Alighiero, who lived during the reign of Emperor Frederick II and was the father of the Dante of whom we are writing. 9

He was born into this large and distinguished family in the 1265th year of Christian salvation, when the Roman imperial throne was vacant owing to the death of the said Frederick and when Clement IV was pope. They say his pregnant mother had a wondrous vision in her sleep shortly before giving birth.[8] She saw herself sitting in a verdant meadow by a clear fountain. There, under a great laurel tree, she gave birth to her son. The latter fed on 10

chis lauri cadentibus tum quoque limpidi fontis aquis egregie nutritus, pastor tandem evadebat, ac dum de frondibus lauri, iam pastor effectus, carpere conaretur, primum cadere, deinde in pavonem postea conversus surgere videbatur.

11 Haec et huiusmodi egregia praegnantium mulierum somnia, in praecipuis praesertim liberorum partubus, vera esse vel facile crediderim. Nam et de Dionysio Siciliae tyranno et de Marone nostro poetarum omnium praestantissimo, et de nonnullis denique aliis praestantioribus viris, praegnantes eorum matres per quietem egregia quaedam vidisse ab optimis auctoribus scriptum esse constat. Quippe praegnans Dionysii mater satyriscum parere visa est; consulti harioli ceterorum omnium potentissimum clarissimumque futurum responderunt. Virgilii itidem mater, puerperio propinqua, laureum ramum edere videbatur, quem quidem coalitum in mirabilem maturae arboris speciem paulo post excrevisse ac variis pomis floribusque refertum esse cernebat. Postridie vero Maronem enixa est. Cum haec igitur aliaque huiusmodi ab optimis auctoribus scripta esse videantur, non sane intellego cur de poeta nostro tam eximio tamque celebrato eiusmodi somnia in eodem prope visionum genere nedum vera extitisse credere, sed pro comperto habere ac vera fuisse oracula per ea quae postea subsecuta sunt existimare certissime debeamus, praesertim cum a gravi quodam auctore et imprimis omnia poetae gesta observante scriptum esse manifestissime appareat.

12 Infantem itaque per hunc modum egregie admodum natum ac laeta satis patrimonii fortuna receptum, quasi de industria factum esset, recto nomine faustisque ominibus Dantem, ceu futura praesagentes, appellarunt, quem optimae ac propemodum divinae indolis fuisse tradunt. Nam ut primum per aetatem discere potuit, mox prima litterarum elementa—quamquam cuiusdam formosissimae puellae, mirabile dictu, ardentissimis amoribus teneretur—mirum tamen in modum ob quandam ingenii sui excellentiam celeriter arripuit. In quos quidem amores, quoniam mirabile quid-

the berries falling from the laurel tree and the water of the clear fountain, until he grew up and became a shepherd; once a shepherd, he tried to pick the laurel branches but fell and turned himself into a peacock, flying away.

I tend to regard as true these remarkable dreams of pregnant women and other such things, especially if they are pregnant with babies who will become important men. Excellent authors, in fact, tell us of the amazing dreams of the mother of Dionysus, tyrant of Sicily, and of our Vergil, the most outstanding of all poets, as well as those of other famous men.[9] The mother of Dionysus dreamt that she was giving birth to a baby satyr; having consulted the augurs, they responded that he would become the most powerful and most famous of all men. Likewise, on the verge of childbirth Vergil's mother dreamt that she was giving birth to a laurel branch, which grew in a remarkable way until it became a fully grown tree laden with fruits and flowers. The following day she was delivered of Vergil. Since such things and the like are attested by excellent auhors, I do not understand why — far from doubting the authenticity of such dreams concerning our most distinguished and celebrated poet — we should not take them as unquestionably true and reliable foretokens of what was going to happen, especially when the source is a serious author writing unambiguously about the poet from first-hand information. 11

Born in such a remarkable way into a fairly rich family, his parents, as if foreseeing the future, deliberately chose for him — who, they say, was endowed with an excellent, almost divine nature — the right name and one of good omen: Dante. In fact, once old enough to start learning, he went through grammar school with incredible speed thanks to his remarkable intelligence, despite be- 12

dam visum est, quemadmodum tam parvulus tamque repente inciderit, non alienum fore putavi, singula vitae suae gesta per ordinem prosecutus, huic loco opportune inserere, praesertim cum ipse quodam librorum suorum loco praecipuam quandam eius rei mentionem fecerit.

13 Erat per ea tempora inveterata civium consuetudo quotannis kalendis Mai catervatim per vicos ac vicinias mulieres atque viros, una congregatos, domi cuiusdam ex finitimis splendidissime epulari festumque diem pro more choris, cantibus, symphoniis, variis denique omnifariam instrumentorum sonis speciosissime celebrare. Quocirca nobilis quidam civis e clara Portinariorum familia, nomine Fulcus, hunc veterem celebrandi ritum egregie secutus, forte mulierum virorumque catervas ea die domi suae congregaverat. Inter ceteros vero Aligherus, quem Dantis nostri parentem diximus, velut hospiti finitimus, aderat, ac secum parvulus filius, nono fere aetatis suae anno, forte accesserat. Solemni deinde convivio celebrato mensisque remotis, Dantes seorsum, ut pueri solent, cum aequalibus ludebat; cetera vero turba maior natu choris, cantibus, sonis dedita erat.

14 In magno alludentium puerorum coetu forte parvula quaedam hospitis filia consistebat; Bicem appellabant, quamquam ipse pro 'Bice' semper 'Beatricem' significantius soleat appellare. Haec quidem ita generosa, ita venusta, ita denique morigera erat, ut eam octavo circiter aetatis suae anno, quemadmodum ipse quodam loco scriptorum suorum manifeste testatur, moribus egregie praeter ceteras aequales uti videretur. Haec itaque et huiuscemodi praecipua in generosa puella divinae indolis puer vehementer admiratus, eius amoribus, incredibile dictu, illico captus est, et ita quidem captus, ut huiuscemodi amores, teneris pueri ossibus ac medullis impressi inustique, vehementius inhaererent. Quin immo usque adeo inhaeserunt, ut non modo dum puella viveret numquam dimitteret, sed, quod certe mirabilius est, post acerbum eius obitum, quae vigesimo quarto aetatis anno e vita decessit, ad extre-

ing deeply in love, wondrous to say, with a beautiful little girl. This love of his—which was truly amazing, especially considering his very young age and how quickly it struck him—we think fit to discuss here, following the order of the events in his life, especially in view of the great attention he pays to it in one of his books.

It was an old civic custom of the time for citizens, once a year 13
on the first of May, to gather together from nearby streets and alleys at the house of some neighbour and dine lavishly, men and women, celebrating the festive day with dances, songs, and music played with all sorts of instruments. So it happened that one day a nobleman of the distinguished Portinari family, a certain Folco, following this old tradition, invited a large number of men and women to his house. Among the other neighbours gathered there was also Alighiero, the aforesaid father of our Dante, together with his little son, who was then almost nine. After dining lavishly and clearing the table, the children as usual went off to play by themselves, Dante with them, while the adults danced, sang, and played music.

Among the many children playing was also one of Folco's 14
daughters, called Bice, though Dante, instead of calling her Bice, prefers the more meaningful name Beatrice. This girl was so sweet, pretty, and well-mannered that, as he attests in one of his books, she seemed by far superior to all the other children when she was but eight years old. Struck by these and similar qualities of the little girl, Dante, a boy of divine nature, immediately fell in love with her. Indeed, he was so captivated by her that, wondrous to say, love penetrated and burned deeply into his tender boyish bones and marrow. It took hold there so tenaciously that, far from abandoning him when she was alive, it continued, which is even

mum usque vitae suae diem semper retinuerit, cum ipse multos post annos vixerit.[3] Tantus tamen ac tam vehemens amorum ardor ita invicem honestus fuit, ut ne minimus quidem aspectus inter se turpis ullo umquam tempore apparuerit.

15 Cum igitur egregius prae ceteris puer tanto mentis ardore vehementius angeretur, litterarum tamen ludo deditus mirum in modum, ut supra diximus, prima earum elementa percepit. In extrema deinde pueritia, mortuo iam patre, artibus libero dignis, quas liberales vocant, propinquorum consilio et imprimis Brunetti Latini, viri per ea tempora eruditissimi, operam dedit. In quibus profecto incredibile dictu est quantum in singulis brevi tempore profecerit. Dialecticae namque ac rhetoricae magnam omnium mathematicorum cognitionem mirabiliter adiunxit. Poeticam insuper, adulescens effectus, prae ceteris omnibus adamavit, atque tantam eius peritiam celeriter hausit, ut omnia nostrorum poetarum quam primum sibi familiarissima essent, de qua plura fortasse suo loco opportunius dicemus.

16 Atque haec omnia artium studia teneris adhuc annis Florentiae prosecutus est; quibus quidem studiis, quamquam vehementer deditus esset, se tamen a ceteris officiis libero dignis minime abstinebat. Nam et cum coequalibus conversabatur, et omnia suae aetatis munera obibat, ita ut in memorabili illo proelio quod Florentini adversus Arretinos in quodam campestri eorum agro ('Campaldinum' incolae vocant) prospere gesserunt, pugnare in prima acie pro patria minime detractarit, quemadmodum ipse in epistola quadam diligenter describit, eius proelii formam accurate demonstrans. In hac atroci dimicatione magna vitae suae discrimina adivit; nam anceps proelium aliquamdiu et dubia victoria fuit. Arretini quippe equites primo impetu in equestres Florentinorum acies furentes eos adeo superarunt ut ad pedites suos confugere cogerentur. Hic pedestris Florentinorum acies non modo rem florentinam restituit, sed Arretinos etiam, in fuga nostros — passim omissa suorum pe-

more amazing, well after her untimely death at the age of twenty-four, until the end of his own life, although he outlived her by many years. Yet this intense and passionate love was so pure on their part that neither one of them ever stained it in the least.

Although deeply troubled by this intense passion, Dante, being 15
an extraordinary child, managed to do incredibly well in grammar school, as we said above. Toward the end of his childhood, after his father passed away, he turned to the arts worthy of a free man, which are called the liberal arts, following the advice of his relatives and above all of Brunetto Latini, the most erudite man of that time. It is unbelievable how much progress he made in each of these studies in a short time. Amazingly, he added a complete knowledge of mathematics to an understanding of dialectic and rhetoric. Furthermore, once out of childhood, he started to adore poetry more than anything else; eventually, he mastered it so quickly that he soon had an intimate knowledge of all the works of our poets, as we will show in greater detail at the right time.

He pursued the study of all these arts as a boy in Florence. Yet 16
though he was a dedicated student, he never abstained from participating in those activities befitting a good citizen. In point of fact, he spent time with other youths and did all the tasks expected of people his age. For example, he did not shrink from fighting for his country in the front line during that memorable battle in which the Florentines defeated the Aretines, in the field the locals call Campaldino, as he himself writes in an epistle describing the battle in detail.[10] In this fierce fight he seriously risked losing his life. The battle in fact was very close and it was long in doubt who would win in the end. At first, the Aretine knights charged the ranks of the Florentine cavalry most violently and routed them, forcing them back to the line of their foot soldiers. The Florentine infantry then not only saved the day but even managed easily to defeat the Aretines who, having left their own foot soldiers far behind, were chasing our routed knights. This

destri acie—persequentes, facile devicit; quo facto e vestigio ad pedites eorum contendentes, itidem nullo negotio superarunt. Ita per hunc modum nostri tamquam ovantes cum magna profligatorum hostium victoria domum reverterunt.

17 Interea puella quam unice adamabat e medio, ut supra diximus, acerba morte rapitur. Quod ipse, iam florenti aetate, supra quam dici potest permoleste tulit. Nam et lacrimis et lamentationibus et eiulatibus assiduis diutius indulsit quam tanto futuro viro convenire videretur. Adeoque vehementia doloris per ea ipsa mortis suae tempora agitatus fuisse dicitur, ut parum comederet, minus etiam dormiret. Proinde, gracilis effectus, valitudinarius erat; qua in re multiplices amicorum, propinquorum, agnatorum cohortationes nullatenus proderant, quin in dies vehementius afflictaretur. Cum per multos igitur menses acrius in dies angeretur, non multo post tempore amicis et propinquis cohortantibus ut tantum dolorem leniri pateretur aures paulo liberius tandem aliquando praebere coepit. Atqui propinqui et agnati de eius salute, ut par erat, solliciti, tempus accipiendae uxoris opportunum venisse rati, quod tantorum dolorum unicum remedium fore censebant, summis precibus rogant <ut> uxorem accipiat. Quibus quidem, cum diutius repugnasset, assiduis demum eorum precibus oppugnatus, non multo post adamatae puellae obitum, vigesimo sexto circiter aetatis suae anno, uxorem accepit.

18 Nec tamen id cuius gratia uxorem acceperat assecutus est; in quo nimirum omnipotens fortuna sibi adversata videtur. Nam uxorem habuit e clarissima Donatorum familia, nomine Gemmam, morosam admodum, ut de Xanthippe Socratis philosophi coniuge scriptum esse legimus. Proinde magnae amorum sollicitudini altera ingens morosae uxoris cura accesserat, tantumque abfuit ut aegritudinis solatia exinde provenirent, ut maximis quoque angoribus ob rem uxoriam iugiter angeretur. Perversos quippe uxoris mores domi tolerare nitebatur, ne foris temerarias mulierum petulantias subire cogeretur. Diutius itaque stultam uxoris pervi-

done, they immediately turned to the Aretine foot soldiers and vanquished them without difficulty. In this way our soldiers returned home in triumph, having won a great victory and put the enemy to flight.

In the meantime, the girl he loved so deeply met, as we men- 17
tioned, with an untimely death. Dante, then in the flower of youth, suffered from it tremendously. For a long time, he gave himself up to tears, lamentations and incessant groaning—more indeed than seemed fit for a man destined to great things. It is said that he was so distressed by her death that he ate little and slept even less. Consequently, he started losing weight and fell sick; and in this condition the frequent exhortations of his friends, relatives, and neighbours did nothing to abate his progressively more violent affliction. After many months of bitter anguish, he at length began to give ear to friends and relatives who urged him to moderate his great sorrow. His friends and relatives, rightly concerned about his health, thought it was time for him to marry, believing this to be the only possible remedy for such a great sorrow. So they urged him strongly to take a wife. After a long struggle he gave in to their ceaseless prayers and finally married at the age of twenty-six, not long after the death of his beloved girl.

Yet he did not obtain that for which he had married. In this re- 18
gard, omnipotent Fortune showed herself his enemy. The truth is that the woman he married from the noble Donati family, called Gemma, was no less difficult, as written sources tell us, than Xanthippe, the wife of the philosopher Socrates. Hence the anxiety caused by an intractable wife was added to the great sorrow of his lost love, so that, far from bringing him relief, his marriage caused him endless stress and great anxiety. At home he tolerated his wife's perverse behavior as best he could so as not to be subjected to rude remarks by heedless women in public. They say he put up with his wife's foolish stubborness for a long time, until fi-

caciam per hunc modum pertulisse dicitur, sed cum ulterius intolerandam eius impudentiam tandem ferre non posset, susceptis exinde pluribus liberis, ab ea ita demum discessit ut, quasi divortio inter se facto, amplius posthac videre vix substinuerit.

19 Accepta igitur, quemadmodum supra diximus, uxore susceptisque iam liberis, nova rei familiaris cura, sicuti est natura mortalium, hominem invitavit ut ad rem publicam se conferret. Cui quidem tricesimo ferme aetatis suae anno vehementer deditus ita se gessit ut paulo post magnus civis, ob singulares virtutes suas, consensu omnium haud immerito haberetur. Non multo deinde post plura ac maxima civitatis munera egregiosque magistratus magno cum honore obivit. Nam ut ad gubernacula rei publicae se contulit, ad summum civitatis magistratum, qui 'prioratus' vulgo nuncupatur, ob admirabiles virtutes suas non immerito assumptus atque delectus est. Eo quippe tempore magistratus, veteri Romanorum more, per electionem suffragiis, non per sortem, ut nunc, creabantur. Ad hunc vero magnum dignitatis gradum trecentesimo supra millesimum christianae salutis anno delectum fuisse constat. Si itaque ducentesimo sexagesimo quinto supra millesimum humanae salutis anno natus est, millesimo deinde post trecentesimo in prioratu consedit, manifestum est ipsum tricesimo quinto aetatis suae anno ad eam dignitatem assumptum accessisse. Cum igitur in hoc suo magistratu magnum quoddam civitatis dedecus nullatenus tolerare posset, factum est ut egregii quidam cives ac sane nobiles, eo ipso imprimis cooperante, urbe exigerentur. Atque ut res ipsa clarius appareat, huius relegationis causas paulo altius ab origine repetemus.

20 Longe ante haec ipsa relegationis tempora Florentiae coeptae erant in civitate factiones duae, quarum una Guelforum, altera vero Gibellinorum vulgato nomine appellabatur. Quibus varie inter se invicem conflictatis, Guelfarum partium homines — adversariis partim relegatis, partim vero qui remanserant in calamitatibus constitutis — multum admodum praevalebant. Verum enimvero

nally, after she had borne him several children, he parted with her, unable to stand her unbearable insolence any longer. Having in a manner divorced her, he could scarcely bear to see her again after that.

After the marriage of which we have just spoken and the birth of his children, the needs of family life, as is the nature of mortal men, pushed him to enter politics. He started devoting himself to public life when he was about thirty, and soon earned a well-deserved reputation as an important citizen by virtue of his outstanding qualities. Shortly thereafter he accepted many important civic commissions and served in the highest magistracies with great honor. Indeed, once he had devoted himself to governing the state, his admirable qualities won him appointment and election to the highest civic magistracy, which is called the *priorato* in the vernacular. At the time, be it noted, officials were elected on the basis of voting, according to the old Roman custom, not by lot, as happens today. It is known that he was elected to this high post in the 1300th year of Christian salvation. Therefore, if he was born in the 1265th year of Christian salvation and served as Prior in 1300, it is clear that he was raised to that post at age thirty-five. Since he would not tolerate that any discreditable deed should be done in the state during his magistracy, he played a crucial role in the decision to have some influential and noble men banished from the city. In order to explain the situation more clearly, I will recount the reasons behind his exile from the beginning. 19

Long before his exile, two factions arose in Florence, one of which was called in the vernacular the Guelfs, the other the Ghibellines. After a series of losses and victories on both sides, the members of the Guelf Party[11] managed to prevail; they banished 20

per haec ipsa tempora quibus Guelfi adeo praevalebant, alia quaedam factio praeter duas paulo ante commemoratas, e Pistorio originem ducens, hac ipsa prioratus tempestate, per hunc modum Florentiam applicuit. Genus quoddam erat Pistorii prae ceteris egregium ac sane nobile; vulgo 'Cancellarios' ab auctore generis nuncupabant. Huius familiae homines, natis primum inter se discordiis, in diversum abire coeperunt. Paulo deinde post, cum graves inimicitiae invicem exercerentur, ad civilis tandem sanguinis effusionem utrimque devenere, ex quo universa Pistoriensium civitas bifariam divisa fuit: vulgo, ut fit, hos 'Albos,' illos 'Nigros' novis nominibus appellabant. Ceterum Florentini id conspicati, ac permoleste ferentes tam pulchram sibique tam finitimam civitatem in ultimum sui discrimen ob civiles dumtaxat discordias procul dubio deventuram, suscepta eius cura, principes factionum urbe amoverunt amotosque Florentiam deduxerunt.

21 Haec quidem Pistoriensium deductio primum Florentiam inficere coepit. Paulo deinde post, velut quaedam tabes, universam paene civitatem corrupit; alii namque Albis, alii vero Nigris favebant. Quid verbis opus est? Ex una tandem Guelforum factione duae Florentiae propalam consurgunt, quas inclitus poeta noster, optimus sane civis, propterea sedare admodum cupiebat, quod ad perniciem civitatis, si paulo diutius obdurassent, vel maxime machinari verebatur. Id cum frustra saepe tentasset, statuit de cetero a rei publicae muneribus abstinere, ac secum privatim in otio vivere. Quod postea non fecit, victus partim gloriae cupiditate (cuius suapte natura avidus erat), partim vero aura populari, insuper et precibus amicorum fatigatus, dissuadentes enim ne a rei publicae gubernaculis cessaret; aperte ostendebant ipsum multo facilius publico civilium discordiarum malo posse resistere si publice quam si privatim viveret. Proinde, re publica retenta, ei demum parti adhaesit quae plus honestatis habitura videbatur. Quocirca Albis adhaerere non dubitavit. Ita per hunc modum perniciosus civilium

some of their opponents and ruined the ones who remained. Right at that time, when the Guelfs had prevailed and the aforesaid priorate was in office, two other factions, originally from Pistoia, came to Florence in addition to the ones mentioned above. There was in Pistoia a distinguished noble family, called the Cancellieri in the vernacular from the name of their progenitor. The members of this family first split into two groups owing to mutual discords. Shortly afterwards, their relationship soured even more until they took up arms and blood was spilled on both sides, causing the whole city of Pistoia to split into two groups. These were called, using two new vernacular terms, the Whites and the Blacks. Seeing what was happening and fearing that such a lovely neighboring town was bound to be ruined by civil strife, the Florentines decided to intervene, so they removed the leaders of the two factions and brought them to Florence.

This transfer of citizens from Pistoia immediately started poi- 21
soning Florence. Shortly afterwards, like some kind of infection, it contaminated the whole city, for some supported the Whites, others the Blacks. To make a long story short, the Florentine Guelf faction split into two, a situation which our famous poet, model citizen that he was, did his best to mitigate, fearing that the ruin of the whole city would certainly follow if these factions should endure. When his efforts ended in failure, he resolved to abstain thereafter from public office and live as a private citizen at leisure. This, however, he did not do, partly because of his desire for glory (to which he was inclined by nature), partly because of popular favor, and finally because of the pressure put on him by his friends. They dissuaded him from leaving the government of the state, showing him in clear terms that it would be much easier for him to resist the scourge of civil strife if he lived as a public figure rather than as a private citizen. He thus remained in politics, joining what he thought to be the more honorable party, and so, without hesitation, he joined the Whites. This is how the destructive

discordiarum morbus per universam prope civitatem pervagatus est, adeo ut nulla fere domus paulo insignior ab hac labe se continuere potuerit.

22 Quapropter veriti Guelfarum partium duces ne, ob hanc pertinacem inter suos homines dissensiones, Gibellinorum factio rursus vires in civitate resumeret, ad Bonifacium octavum summum pontificem confugerunt, pie admodum obsecrantes ut huic nascituro, vel potius iam quasi nascenti malo, auctoritate apostolica mederetur. Quod cum pontifex frustra tentasset, graviores postea contentiones secutae sunt; iamque adeo invaluerant ut ad arma saepius iretur atque ea pars civium qui Nigri vocabantur, adversarios suos in rei publicae gubernatione seipsis longe potentiores conspicati, aequo animo hanc adversariorum excellentiam ferre non poterant. Quin immo graviter ferebant ut ex adversariorum numero omnes civitatis magistratus ut plurimum legerentur. De quo quidem saepenumero inter se conquesti, demum consultandi gratia ad Trinitatis aedem convenerunt, ubi multis hinc inde varie — ut in coetu hominum plerumque fieri consuevit — agitatis, summam tandem consilii fuit: pontificem adiretur postulatum, ut principem quendam regii generis ad tollendas civiles discordias statumque civitatis componendum mittere dignaretur. Id consilium, quia privatim de republica erat habitum, ubi Priores, ex adversae factionis hominibus qui arma illico sumpserant, resciverunt, perindigne tulerunt.

23 Dantes autem, qui in numero Priorum erat, prae ceteris id consilium indigne ferens de aliquo principe in urbem evocando, propterea quod ingenio et eloquentia plurimum poterat, collegis suadet uti animum capesserent libertatemque civitatis animose admodum defenderent, atque pernitiosi illius consilii auctores, perinde ac si eorum praesentia civitatis libertas quotidie turbaretur, imprimis urbe ipsa expellerent. Id ex eo facile persuadet, quod eius voluntatem nutumque omnes maxime spectabant. Ita per hunc modum eius consilii auctores, egregios quosdam homines (atque

disease of civil strife spread through nearly the whole city, so much so that almost none of the main families remained immune to that infection.

Fearing that this lasting breach between their party members 22
would eventually resurrect the local Ghibelline faction, the leaders of the Guelf Party turned to Boniface VIII for help, begging him to remedy this potential—or rather nascent—danger with his apostolic authority. The pope's efforts were in vain, and even harsher conflicts followed. The hatred grew so virulently that arms were often taken up. Eventually the faction called the Blacks could no longer tolerate their enemies' political supremacy. They could not stand to see their enemies almost inevitably elected to all city offices. Having often complained about this among themselves, they resolved to hold a meeting in the church of Santa Trinita, where, after discussing many different proposals, as is typical on such occasions, they finally came to the following decision: to approach the pope and ask that he might deign to send a prince of royal blood to eliminate civil strife and bring back peace to the city. The priors were indignant when they found out that a private meeting had been held about matters of state by members of the opposite faction who had taken up arms in that place.[12]

Dante, who was then one of the priors, was particularly out- 23
raged by the decision to call a prince into town, and relying on his great intelligence and eloquence, he infused his colleagues with courage and convinced them to fight bravely to defend the city's freedom by first of all exiling, as though their presence was a constant threat to civic freedom, the men who had made that dangerous decision. It was easy for him to convince them, for everyone had the highest regard for his good will and leadership. That is how the men who had made this decision—who were all influen-

imprimis Cursium Donatum, praestantem equestris ordinis virum, et Gerium Spinam et Giachinottum Patium et Russium Tosam) aliosque nonnullos Nigrarum partium duces urbe ipsa exegerunt exilioque mulctarunt; et ut in turbulentis civium dissentionibus plerumque evenire consuevit, non modo commemorati Nigrarum partium duces, sed Albarum etiam quidam principes exilio damnati sunt. Nam et Gentilis et Torrigianus Circuli,[4] equestris ordinis viri, et Guido Cavalcantes et Bastiera Tosa et Baldinaccius Adimares una cum illis exularunt.

24 Non multo deinde post, cum nullus discordiarum modus esset, Dantes ipse ad Bonifacium pontificem orator concordiae causa missus est. Ceterum in hac ipsa suae legationis tempestate Cursius Donatus urbem ingressus iam Florentiam reverterat; qua de re, paulo post eius reditum Dantes ipse—qui sui, quemadmodum supra diximus, quasi sola relegandi causa fuerat—varie fortuna volvente vices una cum quibusdam aliis egregiis civibus in exilium truditur ob eam quam suo prioratu invidiam contraxerat. Nam cum commemorati exules Albarum partium duces, Nigris foris dimissis, ab exilio revocarentur, hanc civium inaequalitatem Bonifacius pontifex perindigne tulit. Hac ergo indignatione motus, Carolum quendam Galliae principem Florentiam misit; qui cum, ob venerationem summi pontificis tum etiam ob reverentiam nominis gallici, benigne in urbe susceptus, non multo post Nigros ab exilio revocavit et Albos quoque propter relationem quandam Petri Ferrantis, satrapis sui, urbe ipsa exegit. Is namque tres quosdam Albos summopere ab eo postulasse asserebat cum Carolo ita ageret ut pars sua superior in civitate remaneret; id si faceret, ipsos Pratum oppidum pollicitos fuisse in manu sua tradere prae se ferebat. Huius postulationis litteras petentium sigillis obsignatas demonstrabat, quae cum aliis quibusdam publicis scriptis etiam nunc temporibus nostris in palatio visuntur.

25 In hac Alborum relegatione, quamquam Dantes orator ad summum pontificem civilis concordiae causa legatus esset, ob infausta

tial men, among them Corso Donati, a famous knight, Geri Spini, Giacchinotto de' Pazzi, and Rosso della Tosa—were expelled from the city and condemned to exile together with some other important members of the Blacks. As often happens with fierce civil discords, not only the above-mentioned leaders of the Blacks but also some important party members of the Whites were condemned to exile. For Gentile and Torrigiano de' Cerchi, both knights, Guido Cavalcanti, Baschiera della Tosa, and Baldinaccio Adimari were exiled with them.

Shortly thereafter, since there was no end to the discord, Dante 24
himself was sent to the pope to plead the cause of peace. While he was on this mission, Corso Donati came back to Florence. Because of this, soon after his return, Dante—who, as we said above, had been almost single-handedly responsible for that banishment—was in turn sent into exile, together with other leading citizens, in retaliation for his actions during his priorate. Pope Boniface VIII, in fact, was outraged at the discrimination against the Black exiles, who, unlike the aforesaid leaders of the Whites, had not been called back from exile. Indignant, he sent Prince Charles of France to Florence.[13] The latter received a warm welcome both because of the authority of the pontiff and out of respect for the French royal house, and soon called back from exile the Blacks while banishing the Whites on the basis of a report by his satrap Pierre Ferrant. The latter, in fact, claimed to have been solicited by three Whites to make Charles let their party stay in power in the city. If he had done so, Ferrant said, they promised to hand the town of Prato over to him. As proof of that offer, he showed a letter bearing the seals of the those offering the bribe, which can still be seen today, alongside other official documents, in the Palazzo Vecchio.

It was at the time of this exile inflicted on the Whites that 25
Dante, though serving as orator to the sovereign pontiff to plead the cause of peace, was condemned because of unfortunate meet-

tamen prioratus sui comitia, ut ipse quodam loco dicit, exilio per iniquissimam quandam ac perversissimam legem damnatus est, qua cavebatur ut praetor urbanus de erratis quondam in prioratu perpetratis, quamquam absolutio praecessisset, cognoscere tamen et punire teneretur. Hac ergo lege Dantes citatus, cum non compareret, exilio et proscriptione iniquissime damnatur. Quocirca plebs ipsa, novarum rerum cupida, paucis post diebus ad domos nuper relegatorum diripiendi causa concurrit; unde urbanas eorum aedes paene vacuefecit, praesidia vastavit, singula denique ipsorum bona vel in aerarium redacta vel certe victoribus condonata.

26 Sed utinam, Florentia mater, scelestum hoc facinus nequaquam perpetrasses, ne in tantam ac tam singularem ignominiae notam perpetuo incidisses! Hoc equidem poetae tui exilium tibi ac nomini tuo tam infame tamque ignominiosum nequeo pro virili mea etiam nunc aequo animo tolerare. Si itaque hoc loco 'me diutius continere non possum quin vehementer exclamem,' ut ait ille, parce, precor, Florentia mater. O stultas hominum mentes! O ingratas civium contentiones! O iniustas mortalium actiones! Quid consequi putabas, Florentia parens, si tantum ac tam singularem poetam, praestantem civem tuum atque de te optime meritum, in exilium egisses? 'Gloriam et honorem,' si loqui posses, te dicturam arbitrarer. Atqui vide, etiam atque etiam considera, tametsi haec tua praesens consideratio nihil prodesse possit quominus tuum illud gloriosum nomen per universum paene terrarum orbem dedecoratum esse videatur. Vide, inquam, quam haec tua gloriosa cogitatio inanis, frivola ac vana extiterit; tantum enim abest ut ex hoc poetae tui exilio gloriam consequaris, quod maxima incredibilique ignominia apud omnes orbis terrarum nationes non iniuria notata esse videaris.

27 At fortasse dices civilium partium studia haec atque huiusmodi facinora perpetrare consuesse; quod, pace tua dixerim, quantum ad hoc exilium spectat, verum esse non puto. Nam et generosum civem et summum poetam et de patria optime meritum perpetuo

ings that had taken place during his priorate, as he himself writes, on the basis of a most unjust and perverse law which forced the city praetor[14] to investigate and punish any irregularity by a former prior, even when there had been an acquittal. Having been summonsed because of this law and having failed to appear, Dante was then most unjustly condemned to exile and his property was confiscated. Consequently, a few days later the populace, being eager for a riot, rushed to the houses of the ones who had just been exiled and looted them. They emptied their town houses and wrecked their defenses. In short, all their goods were either confiscated or at any rate became the property of the victors.[15]

Mother Florence, I wish you had never committed this hei- 26
nous crime! Would that your reputation had not been eternally branded by such a uniquely shameful act! Even at this date I cannot bear with equanimity the exile of your poet, an act which defames and disgraces your good name. So pray forgive me, mother Florence, if here "I cannot control myself and refrain from violent clamor," as that character says.[16] O the folly of the human mind! O the ingratitude of civil discord! O the injustice of mortal deeds! What did you think you would gain, Mother Florence, by sending into exile so extraordinary a poet, so fine a citizen who deserved nothing but the best from you? If you could speak, I suppose you would answer, "Glory and honor." But look, turn the matter over in your mind—though all this brooding shall not now keep your glorious name from being held in universal contempt. Look, I say, how foolish and vain that glorious design of yours has turned out to be. Far from obtaining glory through the exile of your poet, you have rightly been branded with the greatest imaginable shame among all the nations of the world.

You might reply by saying that things of this sort are the usual 27
consequences of civil strife. With all due respect, I do not believe that to be true in the case of this exile. I do not remember ever reading of a noble citizen and great poet, whose conduct toward

exilio multatum neque apud domesticas neque apud exteras nationes ullo umquam tempore legisse memini. Quin immo domesticae exteraeque nationes poetas suos non modo patria non expellebant sed magno etiam in honore eos ipsos habebant. Quin immo tanto in honore apud omnes sacrum ac venerandum poetae nomen habebatur, ut peregrinos externosque poetas et viventes saepenumero civitate donarent et mortuos quoque civitatis insignibus condecorarent. Nam, ut inquit Cicero in ea quam pro Archia poeta oratione habuit, 'Homerum Colophonii civem esse dicunt suum, Chii suum vindicant, Salaminii repetunt, Smyrnaei suum esse confirmant, itaque etiam delubrum eius in urbe dedicarunt. Permulti alii praeterea pugnant inter se atque contendunt,' quod etiam graeca cuiusdam veteris poetae carmina aperte declarant; nam has septem praeclaras Graeciae civitates, Samon scilicet, Smyrnas, Chion, Colophona, Pylon, Argon et Athenas de Homeri origine diutius inter se contendisse testantur. In quo quidem hi Graeciae populi Platone suo, pace tanti philosophi dixerim, longe melius iudicarunt. Hic enim in politia quam finxit poetas et vivos et domesticos censet urbe pellendos. Illi vero et alienos et mortuos civitate donandos multo rectius putaverunt. 'Sed haec Graeci,' forsan dicet quispiam. Quid Romani, maiores tui, posteaquam omni doctrinarum genere valuerunt, nonne Archiam Antiochensem, pro quo extat pulchra Ciceronis oratio, ob id solum quod summus poeta erat civitate donarunt permultosque alios egregios poetas exteros atque alienigenas, ut arbitror, sua civitate decorarunt?

28 Quod si praestantes Graeciae civitates fere omnes Homerum, quamvis alienum, quia tamen poeta erat, etiam post mortem tantopere repetiverunt, ut de eo habendo certatim inter se contende-

his country had always deserved the highest praise, being condemned to perpetual exile by any people, whether Italian or foreign. On the contrary, both domestic and foreign peoples, far from expelling their poets, held them in the highest esteem. Indeed, the sacred and venerable name of poet was held everywhere in such great honor that foreign poets were often granted citizenship during their lifetimes, and upon their death were even granted civic honors. In fact, as Cicero writes in his oration for the poet Archias, "the inhabitants of Colophon assert that Homer is their fellow citizen, the Chians claim him for their own, the Salaminians appropriate him, while in Smyrna they are so confident that he belongs to them that they have dedicated a temple to him. Many others, too, fight over him, vying with one another."[17] This is shown by the verses of an old Greek poet, attesting to the age-old competition among these seven famous Greek cities — that is, Samos, Smyrna, Chios, Colophon, Pylos, Argos, and Athens — over Homer's birthplace. In so doing, these Greek peoples have shown much better judgement than Plato, with all due respect to the great philosopher. In the polity he devised, in fact, he holds that all poets, living and domestic, should be expelled from the city.[18] The Greek cities proved much wiser, believing that poets, even foreign ones, even dead ones, should be granted citizenship. "But these are Greeks," some may say. Well, didn't your ancestors, the Romans, after they had become dominant in every branch of learning, grant citizenship to the poet Archias of Antioch, in whose defense Cicero gave that beautiful oration, for the sole reason that he was an outstanding poet? Didn't they embellish their city with many other distinguished foreign-born poets, as I believe?

Now, since almost all the major Greek cities laid claim to 28
Homer, even after his death, for the sole reason that he was a great (though foreign) poet, and competed with one another to claim him, and since the Romans, your ancestors, granted citizen-

rent, et Romani, maiores tui, alienigenas poetas civitate donarunt, quonam modo tu, Florentia parens, hunc tuum poetam tam egregium tamque praestantem, qui et vetusta origine et singulari quadam erga te caritate tuus erat, ita repudiare potuisti ut eum perpetuo exilio multares? Sed haec satis, praesertim nunc, cum nullam utilitatem possunt afferre quominus semper ob hoc tam infame poetae tui exilium dedecorata esse videaris. Ea exilii tempestate forsan perutilia fuissent ne ipse insons, magno cum florentini nominis dedecore, in exilium ageretur.

29 Ceterum, quando quidem facta infecta fieri non possunt, saltem, quod nunc in te est, civis equidem tuus ut facias etiam atque etiam rogo: sacra poetae tui ossa tandem aliquando ab exilio revoca, ubi ipsum, multos annos postea viventem, ab exilio numquam pertinaciter nimis revocare voluisti. Quod si feceris, non modo aliqua ex parte infamia levaberis, sed gloriam etiam et honorem ex hac tua sacrorum cinerum revocatione nimirum consequeris. At si haec te consecuturam forte haudquaquam arbitraris, illud profecto assequeris, ne id tibi umquam de tuo summo poeta merito obici possit quod Romanis Scipio Africanus exilio indignissime multatus non immerito obiecisse fertur; quamquam enim multa egregia pro romana re publica facinora edidisset atque Hannibalem ipsum, Romanorum antea victorem, gloriosius superasset, postremo Carthaginem, Romani imperii emulam, dictioni Romanorum subactam gloriosissime delevisset, ob magnorum tamen gestorum suorum invidiam (perpetuam singularissimarum virtutum comitem) iniquissime in exilium actus <cum> esset, in haec verba indignabundus ad extremum vitae prorupisse traditur: 'Ingrata patria, non habebis ossa mea,' et quae sequuntur. Sed redeamus, quando quidem nostro erga te officio functi esse videmur, unde digressi sumus.

30 Summus igitur poeta (o scelus indignum!), quamquam Romae ad summum pontificem florentini populi nomine civilis concordiae causa legatus esset, exilio tamen iniquissime damnatur. Proinde il-

ship to foreign poets, how could you, Mother Florence, disown your own excellent and outstanding poet—yours both because of his ancestry and because of his unusual love for you—to the point of sending him into exile forever? But enough of this, especially at this point in time, since no consideration of utility can spare you the eternal infamy of having exiled your poet. At the time of his exile, perhaps, it might have been very useful indeed, so as to avoid banishing an innocent man, to the dishonor of the Florentine name.

However, since what is done cannot be undone, I now implore you, as a citizen of yours, to do at least one thing you are certainly capable of doing: summon back at last your poet's sacred remains from exile—from the place where you stubbornly refused to recall him from exile for many a year while he was still alive. If you do recover those sacred ashes, you will not only to some extent cleanse yourself of the stain of infamy, but also, surely, acquire glory and honor. If perhaps you believe you shall not achieve this goal, you will assuredly succeed in giving others no right to blame you concerning your great poet the way Scipio the Elder, after his undeserved punishment, is said to have rightfully blamed the Romans. For despite all his great deeds on behalf of the Roman republic—among which were his glorious victory over Hannibal himself, previously Rome's conqueror, and afterwards the glorious conquest and destruction of Carthage, the Roman Empire's rival—envy, the inevitable companion of great virtue, still drove him into exile with the greatest injustice. It is reported that at the end of his life he was seized with righteous anger and burst out with these words: "Ungrateful country, you shall not have my bones," etc.[19] But let us now end this digression and resume the story, since we would appear to have fulfilled our duty toward you. 29

So, the excellent poet (O most heinous crime!) is most unjustly condemned to exile despite his being in Rome at the time to plead the cause of peace before the supreme pontiff on behalf of the 30

linc abiens, Senas contendit; ibi de calamitate sua certior factus, cum omnes redeundi in patriam aditus post aliquot annos[5] interclusos animadverteret, ceteris exulibus adhaerere statuit. Itaque cuncti exules Gargonsae congregati, sedem suam Arretii constituerunt. Ibi ducem belli Alexandrum Romenae comitem delegerunt duodecimque consiliarios gerendis rebus praefecerunt, e quorum numero Dantes fuit. Atque per hunc modum spem suam in patriam revertendi in dies perpetuo pascebant, donec magna complicum manu comparata reditum enixe tentarent. Ingenti etenim multitudine non modo exulum sed familiarium etiam ex Bononia et Pistorio congregata, urbem incautam subito aggrediuntur, siquidem unam eius portam animose arripientes urbem intrarunt. Ad extremum tamen superati, insalutato ut dicitur hospite, exinde fugientes recesserunt.

31 Dantes autem, ob hos irritos exulum conatus spe redeundi amissa, ex Arretio Veronam se contulit, quo in loco ab Alberto Scala, Veronensium principe, benigne admodum receptus est; ibique aliquamdiu commoratus, aliam revertendi viam tentare statuit. Nam benigne et humane erga populum florentinum se gerens, per spontaneam revocationem in patriam remeare quaerebat. Quocirca in hoc proposito perseverans, complures epistulas et ad privatos cives et ad populum conscripsit. Principium epistulae ad populum scriptae huiusmodi est: 'Popule mee, quid tibi feci?' et quae sequuntur. Bononiam postea perrexit, ubi, etsi parum commoraretur, philosophiae tamen operam dedit. Patavium deinde contendit. Inde rursus Veronam repetens variis cogitationibus ob multiplices exilii curas agitabatur.

32 Postea vero quam undique sibi praeclusam reversionis suae spem atque in dies inaniorem fieri animadvertit, 'in gratiam rursus cum libris,' ut inquit Cicero, 'redire' statuit; cum quibus primum tot annos[6] ob rei publicae gubernationem, ob civiles deinde discordias, ob varias denique exilii curas diuturnum bellum iampridem indixerat. Proinde non Etruria solum sed universa quoque Italia

Florentine people. Leaving Rome, he went to Siena, and there, having learned more about his misfortune, he tried in vain for several months[20] all possible ways of returning to his homeland, until he finally resolved to join the other exiles. Meeting in Gargonza, the exiles chose Arezzo as their base. There they elected Count Alexander of Romena as their military leader and also created twelve counsellors, among whom was Dante himself, to supervise their affairs. In this way they kept nurturing their hopes of returning to their homeland, waiting to have an army big enough to do it by force. Having gathered a large number of exiles and friends from both Bologna and Pistoia, they attacked Florence by surprise, and even succeeded in entering it after bravely seizing one of its gates. In the end, however, they were defeated and fled in retreat without ceremony.

Having lost all hope of coming back after such vain efforts by 31
the exiles, Dante went from Arezzo to Verona, where he was most kindly received by Alberto della Scala, the prince of that town.[21] Staying there a while, he decided to try another way to come back. By behaving with good will and kindness towards the Florentine people, he strove to return to his country through a voluntary act of restoration. Persevering in this purpose, he wrote many epistles both to private citizens and to the whole people. The beginning of one such epistle reads as follows: "O fellow-citizens, what did I do to you?"[22] He then went to Bologna where, though his stay there was brief, he studied philosophy. Afterwards, he moved to Padua, then to Verona again, always stirred up by various ideas thanks to the numerous cares of exile.

Finally, having realized that his hope of restoration had been 32
shut off on every side and was becoming weaker every day, he decided, as Cicero says,[23] "to make his peace with books again," after having declared war on them continuously for many years. He had done so first because of his responsibilities as a magistrate, then because of civil discords, and finally because of the various cares of

derelicta, in Parisiensium urbem—studiorum dumtaxat gratia—se contulit, quippe in hoc loco humanarum et divinarum rerum studia ceteris orbis terrarum locis celebratiora, consensu omnium, ferebantur. Ibique ceteris omnibus posthabitis, naturalium ac divinarum rerum studiis assiduam et paene incredibilem operam navavit, in quibus usque adeo profecit ut in frequentissimis memoratarum rerum disceptationibus, pro more civitatis, et magnos quidem philosophos et quos etiam 'theologos' vocant, una voce omnium, saepenumero superaret.

33 Dum itaque in huiusmodi humanitatis studiis quietissime simul atque securissime viveret, ecce nova quaedam cogitatio, ut est natura nostrarum rerum fragilis atque caduca, subito irrepsit, quae quidem sua haec pertranquilla ac divina studia importune admodum perturbavit atque pervertit. Herricus enim nuper ad imperium legitime delectus Imperatorque, populorum paene omnium consensu, Augustus appellatus, e Germania abiit, Italiam infesto exercitu petiturus; quem ubi Dantes iam Italiam intrasse Brixiamque, non parvam citerioris Galliae urbem, ingentibus equitum ac peditum copiis obsedisse accepit, tempus opportunum sui reditus venisse ratus, statuit rursus Italiam repetere. Quamobrem una cum pluribus et Guelfarum et Nigrarum partium infestis hostibus, Alpibus superatis, Herrico quoquo modo suadere nitebatur ut, Brixiae obsidione omissa, Florentiam faustis exercitibus suis peteret. Id propterea facile impetrasse visi sunt, quod Herricus ab initio suae electionis legatos Florentiam miserat ut eius in Italiam adventum Florentinis nuntiarent postularentque ut in urbe sua receptaculum sibi praepararent, ac bello, quod tunc adversus Arretinos forte gerebant, se abstinerent. Haec legatio quamquam benigne admodum publice, ut ab eis efflagitatum fuit, audita esset, quantum tamen ad sua postulata pertinere videbatur spreta ac neglecta est. Huius rei hac ipsa tempestate memor, Herricus Florentinorum exulum variis persuasionibus cedere constituit.

exile. Hence, having left not only Tuscany but Italy itself, he went to Paris for the sole purpose of studying, for at the time that city was generally regarded as the best place in the world to study all things human and divine. Putting everything else aside, he studied with incredible zeal and dedication both natural and divine sciences, learning so much that in many of those debates which are commonly held there on these subjects he managed to surpass, as everybody agreed, some great philosophers and even some of those who are called "theologians."

While he was leading this sort of life, safely and quietly im- 33
mersed in the study of the humanities, a new idea, as is typical of our frail and fleeting human nature, suddenly got hold of him, disturbing and diverting his calm and holy studies in a most untimely way. Henry—who had just been legitimately raised to the imperial throne, receiving by almost universal consent the title of "Augustus"—had left Germany to invade Italy with an attacking army. As soon as Dante heard that he had reached Italy and was besieging Brescia, a fairly big town of Cisalpine Gaul, with a large force of knights and infantry, thinking that it was the right time for him to come back, he resolved to return again to Italy. Once past the Alps, together with many bitter enemies of both the Guelfs and the Blacks he tried to convince Henry to abandon the siege of Brescia and head for Florence with his army of good omen. They believed Henry would be ready to satisfy their request, since shortly after his election Henry had sent an embassy to Florence to announce his imminent coming to Italy, to request that they prepare a reception for him in town, and to stop fighting the Aretines.[24] Although in public this embassy had been listened to with good will, as requested, in practice its injunctions seemed to have been scorned and ignored. Mindful of that, Henry decided to yield to the various arguments of the Florentine exiles.

34 Quocirca, Brixiae obsidione penitus omissa, Florentiam versus ire contendit. Per Ligures igitur iter faciens Tyrrhenumque mare ingressus, cum triginta navibus longis Pisas devenit atque inde Romam versus, ut imperii coronam assumeret, iter arripuit. Quoniam vero, propter multiplices rei publicae discordias, recta ire non dabatur, Viterbii commoratus est; atque inde post Romam petens, urbem tandem intravit. Ibique, tametsi ab adversariis imperatorii nominis crebra proelia commissa essent, demum adversariis enixe repugnantibus imperii coronam assumpsit; in cuius quidem assumptione Robertus inclitus Siciliae rex ac Florentini imprimis sibi admodum repugnaverant.

35 Corona itaque imperii per hunc modum assumpta, hanc adversariorum repugnantiam perindigne ferens, paulo post Tibur se contulit. Erat enim imperatoris animus in adversarios, pro illatis sibi Romae impedimentis, vehementer infensus, sed praecipue in Robertum Siciliae regem ac Florentinos, utpote egregios suorum impedimentorum principes, ardebat animus. At cum e vestigio Robertum haud facile ulcisci posset, in Florentinos conversus, per Sabinos et Umbros iter faciens, Etruriam ingreditur; per perusinum inde et cortonensem et arretinum agrum ducens, Florentiam usque perrexit, castrisque prope Salvianum templum positis, non longius ab urbe trecentis fere passibus, infestissimis exercitibus Florentiam obsedit. Ad eum igitur ita prope urbem castrametatum universi Florentinorum exules undique confluebant. Proinde Dantes quoque se ulterius continere non potuit quin, ingenti spe plenus, epistulam quandam 'ad Florentinos,' ut ipse vocat, 'intrinsecos' contumeliosam sane scriberet, in qua eos acerbissime insectatur, cum antehac de ipsis honorificentissime loqui solitus esset.

36 In hac autem florentinae urbis obsidione Herricus complures dies commoratus, crebra cum Florentinis proelia committebat; sed cum ab ipsis, frequentibus proeliis lacessitis, totiens egregie admodum repugnaretur, peracto demum nihilo memoratu digno, Romam rursus repetere statuit. Verum in hac sua itineratione, ad

So he abandoned the siege of Brescia and headed for Florence. 34
Passing through Liguria, he set sail for Pisa with thirty galleys on the Tyrrhenian Sea; upon landing there, he made for Rome to receive the imperial crown. Since civil wars prevented him from the direct route, he stopped in Viterbo; eventually, he resumed his trip to Rome and entered the city. There he fought many battles against the opponents of the empire and finally received the imperial crown despite strenuous opposition. It was above all the famous King Robert of Sicily and the Florentines who opposed his coronation.

Soon after receiving the imperial crown in this fashion, he went 35
to Tivoli in a rage at his enemies for their opposition. The emperor was angry at his adversaries for the impediments they had raised against him in Rome, and above all, he was hostile to King Robert of Sicily and the Florentines, for they had been principally responsible for those impediments. Since it was not easy to avenge himself immediately on Robert, he turned on the Florentines. He left Sabina and Umbria behind and entered Tuscany. Passing through the territory of Perugia, Cortona, and Arezzo, he finally reached Florence, and encamping near the church of San Salvi, no more than three hundred yards or so away from the city walls, he laid siege to Florence with his extremely dangerous army. Thereupon Dante was filled with hope and gave vent to his feelings by writing an abusive epistle against what he calls "intrinsic Florentines."[25] In this letter he inveighs against them bitterly, whereas before he had always spoken of them with the greatest respect.

Henry's siege of Florence lasted for many days, during which 36
he often engaged the Florentines in battle. The latter, however, fought off his many attacks with great distinction. At last, having accomplished nothing worthy of record, he resolved to return to Rome. It was during this trip, while stopping in the Sienese town

Bonconventum, quoddam Senensium oppidum, divertens, ibi e vita decessit. Quocirca exules qui Herricum viventem sequebantur, de suo in patriam reditu post mortem eius omnino desperantes, destituta prorsus omni revertendi spe, novas sibi sedes varie pro hominum ingeniis perscrutabantur.

37 Dantes itaque, Apennini montibus superatis, Flaminiam contendit. Ea forte tempestate Guido Novellus Ravennae, ceterarum urbium eius provinciae vetustissimae, praesidebat, vir in omni doctrinarum genere prae ceteris principibus eruditus. Hic pro sua quadam erga doctos homines benignitate eruditissimos viros summe colere et observare solebat. Ubi ergo Novellus hunc praestantem poetam, cuius maxima fama non Italiam solum sed universum etiam paene terrarum orbem iam peragraverat, Flaminiam accessisse accepit, statuit hominem Ravennam, ut secum familiariter viveret, quovis modo benivole et amice accersire. Quamobrem ipsum de hoc sui vehementi desiderio seu per epistulas seu per legatos certiorem fecit, rogans etiam atque etiam ut secum, quando quidem in patria habitare non dabatur, vitam degere nequaquam denegaret; quod ut facilius ab eo impetraret, 'non modo,' ut ait terentianus ille, 'montes aureos' pollicebatur. Haec autem ubi Dantes cognovit, conspicatus magnanimi viri generosum animum, confestim se Ravennam contulit, ut tam digno principi quamprimum obsequeretur atque secum, omissa omni ad patriam redeundi spe, perpetuo familiarissime degeret.

38 Ravennae ergo a Novello per hunc modum benignissime receptus, aliquot annos permoratus est, donec ad ultimum vitae suae diem pervenerit. Nam Ravennae eum obiisse constat, quo in loco et tempore 'rursus cum libris in gratiam rediens', partim legendo, partim alios erudiendo, partim etiam cogitationes suas litteris mandando, humanitatis studia — retenta semper animo, <licet illis> temporibus ob multiplices variarum rerum curas inter-

of Buonconvento, that he passed away. After Henry's death the exiles who had followed him despaired of ever returning to their country, and started looking for new homes for themselves, each according to his inclinations, having lost all hope of returning to their homeland.

Thus Dante, having crossed the Apennines, headed for the 37
Romagna. At the time, Ravenna, the most ancient city of that region, was ruled by Guido Novello, a man far more cultivated in every branch of learning than other princes. Because of his goodwill towards learned men, he tended to cultivate and show respect for great scholars. As soon as Novello found out that such a notable poet, whose immense fame had already spread well beyond Italy to almost the entire world, was coming to the Romagna, he decided he must induce the man, by whatever means generosity and friendship could devise, to live with him in Ravenna as a member of his household. He thus sent him letters and deputations to communicate his fervent wish to have him, begging Dante repeatedly to live with him, seeing that the poet was no longer allowed to dwell in his native town. To sweeten his offer, he promised him "not only mountains of gold," as the famous verse by Terence goes.[26] When Dante learned of this, recognizing the generosity of this nobleminded man, he immediately went to Ravenna to pay homage to such a praiseworthy prince and, having lost all hope of returning to his native city, he lived with him ever after as a member of his household.

Having been welcomed in this most kindly way to Ravenna by 38
Novello, he spent a number of years there until the very end of his life. It is known, in fact, that he died in Ravenna, and it was there, in that period, that he "made peace with books once again," in part through reading, in part through teaching students, and in part through committing his own thoughts to writing. Up to the end of his life, he diligently pursued humane studies — of which he had always been fond, even when his many cares had forced him to

missa — magna cum diligentia mirum in modum usque ad extremum vitae prosecutus est. Quod si quietiora ac tranquilliora, non autem fluctuantia et procellosa studia divinus poeta habuisset, qualem et quantum virum futurum coniectura augurari possumus, quando quidem ipsum, tot magnarum rerum curis impeditum, ad summum omnium doctrinarum cumulum ex celebratioribus scriptis suis pervenisse luce clarius apparet.

39 Ravennae igitur, ut supra diximus, complures annos reliquum vitae suae tempus commoratus, nonnullos sane homines egregiosque viros poeticam egregie prae ceteris docuit; compluresque egregios praestantis ingenii viros materno sermone ita erudivit, ut nonnulli ex his 'vulgares,' ut aiunt, non vulgares poetae haberentur. Hanc suam materni sermonis poeticam hic noster poeta primus apud Italos, perpaucis ante annis adinventam, uno paene omnium consensu non secus nobilitavit quam aut Homerus graece apud Graecos aut Virgilius latine apud Latinos quondam suam quisque apud suos illustraverit. Hic enim primus in hac sua poetica, florentino idiomate prae ceteris egregie admodum nobilitato, magnam humanarum et divinarum rerum cognitionem una voce omnium tradidisse perhibetur, cum prius levia quaedam frivolaque dumtaxat, gravioribus omissis, vulgares poetae suis carminibus prodidissent. Hanc quoque magnam tantarum rerum gravitatem singulari quodam ac paene incredibili dicendi lepore in hoc suo divino poemate mirabiliter condivit. Talia igitur et huiusmodi agentem ac meditantem mors importuna praevenit; de qua priusquam dicere incipiam, non alienum fore putavi ea summatim exponere quae ad eius formam, habitum, cultum et mores pertinere videantur.

40 Fuisse traditur inclitus hic poeta mediocri et decente[7] statura, facie paululum oblonga, oculis paulo grandioribus, naso aquilino, latis pendentibusque maxillis, inferiori labio aliquantulo quam altero supereminentiori, colore fusco, capillis ac barba prolixis, nigris subcrispisque. De quo quidem, si quis etiam rerum minimarum

abandon them for a time—in a truly remarkable way. We can only imagine what an extraordinary man this divine poet could have been if he had been granted the opportunity to study with greater calm and tranquillity, rather than in such uncertain and tempestuous conditions, for his more celebrated writings clearly testify to the outstanding level of erudition he attained, even though hampered by so many cares.

In the many aforesaid years he spent in Ravenna before his 39
death, he became a distinguished teacher of poetics in particular, teaching it to a number of gentlemen. He educated in the common speech several brilliant and eminent men, in such a way that some of these "commoners", as they are called, gained a reputation as uncommon poets. It is generally agreed that this poet of ours was the first Italian to ennoble the art of writing poetry in the vernacular, which in Italy had been discovered only a few years earlier, just as Homer had elevated Greek poetry among the Greeks, and Vergil Latin poetry among the Latins. He was reputed the first to have ennobled the Florentine vernacular above the rest in his poetry, expressing in a unique idiom a vast knowledge of all things human and divine, whereas previous vernacular poets had only touched on matters of little importance in their verse, leaving weighty subjects aside. Moreover, in his divine poem he seasoned marvelously the high seriousness of his subject matter with an incredibly charming and elegant style. An untimely death prevented him from working and meditating on similar subjects. Before speaking of his death, however, I believe it is relevant to describe in summary fashion his appearance, his bearing, his way of life and his character.

They say that this renowned poet was of middling stature and 40
had a particularly long and narrow face, rather large eyes, a hooked nose, broad and pendulous cheeks, a slightly protruding lower lip,

nimium curiosus forte dubitarit, paucis accipiat quid ob hanc ipsam capillorum et coloris qualitatem sibi Veronae tunc commoranti accidisse quidam memoriae prodiderunt. Quadam namque die urbem perambulans prope ianuam cuiusdam domus forte pertransibat, ubi nonnullae matronae pro more civitatis consedentes confabulabantur, quarum una, ubi Dantem pertranseuntem conspexit, confestim ad alteram propiorem conversa 'Vide,' inquit, 'vide hominem qui ad inferos proficiscitur indeque umbrarum illic assistentium nova ad vivos refert' (iam enim fama primae partis suae *Comoediae* percrebuerat). Ad hanc ita loquentem illa suo sermone lacessita subito insulse nimis ac muliebriter, ut solent, in hunc modum respondisse fertur: 'Vera, soror, narras; siquidem barba eius subcrispa et ater color propter obscuriorem quendam inferorum colorem nebulosumque fumum sententiam tuam veram esse aperte testantur.'

41 Incessu insuper gravis, severus, tristis semperque cogitabundus erat; proinde subcurvus provecta aetate aliquantulum incedebat. Sunt qui dicant[8] ipsum gratioris aspectus fuisse; ceterum eius effigies et in basilica Sanctae Crucis et in cappella praetoris urbani utrobique in parietibus exstat ea forma qua revera in vita fuit a Giotto, quodam optimo eius temporis pictore, egregie depicta. Induebatur etiam antequam exularet mediocriter, non speciose admodum, uti tanti viri gravitatem decere vel maxime videbatur. Ea enim tempestate patrimonium non modicum possidebat; nam et domos splendidas Florentiae et aliquot praedia urbis moenibus finitima variis in locis habebat. Cibi quoque potusque parcissimus erat; delicatos laudare solebat, grossioribus vero plurimum vescebatur. Ventri deditos, quos 'gastrimargos' Graeci vocant, vehementer obiurgabat; etenim ex illa veteris cuiusdam sapientis sententia eos qui talia agerent potius vivere ut essent, quam esse ut viverent, dictitare consueverat.

42 In adulescentia vero sonis cantibusque usque adeo oblectabatur ut cum eius temporis peritioribus artis musicae magistris frequen-

dark skin, and a black, curly beard and hair. For those over-curious persons who may have doubts about even these small details, I will briefly report an episode concerning his dark skin and hair that occurred, according to certain accounts, when he lived in Verona. One day, as he was walking through the streets, he happened to pass in front of a house where a group of women sat chattering by the door, as is the Veronese custom. One of them, seeing Dante pass by, turned to the woman beside her and said: "Look, it's the man who travels to Hell and reports back to the living the news he's heard from the shadows dwelling there." (By this time, in fact, the first part of his *Comedy* had become quite famous.) The other woman immediately replied, in that stupid way so typical of women: "You speak the truth, sister: his curly beard and his skin, blackened by the darkness and thick smoke of Hell, clearly show that you are right."

He was a man of grave and lofty bearing, often sad and ab- 41
sorbed in his thoughts; in his old age he walked hunched over. Some say he was better looking than this; but excellent portraits of him, showing what he really looked like, were painted by Giotto, an outstanding painter of the time, on the walls of the church of Santa Croce and in the chapel of the *podestà*,[27] where they can still be seen. Even before his exile he dressed plainly, not ostentatiously, as befitted the serious demeanor of such a distinguished man. The patrimony he possessed at the time was by no means small, for he had some fine houses in Florence and estates in various places just outside the city walls. He was temperate in eating and drinking; he would praise elegant dishes but usually ate frugal meals, rebuking those who were devoted to their bellies—the *gastrimargi*, as the Greeks call them. He used to say, following the maxim of a certain ancient sage, that these men do not eat to live, but live to eat.[28]

In his youth he was so fond of melodies and singing that he of- 42
ten conversed with the greatest musical experts of his time. He

tius conversaretur. Quorum nimirum summa quadam voluptate allectus atque exhilaratus, florentino idiomate et soluta oratione et carmine multa egregie composuit. Quo quidem dicendi genere non solum ceteros omnes, pace cunctorum dixerim, facile superavit, sed posteros, etiam praestantis ingenii viros, quadam incredibili dicendi suavitate et copia, imitandi tam suave dicendi[9] genus percupidos accumulatissime reddidit.

43 Lascivis aliquantulum amoribus obnoxius plus indulsisse visus est quam viro philosopho convenire videretur; quod equidem potius gratiosae hominis naturae quam cuidam gravissimi viri levitati mea sententia ascribendum non iniuria putavi, ut de Socrate, philosophorum omnium severissimo, scriptum esse constat, quem in libidines proniorem fuisse nonnulli memoriae prodiderunt. Cum enim ab egregio quodam illius temporis physionomo, qui ex habitu et forma corporis animorum motus et perturbationes se intelligere ac demonstrare profitebatur, ipsum libidinibus obnoxium iudicatum esset,[10] admirantibus cunctis cachinnationibusque suis physionomum deridentibus, Socrates dixisse fertur huiusmodi physionomi de se iudicium verum extitisse, asserens se natura ad libidines proniorem, magna tamen modestia non solum illam inclinationem naturalem temperasse, sed penitus vicisse ac superasse.

44 Raro nisi interrogatus loquebatur, idque non temere sed ab intimo, ut aiunt, pectore longe ante praemeditata edere videbatur. In cognitione rerum ita vigilantissimus erat, ut in mediis viis nonnumquam lectitare consuesceret. Quocirca 'helluo libri,' quemadmodum de Catone scribit Cicero, non immerito appellari poterat. Ut enim Cato, quamvis vir gravissimus ac sapientissimus esset, in ipsa tamen curia quandoque legere consuerat antequam senatus cogeretur, sic iste vir singularissimus in mediis, ut aiunt, viis interdum lectitabat. Nam cum ei libellus quidam non antea a se visus Senis, prope cuiusdam opificis tabernam, forte oblatus esset, ita cupide et attente lectitavit ut suavissimi variique multiplicum in-

was attracted and exhilarated by the pleasure of music and composed in the Florentine vernacular many excellent writings both in prose and verse.[29] In this form of writing he not only easily excelled everyone, if I may say so without offense, but his incredibly sweet and rich style also made later writers, even men of outstanding genius, immensely eager to imitate his sweet manner of speech.[30]

He seems to have indulged somewhat in frivolous love-affairs, 43
more than is suitable to a man of philosophical temperment, a fact which I think should be attributed more to his charming nature than to any levity on the part of such a serious man. The same is written of Socrates, the most austere of all philosophers, who according to some authorities was overly given to lechery. This inclination to lechery in Socrates was noticed by a famous physiognomist of that time who claimed to be able to tell the nature of a person from his bearing and physical appearance. They say that while everyone was surprised and laughed at the physiognomist, Socrates said that his opinion was correct, and admitted that he was naturally inclined toward lechery, but had managed not only to curb this natural inclination but also to overcome and extinguish it completely.[31]

Dante seldom spoke unless he was asked a question, and his 44
words were never uttered thoughtlessly. On the contrary, they seemed to come, as it were, from the heart and after deep reflection. He was so absorbed in his studies that he even used to read in the middle of the street. So he might justly have been called "a glutton for books," as Cicero writes of Cato.[32] Just as Cato—despite his being a most serious and wise man—used to read at times in the very Senate-house before its sessions had begun, so too, it is said, this extraordinary man was wont to read in the middle of the street. Once, for instance, near an artist's workshop in Siena, he was offered a booklet he had never seen before. He started reading it with so much attention and enjoyment that

strumentorum soni ab eius perpetua lectione vel paulisper dimovere numquam potuerunt quin totum legendo percurreret, tametsi eo tempore forte dies festus, pro more civitatis, universo populi concursu, omni cum consonantium instrumentorum genere prope eum locum, ubi legebatur, speciosissime celebraretur. Et quod mirabilius videri debet, interrogatus quonam modo se umquam continere potuerit quin tam celebre ac tam solemne festum prae oculis celebratum aliquantisper saltem non conspexisset, nihil se audisse sane respondisse fertur.

45 Elegantissimum in orando fuisse perhibent, quod frequentes eius legationes ad multos cum illustres principes tum ad summos pontifices manifeste declarant. Ad haec accedit quod perinde ac semiprinceps quidam in re publica ob summam eius elegantiam regnare videbatur. Fuit praeterea et acerrimi ingenii et fidelissimae memoriae, quorum complura testimonia afferre possem si liberet; sed nimiam prolixitatem veritus, uno solo, et eo quidem peregregio testimonio, contentus ero. Parisiis forte aderat, quo se, post Federici[11] Augusti obitum, ut antea diximus, mox retulerat, ibique in magna excellentissimorum virorum turba solus cum ceteris de rebus divinis altissime simul atque subtilissime disputabat. Proinde cum multa ac inter se diversa super variis de rebus altissimis quaestionibus (numero, ut ferunt, quattuordecim) adversarii in medium adduxissent, omnia sigillatim eo ordine, quo proposita fuerant, non sine singulari quadam omnium admiratione, et fideliter replicavit et admirabilius persolvit.

46 Honoris insuper et gloriae cupidior fortasse fuit quam tanto ac tam gravi philosopho convenire videretur. Sed et magni philosophi et severi etiam theologi a naturali gloriae cupiditate — ob rei quandam incredibilem, ut aiunt, suavitatem — se abstinere non potuerunt, quamquam multa de contemnenda gloria libris suis memoriae mandarint. Hac ergo gloriae cupiditate natura hominibus insita poeta noster inflammatus, prae ceteris, ut arbitror, poeticam adamavit. Etenim poetae boni ea tempestate quam aut philosophi

the most pleasant and varied music being played there did not distract him or stop him from reading even for a second; and so he read through the whole work, even though the entire community was celebrating a traditional feast that day in a spectacular fashion, to the accompaniment of all sorts of instruments, exactly on the spot where he was reading. Even more astonishing is that when he was asked why he had not paid the slightest attention to the famous and solemn festivity being celebrated right in front of his eyes, he replied that he had not heard a thing.

They say he was an excellent orator, as is attested by his many 45
missions to various illustrious princes and supreme pontiffs. Moreover, he seemed to rule almost as a prince in the republic by virtue of his unparalleled eloquence. He possessed, furthermore, a sharp mind and an excellent memory. I could give numerous examples of this if I wanted to, but to avoid prolixity I shall restrict myself to just one remarkable anecdote. Once in Paris, where he had gone, as we said above, right after the death of Emperor Henry,[33] he happened to be disputing all alone against a large group of distinguished men over some extremely difficult and subtle theological problems. After his adversaries had raised many different questions about various highly abstruse matters (it is said there were fourteen of them), he accurately replied to all of them in the exact order in which they had been raised, and then solved them in a most admirable way, arousing the wonder of all present.[34]

He was perhaps more eager for honor and glory than would 46
seem appropriate to a great and serious philosopher. Yet despite their many writings on despising fame, even great philosophers and stern theologians have not managed to remain immune to the natural desire for glory, yielding to what people call its incredible sweetness.[35] It was the natural desire for glory, in my view, that kindled a special love of poetry in our poet. Good poets, in fact, were at the time more difficult to find than philosophers, mathe-

aut mathematici aut denique theologi longe pauciores erant, quod etiam antea, a conditione orbis terrarum usque ad haec nostra tempora, repetitum fuisse constat. Semper enim poetae boni et oratores paucissimi fuerunt. Laurea insuper poetae Caesaresque, vetusto Graecorum Latinorumque more, per ea adhuc tempora coronari consuerant. Huius quidem laureae, de qua loquimur, se cupidissimum fuisse non modo ipse non inficiatur, sed pluribus quoque scriptorum suorum locis saepenumero manifeste testatur; quod sibi profecto non immerito contigisset ut laurea corona sua tempora insignitus fuisset, si ullo umquam tempore ab exilio revocatus esset. Sed in exilio degens, lauream quam tantopere cupiebat, suscipere (non iniurie mea quidem sententia) neglexit.

47 In hac poetica quantum ipse valuerit longe facilius iudicari quam plane explicari posse crediderim. Quippe poeticam, diu antea per noningentos circiter annos vel demortuam vel sopitam, summus hic poeta primum in lucem excitavit, iacentemque ac prostratam ita erexit ut vel ab exilio per eum revocata, vel postliminio reversa, vel e tenebris in lucem excitata fuisse videatur, cum iampridem tot annos demortua iacuisset. Ac non solum primum eam in lucem excitavit, sed cum sana etiam catholicaque nostrae fidei doctrina convenire mirabiliter demonstravit, perinde ac veteres poetae divino quodam spiritu afflati fuissent ac sanam et veram doctrinam cecinissent. Praeter haec quoque divinus poeta illud effecit, ut non modo eruditissimis viris, sed plebeis etiam et idiotis, quorum plena sunt omnia, velata poemata placerent, ne ii qui ad eloquia latina aspirare non possent poeticae omnino expertes essent.

48 Fuit praeterea et generosi et alti animi. Nam cum ad patriam remeare ardentissime cuperet, propterea tamen reverti noluit quod ab unico redeundi remedio, ob solam animi magnitudinem, suapte natura abhorrebat. Quidam namque eius amici, primum quia ipsum unice adamabant, deinde ut sibi frequentius oranti obsequerentur, suam in patriam reversionem apprime exoptabant; ac prop-

maticians and even theologians — as has always been the case since the world's inception. Good poets and orators have always been very rare.[36] At the time it was still common to crown poets and generals with laurel, following the ancient Greek and Latin custom. Far from denying his eagerness for the laurel crown of which we speak, he openly confesses it in many of his works. His forehead would certainly have been graced with a well-deserved laurel crown if he had ever returned from exile. However, being in exile, he was right, in my opinion, to make no effort to obtain the laurel he so much coveted.

His excellence in poetry, I believe, can be far more easily assessed than explained. This exceptional poet was the first to awaken poetry to life after it had been moribund or asleep for about nine hundred years. He raised it from the ground where it was lying prostrate, so that he seems to have recalled it from exile or restored its civic rights or brought it back to the light after it had lain in the darkness of the grave for many years. And not only did he bring it back to light, but he proved it to be perfectly consistent with our Catholic faith, just as if the ancient poets had somehow been divinely inspired to sing the sound and true doctrine. Furthermore, this divine poet rendered poetic veils attractive not only to the most learned, but also to commoners and laymen (who are everywhere), so that even men who may not aspire to Latin eloquence might not be completely ignorant about poetry. 47

He was, moreover, a noble and high-minded man. For instance, despite his intense desire to return to his native land, his loftiness of spirit alone made him decide not to, since his nature abhorred the only possible means of doing it. Some friends of his, moved both by their sincere love for him and in order to honor his continual requests, were eager to see him return to his native town. To 48

terea cum nonnullis principibus civitatis de hoc ipso diligentius pertractaverant omnemque eorum pertractationem penitus irritam fore apparuerat nisi ipse magnum quoddam dedecus submisse nimis et abiecte subiret. Id huiusmodi esse videbatur: ut primum multum admodum mansuesceret; a suis deinde adversariis summis precibus veniam peteret; ad publicos quoque carceres per aliqua temporum curricula commorandi gratia se sponte conferret. Ad haec omnia extrema insuper accedebat quod, exactis eorum temporum curriculis, e carceribus postea liberatus, in cathedrali florentinae urbis basilica, ceu in magnis civitatis solemnitatibus de nonnullis perditis hominibus fieri consuevit, immortali Deo solemniter offerretur. Ceterum ubi ipse de his omnibus ab amicis certior factus est, numquam adduci potuit ut tanta et tam intoleranda abiectionis onera ferre pateretur; quin immo id ipsum usque adeo perindigne tulit ut mori in exilio quam tam ignominiose in patriam redire maluerit.

49 Arrogans aliquantulum fuisse perhibetur, quod ipsum tunc vel maxime declarasse dicunt, cum Bonifacius, summus pontifex, per id temporis Gibellinorum exulum precibus fatigatus, Carolum quendam, vel Philippi Francorum regis fratrem vel potius propinquum, ad componendum civitatis statum mittere constituerat. Quod Guelfarum partium duces, qui ea tempestate rem publicam gubernabant, permoleste ferentes consultandi gratia convenerunt. Summa consilii fuit ut aliquot legati ad Bonifacium mitterentur, cuius legationis princeps, universo omnium consensu, ex eo Dantes designabatur quod ceteris ingenio et eloquentia facile praestabat. Id ubi ipse animadvertit dixisse fertur: 'Si sententiae vestrae, ut par est, acquievero iniunctaeque legationis munus vobis obtemperans obiero, quis ad rei publicae gubernationem remansurus est? Sin minus, quis huius legationis dignus princeps et caput erit?' Sed ea quae materno sermone dixisse perhibetur lepidiora sunt.

50 Haec et huiusmodi eius verba ad singularem quandam hominis arrogantiam vulgo omnes adscribunt. Verum si paulo diligentius

this purpose, they had carefully discussed the matter with some leading fellow citizens, but all their efforts seemed destined to come to naught unless Dante would submit to a most dishonorable and humiliating procedure. It seems to have been something of this sort: first, he would have to greatly soften his attitude, and second, he would have humbly to beg his enemies for their pardon and voluntarily give himself up to serve a term in the city prison. In addition to such extreme measures, he also had to go to the cathedral in Florence upon being released from prison at the end of his sentence and make a solemn offering to God, as condemned criminals used to do on the occasion of important civic feasts. After being informed of all these conditions by his friends, he refused to submit to such degrading and intolerable demands; and indeed he was so offended at the proposal that he preferred to die in exile rather than return to his native land in such an ignominious way.

He had the reputation of being rather arrogant. He showed this particularly, they say, when the sovereign pontiff Boniface VIII, wearied by the entreaties of the Ghibelline exiles, resolved to send Charles—a brother, or rather a close relative of King Philip of France—to bring peace to Florence. Enraged at this decision, the leaders of the Guelf Party, who then ruled the state, gathered to discuss it. The upshot of the meeting was that some ambassadors should be sent to Boniface, and as the head of this mission they unanimously elected Dante, as he easily excelled the rest in intelligence and eloquence. It is said that upon being informed of this he asked: "If I obey your order, as is fit, and leave to carry out the mission with which you have entrusted me, who will be left here to govern the state? If, on the other hand, I stay, who will be fit to act as the leader and the head of this mission?" The response he is reported to have made is wittier in the vernacular, however.[37] 49

Everyone commonly ascribes these and similar remarks to some sort of unusual arrogance on his part. Yet if you weigh the matter 50

et res ipsa et tempora, ut decet, pensitabuntur, vel ex magna rei publicae caritate vel ex altitudine quadam animi fortasse ab eo dicta verosimilius accipi poterunt. Nam si quis etiam atque etiam considerarit quanta et quam varia mala pestifera civilium partium studia iampridem Florentiae intulerant, si deinde postea animadverterit Dantem, in suo illo praeclaro prioratu, nonnullos magnae auctoritatis viros ob cuiusdam principis evocationem relegandi, ut supra diximus, auctorem extitisse, si denique eo spectare pontificis decretum excogitaverit, ut adversariarum partium exules ab exilio ad patriam revocarentur, mirari fortasse desinet; quin immo haec eius verba, quae quibusdam parum momenta temporum, ut par est, considerantibus tumida nimis videri solent, in bonam partem ab eo prolata fuisse censebit.

51 Complura volumina bifariam conscripsit, quorum quaedam materno, quaedam vero latino sermone composuit. Materna quoque partim florenti, partim autem provecta aetate edidisse manifestum est. Nam praeter solutos quosdam rhythmos compluresque solutas cantilenas, adulescens duo egregia opera litteris mandavit: horum alterum *Vita Nova*, alterum vero *Convivium* inscribitur, in quibus quidem opusculis claras quarundam cantilenarum suarum expositiones congregavit. Provecta deinde aetate, suum illud divinum potius quam humanum *Comoediae* poema, tametsi latine heroicis carminibus primum ab initio in hunc modum incoepisset:

Ultima regna canam fluido contermina mundo,

et quae sequuntur, ac satis eleganter per plura latina carmina processisset, cum postea non recte principiis reliqua convenire viderentur, genere dicendi permutato, rursus ab initio resumens materno sermone egregie incohavit atque elegantissime absolvit.

52 In hoc divino, ut dixi, poemate non modo poetica ipsa et quae proprie ad poetas pertinent, sed moralia quoque et naturalia ac divina, ingenti legentium admiratione, congessit. Quocirca quinque

itself and the circumstances more carefully, as you should, you might accept that his words were more likely dictated either by his great love for the state or by a kind of high-mindedness. For if you consider carefully how many terrible evils of all sorts partisanship had brought to Florence, and then remember that Dante, while serving in that famous priorate, had been responsible for exiling some influential citizens, as we said above, for having called in a foreign prince, and if, finally, you take into account that the aim of the pope's decision was to recall Dante's enemies from exile, you will perhaps not find his behavior all that surprising. Indeed, you will conclude that these remarks of his were well taken, and not swollen with arrogance as certain people think who have taken too little account of the circumstances.

He wrote many books, which may be divided into two classes: 51
those written in his native tongue, and those in Latin. It is obvious that he authored some of his vernacular writings in his prime, others at an advanced age. Besides some sonnets and many ballads, in his youth he wrote two outstanding works, whose titles are *New Life* and *The Banquet*. Both these booklets contain a selection of his poems accompanied by a commentary. Then in his maturity, he composed his *Comedy*, a poem more divine than human. He actually started it in Latin in an heroic meter, the first verse running as follows:

Ultima regna canam fluido contermina mundo.[38]

Later, however, after completing several cantos in rather elegant Latin, he resolved to change the type of diction he was using, since the first part of the poem seemed not to match the rest. Admirably, he began again in the vernacular, and eventually completed the poem in a most elegant way.

In this poem that I have called divine, Dante not only touched 52
on subjects proper to poetry and poets, but also on ethics, natural science, and theology, thus inspiring enormous admiration in his

supra viginti circiter annos huiusmodi opus scripsit atque emendavit, quippe antequam exularet iam septem eius *Comoediae* cantus expleverat, quos Graeci odas appellant. Eiusmodi cantus, quamquam in direptione et depredatione domus suae una cum multis aliis libellis chirographisque inter magnam quandam suorum librorum congeriem in penitiori parte aedium abstrusi fuissent, sedato tamen paucis post diebus populi furore, non dedita opera in hunc modum reperti fuisse dicuntur. Cum enim uxor eius de chirographo dotis suae sollicita esset, ad quaerendum idoneum quendam virum adhibuerat. Hic cum inter illam librorum atque chirographorum congeriem, quam reconditam fuisse diximus, de dotis chirographo diligenter quaereret, inter quaeritandum oblatus est libellus quidam in quo septem illae memoratae odae continebantur, quas cum legeret, novitate rei admiratus, domum suam asportavit. Ibique saepenumero lectitans, mira quadam legendi suavitate exhilaratus, ad poetam exsulantem demum transmisit; quos cantus postea poeta[12] prosecutus, subsequenti oda his verbis manifestissime expressit: 'Equidem prosequens inquam,' et reliqua.

53 Non multis deinde ante mortem suam diebus ultimas manus divino poemati imposuit absolvitque. Id ex eo constat, quod post obitum suum mirabilia quaedam contigisse dicitur, quae hoc ipsum apertissime declararunt. Nam cum scripta quaedam, in quibus aliquot ultimi *Paradisi* cantus continebantur, nondum integro volumini apposuisset sed in quodam occulto aedium loco abscondisset, ut forte opportunum componendi tempus praestolaretur, ac per hunc modum opus imperfectum appareret, ecce umbra defuncti poetae Jacopo, cuidam ex filiis suis maiori natu et imprimis de imperfectione operis sollicito atque ansio, in somniis apparuisse fertur; qua quidem visione filium admonitum fuisse dicunt ubi illa ultima *Comoediae* scripta abstrusa laterent, ac per hunc modum ab eo postea summo mane quaesita, ut in somniis fuerat admonitus, tandem adinventa fuisse. Sed quorsum haec tam multa de huiusmodi[13] somniis dicet quispiam? Ut luce clarius appareat id quod

readers. He wrote and polished this poem for more than twenty-five years; indeed, even before his exile he had already completed seven cantos (which the Greeks call "odes") of the *Comedy*. The following story is told about these cantos, which had been hidden in a remote part of his house, thrown into a great pile along with many other books and documents when the house was being looted. They were discovered a few days later when popular fury had had a chance to subside. His wife had become concerned about the document recording her dowry, and asked a suitable person to make inquiries. While searching for the document among the great pile of books and papers hidden there, this person came upon a booklet containing those seven cantos. He started reading them and was so impressed with their originality that he took them home with him. There he kept reading and rereading them, enjoying their marvelous sweetness, until finally he sent them to the poet who was then in exile. Dante afterwards continued on from those verses, as he clearly indicated in the first line of the following canto: "Continuing on, I say," etc.[39]

It was only a few days before his death that he put the final 53
touches on the divine poem and completed it. The clearest possible evidence of this is offered by the miraculous episodes that are said to have taken place after his death. In fact, he had hidden in a cranny of his house some sheets containing the last cantos of *Paradise*, waiting for the right time to add them to the rest of the poem—which for this reason seemed still incomplete. The story is told that one night the shade of the dead poet appeared in a dream to Jacopo, his eldest son, who was the person most concerned and anxious to see the poem finished. They say that in this vision the son was told where those last cantos of the *Comedy* were hidden. Early the following morning he started looking for them and finally found them, exactly as he had been told in the dream. Some may wonder why I speak so much of dreams like this. I do so in order to give the clearest proof of my earlier claim, namely, that it

paulo ante expressimus: vigintiquinque circiter annos illud divinum poema fuisse absolutum atque emendatum. Nam si poeta ante exilium suum septem illas odas perfecerat et ultimo vitae suae anno opus absolverat, cum tricesimo quinto aetatis anno exularet obiretque quinquagesimo sexto, constat ipsum per tot fere annos quos supra expressimus absolvisse; nam aliquot annos in septem illarum odarum absolutione consumpsisse credendum est.

54 In latino vero sermone nonnulla insuper opera composuit. Etenim, praeter multas eius epistulas, *Bucolicum carmen* scripsit. Soluta quoque oratione praeclarum quoddam opus edidit, quod *Monarchia* inscribitur; id in tres libros ob tria pulcherrime quaesita speciosissime distinxit. In primo namque eius operis libro, more dialectico disserens, perscrutatur an ad bonum orbis terrarum statum unius dominatus, qui 'monarchia' graece appellatur, necessario requiratur; in secundo vero an populus romanus hunc unius dominatum sibi non iniuria asciverit; in tertio denique an eiusdem dominatus a solo Deo vel ab aliquo eius ministro dependere videatur. Ob hoc tam singulare opus, propterea quod adversus romanae ecclesiae pastores editum esse videbatur, poenae haeresis, ut magnus quidam legum interpres manifeste testatur, damnatus fuisse dicitur.

55 His igitur omnibus, ut diximus, egregie admodum peractis, quinquagesimo sexto aetatis suae (trecentesimo autem et vicesimo primo supra millesimum christianae salutis anno) Ravennae obiit. Hanc mortis suae causam nonnulli extitisse tradidere. Quippe Veneti adversus memoratum Novellum, Ravennatum praesidem, bellum gerebant; quocirca factum est ut a Novello, ob singularem quandam viri elegantiam, ipse ad Venetos orator mitteretur. Ubi ergo Venetias applicuit, oratoris officio accurate fungi cupiens, postulavit ut sibi publicum auditorium praeberetur; id cum saepenumero frustra tentasset, plane animadvertit, ob singulare quoddam et ardens Venetorum in Novellum odium, omnes conatus suos tandem aliquando ad nihilum evasuros. Proinde, re infecta,

took him about twenty-five years to finish and polish that divine poem. For if the poet had completed those seven cantos before his exile and had finished the whole work in the year of his death, and if, moreover, he was exiled at thirty-five and died at fifty-six, it is clear that it took him about the number of years we said to finish it. Besides, it is very likely that he spent some years finishing the first seven cantos.[40]

He also composed several works in Latin. Apart from his nu- 54
merous letters, he wrote a *Pastoral Poem*. Furthermore, he authored an excellent work in prose entitled *Monarchy*, which he strikingly divided into three books, each one dedicated to a famous problem. The first book of this work contains a dialectical discussion aimed at assessing whether the rule of one, which in Greek is called *monarchia*, is necessary for the good of the whole world; the second whether the Roman people justly claimed this monarchical lordship for itself, and the third, finally, whether this rule derives from God alone or from one of His ministers. It is said that Dante was condemned to be punished for heresy, as a certain great professor of law clearly testifies, on account of this unusual work, because it seemed to be directed against the shepherds of the Roman church.

Having accomplished all these excellent things, he died at the 55
age of fifty-six in Ravenna, in the 1321st year of Christian salvation. Some have reported that the cause of his death was as follows. The Venetians were waging war on the aforementioned Novello, ruler of Ravenna, who on that account decided to send Dante as ambassador to the Venetians because of his unusual elegance and refinement. Upon his arrival in Venice, being eager to perform in the best possible manner the task with which he had been entrusted, he immediately asked to be granted a public audience. Having repeatedly tried in vain to obtain one, he finally realized that all his efforts were going to come to nothing thanks to the Venetians' unique and burning hatred for Novello. He acknowledged

quamprimum Ravennam redire statuit. Verum iter maritimum veritus — quod a praefecto magnae Venetorum classis mare ea parte, qua Ravennam ibatur, vehementer vexari acceperat — terrestre iter assumpsit. Quo quidem in itinere, cum ingenti animi sollicitudine (quod irrita omnino sua legatio extitisset) tum quoque ob varia ac multiplicia terrestris itineris incommoda, febris, antequam Ravennam ingrederetur, hominem repente invasit, a qua usque adeo acerbe vexatus est ut paucis post diebus e vita decederet. Huiusmodi ergo fuit praeclari poetae finis.

56 Sepultus est Ravennae in sacra Minorum aede, egregio quodam atque eminenti tumulo lapide quadrato examussim constructo, compluribus insuper egregiis carminibus inciso insignitoque. Epitaphium ab initio huiusmodi in quadrato sepulcri lapide incisum fuit:

Theologus Dantes nullius dogmatis expers
   quod foveat claro philosophia sinu,

et quae sequuntur. Cum deinde postea sex dumtaxat carmina, longe prioribus illis elegantiora, a doctissimo quodam viro edita essent, veteribus e tumulo abolitis, nova haec incisa fuerunt. Carmina huiusmodi sunt:

Iura monarchiae, superos, Phlegethonta lacusque
lustrando cecini, voluerunt fata quousque.
Sed quia pars nostri melioribus edita castris
auctoremque suum petiit felicior astris,
hic claudor Dantes patriis extorris ab oris
quem genuit parvi Florentia mater amoris.

the failure of his mission and decided to return to Ravenna as soon as possible. Afraid of travelling by sea, and having heard that the expanse of sea between there and Ravenna was being harried by the admiral of the great Venetian fleet, he went by land. On that trip, both because of the deep disappointment he felt over the complete failure of his mission and also owing to the many discomforts of travelling by land, he suddenly fell sick with fever before reaching Ravenna. The fever was so violent that within a few days he passed away. Such was the death of this illustrious poet.

He was buried at Ravenna in the church of the Franciscans, in 56
a splendid and imposing tomb built of finely hewn square stones. It was marked with a long and splendid verse inscription. Originally, an epitaph was carved on the square tombstone as follows:

Dante the theologian, well-versed in all the principles
that Philosophy may nurture at her noble breast,

and so on.[41] Afterwards, a learned man wrote six verses much more elegant than these earlier ones. The latter were then erased and replaced by the new ones, which read as follows:

The rights of monarchy, the gods, the lake of fire
in song did I describe so long as Fate allowed me.
But part of me then left for better campaigns,
To seek its creator happily amid the stars.
Here I, Dante, am enclosed, in exile from my native land,
whom Florence bore, a mother of little love.[42]

Vita Francisci Petrarchae

1 Franciscus, Petrachi cuiusdam scribae filius, cognomento Petrarcha (a Petracho patre 'r' littera sive euphoniae sive potius, ut quibusdam placet, amplificandi nominis sui causa interposita), trecentesimo quarto supra millesimum christianae salutis anno, illucescente vigesimae diei quintilis mensis aurora, Arretii natus est, in vico quodam qui vulgo 'Orti' vicus dicitur. Hac forte die, eadem fere nativitatis suae hora, exules florentini populi, qui iam pridem patria extorres se Arretium Bononiamque contulerant, contractis undique auxiliis, ad portas patriae, si qua fors fuisset, ulciscendi gratia certatim contenderunt. Haec enim omnia ipse in epistula quadam ad Ioannem Boccacium, eius temporis egregium poetam, manifeste testatur. Vetusta eius origo supra Parenzum quendam avum suum ab Ancisa, propinquo Florentinorum oppido, repetita traducitur.

2 Petrachus igitur pater, quamquam Ancisae oriretur, Florentiae tamen habitavit, ubi prae ingenii excellentia ac singulari linguae elegantia ad magnos Italiae principes primum florentini populi nomine pro arduis rebus oratoris officio elegantissime usus est. Scriba deinde ad magistratum Reformationum ex magno eiusmodi hominum numero, ceteris omnibus non iniuria ob ingenii acrimoniam et linguae elegantiam praepositus, ipse unus deligitur. Quo in magistratu, tametsi aliquot annos officio suo diligenter atque integre fungeretur, in magna tamen illa civili et turbulenta dissensione quae inter Albos et Nigros, duas diversas civitatis factiones, invaluit, quemadmodum in Dantis vita latius descripsimus, propterea quod Albis adhaesisse videretur, una cum ceteris Albarum partium fautoribus urbe exactus, Arretium concessit. Ac dum fallaci spe Florentiam redeundi in hoc loco aliquamdiu commoraretur, factum est ut filium ex uxore sua susciperet, quem diminute, veteri quodam infantilis indulgentiae ritu, pro Francisco 'Checcum'

Life of Francesco Petrarca

Francesco Petrarca, son of a notary named Petracco—eventually an 'r' was added to his father's name, either for the sake of euphony or, as some prefer, to make it sound more impressive—was born in the 1304th year of Christian salvation, at dawn on July 20th in Arezzo, in a part of town called "Dell'Orto" in the vernacular. On that same day, around the hour of his birth, the Florentine exiles (who had been banished some time before and had gone to Arezzo and Bologna) were heading for the gates of their native town. Hoping to avenge themselves, if good fortune would allow it, they had gathered support on every side. This is what Petrarca himself attests in an epistle he wrote to Giovanni Boccaccio, an excellent poet of the time.[1] As for the origins of his family, it is possible to trace them as far back as his grandfather, a certain Parenzo from a village close to Florence called Incisa. 1

Though born in Incisa, his father Petracco lived in Florence. 2
There, thanks to his intelligence and unusual eloquence, he had been entrusted with some difficult missions to important Italian princes, which he scrupulously carried out. Later he was chosen from among a large number of candidates to serve as secretary to the Riformagioni,[2] a preferment he merited by virtue of his keen intellect and correct use of language. After serving with zeal and integrity in this office for several years, at the time of that great and turbulent civil discord (which, as we described at length in Dante's life, split the city into the White and Black factions), he was exiled, along with the other Whites, for having supported that faction. He then went to Arezzo, where he dwelt a rather long time in the vain hope of returning to Florence. It was in that town that his wife bore him a son, Francesco, whom he used to call by the diminutive "Checco," an old form of indulging children. At the time he already had another son, Gherardo—the same Gherardo

appellavit, cum alterum nomine Gerardum iam pridem habuisset. Hic est ille Gerardus qui infinitis paene saecularis vitae, ut ita dixerim, incommodis posthabitis, arduum illud Cartusiensium monasterium intrare non formidavit; ibi monasticam vitam, iuxta asperiores quasdam eius religionis constitutiones, asperrime usque ad extremum ducens, in aeterna pace quievit.

3 Paucis deinde annis post hanc filii sui nativitatem, Petrachus omnes exulum cum quibus conspiraverat conatus in irritum hactenus evasisse atque ad nihilum recidisse conspicatus, in Galliam Transalpinam versus, Avinionem, ubi forte ea tempestate summus pontifex residebat, simul cum universa familia sua perrexit. Hic sedem suam constituens, ubi Franciscum primis pueritiae annis iam ad discendum aptum prospexit, in parvam quandam Provinciae urbem[1] transmisit cuius nomen Carpentoras dicebatur, ut ibi a praeceptore nescio quo egregie erudiretur. Inde quadriennio grammaticis eruditus, postea quam prima illa puerilia studia transegit e vestigio ad Montem Pesulanum, oppidum per ea tempora florentissimum, ut ius civile cognosceret (non sine molestia, quod suavibus Ciceronis et Maronis libris iam mirum in modum oblectaretur) vicina iam pubertate traducitur. Ubi quadriennio etiam in cognoscendo iure civili consumpto, non iniussu patris Bononiam proficiscitur, quo in loco alterum itidem quadriennium in cognitione iuris prope contrivit. Septem namque annos in studiis civilibus incassum amisit, ut ipse in epistula quadam aperte demonstrat, in qua de hac tanta temporis iactura vehementius conqueritur, quamvis nonnullos Ciceronis et Virgilii libros clanculum, ne pater rescire posset, hoc interim tempore legisset.

4 Post obitum vero patris, utpote tunc primum sui iuris effectus, cunctis iuris civilis codicibus eiusque ineptis commentationibus abdicatis, circa primos adulescentiae suae annos humanitatis studiis omnino se dedicavit, quocirca studiorum gratia Tolosam concessit. Inde quarto anno reversus, Parisiensium urbem contendit. Quarto rursus anno, Neapolim eo tempore opportune adivit

who did not hesitate to renounce the innumerable cares of secular life so as to join the stern Carthusian order.[3] He thus led an extremely strict monastic life, following the demanding rules of that congregation, until he was blessed with eternal rest.

A few years after the birth of his second son, Petracco saw that all the efforts of the exiles with whom he had conspired were vain and had come to naught. So he resolved to leave with all his family for Avignon, in Transalpine Gaul, where the supreme pontiff happened to be living at the time. Having settled there, in due course he saw that little Francesco was ready to be educated, so he sent him to Carpentras, a small town in Provence, in order that he might receive there an excellent education from a teacher whose name I don't know.[4] After studying Latin for four years and completing his primary education, he was now approaching puberty and was sent to Montpellier, at that time a flourishing city, to study civil law. This he disliked, for he already delighted to an amazing extent in the delicious books of Cicero and Vergil. After spending another four years there in the study of civil law, he complied with his father's wishes and went to Bologna, where he wasted a further four years learning civil law. He thus spent about seven years in the study of civil law to no purpose, as he attests in a letter where he complains bitterly about having thrown away so much time.[5] Nevertheless, in those years he managed to read several works of Cicero and Vergil in secret, hiding it from his father. 3

Upon his father's death, having finally become independent, he rid himself of all civil law texts and their foolish commentaries. He was then in the early years of his adolescence and decided to dedicate himself completely to the study of the humanities, to which end he left for Toulouse. He came back from that town in the fourth year of his studies and betook himself to Paris. After four years (again) he went to Naples. It was a good time to go, for the famous king Robert of Sicily happened to be there at the time. After another four years — he divided the course of his studies into 4

quo Robertus inclitus Siciliae rex forte convenerat. Hinc postea abiens quarto quoque anno, sic studiorum suorum cursum per quadriennia partiebatur, eodem remeavit.

5 In Galliam deinde Cisalpinam profectus, Veronae primum, mox Parmae ac Ferrariae, demum Patavii aliquamdiu fuit; Mediolanum post haec ac Ticinum venit. Pisas et Arretium, dilectum primi exilii et originis suae locum visendi gratia, petiit. Venetiis denique aliquantulum permansit, ut ipse haec omnia in epistula quadam ad Guidonem archiepiscopum Ianuae, omnem studiorum suorum cursum prosecutus, apertius ostendit.

6 In his igitur humanarum et divinarum rerum studiis diutius per varia et diversa loca, quemadmodum diximus, versatus, usque adeo profecit ut inter ceteros praecipuos laborum suorum fructus primus dicendi elegantiam, iam supra mille annos paene defunctam (ob inhumanam quandam primo Romanorum imperatorum crudelitatem, qui urbem Romam omni saevitiarum genere, crebris proborum et doctorum virorum trucidationibus, nefarie nimis vexaverant, ob saevissimum deinde Longobardorum dominatum, qui totam Italiam quattuor supra ducentos circiter annos occupatam penitus devastaverant), praecipua quadam ac prope divina ingenii excellentia e tenebris in lucem revocavit. Nam et primus complures Ciceronis libros per multa saecula Italis antea occultos ac propemodum amissos sua singulari diligentia nobis restituit, atque eius epistulas, prius hinc inde varie dispersas, eo ordine quo nunc videmus in sua volumina redegit.

7 Et suo quodam excellentiori dicendi genere seipsum posteris in soluta oratione et carmine ad imitandum praestitit, quod nulli alio usque ad tempora sua contigisse legimus ut in utroque dicendi genere praevaleret. Etenim si duo apud Latinos et totidem apud

four-year periods in this way—he left that city, too, and returned to Avignon.[6]

Then he set out for Cisalpine Gaul.[7] He stopped first in Ve- 5
rona, then Parma and Ferrara, and finally in Padua for a short time. Afterwards, he went to Milan and Pavia. He also visited Pisa and Arezzo—the latter out of a desire to see his beloved birthplace and his first place of exile. He then stayed for some time in Venice, as he himself writes in an epistle to Guido, archbishop of Genoa, in which he describes all these travels, following the whole course of his studies.

Thanks to his uncommon and almost divine genius, Petrarca 6
made great progress in the study of things human and divine—which, as we have just said, he pursued for a long time in many different places. Among the many remarkable fruits of his studies the principal one was his revival of correctness and good taste in Latin diction, which he brought back to light out of darkness after it had been nearly defunct for over a thousand years. It had died, in the first place, because of the inhuman ferocity of the Roman emperors, who had wickedly oppressed the city of Rome with every sort of cruelty, slaughtering numerous upright and learned men, and secondly because of the savage rule of the Lombards, who sacked all of Italy during their two-hundred-and-four-year occupation.[8] It was Petrarca, in fact, who first restored to us, by virtue of his unremitting zeal, a large number of Cicero's works that had been unknown and almost lost to the Italians for many centuries, and it was Petrarca who also collected his scattered epistles in the order in which we now read them.

Furthermore, his unparalleled eloquence rendered him a model 7
for future writers both in prose and verse. We know of no one prior to his time who excelled in both forms of writing. Indeed, if, as it seems, the two greatest thunderbolts of genius among both the Latins and the Greeks excelled in just one form of writing, failing in the other, what should we think of the lesser lights? It is

Graecos humanorum ingeniorum fulmina alter ab altero dicendi genere destituta videntur, quid de ceteris putandum est? Quippe immortalia illa Demosthenis et Ciceronis ingenia, quae quidem in soluta oratione, velut in regno suo, dominantur ac triumphant, in carminibus manca ac debilia fuisse conspicimus; et veneranda in versibus Homeri et Virgilii maiestas, in prosis orationibus ita claudicat ut qui ab eis dicta fuisse ignoraret, eorum esse perpetuo contenderet. Quod in ceteris quoque artium studiis evenire perhibetur, ut nullus in pluribus excellat. Id propterea natura comparatum esse arbitrantur, ut si ipsa parens rerum uni vel omnia vel plura largiretur, unde postea alteri traderet habere non posset.

8 Solus igitur Petrarcha, hac praecipua et paene divina gratia praeditus, in utroque dicendi genere valuit. Proinde tanto in honore apud omnes habebatur, ut non amplius Franciscus Petrachi sed Franciscus Petrarcha, amplificato nomine, ubique appellaretur. Cuncti etiam paulo humaniores omnium gentium populi eius nomen venerari videbantur. Unde Arretini, cum ipsum e Roma revertentem — quo Jubilaei gratia perrexerat — Arretium divertere accepissent ut dilectum nativitatis suae locum viseret, sibi adventanti ante urbis moenia populariter occurrerunt tanta omnium congratulatione ut regi aut magno principi amplius, sicut ipse in epistula quadam commemorat, fieri non potuerit. Florentini quoque, qui Petrachum patrem antea relegaverant, paternae relegationis contumaciam revocantes, filio (tanto et tam singulari viro) omnia patris errata gratis condonarunt; de quo quidem tam praecipuo et tam peculiari erga se beneficio ipse florentino populo gratias agens, epistulam quandam laudibus et gratiis refertissimam scribit.

9 Incliti insuper principes, admirabili et paene incredibili virtutum suarum fama pertracti, personam suam ita observabant ut inter se de eo habendo certatim fere contenderent. Summus namque pontifex ipsum ad sanctitatem suam saepenumero per epistulas accersivit, magnos sibi dignitatis gradus, si accederet, ultro pollicitus. Quod etsi primam, sicut dicitur, tonsuram iampridem acce-

obvious that the immortal geniuses of Demosthenes and Cicero, which dominate and triumph in prose as though in their own kingdom, are lame and feeble in verse. As for Homer and Vergil, while their verse is solemn and majestic, their prose speeches are so awkward that any person who didn't know they had written them would invariably challenge their authorship.[9] The same is true of all the other disciplines: no one excels in many fields. They say that nature is the cause of this, for if like a mother she bestowed all or most of her gifts upon a single person, nothing would be left for the others.

Only Petrarca, therefore, was endowed with the peculiar and almost divine grace of excelling in both forms of writing. Hence he was universally held in such esteem that everyone started calling him "Francesco Petrarca" instead of "Francesco di Petracco," making his name more impressive. All the peoples of every country possessing some degree of culture seemed to venerate his name. The Aretines, for instance, having heard that he was visiting their city on his way back from Rome—where he had been for the jubilee—so as to see his beloved birthplace, came out en masse to meet him before the city walls with such enthusiasm that even a king or a great prince, as Petrarca himself writes in an epistle, could not have been better received.[10] Even the Florentines, who had once exiled his father Petracco, revoked the insult of his father's banishment and freely forgave all the father's wrongs for the sake of his son, that great and extraordinary man. To express his gratitude to the Florentine people for such a substantial and extraordinary privilege, he wrote a letter filled with praise and thanks.[11] 8

Famous princes, too, drawn by the remarkable and almost incredible fame of his virtues, esteemed his person so much that they competed with one another to retain his services. The supreme pontiff himself often summoned him before his holy presence by letter, promising him high honors if he would come. Al- 9

pisset, ut facilius iuxta vota sua, tenuitate patrimonii cogente, in otio viveret, maiora tamen haec summi pontificis oblata, utpote tranquillam studiorum suorum quietem perturbatura, recusare non dubitavit. Id ipsum et potentissimum Mediolanensium ducem et illustrem Patavii principem nonnumquam fecisse constat, ut ingentia sibi munera ultro pollicerentur si secum conversari atque habitare vellet.

10 At ipse cum quibusdam praeclaris principibus aliquamdiu vixit. Penes enim summum pontificem tempore iuventutis suae aliquantulum commoratus est; sed ingenti quodam curialis, ut aiunt, vitae taedio postea affectus, ita inde abiit ut numquam in posterum redire voluerit, quamvis saepius ab ipso pontifice per epistulas et apostolicas oblationes multum admodum invitaretur. Et cum Galeatio Vicecomite, Mediolanensium ductore, aliquot annos permansit; et cum quibusdam denique aliis egregiis[2] principibus conversatus, tria (et ea quidem praecipua) legationis munera his temporibus dignissime obivit: Venetias quippe causa pacis inter Venetos et Ianuenses reformandae, et ad serenissimum etiam Romanorum regem, in extrema barbarie forte degentem, 'pro ligustica pace,' ut eius verbo utar, et ad gratulandum denique Ioanni Francorum regi, britannico tunc carcere liberato, orator missus est, quemadmodum ipse ad Ioannem Boccacium in epistula quadam scribit. Tantoque in honore memorati principes eum habebant, ut de praelationibus et praecessionibus, velut in ambulationibus fieri consuevit, vicissitudinaria inter se controversia crebro oriretur. Verum ille, quoniam erat singulari prudentia nec minori modestia praeditus, numquam adduci potuit ut tantis et tam praestantibus populorum ductoribus se in honore praeferri pateretur.

11 Quid plura de maximo eius honore dicam, cum sexcenta sint eiusmodi quae ingentem eius gloriam fuisse aperte declarent? Sed ceteris omnibus brevitatis causa omissis, unum tacitus praeterire

though he had already received the so-called first tonsure, so as to fulfill more easily his wish to lead a leisurely life despite the meagerness of his patrimony,[12] he did not hesitate to turn down the supreme pontiff's grand offers, fearing that they would disturb the tranquillity of his studies. As is well known, the most powerful duke of Milan and the illustrious prince of Padua did the same, promising him enormous gifts if he would come and live at their courts.

Admittedly, he did spend time with certain renowned princes. 10
In his youth, for instance, he waited upon the supreme pontiff for a while. But afterwards he left in disgust at the immense boredom of curial life, they say, so that he never returned despite the pontiff's frequent personal letters and apostolic offerings inviting him. He also spent some years with Galeazzo Visconti, the Milanese condottiere, and frequented the courts of other noble princes. While doing so he distinguished himself by service on three very important diplomatic missions. He was sent as ambassador first to Venice to negotiate a peace agreement between the Venetians and the Genoese; then to represent the "Ligurian peace" (to use his own expression) before His Most Serene Highness, Emperor of the Romans, who happened to dwell in a remote barbarous country; and finally, as he himself writes in an epistle to Giovanni Boccaccio, to congratulate King John of France on his release from British captivity.[13] The aforesaid princes held him in such esteem that successive controversies often arose between them on matters of preference and precedence, as generally happens when there are processions. Being an unusually prudent and modest man, however, he was never drawn into allowing himself to be given precedence over those important and distinguished leaders.

There is no point in continuing to describe the great honor in 11
which he was held, as I could give six hundred examples of this kind which would clearly reveal his extraordinary fame. But leaving them aside for brevity's sake, I cannot pass over in silence this

non possum, quod ita mirabile est ut quiddam huic nostro simile mirata antiquitas pro miraculo litteris mandaverit. Etenim dum in Gallia Cisalpina admodum adulescens degeret, non modo de Italia sed de ulteriori etiam Gallia nobiles quosdam et ingeniosos viros, sola visendi gratia, in epistula quadam ad seipsum venisse testatur. Et quod mirabilius est et vix credibile, nisi ab eo ipso vel idoneo veritatis assertore ibidem confirmaretur, caecum namque grammaticum per totam ferme Italiam ipsum quaeritasse ac tandem aliquando convenisse tradit; atque prae nimio conveniendi sui desiderio ipsum sublatum manibus filii et discipuli, quibus ambobus pro vehiculo utebatur, caput eius et dexteram manum crebris osculationibus petiisse describit, quasi tactu ipso eximio et paene insatiabili sui desiderio satisfaceret, quandoquidem visu satiari non posset. Haec omnia ipse, ut diximus, in epistula quadam ad Doninum grammaticum placentinum aperte commemorat. Quamobrem de ultimis Hispaniae Galliarumque finibus usque ad urbem Romam quosdam venisse nobiles sola visendi doctissimi viri causa minime mirari se dicit, quod de Tito Livio scribit Hieronymus, cum sibi superiora provenerint.

12 Ad haec omnia vel maxima gloriae insignia nihil deesse videbatur ad gloriosum hominis cumulum nisi ut laurea corona insigniretur, qua apud veteres Graecos et Latinos imperatores egregiosque poetas tantummodo coronatos fuisse constat. Id ne consummatae hominis gloriae deesset, magna quadam ac solemni celebritate Romae coronari meruit. Hanc poeticam lauream—per quinquaginta supra noningentos circiter annos a Claudiani temporibus (qui imperante seniore Theodosio floruit) usque ad hunc nostrum Petrarcham perpetuo intermissam—solus ipse non immerito assumpsit, ut quod florentinus et vetus poeta iamdiu antea ultimo accepisset, florentinus et novus vates eodem modo accipiens post tot annorum curricula renovaret.

one wondrous episode, for antiquity marvelled at an episode like this, recording it as a miracle. When he was still a youth in Cisalpine Gaul, as he writes in a certain letter, noble and clever men came not only from other parts of Italy, but also from Transalpine Gaul for the sole purpose of seeing him. What he adds in the same epistle is even more prodigious, and it would be hard to believe were it not reported by him or another such trustworthy claimant. He writes how a blind grammar school teacher finally succeeded in meeting him after having searched for him all over Italy. He describes how the man was so overcome with the desire to meet him that he had his son and his pupil, who were carrying him, lift him up in their arms so that he might cover the poet's head and right hand with kisses, as though, being unable to see him, only actual physical contact with him would satisfy his extraordinary and almost insatiable desire. He narrates all this, as we said, in an epistle to a grammar school teacher, Donino of Piacenza.[14] This is why, he says, he wasn't surprised that certain noblemen would come all the way to Rome from the most distant regions of Spain and Gaul just to see a great scholar, as Jerome writes of Livy—for even more remarkable things had befallen himself.[15]

The only emblem that seemed to be lacking in the man's glorious accumulation of honors and success was the bestowal of the laurel crown, which among the ancient Greeks and Latins was conferred solely upon emperors and the greatest poets. Lest the consummation of his glory be wanting in any way, he earned his coronation at a great and solemn ceremony in Rome. He alone deserved to be crowned poet laureate, a title which had not been granted for over nine hundred and fifty years, from the time of Claudian, who flourished under the elder Emperor Theodosius, until our Petrarca. Hence an honor that long ago an ancient Florentine poet had been the last to obtain was renewed in like manner by a modern Florentine bard, who received it after the passage of many years.[16] 12

13 Cum haec igitur humanitatis studia per longinqua ac diversa terrarum loca (Pythagoram et Platonem, duos summos philosophos, egregie imitatus) diutius perscrutaretur atque propterea in maximo honore apud omnes fere orbis terrarum gentes, quemadmodum supra diximus, haberetur, demum vitam solitariam, utpote huiusmodi humanarum ac divinarum rerum studiis accommodatiorem, adamavit. Proinde, ceteris omnibus mundi pompis et honoribus posthabitis, in Euganeis collibus, non amplius quam decem milia passuum a Patavio urbe distantibus, se in otium contulit; ubi et domum parvam, solitudinis gratia, instruxit et aliquot oliveta nonnullasque vineas parvo emptas adiunxit. In hoc tam opportuno atque tam[3] accommodato loco in studiis suis usque ad extremum vitae longius versatus, multa memoriae mandavit; de quibus omnibus antequam mentionem faciamus, formam et habitudinem corporis et domesticos mores eius parumper enarrare satius esse censemus.

14 Forma eius ita decora fuisse dicitur ut per omnem aetatis partem maiestatem quandam prae se ferre videretur. Nam, praeter singularem quandam corporis pulchritudinem, hilari facie gravitate condita et statura procera adeo ornabatur ut praecipuam ac censoriam personae dignitatem visentibus demonstraret. Ad naturalem quoque gravitatem acerba et immatura in adulescentia canities accedebat, quod licet ipse ab initio moleste ferret, seipsum tamen praeclarorum virorum exemplis consolabatur quibus adulescentibus hoc idem contigisset. Siquidem et Numae incana menta et Vergilii iuvenis barba candidior et Domitiani adulescentis coma senescens et Stilichonis festina et postremo intempestiva canities[4] Severini sibi ipsi interdum consolandi gratia ante oculos proponebat.

15 Valitudine prosperrima usque ad senectam usus est; tanta enim corporis agilitate ac dexteritate praevalebat ut vix ab aliquo superari posset. In senectute autem postea tantis languoribus vexabatur ut, agmine facto, sicut ipse quodam loco dicit, omnia morborum

Having long pursued the study of the humanities in many different and distant lands (following the example of Pythagoras and Plato, those two supreme philosophers)[17]—thus eliciting, as we said above, the deepest admiration from almost all the nations of the world—he finally embraced a solitary life as more befitting the study of things human and divine. Accordingly, he renounced all worldly pomp and honors and went to live a retired life in the Euganean Hills, no more than ten miles away from the city of Padua. There he built himself a small house to protect his privacy and also purchased cheaply a few olive groves and some vineyards. In this place, perfectly convenient and suited to his studies, he spent the rest of his long life, composing a large number of works. Yet before we speak of them all it will be well to say a few things about his bearing and physical appearance as well as his daily habits. 13

They say he was so handsome that throughout his life he seemed to project a kind of majesty. He added to his unusual physical beauty a grave yet pleasant face and a body of imposing height, which were such as to inspire onlookers with a sense of his extraordinary personal dignity and austerity. His natural gravity was enhanced by his white hair, which came upon him distressingly early in his youth. He deplored this at first, but eventually found comfort in the examples of famous men who had had a similar experience in their youth. So, from time to time, he consoled himself by thinking of Numa's "hoary chin,"[18] the "too-white beard" of the young Vergil, the young Domitian's "aging hair," as well as the untimely whitening of Stilicho and Severinus' hair.[19] 14

He enjoyed robust health until old age, and his physical quickness and dexterity were almost unsurpassed. In old age, however, he was beset with so many ailments that, as he himself writes, it was as if all kinds of illnesses had closed ranks and were leaping to attack him on all sides.[20] Thus by the age of sixty-six his body was so weak that he could not walk without the help of his servants. 15

genera circumsilirent atque invaderent. Itaque sexto et sexagesimo aetatis suae anno tanta corporis imbecillitate tenebatur ut absque ope famulorum nullatenus ambularet. Huius rei causam medici partim aquae potum extitisse aiebant, qua quotidie vesceretur, partim vero quotidiano pomorum esui et inediae carnium et assiduis ieiuniis hanc eius debilitatem imputabant.

16 Nec minor animi sui decor quam corporis fuit; nam in moribus semper usque a primis pueritiae annis gravitatem servavit, et quamquam florenti aetate in odis suis, quibus natura aptissimus erat, lascivis amoribus indulsisse videretur, a gravitate tamen censoria ungue latius, ut dicitur, non recedebat; quod quidem complura ab eo per omne tempus aetatis diligenter servata manifestissime probant. Siquidem ieiunium a pueritia animose coeptum usque ad extremum fere vitae suae annum accuratissime simul atque constantissime sine intermissione retinuit; idque ieiunium ita accurate custoditum, inedia sextae feriae, cum solo aquae potu, quasi acriori sale, condiebat. Media insuper nocte ad dicendum Christo laudes iugiter surgebat, qui mos ab eo magna cum cura servabatur nisi forte aliqui morbi nonnumquam interrupissent.

17 Quid plura? Tantum abest ut ipse lascivis amoribus inhaereret ut ob religiosam quandam vitae continentiam atque severitatem et sanctimoniam morum non defuerint qui ipsum perpetuam castitatem ac virginitatem continuisse traderent; quod forte mirari desinemus, si abstinentiam et asperitatem victus, si aquae haustum, si crudas herbas, si pomorum esum, si praeterea quotidianum et perpetuum ieiunium, quibus non modo non offendebatur sed vehementius oblectabatur, nobis ante oculos proposuerimus. Quod si haec vera sunt, ipsum aliud profecto in memoratis odis quam nuda eius verba sonare videantur poetico more intellexisse manifestum est.

18 Acerrimi et ardentissimi ingenii ac tam fidelissimae memoriae fuisse traditur, ut in miraculum usque procederet; siquidem nonnulli ipsum supra viginti milia versuum, quandocumque recitare

The doctors ascribed his debilitation to his habits of drinking water and eating fruit every day, to his avoidance of meat and to his frequent fasts.

His soul was no less beautiful than his body. Ever since child- 16
hood, in fact, he had adopted a serious way of life, and even in his prime, when he seems in his lyrics to have indulged amorous passions (to which he was highly inclined by nature), he actually never departed more than a finger's breadth, so to speak, from the most austere gravity. This is manifestly proven by many practices he preserved carefully throughout his life. From adolescence to almost the last year of his life, for instance, he maintained a fixed regime of fasting. In addition to fasting on Fridays he also drank only water, as though seasoning his fasts with bitter salt. He used to rise faithfully in the middle of the night to sing the praises of Christ, a habit he always observed with great care, except in case of illness.

In short, he was so far from indulging amorous passions that, 17
owing to his almost religious self-control and his severe, holy habits of life, not a few people claimed that he observed perpetual chastity and virginity. Such claims will not surprise us if we bear in mind his plain and meager diet, his habits of drinking water and eating just uncooked vegetables and fruit, his regular and unremitting fasts—all of which, far from harming him, brought him intense pleasure. If all this is true, it is clear that those afore-mentioned poems are meant to be understood in a sense other than their literal meaning, after the fashion of poets.

His mind was so keen and eager and his memory so powerful 18
that it was almost miraculous. Some write that he was able to recite more than twenty thousand verses whenever he pleased. Throughout his entire life, he was subject to an inexhaustible desire to read, a real insatiability which, as he writes somewhere, na-

placuisset, rettulisse scribunt. Per omnem aetatem suam inexhausta quadam legendi cupiditate ferebatur, cuius nimirum insatiabilem, ut ipse quodam loco dicit, natura ipsum finxerat. Itaque non contentus latinae linguae libris qui per id tempus vulgo habebantur, vetustos codices quos et Varronem et Ciceronem aliosque doctissimos viros quondam posteris scriptos reliquisse noverat assidue perquirebat. Unde inter Belgas et Helvetios, sicut ipse testatur, viginti quinque aetatis annos natus accuratissime quaeritabat, ubi praeter epistulas et nonnullas Ciceronis orationes duos illos praeclaros eius *De gloria* libros, in extremo fere Germaniae angulo abstrusos, post multos quaerendi labores demum inveniens e tenebris in lucem eruit; ipsosque coetaneis suis singulari eius diligentia restitutos, incuria eorum nobis ablatos satis admirari non possum.

19 Neque hoc etiam insatiabili et inexhausto legendi desiderio ullatenus satisfecit, quin immo linguam graecam, per ea tempora omnino novam et peregrinam atque, ut ita dixerim, ab Italia longe abhorrentem, discere concupivit, ut per maximam quandam graecorum librorum copiam suo illi lectitandi desiderio satisfaceret, quandoquidem in quotidiana et perpetua latinorum voluminum pervolutione satisfacere non posset. Quocirca primus a Barlaam, monacho litterarum graecarum imprimis peritissimo, vel potius tantummodo doctissimo, Catonem Censorium imitatus—qui in senectute litteras graecas discere non erubuit—graece edoceri coepit. In his peregrinis alienarum litterarum studiis multum admodum, ut arbitror, prae singulari ingenii ac memoriae excellentia diligentia adhibita profecisset, quamquam ipse moderate, ut cetera, se forte profecisse dicat, nisi importuna memorati praeceptoris mors sibi ipsi iam discere incipienti invidisset.

20 Proinde ad lectionem latinorum librorum reversus, simul ac[5] cuncta profana gentilium volumina legendo percurrit, postremo sacris codicibus operam dedit, quorum veneranda lectione incredibiliter delectabatur. Unde et cum religiosissimis simul atque doctissimis eius temporis viris magnam per epistulas familiaritatem

ture had impressed upon him.[21] Hence, dissatisfied with the Latin books commonly available at the time, he set out to search tirelessly for ancient manuscripts that would contain the works he knew to have been written by Varro, Cicero, and other learned men. At the age of twenty-five, for instance, he was in Belgium and Switzerland, as he himself attests, seeking books with great care. There, in addition to the epistles and several orations of Cicero, he brought to light the Roman orator's two famous books *On Glory,* which he found after much laborious searching in a remote corner of Germany.[22] I am continually amazed how these books, which his strenuous efforts had restored to his contemporaries, were then lost to us again because of their negligence.

So great was his insatiable and bottomless longing to read that 19
he conceived the desire to learn Greek — a language utterly unusual and foreign at that time and, so to speak, repugnant to Italy. He hoped that the great quantity of books written in that language would finally satisfy his intense desire to read, since the regular and constant perusal of Latin texts had not done so. To this end, he began to learn Greek under Barlaam, a monk especially knowledgeable about Greek letters — or rather just learned enough. In doing so, he imitated Cato the Elder, who was not ashamed to study Greek in old age. I believe that his unique intelligence and outstanding memory would, with due application, have allowed him to make great progress in the exotic study of this foreign language (although as usual he says that he made little progress) if the untimely death of the aforesaid tutor had not hampered him just as he was beginning to learn.[23]

Accordingly, he returned to reading books in Latin, and as soon 20
as he had run through all the secular writings of non-Christian authors, he at length devoted his efforts to sacred letters, taking incredible pleasure in reading those venerable pages. By exchanging letters he formed close relationships with the most holy and learned men of his time, and he often asked them in his letters to

contraxerat, ita ut eos crebro per litteras precaretur ut sui in divinis eorum orationibus, maxime vero in consecratione dominica, sine intermissione meminissent.

21 Cum itaque formam et habitudinem corporis et domesticos mores eius, sicut promisimus, breviter attigerimus, reliquum est ut egregia scripta sua deinceps recenseamus, si prius tamen quendam Sorgiae fontem parumper descripserimus; nam hic et Arquadae quadam, ut diximus, Patavii villa magnam suorum operum partem adumbravit ac confecit. Sorgiam igitur nobilissimum Narbonensis provinciae fontem esse aiunt, cuius origo e specu quodam saxei montis tanta clarissimarum aquarum copia emanat, ut fluvium eiusdem nominis, cum in planitiem largius descenderit ac se in lata camporum aequora effuderit, optimis piscibus abundantem efficiat. Ubi ergo se in campos latius effudit, in fundo suo laetas herbas ita suaves producit ut boves, vel bibendi vel adaquandi vel pascendi spatiandive gratia eo adductae, cum illam limpidarum aquarum claritatem prospexerint, a fundo ipso, mersis usque capitibus, petere ac carpere conentur.[6] Per planitiem deinde, parvo cursu contentus, penes Avinionem oppidum in Rhodanum effluit. Hic itaque fons—licet aquarum copia, abundantia piscium, herbarum fertilitate non ignobilis et incolentibus et transeuntibus esse videatur—longius tamen diuturno praestantissimi poetae incolatu omnibus et doctioribus et semidoctis innotescit. Pluribus quippe scriptorum suorum locis perpetuam quandam huius amoenissimi fontis mentionem fecit; magna etenim huius fontis amoenitate captus, complures ibi annos quietissime habitavit atque studia sua ita peregit ut multa memoriae mandaret. Proinde hunc locum, ubi memoratus Sorgia ('rex fontium,' ut ipse dicit) oriebatur, 'transalpinum Eliconem' suum appellare solebat.

22 Ea igitur quae in hoc loco scripsit una cum reliquis scriptis suis apud nos extant. Nam praeter odas materno sermone compositas, quas cantilenas et sonetia vulgato nomine dicunt, plura etiam litteris tradidit. Eglogas enim duodecim egregiis bucolicis carminibus

remember him unceasingly in their prayers—especially, of course, at Mass on Sunday.

21 Having briefly discussed, as we promised, his physical bearing and appearance as well as his daily habits, it now remains to touch on his excellent writings. First, however, we would like to spend a few words describing the spring called "the Sorgue", for it is there and in the village of Arquà, near Padua (as we said), that he conceived and wrote most of his works. The Sorgue, they say, is a celebrated spring in the province of Narbonne, whose source is a cave in a rocky mountain. From there it tumbles with an abundance of crystal clear water down to the plain below where it becomes a river of the same name and spreads out into wide pools in the fields, making it an excellent place to fish. There in the fields where the river is broadest, its bed produces grass so luxuriant and sweet that cows, attracted there to drink, bathe, graze, and walk about, gaze into the clear, limpid waters, and try to reach and graze in the river bed itself, sinking up to their heads. Thence it flows through the plain and after a short stretch feeds into the Rhone near the city of Avignon. Although already quite well known both to the natives and to travellers for its wealth of water, fish and and fertile pasture, the spring has long been made famous among all learned (and half-learned) men for the extended residence there of this most excellent of poets. He makes continual mention of this delightful spring in many places in his writings. Taken by the beauty of this place, he led a retired life there for many years, completing the studies that enabled him to leave behind him so many works. That is why he used to refer to the place where the Sorgue rises ("the king of fountains," as he calls it) as his "transalpine Helicon."[24]

22 What he wrote there has come down to us together with the rest of his writings. Besides the poems in his native tongue, which are called *canzoni* and *sonetti* in the vernacular, he composed many other works. He published twelve eclogues in fine bucolic verse.

edidit; epistulas multas scripsit numero circiter quadringentas — mille aliis, ut eius verbis utar, non ob aliam causam quam quia locus non caperet omissis — easque in duo volumina, instar tullianarum, ipse digessit. Horum alterum *Rerum Familiarum,* alterum *Rerum Senilium* nuncupavit; tertium quoque ad Barbatum quendam sulmonensem versibus dictatum adiunxit. Invectivas in gallum et in medicum composuit. Scripsit insuper *De remediis ad utramque fortunam* libros duos; *De vita solitaria* ad Philippum Cavallacensem episcopum item duos;[7] *De otio religioso* unum; *Rerum memorandarum* libros quattuor; *De ignorantia sui et aliorum* ad Donatum nescio quem librum unum; *De secreto conflictu curarum suarum* et *Contra clericos* libros; *De viris illustribus* unum, licet quidam nomine Lombardus post eius obitum alterum suppleverit. Cunctas praeterea superioris Africani laudes, in uno volumine per libros novem distincto, hexametris carminibus mirabiliter congessit, quem librum *Africam* inscripsit, licet morte praeventus ei ipsi iam immature edito ultimas, ut cupiebat, manus imponere non potuerit. Quas ob res in hac tanta scriptorum suorum confectione id praecipue curasse visus est, ne moriens minorem, vel maiorem potius, nominis sui gloriam relinqueret quam vivens reportasset; siquidem paulo ante quam moreretur et *Africam* ipsam emendabat et nova, ut aiunt, opera cudebat.

23 In hac itaque tam gloriosa et tam felici vita usque ad septuagesimum aetatis suae annum in magnarum ac variarum rerum studiis versatus, Arquadae obiit, quo, ut diximus, se in otium contulerat. Hunc ultimum eius finem a reliqua anteacta vita nullatenus discrepasse aiunt. Nam quemadmodum ab ineunte aetate usque ad medium fere annorum suorum cursum probitate morum atque excellentia doctrinae ab initio in maximis honoribus vivebat, et mox inde usque ad extremum in continua quadam altissimarum rerum contemplatione simul atque diuturna aeternae vitae praemedita-

He wrote many epistles, and collected about four hundred of them — omitting a thousand more, he says, simply for lack of space —[25] into two volumes, following Cicero's example; the first he called *Letters to His Friends*, the other *Letters of Old Age*. He then added a third volume, in verse, which he dedicated to Barbato of Sulmona. He composed two invectives, one against a Gaul, the other against a doctor. He also wrote the *Remedies for Good and Bad Fortune*, in two books; *The Life of Solitude*, to bishop Philippe de Cabassole, also in two books; *Religious Retirement* in one book; then the four books of *Things Worth Remembering*; [the invective] *On His Own Ignorance and that of Others* in one book, dedicated to a certain Donato;[26] the books *On the Secret Conflict of My Anxieties* and *Against the Clergy*; and the *Illustrious Men*, in one book, though a certain Lombardo added another one after his death. Furthermore, he collected all the great deeds of Scipio Africanus the Elder in a wonderful work in hexameters, consisting of nine books, which he entitled *Africa*. However, he died before he could put the final touches, as he desired, on this work which had been published before it was ready. His chief concern in composing these many writings seems to have been to bequeath a glory after death not at all inferior to the one he enjoyed in his lifetime — nay, an even greater one. Suffice it to say that shortly before his death he was still polishing the *Africa* and, reportedly, hammering out new works.

Thus, having led such a glorious and happy life devoted to the study of various important subjects, at the age of seventy he died in Arquà, where he had gone to live in retirement, as we said above. They say that the last part of his life was by no means inconsistent with his earlier years. From earliest youth until about middle age his moral integrity and pre-eminent learning had brought him great honors, and from then until the very end he dwelt sweetly in uninterrupted contemplation of the holy mysteries and in long meditation on eternal life, as though in some de- 23

tione, tamquam in iocundo quodam diversorio, suavissime commorabatur. Sic demum in Dei gratia, quantum per ea quae in morte apparuisse ferunt coniectura augurari possumus, gloriosissime defunctus, ex hoc caliginoso carcere in caelos ad patriam remeavit. Peregregium namque discipulum suum nomine Lombardum, quem ipse unice diligebat in cuiusve[8] sinu moriens expiravit, haec de eo, paulo post obitum suum, retulisse perhibent. Ipsum scilicet moribundum in extrema ultimi spiritus sui efflatione aerem quendam tenuissimum in candidissimae nubeculae speciem exhalasse, qui instar incensi thuris usque ad laquearia tabulati altius elatus ibidem vel paululum requievit; postremo in aerem limpidissimum paulatim resolutum evanuisse. Hoc adeo mirabile, ubi et auctoritate memorati discipuli et aliorum qui aderant testimoniis comprobatum ac creditum est, pro miraculo habitum, divinum poetae spiritum ad Deum revertisse propalam indicavit. Etenim in quotidianis et pervulgatis hominum mortibus, quos vita communis ferre consuevit, vel haec vel his similia nullo umquam tempore contigisse legimus.

24 Per hunc igitur modum poeta noster gloriosissime defunctus, ibidem in arca quadam marmorea sepultus esse dicitur, quam his tribus eius humillimis versibus insignitam exstare tradunt. Epigramma plenum modestiae eiusmodi est:

Frigida Francisci lapis hic tegit ossa Petrarchae.
Suscipe, virgo parens, animam, sate virgine parce,
fessaque iam terris caeli requiescat in arce.

De hac praecipua eius morte Colucius, non ignobilis nostri temporis poeta, libellum quendam composuit.

lightful hospice. Thus at last he died gloriously in the grace of God—so much we may suppose and hope, thanks to the signs that were said to have appeared at his death—and returned from this shadowy prison to his heavenly home. They say that a distinguished student of his, Lombardo, whom he held particularly dear and in whose arms he passed away, reported the following things right after his death. He said that when Petrarca breathed his last sigh he exhaled something like a surpassingly white cloud that, like burning frankincense, went up to the roofbeams and stayed there for a short while before vanishing little by little into the limpid air. This extraordinary event, whose authenticity is proved and attested by the authority of the aforementioned student and of others who were present, is considered a miracle, clearly confirming that the divine spirit of the poet returned to God.[27] And indeed I have never read that this or anything like it has ever happened in the case of the common and familiar deaths of the persons with whom ordinary life normally presents us.

Having departed this life in such a glorious way, our poet was 24
buried in Arquà in a marble vault, upon which were engraved these three humble verses of his. The epigram, full of modesty, goes like this:

> This stone covers the cold bones of Francesco Petrarca.
> Virgin mother, receive his soul; seed of the Virgin, have mercy upon it.
> Weary of the world, may his soul now find rest in the vault of heaven.

Coluccio [Salutati], a notable poet of our time, wrote a short book about his remarkable death.[28]

Vita Ioannis Boccacii

1 Ioannes Boccacius, egregius sui temporis poeta, ita Petrarchae in poetica successisse visus est, ut ipse Danti paulo ante successerat. Nam sicut Petrarcha septem supra decem annos natus erat quando Dantes ex hac vita decessit, sic ante Boccacium per novem annos nascens eius nativitatem praecesserat. In hac itaque vicissitudinaria horum praestantium poetarum successione, huiusmodi acerrima eorum ingenia ideo iisdem paene temporibus ex ipsa natura pullulasse arbitror, ut in quo humanum genus per mille circiter annos destitutum fuisse videbatur, in eo — quasi opportune post tot saecula aliquantisper dedita opera — restauraretur, ne poetica ab hominibus omnino recessisse crederetur, si diutius in tenebris iacuisset.

2 Ioannes igitur, cognomento Boccacius, a Boccacio patre e Certaldo — quodam propinquo Florentinorum oppido — oriundo, viro in primis honesto atque mercatore, nascitur, quemadmodum ex pluribus scriptorum suorum locis et ex[1] epitaphio suo, quod ipse dictaverat, evidentissime apparet. Ut autem post infantiles parentum indulgentias puer discendi per aetatem capax fuit, a genitore, vetusto maiorum more, ludo litterarum deditus, sub Ioanne grammatico, Zenobii cuiusdam non ignobilis eius temporis poetae patre, Florentiae erudiebatur, donec paterna congregandae pecuniae cupiditas ipsum, vel paululum eruditum, ex florenti paene discendi cursu, mutata voluntate, revocaverit; quae usque adeo vehemens fuit ut eum vix prima litterarum elementa, quamvis acri ingenio praeditus esset, percipere permiserit. Unde ex ludo grammatici circa primos pueritiae suae annos ad scholas arithmetici, iuxta florentinam consuetudinem, traducitur. Inde, paucis post annis, nondum adulescentiam ingressus, ut ipse testatur, cuidam maximo eorum temporum mercatori traditur ut in mercatura eru-

Life of Giovanni Boccaccio

Giovanni Boccaccio, an excellent poet of his time, seems to have succeeded Petrarca in poetry the way the latter succeeded Dante. Just as Petrarca was already seventeen when Dante departed this life, Boccaccio was born nine years after Petrarca. I believe this succession of distinguished poets to be the work of nature herself, which caused those extraordinary geniuses to flourish around the same time, so that what had been lacking to the human race for almost a thousand years — namely, poetry — might be restored to it, after so many centuries, at an opportune moment, almost as though on purpose. Otherwise, if it had lain in darkness any longer, poetry might be thought to have abandoned the human race completely.[1] 1

Giovanni, whose surname was Boccaccio, was the son of Boccaccio, a gentleman merchant, and came from Certaldo, a village close to Florence, as one can clearly see from many passages in his writings and from his own epitaph, which he himself dictated. After being indulged as a child, the boy reached an age where he was capable of learning, and was sent by his father in the customary way to be educated at a grammar school in Florence. He studied under Giovanni the Grammarian, the father of that Zenobi who was a poet of some repute at the time.[2] Shortly afterwards, his father's lust for moneymaking made him change his mind and withdraw young Giovanni from school. He had been doing well, but had just started his education. His father was so imperious on this point that his son, though endowed with a sharp intelligence, barely had the chance to learn the alphabet. So from grammar school he was transferred, in the early years of his boyhood, to a counting school,[3] in accordance with Florentine custom. After a few years, before entering adolescence (as he himself attests), he was apprenticed to a great merchant of the time to learn about 2

diretur. In hac institoria arte cum memorato illo mercatore per sex annos commoratus, se nihil aliud egisse quam irrecuperabile tempus incassum contrivisse confirmat, quoniam suapte natura ab huiuscemodi quaestoriis artibus abhorrebat ac litterarum studiis aptior videbatur. Quocirca rursus e taberna institoria ad cognitionem iuris pontificii (non iniussu patris, ut cetera) invitus in canonicum gymnasium detruditur; quod Petrarchae in iure civili itidem in eius vita contigisse diximus.

3 Huiusmodi igitur iuri cognoscendo a patre destinatus, totidem fere quot in mercatura annos, magna cum molestia, frustra consumpsit. Nihil enim in illis studiis se profecisse dicit, quod has pontificum sanctiones atque quascumque ineptissimas commentationes mens sua indignabunda multum admodum fastidiret. Proinde ubi per aetatem sui iuris effectus esse visus est, statuit quoquo modo huiusmodi studia dimittere et ad poeticam, ceteris posthabitis, se conferre; quod, repugnantibus et patre et clarissimo quodam praeceptore suo et nonnullis eius familiaribus, postea fecit. Nec mirum cuiquam videri debet si nec reverentia patris, nec praeceptoris auctoritas, nec amicorum preces ipsum continere potuerunt quin pontificia iura dimitteret et ad poeticam se conferret, quoniam ad ipsa poetica ita natus erat, ut paene ab ipso Deo factus ad haec sola fuisse videretur, atque a ceteris omnibus abhorreret. Quod ut evidentius appareat, nonnullas sententias suas, certa quaedam ac fidelia tantae aptitudinis testimonia, in medium adducemus.

4 Ipse quippe in ultimo *Genealogiarum* libro de universali studiorum suorum cursu loquens, cum se a patre primum arithmeticae, mox mercaturae, deinde memorato iuri lucrandi gratia traditum memoraverit, postremo, 'matura paene aetate' (his enim verbis utitur) ceteris omissis, poeticae operam dedisse scribit, ad quam suapte natura ita natum fuisse testatur, ut nondum septimum aetatis annum ingressus (quo quidem tempore nec poemata per se ipsum capere nec poetas ab aliis audire potuerat, quin immo vix

commerce.[4] He asserts that the six years he spent learning the arts of shopkeeping under this merchant turned out to be nothing but an irreparable waste of time, for his nature abhorred these money-grubbing arts and seemed to be particularly suited to literary studies. So, once again complying with his father's wishes, he was taken out of the shop and forced to study canon law[5] at a university—just as had happened to Petrarca with respect to civil law, as we said in his life.

Being thus put by his father to study law, he wasted on it, much 3
to his annoyance, almost as many years as he had on commerce. He claims to have made no progress whatsoever in those studies, for his intellect rebelled at all those pontifical decrees and mindless commentaries and scorned them. Therefore, as soon as he came of age and was independent, he resolved to quit those studies somehow and turn to poetry, putting aside all other preoccupations. This he eventually did, despite opposition from his father, a certain famous teacher of his, and some of his intimates. Nor should anyone be surprised that neither respect for his father, nor his teacher's authority, nor his friends' entreaties kept him from quitting canon law and turning to poetry, since he was so born for poetry that he seemed to have been created by God for it alone, finding every other calling repugnant. Let us show this more clearly by reporting some statements of his as certain and reliable proof of his remarkable aptitude.

In the last book of the *Genealogies*, speaking of the entire course 4
of his studies, after mentioning how his father, for the sake of gain, sent him first to study arithmetic, then commerce, and finally the aforementioned kind of law, he himself says that, "close to maturity" (to quote his words), he put everything aside and devoted himself completely to poetry, to which he was so inclined by nature that even before he was seven years of age (at a time when he was still unable to understand poems for himself, and could not have studied the poets with others as he had barely learned the al-

prima litterarum elementa perceperat) nonnullas, mirabile dictu, fabellas composuerit; et, quod mirabilius est, ante quam poemata intelligere posset, propter singularem tamen quandam fingendi aptitudinem 'poeta' vulgo ab omnibus vocabatur. Et paulo post: 'Iam fere,' inquit, 'maturus aetate ac mei iuris effectus, nullo suasore, nullo praevio doctore, quin immo patre repugnante et eiusmodi studia velut frivola et inutilia damnante, poetas dumtaxat aggredi non dubitavi; nec ambigo, si florenti aetate haec ipsa poetarum studia attigissem, quin unus inter celebres poetas tandem evasissem.' Haec propterea ab eo dicta fuisse constat, ut se suapte natura ad poeticam natum apertius posteris demonstraret.

5 In his igitur vatum studiis, ceteris aliarum artium omissis, ita assidue versatus est ut, quamvis multa alia praeter ipsa poemata sibi admodum placerent, omnibus tamen posthabitis solam poeticam[2] retinuerit. In mathematicis quippe sub Andalone quodam ianuensi viro, eius temporis omnium in illis artibus peritissimo, aliquot annos audivit. Sacros quoque Sanctarum Scripturarum libros libentius avidiusque perlegit, et quamquam haec omnia peravide[3] legeret, retentis tamen vatum dumtaxat studiis, postea dimisit. Huiusmodi ergo vatum cognitioni per hunc modum sero nimis addictus,[4] dici non potest quantum brevi tempore cum corpore tum animo elaboraverit ut per assiduam quandam veterum poetarum lectionem ac multiplicem librorum latinae linguae transcriptionem in certam mysteriorum suorum notitiam facilius perveniret. Quocirca cum libros non haberet nec unde emere posset, tenuitate patrimonii cogente, <ut> sibi suppeteret, multa non modo veterum poetarum sed oratorum etiam et historicorum volumina, quicquid paene in latina lingua vetustum inveniri potuit, propriis manibus ipse transcripsit, adeo ut copiam transcriptorum suorum intuentibus mirabile quiddam videri soleat hominem pinguiorem, ut eius corporis habitudo fuit, tanta librorum volumina propriis manibus exarasse ut assiduo librario, qui nihil aliud toto fere vitae suae tempore egisset, satis superque esset, nedum homini

phabet) he had composed, wondrous to say, some stories; and, more wondrous still, even before he could understand poetry, everyone called him "poet" because of his unusual creativity. And a little later he writes: "When I reached maturity and became independent, without anyone either urging me or teaching me — indeed, my father disapproved of my decision, holding these studies in contempt as frivolous and useless —, I did not hesitate to turn to the poets alone; and I am sure, had I started studying the poets early in my life, I would have become a famous poet myself." These things he said in order to show more clearly to posterity how he was naturally inclined to poetry.[6]

5 He immersed himself so much in the study of the poets, leaving all other arts aside, that, despite his enjoyment of many things apart from poetry, he devoted all his time to poetics alone and nothing else. He was taught mathematics for a few years by a certain Andalò, a Genoese, the greatest expert of the time in that subject.[7] He also read the Bible with great interest and pleasure; nevertheless, after reading all such things with great avidity, he afterwards gave them up to focus entirely on the study of poetry. Having come very late to the study of the poets, as we said, it is incredible how much effort he put in it, laboring physically and mentally, so that in a short time, by reading carefully the ancient poets and transcribing many Latin texts, he attained quite easily a sure knowledge of their mysteries. Lacking both books and the means of buying them owing to his slender patrimony, he copied down in his own hand many volumes not only of ancient poets but orators and historians as well — virtually any ancient Latin text he could find. It is really amazing, if one considers the quantity of books he transcribed, that a rather fat and corpulent man such as he was succeeded in copying on his own so many volumes, an accomplishment that would have been difficult for a hardworking

circa cognitionem humanarum et divinarum rerum propterea occupatissimo ut cogitationes suas litteris postea mandaret; quod a poeta nostro egregie factum fuisse constat, ceu posterius apparebit.

6 Nec hac nostra latinorum librorum copia, vel inopia potius, contentus, graecas litteras discere concupivit, ut per earum cognitionem in his quae latinae linguae deesse videbantur pro virili sua opitularetur. In quo quidem Petrarcham, ut arbitror, imitatus, plus alienae linguae quam ipse consecutus est. Etenim sicut ille Barlaam, Basilii Caesariensis monachum litterarum graecarum imprimis peritissimum, audire voluit, ut suo insatiabili legendi desiderio per graecorum librorum lectionem penitus satisfaceret quando latine legens satiari non poterat, sic iste Leontium quendam Pilatum thessalonicensem—peregregium primo memorati monachi discipulum, mox virum eruditissimum atque in omni Graecorum facultate doctissimum—triennium, dum graece legeret, publice ac privatim audivit. Siquidem hunc e Venetiis longe alio contendentem, suis consiliis mutato eundi proposito, Florentiam ubi habitabat pollicitationibus suis revocavit. Illum namque in propriam domum ab initio honorifice suscepit susceptumque postea diuturnum hospitem habuit atque ita curavit ut publica mercede ad legendum codices graecos publice conduceretur; quod ei primo in civitate nostra contigisse dicitur ut graece ibidem publice legeret. Non multo post, maiori graecarum litterarum aviditate tractus, suis sumptibus, quamquam inopia premeretur, non modo Homeri libros sed nonnullos etiam codices graecos in Etruriam atque in patriam (e media, ut aiunt, Graecia) reportavit, quod ante eum nullus fecisse dicebatur ut in Etruriam graeca volumina retulisset. Huiusmodi veteres duorum tam insignium poetarum graecarum litterarum primitiae quasi seminarium quoddam extitisse videntur, quod uberiorem terram postea nactum gradatim adeo in dies pullulavit ut, temporibus nostris florens, uberrimos iam fructus peperit. Id ut evidentius appareat, graecorum studiorum progressum,

scribe who devoted his whole life to such a task, let alone a man intensely involved in the study of things human and divine and striving to commit his thoughts to writing—which, as we shall see, our poet did with great success.

Not content with our abundance—or rather paucity—of Latin 6
books, he grew eager to learn Greek in order to compensate as best he could for what was lacking in Latin texts. I believe that in so doing he followed Petrarca's example and eventually learned Greek better than the older poet had. Just as Petrarca wanted to be tutored by the Basilian monk Barlaam, a great expert in Greek, in order to satisfy his insatiable desire for books by reading Greek texts (since reading Latin books had not satisfied him), so Boccaccio attended for three years both the public and private lessons of a certain Leontius Pilatus of Thessalonica, an excellent disciple of the aforesaid monk and himself a most learned man and an expert in Greek language and literature. Leontius had already made up his mind to leave Venice for some distant country when Boccaccio's offers persuaded him to come to Florence, where the poet was then residing. At first, in fact, he received him graciously in his own house and had him as his guest for quite a long time. He also saw to it that Leontius was appointed with a public stipend to give public readings of Greek books. He is said to have been the first to give such public lectures in Greek in our city. Not long afterwards, motivated by an increasing desire to study Greek, he brought back "from the heart of Greece," as they say, to Tuscany and his native land not only Homer's books but also various other Greek manuscripts, at his own expense and despite the pressures of poverty. It was said that no one before him had ever brought Greek books back to Tuscany.[8] These first fruits of Greek letters brought forth by the two distinguished poets seem to have provided a kind of seedbed which, finding in later times more fertile ground, germinated gradually day by day until they finally flourished in our times, bearing the richest of fruits.[9] To make this

opportunum dicendi locum in praesentiarum nacti, paucis ab origine repetemus.

7 Ante Petrarchae tempora, posteaquam latina lingua remittere paulatim pristinas vires suas coepit, nulla paene in Etruria graecarum litterarum mentio a nostris hominibus per multa saecula habebatur, sed qui tunc erant homines, suis contenti disciplinis, aliena non quaerebant. Petrarcha igitur, primus ex nostris peregrinas litteras attingere conatus, sub Barlaam monacho (Graecorum omnium, ut diximus, eius temporis peritissimo) erudiebatur; et nisi ei iam discere incipienti importuna praeceptoris mors invidisset, non forte, ut ipse de se loquens modeste dicit, sed procul dubio, prae singulari quadam ingenii ac memoriae excellentia, multum admodum profecisset. Hunc Boccacius, ut arbitror, imitatus, a Leontio quodam thessalonicensi, litterarum graecarum in eadem tempestate doctissimo, triennium eruditus, nonnulla percepit; multo plura, ut ipse testatur, percepturus, si diutius vagus praeceptor, veteri maiorum suorum ritu, in eodem docendi proposito perseverasset. Tantum tamen ex inde hoc suo disciplinae tempore reportavit ut inter cetera *Iliadem* atque *Odysseam*, praeclara Homeri poemata, intellexerit; verum etiam nonnullos alios poetas ab exponente magistro percipiens, multa suo egregio *Genealogiarum* operi opportune admodum inseruerit.

8 Non multo post Boccacii obitum complures docti homines una emerserunt, qui universum latinae linguae campum florenti aetate longius pervagati, recenti Petrarchae et Boccacii (doctissimorum hominum) exemplo graeca ipsa adoriri non dubitarunt. Unde vehementi eorum discendi desiderio satisfacere cupientes, doctissimum quendam virum constantinopolitanum nomine Emmanuelem, e Costantinopoli, ubi degebat, Florentiam usque, non sine magnis variarum rerum pollicitationibus, accersiverunt; accersitumque privata et publica mercede aliquot annos discendi gratia

clearer, we shall seize the opportunity to illustrate briefly the progress of Greek studies from the beginning.

Before Petrarca's time, after the Latin language had slowly be- 7
gun to lose its original vigor, there had been for many centuries almost no mention of Greek letters in Tuscany; the men of that age, content with their own disciplines, did not investigate foreign ones. Petrarca was the first among us to try to learn foreign letters by becoming a student of the monk Barlaam—who, as we said above, was the greatest Greek scholar of the time. If the untimely death of his teacher had not hampered him as he was just starting to learn, he would doubtless (not "perhaps", as he modestly says of himself)[10] have made great progress, thanks to his unusual intelligence and excellent memory. It was in imitation of Petrarca, I believe, that Boccaccio managed to learn quite a lot after three years of study under Leontius of Thessalonica, the best scholar of Greek letters of the time; yet he would have learned much more, as he himself attests, had his tutor, following the erratic traditions of his race, not abandoned his plan of teaching.[11] He did, however, carry away from that period of instruction enough knowledge to understand, among other texts, Homer's renowned poems, the *Iliad* and the *Odyssey*. Moreover, his teacher's lessons acquainted him with the writings of various other poets, of which he made good use later, quoting them often in that excellent work of his, the *Genealogies*.[12]

Not long after Boccaccio's death, many learned men emerged all 8
at once who had explored the whole field of the Latin language and did not hesitate to follow the recent example of those most learned men, Petrarca and Boccaccio, by turning to the study of Greek. Wishing to satisfy their intense desire to learn, they offered inducements of various kinds to bring a most learned man, called Manuel, from his native Constantinople to Florence. Upon his arrival, they provided him with both a public and a private stipend to teach and retained him for several years, up to a point when he

eo usque retinuerunt quoad plures exinde doctiores emanaverint. Quid plura de graecis studiis dixerim, cum eorum ortum progressumque longius enarrasse videamur quam ab initio putaramus? Hic est ille Emmanuel Chrysoloras a quo multi peregregii discipuli primitus profluxerunt, qui postea peregrinam Graecorum linguam non modo per Etruriam sed per nonnullas etiam nobiliores Italiae partes, quasi novum litterarum semen, ita disperserunt ut parvo post tempore, paulatim crescens, iam usque ad nostram aetatem mirum in modum germinasse videatur. Sed quorsum haec tam multa de litteris graecis, dicet quispiam? Quorsum? Ut totum hoc quicquid apud nos Graecorum est Boccacio nostro feratur acceptum, qui primus praeceptorem et libros graecos, a nobis per longa terrarum marisque spatia distantes, propriis sumptibus in Etruriam reduxit.

9 In huiusmodi ergo humanitatis studiis usque ad extremum vitae sine intermissione versatus, multa litterarum suarum monumenta reliquit, quae omnia bifariam scripta apud nos extant. Quaedam enim materno, quaedam vero latino sermone edita habentur. Materna quoque partim carmine, partim soluta oratione bipartita cernuntur. Haec omnia, quamquam ab eo[5] adulescente scripta fuisse constat, tanto tamen lepore tantaque verborum elegantia condita conspicimus ut latinarum litterarum expertes homines, modo mediocri ingenio praediti, magna quadam sermonis sui lepiditate plurimum capiantur. Proinde fit ut suo illo lepido dicendi genere imbuti plerumque elegantes appareant. Scripta latina item bifariam sunt; alia namque versibus, alia vero prosa oratione dictavit. *Bucolicum* quippe *carmen* per sexdecim eclogas egregie distinxit ac nonnullas etiam epistulas carminibus edidit. Reliqua omnia soluta oratione composuit, siquidem *De casibus virorum illustrium* ad Carolum Cavalcantem, egregium equestris ordinis virum ac regni Siciliae praefectum, libros novem scripsit; *De montibus et fluminibus, stagnis ac lacubus et maribus* nonnulla litteris mandavit; *De mulieribus claris* ad dominam Andream de Acciarolis Altae Villae

had produced many learned men. What more should I say concerning Greek studies, since it looks as though we have expounded their origin and progress more than we intended? This Manuel Chrysoloras was the fountainhead from whom many eminent disciples flowed, who afterwards disseminated the Greek language, as though it were a new seed of letters, not only through Tuscany but also through several of the chief regions of Italy as well.[13] Shortly afterwards, it started to grow little by little, flourishing wonderfully in our time, as one can see. But someone might ask: why say all this about Greek letters? What is your point? My point is to show that we owe all our knowledge of the Greeks to our Boccaccio, who first brought back to Tuscany at his own expense a teacher and Greek books which had previously lain far away from us, over land and sea.

Being thus continuously dedicated to the study of the humani- 9
ties until the end of his life, he left many monuments of his literary activity. His books, all of which are extant, are of two kinds: some were written in the vernacular, some in Latin. The ones in the vernacular are partly in verse, partly in prose. Although written in his youth, the charm and the elegance of the language gracing all these works are so great that they fascinate even readers ignorant of Latin, as we see, provided they are endowed with an average degree of intelligence. Thus it happens that, imbued as they are with his charming style, they usually have an elegant appearance. His Latin works are also of two kinds: some he wrote in verse, others in prose. He divided his *Bucolic Poem* into sixteen eclogues and also published some verse epistles. He wrote all the others in prose, namely *The Misfortunes of Illustrious Men* in nine books, dedicated to Carlo Cavalcanti,[14] a distinguished member of the equestrian order and governor of the Kingdom of Sicily; he wrote a book entitled *On Mountains, Rivers, Lakes, Pools and Seas;* a book called *Famous Women,* dedicated to Lady Andreina

comitissam librum unum;[6] postremo praeclarum *Genealogiarum* opus in quindecim libros quam probe partitus ad Ugonem (inclitum Hierosolymae et Cypri regem) dedicavit, quod inter omnia opera sua consensu omnium principatum tenet.

10 Cum igitur originem atque studiorum suorum progressum hactenus pertractarimus, reliquum est ut formam et habitudinem corporis sui ac domesticos mores eius paucis deinceps absolvamus. Habitudo corporis obesa fuisse dicitur, statura procera, rotundiori facie, hilari et iucundo aspectu; sermone ita facetus et comis ut singulis eius verbis dum loqueretur summa urbanitas appareret. In amores usque ad maturam fere aetatem vel paulo proclivior.

11 Paupertate plurimum propterea offendebatur, quod expeditam studiorum suorum viam inde praepediri cernebat qua quidem sibi ad culmen, ut cupiebat, emergendum erat, illam satiricam sententiam crebro expertus:

> Haud facile emergunt quorum virtutibus obstat
> res angusta domi.

Plurima itaque paupertatis adversus gloriam eius impedimenta, paupertatem ipsam abigere non valens, assiduis quantum fieri potuit diurnis nocturnisque laboribus vel tollere vel saltem minuere enixius curavit. Quocirca multa librorum volumina propriis manibus transcripsit, ut per hanc paene assiduam codicum transcriptionem magno legendi, quo tenebatur, desiderio aliqua ex parte satisfaceret. Plurimorumque ab eo transcripta fuere; testis est non ignobilis bibliotheca quam Nicolaus Niccoli, vir apprime eruditus, in basilica sancti Augustini, multis post obitum Boccacii annis, suis, ut dicitur, impensis aedificavit; ubi postea omnes poetae libros, una cum operibus ab eo latine editis, egregie condiderunt, ut perpetuum quoddam maximae ac paene incredibilis in trascribendis codicibus diligentiae testimonium posteris extaret.

12 Suapte natura adeo indignabundus erat ut, quamquam tenuitate patrimonii vehementer angeretur, cum nullis tamen terrarum

Acciaiuoli, countess of Altavilla; and finally the *Genealogies*, a great work nicely divided into fifteen books and dedicated to Ugo, the famous king of Jerusalem and Cyprus. It is, by general consent, the most important of all his works.

Having thus far discussed the beginning and the progress of his studies, there remains for us to describe briefly his bearing, physical appearance and way of life. As for his physical appearance, he is said to have been fat, tall, rather round-faced, with a cheerful and jovial look. He was so sharp-witted and amiable that great urbanity was apparent in his every word. He was a little too inclined to love affairs almost until the age of maturity. 10

He was often preoccupied by his poverty, for he saw it obstructing the smooth course of the studies whose heights he hope to reach. He knew well, from personal experience, that satirist's famous saying: 11

Success is difficult to achieve for those whose virtues
are thwarted by a scant patrimony.[15]

Being unable to flee poverty itself, he strove with all his might, night and day, to remove or at least reduce the many impediments that poverty had strewn in his path to glory. He therefore transcribed many books with his own hand, and so was able to satisfy in some degree his great desire to read through this almost endless transcription of manuscripts. The large number of books he transcribed is attested by the fine library that Niccolò Niccoli, a man of remarkable learning, is said to have built at his own expense in the church of Saint Augustine many years after Boccaccio's death. Eventually all the poet's books were gathered there in an admirable fashion, along with the works he published in Latin, thus serving as an everlasting testimony to posterity of his outstanding and almost incredible diligence in transcribing manuscripts.

By nature he was so irascible and resentful that, though terribly harassed by lack of money, he never consented to live at any 12

principibus commorari vel paululum tolleraret; ex quo factum esse arbitror ut, numquam rebus suis contentus, pluribus scriptorum suorum locis statum suum vehementius deploraret.

13 Ad extremum huiusmodi tam studiosa vita functus, sexagesimo secundo aetatis suae anno gloriose obiit. Sepultus est Certaldi honorifice in basilica sancti Iacobi, lapide quadrato hoc epigrammate, quod ipse dictaverat, insignito:

Hac sub mole iacent cineres atque ossa Ioannis.
Mens sedet ante Deum, meritis ornata laborum
mortalis vitae. Genitor Boccacius illi,
patria Certaldum, studium fuit alma poesis.

Quae quidem carmina cum Colutio Salutato, viro eruditissimo, prae singulari quadam poetae excellentia nimis humilia viderentur, duodecim sua prioribus illis in hunc modum adiecit:

Inclite cur vates, humili sermone locutus,
de te pertransis? Tu pascua carmine claro
in sublime vehis, tu montium nomina tuque
silvas et fontes, fluvios ac stagna lacusque
cum maribus multo digesta labore relinquis
illustresque viros, infastis[7] casibus actos,
in nostrum aevum a primo colligis Adam.
Tu celebras claras alto dictamine matres,
tu divos omnes ignota ab origine ducens
per ter quina refers divina volumina, nulli
cessurus veterum. Te vulgo mille labores
percelebrem faciunt; aetas te nulla silebit.

14 Vita igitur et moribus trium praestantissimorum poetarum ut potuimus hactenus descriptis, reliquum est ut pro brevi quadam dictorum omnium conclusione eos invicem comparemus. Volentes itaque vicissitudinarias horum poetarum excellentias simul con-

prince's court, not even for a short while. That is why, in my opinion, he was never satisfied with his resources and why his writings are filled with bitter complaints about his condition in life.

At the end of this life of study, he died a famous man at the age of sixty-two. He was buried with honor in Certaldo, inside the church of Saint James, under a square gravestone upon which the following epitaph, which he himself composed, is written: 13

Beneath this stone lie the ashes and the bones of Giovanni.
His mind rests before God, embellished by the merits and
labors of his mortal life. Boccaccio was his father,
Certaldo his homeland, poetry his nurse and his passion.

Finding these verses too modest for the unique excellence of such a poet, Coluccio Salutati, a most learned man, added to them twelve of his own, which read as follows:

Distinguished poet, why speak of yourself so humbly,
As though in passing? Your famous verses elevate
pastoral life; the names of mountains,
woods and fountains, rivers, marshes, lakes
and seas you leave behind, most carefully arranged.
Illustrious men and their great misfortunes
you collect together, from Adam to our age.
You celebrate famous mothers in solemn style.
You depict the gods, tracing them all from their obscure
origins, in fifteen divine volumes, yielding to none
of the ancients. A thousand labors have made you famous
among the common people, and no age shall remain silent
about you.[16]

Having described as best we could the lives of these three excellent 14
poets, it remains for us to conclude by comparing them all briefly.
Wishing to compare one by one the excellent qualities of these po-

ferre, id praemittere ante omnia necessarium duximus quod ab omnibus conceditur: duplicem esse vitam in qua humanum genus versaretur, alteram activam, alteram vero contemplativam. Hoc ergo tamquam principio quodam vere in hac nostra comparatione praesupposito, non temere Dantem in utriusque vitae prope omnibus ceteris duobus praeferri oportere censemus. Ipse namque primum pro patria arma ferre atque fortiter pugnare non dubitavit; in gubernatione deinde rei publicae aliquamdiu versatus, optime se gessit. Haec sane ad vitam activam pertinent, quae de Petrarcha et Boccacio minime dici possunt; ipsi enim, omissa penitus re publica, privatim in otio ac litteris totam fere aetatem suam contriverunt, quae vita, communi omnium consensu, contemplativa appellari consuevit.

15 Petrarcha itaque[8] et Boccacius huic soli, ceteris posthabitis, dediti, eum profecto superare debuerunt, quo quidem et diuturniorem et longe quietiorem ac pacatiorem vitam tenuerunt. At id longe secus est; quamquam enim Dantes neque senuerit neque etiam id quod datum est vitae tranquillum habuerit (quin immo partim assiduis rei publicae occupationibus a studiis distractus, partim vero variis exilii curis agitatus plerumque consumpserit), ob quandam tamen divinam[9] ingenii sui excellentiam magnam humanarum et divinarum rerum cognitionem brevi tempore comparavit. Quippe et in mathematicis — quae scientia tum numeros tum dimensiones, tum consonantias, tum astrorum motus et conversiones una complectitur — et in utraque philosophia, quae ad mores et ad naturalia pertinet, et in Sacris denique Scripturis, quae omnem divinitatem penitus comprehendunt, usque adeo profecit ut illis, in memoratarum rerum cognitione, non immerito praeponatur.

16 Dantes ergo in his omnibus, ut diximus, Petrarcham et Boccacium nimirum excellit. Atqui ab ipso Petrarcha[10] cum integra latinarum litterarum scientia, tum etiam certa veterum historiarum perceptione superatur; nam Petrarcha maiorem et clariorem utra-

ets, we find it first necessary to say what everyone agrees on: the human race is subject to a twofold life, namely active and contemplative. This being in truth the chief premise of our comparison, we do not deem it rash to hold that in almost every aspect of both sorts of life Dante should be preferred to the other two. First of all, he did not hesitate to take up arms and gallantly fight for his country. Secondly, he conducted himself excellently while holding office for some length of time in the government of the state. All this obviously pertains to the active life, and it cannot be predicated of either Petrarca or Boccaccio, since they spent almost all their lives in solitary leisure studying literature, withdrawing entirely from public business, a state which is by common consent known as the contemplative life.

Having set everything else aside and devoted themselves solely 15
to that life, Petrarca and Boccaccio should have surpassed Dante, for they led longer, more quiet and peaceful lives. Yet this is not true at all; in fact, although Dante did not reach old age and never enjoyed much tranquillity in his life—rather, he spent most of it either involved in incessant political activities or burdened with the many cares of exile, all of which distracted him from studying—he rapidly succeeded in attaining a vast knowledge of things human and divine, thanks to the almost divine excellence of his intellect. And so, in mathematics—the science that studies numbers, dimensions and harmonics, together with the movements and the revolutions of the stars—as well as in both kinds of philosophy, moral and natural, and finally in the Sacred Scriptures, which embrace all divinity, he so excelled that he is rightly deemed superior to the other two in knowledge of the aforesaid subjects.

Hence Dante surely seems superior to Petrarca and Boccaccio 16
in all these respects, as has been said. He is, however, exceeded by Petrarca in broad knowledge of Latin letters and the sure mastery of ancient history; Petrarca, in fact, possessed a greater and more precise erudition in both fields. He also surpasses Dante in the

rumque rerum notitiam habuit. In carmine quoque et soluta oratione Dantes ab eo itidem vincitur, siquidem eius carmina rotundiora ac sublimiora sunt atque eius oratio longe elegantior apparet. In materno sermone pares paene habentur; etenim si Dantes in odis Petrarcha ipso superior est, in rhythmis ab eo superatur, unde pares in materno dicendi genere non immerito habentur. Ceterum Boccacio ita paene in omnibus prestat ut in paucis admodum ac levibus quibusdam, in graecarum scilicet litterarum cognitione, qua Dantes omnino caruit, et in materna ac soluta oratione, qua pauca scripsit, sibi cedere videatur. In quibus duobus dumtaxat etiam Petrarcham excelluit, cum ab eo tamquam a praeceptore suo in ceteris omnibus vinceretur.

writing of Latin verse and prose, for his verses are more polished and sublime and his prose has a far more elegant appearance. In their native tongue they are considered almost equal, for Dante exceeds Petrarca in his cantos, while he is bested by him in the sonnet form. It seems proper, thus, to judge them equal in their native tongue. Finally, Dante is superior to Boccaccio in almost everything, except for a few things of lesser importance, such as the knowledge of Greek letters, which Dante lacked completely, and the writing of prose works in the vernacular, which he did not practice often. These two are also the only things in which Boccaccio exceeded Petrarca, whereas in everything else he was surpassed by him, as a student by his teacher.

Ex libro
DE ILLUSTRIBUS LONGAEVIS

1 Paucis illustribus poetis qui a principio salutis humanae usque ad haec nostra tempora intercesserunt praetermissis, quoniam in numero longaevorum haudquaquam collocari poterant, ad Franciscum Petrarcham accedamus. Post Varronem enim Vergilium, Horatium, Ovidium, Lucanum, Senecam, Persium, Statium, Iuvenalem, Catullum, Propertium, et si qui alii fuerunt quod ante septuagesimum aetatis suae annum abierint, missos faciamus.

2 Franciscus igitur, Petrachi cuiusdam scribae filius, cognomento Petrarcha (a paterno nomine 'r' littera euphoniae causa, ut arbitror, interposita) trecentesimo quarto supra millesimum christianae salutis anno, illucescente vigesimae diei Iulii mensis aurora, Arretii, in vico quodam qui vulgo 'hortus' dicitur, natus est, qua die eadem ferme nativitatis suae hora exules florentini populi qui iampridem patria extorres se Arretium Bononiamque contulerant, contractis undique — quoad fieri poterat — auxiliis, armati ad portas patriae, si qua fors fuisset, ulciscendi gratia contenderent. Haec ipse in epistula quadam ad Ioannem Boccacium, illius temporis egregium poetam, manifestissime ostendit. Vetusta eius origo supra Parenzum quendam avum suum ab Ancisa, quodam Florentinorum oppido, repetita traducitur. Petrachus pater, quamquam Ancisae oriretur, Florentiae tamen habitavit, ibique prae ingenii magnitudine et singulari linguae elegantia, nonnullis legationibus florentini populi nomine ad magnos Italiae principes antea susceptis, ad magistratum postea Reformationum scriba, ex magno scribarum numero, unus deligitur. Quo in magistratu, licet aliquot annos officio suo diligenter atque integre fungeretur, in magna tamen illa civili

From
ON FAMOUS MEN OF GREAT AGE

Omitting a few famous poets who have happened to live between the birth of Christ and our own time, as they could not possibly be numbered among men of great age, let us come now to Francesco Petrarca. After treating Varro, in fact, we must set aside Vergil, Horace, Ovid, Lucan, Seneca, Persius, Statius, Juvenal, Catullus, Propertius and any other poet who died before the age of seventy. 1

Now Francesco Petrarca, son of a notary named Petracco (Francesco added the letter 'r' to his father's last name to make it sound better, as I believe) was born in the 1304th year of Christian salvation, at dawn on July 20 in Arezzo, in a part of town called "Dell'Orto" in the vernacular. On that same day, around the hour of his birth, the Florentine exiles (who had been banished some time before and had gone to Arezzo and Bologna) were armed and heading for the gates of their native town. Hoping to avenge themselves, if good fortune would allow it, they had gathered as much support as they could. This is what Petrarca himself attests in an epistle he wrote to Giovanni Boccaccio, an excellent poet of the time. His lineage can be traced back to his grandfather, a certain Parenzo from Incisa, a town in the Florentine territory. His father Petracco, though born in Incisa, lived in Florence. There, thanks to his great intelligence and precision of language, he had been entrusted with several missions to great Italian princes on behalf of the Florentine people. Later he was chosen from among a large number of candidates to serve as secretary to the Riformagioni.[1] Though he had served diligently and with integrity in this office for several years, at the time of that great and turbulent 2

dissensione quae inter Albos et Nigros, duas diversas civitatis factiones, invaluit, quod albis adhaesisse videretur, una cum ceteris albarum partium fautoribus urbe exactus Arretium concessit, atque dum ibi spe Florentiam redeundi aliquamdiu commoraretur filium ex uxore sua suscepit, quem diminute, veteri quodam infantilis indulgentiae ritu, 'Checcum' appellavit, cum alterum nomine Gerardum iam antea habuisset.

3 Non multo deinde post, cum exulum conatus irrita evasissent, ceu de reditu desperans in Galliam transalpinam Avinionem, ubi forte ea tempestate summus pontifex residebat, simul cum universa familia sua proficiscitur, quo in loco Franciscus, paucis post annis, iam aetate ad discendum aptus, a pueritia litteris deditus, ubi illa prima puerilia studia transegit e vestigio ex patris mandato ad ius civile non sine molestia, quod Ciceronis et Maronis libris vehementer oblectaretur, se contulisse dicitur. Quibus in studiis septem annos perseveravit, quamvis clam aliquos Ciceronis et Vergilii libros aliquotiens hoc interim tempore legisset, ut ipse in epistula quadam aperte testatur, in qua multum admodum de hac tanta temporis iactura conqueritur.

4 Post obitum vero patris, quasi sui iuris effectus, cunctis iuris civilis codicibus omnibusque eius ineptis[1] commentationibus penitus abdicatis, circa primos adulescentiae suae annos humanitatis studiis omnino se dedicavit, in quibus usque adeo profecit ut inter ceteros laborum suorum fructos primus dicendi elegantiam, iam supra mille annos paene defunctam, praecipua quadam ingenii excellentia in lucem revocaverit. Nam et primus multos Ciceronis libros per multa saecula ante occultos ac paene amissos sua singulari diligentia nobis restituit atque eius epistulas, prius hinc inde dispersas, eo ordine quo videntur in sua volumina redegit et suo excellentiori quodam genere dicendi se ipsum nobis ad imitandum praestitit.

5 Quocirca in tanto honore ob haec ipsa humanitatis studia habitus est ut cuncti paulo humaniores populi eius nomen venerari vi-

civil discord which split the city into the White and Black factions, he was driven out, along with the other Whites, for having supported that faction. He went to Arezzo, and it was while he was staying there for some time in the hope of returning to Florence that his wife bore him a son, whom he called by the diminutive "Checco," employing an old form of indulging children. He already had another son by the name of Gherardo.

Shortly afterwards, once the exiles' efforts had proved vain, 3
Petracco, as if losing all hope of restoration, left with all his family for Avignon in Transalpine Gaul, where the pope happened to be residing at the time. It was there that Francesco, a few years later, being then of an age to learn (though fond of letters from a very early age), completed his early education and was sent by his father to study civil law. This he did, though not without distress, for he was fond of Cicero and Vergil. He spent seven years studying that subject, though during this time he sometimes read in secret some works by Cicero and Vergil, as he openly declares in a letter in which he laments civil law as a tremendous waste of time.

Upon his father's death he became independent and put aside 4
all codes of civil law and the worthless commentaries on them. In the first years of his adolescence he dedicated himself to studying the humanities, and in these subjects made so much progress that among the fruits of his labors the principal one was the recovery of correctness and good taste in Latin diction, then nearly defunct for over a thousand years, which he brought back to light by virtue of his uncommon genius. He was the first to restore to us through his extraordinary diligence many works of Cicero which had been hidden and almost lost for centuries and to collect Cicero's scattered epistles, organizing them in the order in which we now see them. His finer style of diction made him a model for us to imitate.

Thus his study of the humanities brought him such honor that 5
all peoples with some degree of culture, however slight, seemed to

derentur. Incliti vero principes admirabili quadam virtutum suarum fama pertracti personam suam ita observabant ut inter se de eo habendo certatim fere contenderent. Summus namque pontifex ipsum per epistulam saepenumero ad sanctitatem suam accersivit, magnos sibi dignitatis gradus si accederet pollicitus, quod etsi primam, ut dicitur, tonsuram iampridem accepisset recusare tamen non dubitavit. Id ipsum et Mediolanensium ducem et Patavii principem nonnumquam fecisse constat, ut magna sibi munera pollicerentur si secum conversari vellet. Cum quibus omnibus aliquamdiu vixit; penes enim summum pontificem tempore iuventutis suae aliquantulum commoratus est, sed magno curialis, ut aiunt, vitae taedio postea affectus inde abiit ac redire noluit, quamvis saepius ab ipso per epistulas et munera invitaretur.

6 Cum haec igitur et huiusmodi anteactae vitae suae temporibus egregie peregisset, ut latius in eius vita descripsimus, iam senescens Arquadam, quoddam Patavii oppidum, in otium se contulit. Ubi in summa tranquillitate et quiete complures annos degens, ad extremum septuagenarius, quantum ex gestis eius augurari coniectura possumus, in summa pace quievit. Optimae quippe vitae fuit; nam inter cetera a pueritia usque ad extremam aetatem perpetuo primum ieiunasse fertur. Cum religiosissimis deinde illius temporis viris magna familiaritate coniunctus, saepius per epistulas precabatur ut sui in eorum orationibus meminissent. Ad sacros denique libros conversus, sacra eorum lectione incredibiliter delectabatur.

7 Ingens in eo decor corporis erat. Statura enim mediocritatem excedens, formosam et venerandam faciem habebat; corpore valido, ita ut assiduo aquae potu et crudis herbis et variis cuiuscumque generis pomis, quibus per omne tempus aetatis suae magna cum suavitate vescebatur, nullo unquam tempore laedi videretur, nisi quod perpaucis ante mortem suam annis assiduis prope febribus vexabatur.

venerate his name. Famous princes, attracted by the wonderful fame of his virtues, showed respect for his person to the point of vying with one another in order to have him at their courts. The pontiff himself summoned him repeatedly to his holy presence by letter, promising him high offices, which he did not hesitate to turn down, though he had already received the first tonsure. It is well known that the duke of Milan and the ruler of Padua did the same more than once, promising him great gifts if he would associate with them. He lived with all of them for periods of time. In his youth, indeed, he waited upon the supreme pontiff for some time. But afterwards he left, they say, because he was disgusted by court life, and refused to return, despite the frequent written invitations and gifts he received from the pope.

With these distinguished accomplishments behind him, and 6
others like them (we described them in detail in his biography), he retired to Arquà, a village near Padua, as he entered old age. There he lived in the greatest tranquillity and quiet for many years until he turned seventy, when he finally died in the utmost peace, as we may assume from his actions. He led, in fact, a perfect life. Among other things, for instance, it is said that he fasted regularly from adolescence until extreme old age. Then, too, he was on intimate terms with the most religious men of that time, and in his letters often asked them to remember him in their prayers. Finally, having turned to sacred literature, he took incredible delight in pious readings.

He was exceedingly handsome. He exceeded middle height and 7
had a fair and venerable countenance. He was so healthy that despite drinking only water and eating nothing but uncooked vegetables and fruits of various kinds, as he did with great pleasure throughout his life, he never fell ill except in his very last years when he suffered from continual fevers.

8 Ingenii sui complura monumenta reliquit. Nam praeter odas materno sermone compositas, quas 'cantilenas' et 'sonetia' vulgato verbo vocant, multa etiam conscripsit. Eclogas quippe duodecim egregiis carminibus mandavit. Epistulas multas composuit, quas in duo volumina, instar tullianarum, ipse digessit; horum alterum *Rerum familiarum,* alterum *Senilium* appellavit. Invectivas in gallum et medicum edidit. Scripsit insuper *De remediis ad utramque fortunam* libros duos, *De vita solitaria* libros duos ad Philippum Cavallicensem episcopum, *De otio religioso* librum unum, *Rerum memorandarum* libros quattuor, *De ignorantia sui et aliorum* librum unum, *De secreto conflictu curarum suarum* librum unum, *Contra clericos* librum unum, *De viris illustribus* libros quosdam. Cunctas superioris Africani laudes in uno volumine per novem libros distincto hexametris carminibus mirabiliter congessit, quem librum *Africam* inscripsit, licet morte praeventus ei ipsi iam immature edito ultimas, ut cupiebat, manus imponere non potuerit.

9 Itaque ex tam multis scriptis eius et versibus et soluta oratione compositis singularem quandam in utroque genere dicendi gratiam habuisse constat; quod perpaucis, immo ut verius loquar nullis, contigisse manifestum est ut et in carmine et in soluta oratione simul excellerent. Nam et Ciceronem, cui latinae eloquentiae in soluta oratione palma consensu omnium tribuitur, immortale illud ingenium in carminibus destituisse videmus et Maronem, quem latinorum poetarum principem et solum poetam appellare non dubitant, in prosa oratione ita mancum fuisse conspicimus ut paene nullus videretur. Quid de ceteris dicam, cum duo summa in utroque dicendi genere eloquentiae nostrae fulmina alterutrum in altero excelluisse, in altero vero defecisse luce clarius appareat? Proinde solus omnium Petrarcha noster hac ingenti laude dignus esse dicitur.

10 Quocirca laurea dum viveret donatus atque tempora sua Romae speciosissime insignitus magna cum gloria nominis sui septuage-

He left many records of his genius. Apart from the poems he wrote in his native tongue, which are called *canzoni* and *sonetti* in the vernacular, he wrote many other works. He wrote twelve eclogues in fine verse. He also wrote a large number of letters, which he eventually divided into two groups, following Cicero's example; some he called *Letters to his Friends*, others *Letters of Old Age*. He wrote invectives against a Frenchman and a doctor. He also wrote *Remedies for Good and Bad Fortune* in two books; *The Solitary Life*, to Philip, bishop of Cabassole, again in two books; *Religious Retirement* in one book; *Things Worth Remembering* in four books; *On his Own Ignorance and that of Others* in one book; *On the Secret Conflict of His Anxieties* in one book; *Against Clerics* in one book, and *Famous Men* in several books. He collected all the praiseworthy deeds of the elder Scipio in one amazing work divided into nine books and written in hexameters. This book he entitled *Africa*, though death prevented him from putting the final touches he wanted on the work, which had been published prematurely. 8

All the works that he composed in verse and prose attest that he had remarkable gifts in both types of writing. This is an ability that few others have possessed. Indeed (to be more precise) it is clear that no other writer has excelled both in verse and prose. We know, for instance, that Cicero — who, as everyone agrees, deserves the palm of eloquence in Latin prose — is bereft of his immortal genius in verse. Vergil, on the other hand, whom no one hesitates to call the prince of Latin poetry and a unique poet, is so lame in prose that he appears to be almost a nullity.[2] Why speak of the rest, if it is clear that the two stars in the twin genera of Latin eloquence were both excellent in one genus of writing and defective in the other? That is why Petrarca is said to be the only one who deserves to be praised for this great accomplishment. 9

Accordingly, during his lifetime Petrarca received in Rome the laurel crown that graced his brow and died a famous man in 10

simo aetatis suae anno Arquade obiit. Ubi in arca marmorea conditus est quam tribus dumtaxat humillimis eius carminibus sic illustratam cernimus:

> Frigida Francisci lapis hic tegit ossa Petrarchae.
> Suscipe virgo parens animam, sate virgine parce
> fessaque iam terris caeli requiescat in arce.

11 Colucius cognomento Linus, ex quodam Stignani oppido, stirpe antiqua, quam de Salutatis vocatur, oriundus, a patre Piero in ipso adulescentiae sinu post prima litterarum elementa artibus libero dignis, quae liberales appellantur, deditus, excellentia ingenii brevi tempore mirum in modum profecisse videtur. Nam et grammaticam et dialecticam tenera aetate prae ceteris facultatibus prosecutus, plurima veterum grammaticorum et dialecticorum assidua lectione perlegit. Sed non multo post huiusmodi artium studiis penitus omissis, ut genitoris mandatis obtemperaret invitus ad ius civile se contulit.

12 In hac iuris cognitione parumper commoratus est, quoniam ad oratoriam et poeticam, suapte natura et quotidianis quibusdam stimulis, agebatur. Nam earum amore usque adeo flagrabat ut ceteris praetermissis has dumtaxat facultates adamaverit ac tantummodo retinuerit. Quibus quidem in rebus quantum laudis et gloriae consequeretur vix dici potest, siquidem cunctis naturae muneribus ornatus tantam legendi et exercendi sui diligentiam adhibuit ut ceteris sui aetatis hominibus facile praestitisse et quasi ad ea natus et ab aliquo deo factus esse videretur.

13 Testes huius rei sunt plura litterarum monumenta quae in utraque facultate posteris legenda reliquit. In poetica enim praeter plurima ac paene innumerabilia carmina hic inde varie dispersa octo eclogas lepidis versibus conscripsit et opusculum quoddam *De conquestione Phyllidis* hexametris pentametrisque carminibus

Arquà at the age of seventy. There he was buried in a marble vault decorated, as we see, only with these three humble verses of his:

> This stone covers the cold bones of Francesco Petrarca.
> Virgin mother, receive his soul; seed of the Virgin, have mercy upon it.
> Weary of the world, may his soul now find rest in the vault of heaven.

Coluccio Lino, son of Piero, was born in the town of Stignano. A member of the old Salutati family, he devoted himself in childhood, immediately after learning to read and write, to those arts worthy of a free man (the "liberal arts," as they are called). In these studies he soon progressed remarkably owing to his excellent mind. He focused particularly during his youth on the subjects of grammar and logic, and studied the numerous ancient grammarians and logicians long and carefully. Shortly afterwards, however, he abandoned these liberal studies and turned reluctantly to civil law so as to obey his father's commands. 11

He did not pursue the study of the law for long, for he was naturally inclined and constantly spurred to take up rhetoric and poetry. He loved them so much that he put all other studies aside, clinging and devoting himself to these subjects alone. It can scarcely be described how much praise and glory he attained in these disciplines, for to all the gifts that nature had bestowed upon him he added so much diligence in reading and practice that he easily came to surpass all his contemporaries, as if he had been born and made for these studies by some god. 12

The many literary works in both genres that he left for future generations to read bear witness to his excellence. In verse, apart from the almost innumerable poems scattered everywhere, he wrote eight delightful eclogues, a short work in elegiac couples entitled *The Complaint of Phyllis*, and much other poetry. In prose he 13

composuit et multa alia hac poetica facultate litteris mandavit. In soluta quoque oratione epistulas privatas et publicas paene infinitas ita egregie dictavit ut in hoc epistulari genere solus consensu omnium regnare diceretur. *De laboribus Herculis* librum edidit in quo quicquid veteres poetae historicique de Herculibus tradiderunt in unum diligenter et accurate congessit. *De fato et fortuna, De laude legum et medicinae, De tyranno, De morte Petrarchae, De saeculo et religione* ad Hieronymum heremitam, *De verecundia* ad Antonium physicum faventinum libellos conscripsit; invectivam insuper contra Antonium Luscum, a quo florentini populi nomen[2] multis contumeliis et iniuriis lacessitus fuerat, graviter simul atque eleganter respondendi gratia composuit.

14 Atque haec omnia pluraque alia in maximis privatarum et publicarum rerum occupationibus memoriae mandavit. Magnum namque familiae ac decem liberorum onus gubernabat et florentini populi scriba omne civitatis pondus suis humeris sustinebat. Etenim quadragesimo circiter quinto aetatis suae anno ad hunc dignitatis gradum publice delectus, illud munus ultra triginta annos usque ad extremum vitae suae diem magna cum nominis sui gloria exercuit. Nam septuagesimo sexto aetatis suae anno feliciter obiit; quippe amplo satis patrimonio [et] pluribus adulescentibus filiis et magna librorum copia simul cum singulari quadam nominis sui gloria relictis, ob memorata rerum suarum monumenta lauream promeretur; quod sibi ac Petrarchae tantummodo contigisse legimus, ut instar veterum poetarum alter vivus, alter mortuus laurea corona post multa temporum curricula insigniri mererentur.

15 Fuit staturae plus quam mediocris licet aliquantulum recurvus incederet; facie fere rotunda, latis pendentibusque maxillis, tristis ac severus aspectu mirabilisque constantiae, quod, ut alia omittam, in morte duorum adulescentium filiorum, Petri et Andreae, manifestissime demonstravit. Nam in funeribus eorum ita modeste se gessit ut non modo lacrimas non emitteret sed etiam domesticos flentes egregie consolaretur. Idque praecipue in obitu Petri, qui

dictated almost an infinite number of private and public letters with such distinction that by universal consent he is called the reigning king of the epistolary genre. He published a book, *The Labors of Hercules,* in which he collected with great care and diligence everything the ancient poets and historians said about Hercules. He also composed the following works: *On Fate and Fortune, In Praise of Law and Medicine, On Tyranny, The Death of Petrarca, On the Worldly and the Religious* to the hermit Gerolamo, and *On Modesty* to Antonio, a doctor from Faenza.[3] In addition, he composed a grave and elegant invective against Antonio Loschi in reply to the insults and slanders the latter had hurled at the Florentine people.

He wrote all this and much more while deeply involved in both 14
private and public business. He looked after his large family with ten children while carrying on his shoulders the whole weight of the city as chancellor of the Florentine people. He had been publicly chosen for this honorable post at the age of forty-five and served in office with great distinction for over thirty years until the very end of his life. He died happily at seventy-six, leaving a rather ample patrimony to his many young sons, together with a large number of books and the singular glory of his name. His abovementioned books won for him the laurel crown, a thing which was conferred only upon him and Petrarca, so that, just like the ancient poets many centuries earlier, one earned the laurel during his lifetime, the other after his death.

He was much taller than average, though he walked with a 15
slight stoop. His face was quite round, with large and heavy jowls. He always looked grave and serious and possessed remarkable self-control, as he showed with utter clarity (to mention just one episode) upon the death of his two young sons, Piero and Andrea. At their funerals he behaved with such restraint that not only did he refrain from shedding tears, but he even was able to comfort successfully the weeping members of his family. This was particularly

unica spes sua esse videbatur, fecisse dicitur: ab eius namque latere toto aegrotationis suae tempore numquam discedebat ut extremum filii spiritum forte hauriret, quem ut toto pectore accepit, illico supinum cadaver statuit, palpebras oculorum propriis manibus composuit, labia clausit, manus insuper et brachia in crucem constituit. Ad extremum, cum vultus eius etiam atque etiam intueretur, nullum maestitiae signum, mirabile dictu, exinde discedens prae se tulit. Atque haec omnia ipse in epistula quadam in qua de acerba huius filii sui morte ad amicum consolantem rescribens sese fecisse testatur.

16 Nicolaus, ex quodam familiae suae cognomine 'Nicoli' vulgo appellatus, egregiis atque honestis parentibus Florentiae natus est. Et pater quidem mercaturae operam dedit, qua in arte, cum ingenio et diligentia plurimum valeret, ita magnas opes et amplas sibi divitias comparavit ut sex filiis, quos superstites moriens dereliquit, ingens eius patrimonium equis inter se portionibus divideretur. Et tamen ita magnum erat ut in tot partes distributum, pro more civitatis, sua cuique ad bene beateque vivendum portio sufficeret.

17 Huius igitur pater, mercator egregius, cunctos eius natos ad mercatoriam instituebat, sed Nicolaum, ceteris fratribus maiorem natu et iam ad institoriam educatum, statim ut adolescere coepit suo edicto ad mercaturam evocavit atque mercatorem fieri voluit. Per hunc itaque modum Nicolaus, ut paternis iussis pareret, mercatorum exercitio deditus officio suo generose accurateque utebatur. Cum vero in eo vitae genere exercendo aliquot annos contrivisset, ne si aliter fecisset contra paterna imperia facere videretur, tandem taedio ductus, quasi ad altiora et digniora nasceretur, iam adultus aetate, omnibus mercaturis velut frivolis et inanibus rebus praetermissis, ad latinae linguae cognitionem se contulisse dicitur, qua in re prae ingenii acrimonia ac singulari diligentia brevi post tempore multum admodum perfecit.

remarkable behavior in the case of Piero's death, a boy who had seemed his only hope. Indeed, during the whole illness he never absented himself from his son's sickbed, so that he was there to inhale his last breath; but he immediately laid out his son's body, closed his eyelids with his own hands, then his lips, and arranged his hands and arms in the shape of a cross. Finally, having looked at his face again and again, he departed — wondrous to say — without showing any sign of sorrow. He himself records all this in a letter responding to a friend who had written to comfort him for the bitter loss of his son.[4]

Niccolò, whose family name in the vernacular is Niccoli, was born 16
in Florence of fine and respectable parents. His father had devoted himself to commerce, and in this calling he did so well, thanks to his intelligence and hard work, that he accumulated a large fortune. Upon his death, he left his six sons a rich patrimony which was divided equally among them, as is the custom in Florence. Even divided into so many parts, it was still so large that each share was enough for each son to lead a fine and happy life.

Now, his father, this excellent merchant, brought up all his sons 17
to be businessmen, but Niccolò, his eldest son who had already had a commercial education, he commanded to enter business while still a youth, in the desire to turn him into a merchant. Therefore, to do his father's bidding, Niccolò devoted himself to business, fulfilling his tasks worthily and with diligence. After spending several years in this fashion, always careful not to do anything contrary to his father's wishes, he at last grew weary, feeling he had been born for higher and nobler goals. Once out of boyhood, therefore, he put aside all business matters as trivial and useless and turned to the study of the Latin language. In this he soon excelled, thanks to his keen intelligence and outstanding zeal.

18 Cum autem variae essent discendi facultates quibus homines secundum varias eorum conditiones quique sua applicare ingenia solent, post latinarum litterarum eruditionem ceterarum artium studia neglexit quamquam utiliora ac vendibiliora viderentur; humanitatis vero peritiam, unde virtutes eruuntur, unice adamavit adamatamque sibi delegit et voluit. Haec enim humanitatis studia ad virtutem apprime spectare et pertinere manifestum est. Nam in his ipsis prae aliis artium studiis honestum quaeritur quaesitumque haud dubie reperitur. Ex honesto autem iustitia, fortitudo, modestia ceteraeque virtutes emanare et effluere viderentur.

19 Quocirca in familiaritatem et disciplinam cuiusdam Lodovici Marsilii sese recepit, viri per ea tempora et religione et sanctimonia vitae et excellentia doctrinae praestantissimi, ut una cum bonarum artium studiis veram bene beateque vivendi viam exinde perciperet. Huius Lodovici tunc fama et opinio tanta ac tam celeberrima erat ut domus eius egregiis adulescentibus atque praestantibus viris discendi gratia vel maxime frequentaretur, qui ad eum audiendum tamquam ad divinum quoddam oraculum undique confluebant. In huius ergo singularissimi atque eruditissimi viri disciplina deditus, ita in huiusmodi ludo diligenter accurateque perseveravit ut ab eius fere latere numquam recederet. Ex quo factum est ut praeter singularem quandam plurimarum rerum cognitionem, egregios quoque mores et optima instituta vitae ab eo reportaret. Inter cetera namque memoratu digna quae exinde tamquam ex vivo fonte hausisse creditur latinae linguae integritatem, historiarum etiam tam externarum quam nostrarum notitiam, Sacrarum insuper Scripturarum scientiam connumerant, quibus omnibus Nicolaus noster plurimum pollebat.

20 Atque haec ad studia. Ad mores vero alia huiusmodi spectant et pertinent, loquendi videlicet et obiurgandi vaga quaedam ac soluta libertas atque licentia. Quae quidem ab eo non aliter retulit quam illa superius commemorata retulisse dicebamus. Ille enim praeceptor egregius et ad loquendum promptissimus et ad scelerum flagi-

Now men generally apply themselves to various disciplines each according to his own genius and circumstances; as for Niccolò, he disregarded all the other arts, although they might appear to be more useful and profitable, in favor of studying Latin literature. He had a unique love for the humanities, from which all virtues derive, and decided to follow his passion. It is obvious that the principle aim of the humanities has to do with virtue, for in them, much more than in other disciplines, the object is moral rectitude[5] — an object that is always found when truly sought. And it is from moral rectitude that justice, fortitude, modesty and all the other virtues spring forth and derive. 18

Niccolò thus became a friend and disciple of a certain Luigi Marsili — an exceptional man of that time for his piety, holiness, and the excellence of his learning — so as to learn the true path to a good and happy life while studying the humanities. The fame and reputation of this Luigi were then so great and so widespread that his house was full of excellent youths and important men seeking to learn from him; they flocked to him from every direction as though to hear a divine oracle. Having given himself over to learning from this unique and erudite man, he studied with such care and diligence under his guidance that he never left his side. Thus it happened that, in addition to a deep understanding of many different subjects, he also acquired from him an excellent moral character and a fine pattern of life. Among the memorable things he is believed to have drawn from him, as though from a living spring, are a complete knowledge of the Latin tongue, a familiarity with Roman and foreign history, and a knowledge of the Holy Scriptures — all subjects which our Niccolò mastered. 19

So much for his studies. There are other, related matters that pertain to his character, namely a kind of frank and free-wheeling license in censuring others — characteristics that he also acquired from his teacher along with the other qualities we mentioned above. For his distinguished teacher was also reported to be ready 20

tiorumque detestationem paratissimus ferebatur. Fit enim plerumque ut mores eorum imitemur imitatique similitudinem quandam exprimamus cum quibus diutius conversamur; atque id ipsum facilius ac frequentius contingit si cum aliqua observatione et admiratione intuemur.

21 Quid plura? Ita huius doctrina, ita mores, ita instituta mirabili quoddam dicendi lepore condita Nicolao nostro placuerunt ut ceteris vel divitiarum vel honorum vel suscipiendorum liberorum, quae maxime ab hominibus suapte natura expetantur, cupiditatibus posthabitis totum se in otium ad bonarum artium studia converteret. Neque postea ullo umquam tempore aut comparandis opibus, ut cupidi, inhiavit, aut aucupandis honoribus, ut ambitiosi, inservivit, aut rei uxoriae, procreandi prolis gratia, indulsit, sed potius egenus et inglorius et caelebs, omni saeculari cura liber et vacuus, in summa quiete et tranquillitate una cum libris suis feliciter vivebat.

22 Per hunc itaque modum publicis simul atque privatis occupationibus carens otio non desidioso illo et ignobili sed litterato et generoso fruebatur. Proinde partim legendo, partim vetustos codices transcribendo, partim amicorum negotiis impartiendo, quod reliquum erat temporis in cumulandis et congregandis undique voluminibus consumebatur.

23 Mortuo vero hoc de quo loquimur praeceptore suo unde latinam, ut ita dixerim, cognitionem acceperat, graecarum litterarum cupiditate mirum in modum flagrare coepit, sine quibus nostra haec studia manca ac debilia esse videbantur. Proinde cum Colucio Salutato, viro sui temporis integerrimo simul atque doctissimo, cuius vitam paucis paulo ante descripsimus, dedita opera Manuelem quendam Chrysoloram constantinopolitanum, Graecorum omnium facile principem, e Constantinopoli per tot maris terrarumque spatia legendi causa Florentiam usque accersiverant. Si hoc ergo singularissimo magistro et optimo praeceptore in perdiscendis litteris graecis ob familiares ac perniciosas germanorum

of speech and quite prepared to condemn crimes and wicked acts. It commonly happens that we imitate the behavior of those with whom we consort and become a kind of copy of the person imitated, and this happens more easily and more often when we respect and admire such persons.

In short, our Niccolò was so taken with Luigi's learning, his character, and the witty way he expressed his teachings that he put aside all the desires most people naturally have for riches, honors and children and devoted himself entirely to the study of the humanities. From that time on he never longed to amass wealth like the greedy, nor sought honors like the ambitious, nor indulged in matrimony in order to raise a family. Instead, he remained poor, unknown and celibate, entirely free of all worldly cares, living happily with his books in the greatest quiet and tranquillity. 21

Being thus free of all public and private concerns, he enjoyed leisure — not the indolent and worthless kind, but rather leisure of a cultivated and noble sort. Accordingly he spent his time partly reading, partly transcribing old manuscripts, and partly sharing in the business of his friends. Whatever time was left over he spent amassing and collecting books from every source. 22

After the death of his aforementioned teacher, from whom he learned Latin, he began to burn with an all-consuming desire to learn Greek, since without this knowledge the study of Latin seemed crippled and weak.[6] So with this end in view he joined forces with Coluccio Salutati — the most irreproachable and learned man of his time, whose life we have just described — to bring to Florence over land and sea from far-off Constantinople the most distinguished of the Greeks, Manuel Chrysoloras, in order to have him lecture. If the annoying quarrels with his brothers, which hampered his studies both inside and outside his house, 23

suorum discordias, quae non modo externa sed domestica etiam studia perverterant, Nicolao nostro uti licuisset, quantum in illis profecisset ex eo facile iudicari potest, quod ingenio et diligentia plurimum valebat. Missos facio admirabiles quosdam peregrinarum litterarum fructus quos in hominibus nostris per universam Etruriam hinc inde diffusos esse cognoscimus. Nam ab hoc eruditissimo viro multos graece edoctos, velut seminarium quoddam, profluxisse manifestum est, quae omnia a Nicolao nostro accepta referre debemus, qui peregrinum praeceptorem e media, ut aiunt, Graecia Florentiam usque in Etruriam evocavit.

24 Quid multa de studiis suis loquar? Quin immo, ut cuncta huius singularissimi viri studiosa gesta paucis complectamur, latinas litteras ita perceperat ut rectam atque integram earum cognitionem solus habere videretur. Priscas deinde historias ita omnes memoriter tenebat ut ad unguem singula illustrium virorum facta [ad unguem][3] recitaret, si quando libuisset, et ita quidem recitabat ut cunctis ferme actibus interfuisse videretur. Cosmographiae quoque tantam ac tam claram notitiam summa diligentia conquisiverat ut toto terrarum orbe de singulis provinciis, urbibus, locis, sitibus, tractibus denique omnibus melius et apertius loqueretur quam ii ipsi qui in illis diutius habitassent. Sacras insuper Scripturas usque adeo perlegit, usque adeo hausit, usque adeo olfecit ut mirabile quiddam videretur hominem saecularem ac nulla, ut aiunt, religione praeditum tantam earum scientiam percepisse.

25 Ad haec accedebat singularis quaedam et propria eruditissimi viri eloquentia qua communi sermone plurimum poterat. Tum ad iudicandum de singulis auctoribus oratoribusque, utrum eloquentes vel infantes haberentur, ceteris omnibus praestabat. Elegantes quoscumque scriptores oratoresve apprime laudabat, ineptos vero maxime vituperabat. Raro tamen vel numquam latine loquendi latineve scribendi onus suscipere voluit, ea de causa adductus, ut arbitror, quod cum nihil ab eo nisi plenum et perfectum probaretur, neque orationes neque scripta sua sibi ipsi omni ex parte, ceu in

had not prevented our Niccolò from making the most of this exceptionally fine teacher, it is easy to guess, judging from his intelligence and zeal, how much he might have learned. I shall forebear to mention the marvellous fruits of foreign literature which we know to have spread hither and yon among students of Latin throughout Tuscany. It is obvious that the learned Chrysoloras taught Greek to many men, as though planting a seedbed, and that all this is something for which our Niccolò deserves the credit,[7] as it was he who called this foreign teacher to Florence and Tuscany "from the heart of Greece," as they say.

But why dwell so much upon his studies? Indeed, one may em- 24
brace all of this exceptional man's scholarly accomplishments in a few words: such was his grasp of Latin literature that he alone seemed to possess a full and correct knowledge of that subject. Then, too, his memory of the old histories was so tenacious that whenever he wanted he could recite every single deed of great men with perfect precision and in such a way that it seemed, almost, that he had witnessed them personally. He also acquired with great effort such a vast and accurate knowledge of geography that he could talk about every single province, city, locale, place—in short, about any region—better and in greater detail than people who had themselves lived in those places for long periods of time.[8] Furthermore, he pored over, absorbed and investigated the Holy Scriptures to such an extent that it seemed an amazing thing that a layman, who (they say) was not endowed with religious feeling, could possess such a knowledge of them.

Besides, he possessed the exceptional eloquence characteristic 25
of learned men, which made a deep impression whenever he spoke in the vernacular. He excelled all others in judging whether an author or an orator was polished or puerile. He lavished praise on elegant writers and orators while abusing inept ones. Yet seldom or never did he undertake to speak or write in Latin,[9] the reason being, in my opinion, that he approved of nothing unless it were full

aliis hominibus exigebat, satisfactura videbantur. Omnis praeterea antiquitatis, quod hoc loco tacitus praeterire non possum, ita curiosissimus et amantissimus fuit ut eam prae ceteris laudare atque ab oppugnantibus protegere auderet.

26 In huiusmodi igitur bonarum artium studiis sine uxore et liberis, nullo fere privato nec publico negotio impeditus, ab adulescentia usque ad extremum obitus sui diem, septuagesimo tertio aetatis suae anno, diutissime versatus (felicem profecto ac beatam vitam ita probe instituerat), tam diuturno tempore duxisset nisi domesticae fratrum dissensiones interdum supervenissent atque animi sui tranquillitatem impedissent.

27 Haec pauca de studiis suis hactenus dixisse sufficiat. Nunc vero de forma corporis et habitudine eius domesticisque moribus breviora deinceps recensebimus. Statura erat mediocri, habitudine obesa, honesta facie, mira alacritate atque iocunditate, quadam gravitate condita. Hanc naturalem corporis sui pulchritudinem purpureis et egregiis vestibus adornabat. Sensus omnes, praecipue illos ex quibus aliqua disciplina percipitur (auditum et visum), usque adeo delicatos habebat ut nihil audire videreve pateretur quod non aliquid voluptatis afferre videretur. Unde neque rudentem asinum neque secantem ferrum neque muscipulam vagientem sentire audireve poterat; idemque sibi circa oculos contingebat, qui nihil nisi formosum et decorum ac speciosum admittebant. Unius ancillae ministerio, exemplis Socratis summi philosophi atque Ennii veteris poetae multorumque aliorum eruditissimorum virorum, contentus cum libris suis diu ac multum commorabatur. Suis quamquam modicis acquiescens, aliena non quaerebat; innocentia, iustitita, modestia in omni vita sua utebatur. Humanus, comis atque facetus adeo erat ut quandocumque in eruditorum hominum coronas et coetus incidisse, quod crebro requiescendi animi gratia contingebat, ex facetiis et dicacitatibus suis (nam huiusmodi ridiculis iocis suapte natura affluebat) continuos quosdam et perpetuos propemodum risus cunctis audientibus commovebat.

and perfect, and so feared that his own writings, like those of others, would fail to satisfy him completely. Finally, one thing I cannot pass over in silence is his extraordinary curiosity about and love for all things ancient, thanks to which he dared to praise antiquity above everything else and to defend it against its detractors.

Thus, without either wife or children, free of nearly all private and public business, he devoted himself to liberal studies of this kind for a very long time, from his youth till the day he died, in his seventy-third year. Indeed, he laid out for himself a laudably happy and blessed way of life. His happiness would have been unbroken if domestic quarrels with his brothers had not from time to time supervened to spoil the tranquillity of his soul. 26

Let this suffice for his studies. Let us now turn briefly to his appearance, his bearing and his domestic habits. He was of middle height, obese and had a handsome face, lively and jovial, with a touch of gravity. He enhanced his natural good looks with fine, plum-colored garments. All his senses, especially those necessary to the study of some discipline (like hearing and sight), were so refined that he could not stand hearing or seeing anything unpleasant. Hence he could not bear the noise of a braying donkey, a saw, or a mousetrap moving around. It was the same with his eyes: they couldn't stand the sight of things that were not beautiful, appropriate, and splendid. Following the example of the great philosopher Socrates, of the old poet Ennius and many other learned men, he was content with the help of a single serving woman and spent most of his time with his books. Finding comfort in the little he had, he did not seek more; throughout his life he practiced honesty, justice, and restraint. He was so affable, gracious and witty that whenever he joined a discussion of learned men, which he often did for relaxation, his funny stories and mordant raillery (for he naturally overflowed with comic jests) would make all his listeners laugh continuously. 27

28 Priscis picturis sculpturisve plurimum delectabatur. Quocirca nihil in tota fere Italia ab antiquis illis celebratis sive pictoribus sive sculptoribus affabre pictum sculptumve reperiebatur quod domi suae, nullis sumptibus parcens, congregare non conaretur, si ullo quovis pacto prae facultatibus suis licuisset. Unde magnam quandam huiusmodi tabularum ac signorum copiam comparaverat. Tanta in transcribendis codicibus, praesertim priscis et vetustis, voluptate capiebatur ut ab huiusmodi transcriptionibus paucis diebus antequam moreretur se abstinere non posset.

29 Unum in huius vitae suae calce vel summa laude dignissimum non praetermittam. Ita enim veterum scriptorum, maxime eorum qui apud nos culpa temporum perierant, avidus, ita librorum helluo erat ut sua diligentia et magnis sumptibus complura volumina ab extremis usque Germaniae, Galliarum, Graeciaeque finibus ad nos usque in Etruriam referrentur, quorum antea non nisi nomina et quaedam fragmenta tenebamus. Proinde et plures Ciceronis orationes et Nonium Marcellum et Lucretium et Silium Italicum et integrum Quintilianum et omnes quoscumque veteres auctores, maiorum nostrorum incuria amissos, ab eo acceptos referre ac recognoscere debemus. In his igitur et huiusmodi bonarum artium studiis et in hac tabularum signorumque oblectatione toto vitae suae tempore diutissime versatus, felix profecto beatusque fuisset si familiaribus quinque fratrum ('domesticorum,' ut ipse aiebat, 'hostium') suorum dissensionibus caruisset.

30 Hac ergo studiorum tranquillitate, hac facilitate morum, hac denique felicitate vitae usus, septuagesimo tertio, ut diximus, aetatis suae anno, cum aliquando febribus vexaretur, ad extremum defunctus est. Sed cum diem mortis iam iam instare urgereque animadverteret, etsi nihil pecuniarum ac praediorum relinquebat, de singulari tamen et praecipuo librorum suorum peculio, praeclarissimo rerum omnium thesauro, ne forte post obitum suum hinc inde dispergerentur, testamentum conficere voluit. Quamobrem pridie quam moreretur suo testamento instituit ut ex magna libro-

He took great delight in ancient painting and sculpture. Thus there was nothing skillfully painted or sculpted by those celebrated ancient painters or sculptors in nearly all of Italy that, sparing no expense, he did not try to find and collect in his house, if his resources would in any way permit it. This is how he put together so large a quantity of paintings and seals. He took so much pleasure in transcribing manuscripts, especially very ancient ones, that he could not keep himself from doing it until just a few days before his death. 28

There is one truly praiseworthy thing he did that I cannot pass over in silence at the end of this biography. He was so eager to read the ancient writers, especially the ones that time took away from us, he was such a "glutton for books,"[10] that through hard work and at great expense he managed to bring to us in Tuscany, from as far away as Germany, France, and Greece, many books of which before we knew only the titles and a few excerpts. We ought to acknowledge the fact that it is from him we received many of Cicero's orations as well as Nonius Marcellus, Lucretius, Silius Italicus, the full text of Quintilian and all those ancient authors who had been lost because of the indifference of our ancestors. Thus he devoted his whole life to the study of the liberal arts and to his passion for paintings and seals, and he would have been perfectly happy and fortunate had it not been for the quarrels with his five brothers, whom he called his "domestic enemies." 29

Thus he enjoyed the tranquillity of study, easy relations with others and, in short, a happy life—although he was sometimes racked with fevers—until his death (as we said) at the age of seventy-three. But when he realized that the day of his death was fast approaching, though he had no money or lands to bequeath, he decided to draw up his will so as to prevent the dispersion after his death of his unique and remarkable holdings of books—the most splendid treasure one could have. Therefore, the day before 30

rum suorum congerie (qui octingentorum circiter tam graecorum quam latinorum voluminum numerum, pulcherrimam et pretiosissimam omnium supellectilem, transcendebant) publica quaedam bibliotheca fieret quae cunctis eruditis hominibus perpetuo pateret, idque <ut> ab aliquot doctioribus viris, civibus florentinis ac familiaribus suis, curaretur optime atque sapienter commisit.

31 Hanc solam tantorum ac tam nobilium librorum legationem mecum ipse considerans tanti facere soleo ut ex hoc uno eius dignissimo facto satis hominem laudare non posse putem. Qualis enim, omissis poetis et oratoribus, philosophus umquam fuit qui huiusmodi librariae dumtaxat supellectilis testamentum faceret? Sed si de tribus—Platone, Aristotele ac Theophrasto—philosophorum principibus dixerimus, de reliquis non immerito dixisse videbimur. Horum igitur testamenta qualia fuerint, ut cum hoc nostro paulisper conferantur, paucis videamus. Plato inter cetera complures fundos et tres argenti minas et argenteam phialam et nonnullas insuper ancillas Adamantho filio legavit. Idemque fecit Aristoteles, quippe [moriens] Nicomacho eius nato fundos et aedes cum in Chalcide tum in Stagiris moriens reliquit. Theophrastus quoque paene idem fecisse videtur, nisi quod librorum mentionem non praetermisit. Etenim fundum stagiritem Callino et hortum aedesque omnes horto adiacentes amicis et familiaribus, cunctos vero libros, quorum in prioribus duorum philosophorum testamentis nulla mentio habebatur, Neleo cuidam dimisit; non publice, ut Nicolaus noster, bibliothecam fieri et construi voluit, in qua ad perpetuam rei memoriam et ad perennem quandam doctorum hominum utilitatem optime simul atque speciosissime reconderentur. Quare si huiusmodi tam praeclarae ac tam pretiosae supellectilis non privata, sed publica et communis omnium legatio priscis illis temporibus et eruditis, ut ita dixerim, saeculis instituta fuisset, quantis et quam summis in caelum laudibus a scriptoribus efferretur non satis dici posset.

he died he put down in his will that all of his books (which amounted to more than eight hundred, both Greek and Latin, the most beautiful and precious of all furnishings) be used to create a kind of public library which would be open to all scholars in perpetuity. Wisely, he entrusted this project to several learned men, Florentine citizens and friends of his, to be carried out.

The more I think about his bequest of so many noble volumes, 31
the more I am convinced that this admirable act is enough to put him beyond praise. As a matter of fact, leaving aside poets and orators, was there ever any philosopher who bequeathed a library like this? If we speak of just the three leading philosophers—Plato, Aristotle, and Theophrastus—we may justly be deemed to have spoken of the rest as well. Let us look briefly at their wills and compare them with his. Plato bequeathed to his son Adeimantus, among other things, numerous pieces of land, three silver minae, a silver bowl, and some serving girls.[11] Aristotle did the same, on his death leaving to his son Nicomachus some lands and buildings in both Chalcis and Stagira.[12] Theophrastus too seems to have done almost the same, except that he did not forget to mention his books. In point of fact, he gave the land in Stagira to Callino, the garden and all the buildings adjacent to it to his friends and familiars, but all his books (of which there is no mention at all in the wills of those two previous philosophers) to a certain Neleus.[13] He did not, however, intend to establish a public library, as did our Niccolò, in which the books would be splendidly and well preserved as a perpetual memorial to the donor and for the eternal benefit of all scholars. It is impossible to imagine the high praises that writers would have showered on the bequest of such a splendid and precious library—not a private but a public one—if it had been founded in those ancient times, in what might be called the age of learning.

Ex libro sexto

CONTRA IUDAEOS ET GENTES

1 Guido civis florentinus de nobili Cavalcantium genere oriundus vir apprime eruditus fuit. Nam et multarum et magnarum rerum, quantum aetas illa indocta et rudis pati et ferre posse videbatur, cognitionem habuit. Et quia ea tempestate elegantiae latinae et artis oratoriae facultas omnes vires cunctosque nervos suos penitus amiserat, cum in honorem non haberetur, nonnullas peregregias cantilenas materno sermone, qui tunc in pretio putabatur, elegantissime composuit. Quarum unam et quidem omnium aliarum celeberrimam ac subtilissimam Dinus Garbensis, optimus illius temporis philosophus ac famosissimus medicus, et Aegidius Romanus, tunc theologorum princeps et caput, duo praestantissimi et excellentissimi viri, interpretari atque explanare dignati sunt. Itaque ob maximam horum duorum doctissimorum auctoritatem factum est ut ego illius cantilenae in hoc loco aliquam mentionem habere voluerim.

2 Brunectus, cognomento Latinus, Florentiae oriundus, multum ingenio atque arte dicendi valuisse traditur. At cum studio partium, ut fit, ex urbe pelleretur, in Galliam Transalpinam contendit ibique gallicum idioma, tametsi iam provectae aetatis et quasi senex esset, prae ingenii tamen acrimonia atque excellentia memoriae ita apprehendit ut in ea lingua singularia quaedam ac memoratu digna scribere auderet. Celebratum enim et famosum librum suum, qui *Thesaurus* inscribebatur, in tres partes pulcherrime distinxit. In prima namque, quam 'Monetam usualem' appellari et nuncupari voluit, de gestis utriusque Novi et Veteris Testa-

From Book Six of

AGAINST THE JEWS AND THE GENTILES

Guido, a Florentine citizen and a scion of the noble Cavalcanti family, was a highly educated man.[1] He possessed a wide knowledge of important subjects, as much as was possible in that illiterate and uncouth age. Since at that time Latin style and the rhetorical art, not being held in high esteem, had lost all of their strength and vigor, he composed with great elegance some wonderful poems in the vernacular, which at that time was much prized. One of these poems was so celebrated and so subtle that Dino del Garbo, an excellent philosopher of the time and a well-known doctor, and Giles of Rome, who was then regarded as the prince of all theologians — two outstanding and excellent men — deigned to interpret and comment on it. It is exactly because of the great authority of these two learned men that I have decided to mention that poem here.[2] 1

Brunetto Latini was born in Florence and is said to have had a strong intellect and great skill in speaking.[3] As happens, he was expelled from the city owing to partisan passion and went to France. There, though no longer young — indeed, almost an old man — he learnt French so well, thanks to his keen intellect and outstanding memory, that he even dared to write some unusual and memorable works in that language. In fact, he wrote that much-praised and famous book, the *Trésor,* which he neatly divided into three different sections. In the first, which he desired to be known as "Common Currency," he treated with great distinction the events of both the Old and the New Testament: that is, the ages of the world, the kingdoms of the various nations, the 2

menti peregregie tractavit; quippe de aetatibus mundi et regnis gentium, de prophetis, de apostolis, de donatione ecclesiae, de multiplici translatione Romani imperii, de situ ac distinctione provinciarum, de elementis, de piscibus, de avibus, de serpentibus, de bestiis. In secunda, quam 'Lapides pretiosos' inscripsit, de virtutibus moralibus vitiisque oppositis eleganter disseruit. In tertia et ultima, quam vocavit 'Aurum purissimum,' omnem dicendi artem et artificiosam eloquentiam diligenter accurateque edocuit atque huic orandi et persuadendi artificio modos gubernandi civitates principatusque admiscuit. Hoc quodcumque est volumen apud Gallos habetur in pretio et est illud de quo Dantes, insignis poeta florentinus, in *Comoedia* sua praecipuam quandam et singularem, maxima cum nominis sui laude, mentionem facit. [. . .]

3 Petrus, cognomento Berchorius, vir sacrarum litterarum peritissimus extitit, quod quidem in quoddam suo egregio et insigni volumine plane et aperte ostendit, ubi secundum latinorum characterum ordinem cuncta memoratu digna ad Vetus et Novum Testamentum aliquatenus pertinentia explanavit, quod ipse, a dictionibus secundum seriem praedictorum characterum explanatis, *Dictionarium* appellavit.

4 Dantes Aligherius, ex generosa quadam Aligheriorum familia, quae vetustam a Romanis originem traxit, Florentiae natus est. Hic ubi per aetatem discendi capax fuit prae ingenii sui excellentia quam primum litterarum monumenta percepit ac postea cunctas artes libero dignas eadem temporis brevitate mirabiliter apprehendit. Ac per hunc modum eruditus et doctus ad rei publicae gubernacula accessit publicaque civitatis munera et mediocria et magna obivit. Nam et in Prioratu, qui quidem est principalis et primus totius civitatis magistratus, consedit. Sed studio postea partium patria pulsus, cum per plura ac diversa orbis terrarum loca et per

prophets, the apostles, the founding of the Church, the multiple translations of the Roman empire, the location and the peculiarities of each province, the elements, and the species of fish, birds, snakes, and beasts. In the second, which he titled "Precious Stones," he discussed with precision the moral virtues and the vices opposed to them. In the third and last, which he called "Purest Gold," he taught with care and thoroughness the whole art of speaking and the techniques of eloquence, adding to this art of public speaking and persuasion some teachings on how to govern cities and states. This volume, whatever its value, is much admired by the French and is the book which Dante, the famous Florentine poet, mentions in his extraordinary and unique *Comedy*, shedding lustre on Brunetto's name.[4] [. . .]

Pierre Bersuire was a recognized expert on sacred texts, as he showed clearly and unquestionably in an extraordinary and notable book, in which, following the order of the Latin alphabet, he explained all noteworthy things in any degree pertaining to the Old and the New Testaments. Because of the alphabetical order followed in explaining each entry [*dictio*], he called it *The Dictionary*.[5] 3

Dante Alighieri was born in Florence into the noble family of the Alighieri, who trace their origins back to the Romans. There, as soon as he reached an age when he was able to learn, his excellent mind immediately mastered the records of literature, and afterwards, with equal rapidity, he learned wondrously all the arts worthy of a free man. Thus imbued with erudition and learning, he turned to the administration of the state, where he served in both minor and high public offices of the city. For instance, he served in the Priorate, the principle magistracy of the whole city. However, having been exiled from his country owing to political partisanship, he later traveled to many different places and cities ruled by 4

variorum principum urbes—quorum amicitia utebatur—extorris vagaretur, Ravennam ad Guidonem Novellum, illius civitatis praesidem, tandem se contulit, qui pro sua eruditione doctos omnes et eruditos viros mirum in modum adamabat; ubi quinquagesimo sexto aetatis suae anno, cum ex legatione veneta (quo a Novello missus antea fuerat) anxius reverteretur, mortuus est.

5 Complura volumina bifariam conscripsit, quorum quaedam materno, quaedam vero latino sermone composuit. Materna quoque partim ipsum florenti, partim vero provecta aetate edidisse manifestum est. Nam praeter vagos quosdam et solutos rhythmos quampluresque solutas et vagas cantilenas, dum adulescens esset, duo egregia opera vulgaribus litteris mandavit. Horum alterum *Vita Nova*, alterum vero *Convivium* inscribitur, in quibus quidem ambobus opusculis apertas quarundam cantilenarum suarum explanationes congregavit. Provecta deinde aetate suum illud divinum potius quam humanum *Comoediae* poema, tametsi latine heroicis versibus primum ab initio in hunc modum incepisset 'Ultima regna canam fluido contermina mundo' et quae sequuntur ac satis eleganter per plura carmina processisset, cum tamen postea reliqua huic tam nobili principio nequaquam convenire viderentur, genere dicendi permutato, rursus ab initio resumens egregie inchoavit atque elegantissime absolvit.

6 In latino vero nonnulla insuper memorabilia opera edidit. Etenim praeter multas eius epistulas, *Bucolicum carmen* scripsit. Soluta quoque oratione praeclarum quoddam opus confecit, quod *Monarchia* inscribitur. Id in tres libros, ob tria pulcherrima quaesita, speciosissime distinxit. In primo namque eius operis libro, more dialectico disserens, perscrutatur an ad bonum totius orbis terrarum statum unius solius dominatus, qui 'monarchiae' graece appellatur, necessario requiratur. In secundo vero an populus romanus hunc unius solius dominatum sibi non iniuria asciverit. In tertio denique an eius dominatus a solo Deo vel ab aliquo eius ministro dependere videatur.

various princes with whom he was on friendly terms. Finally, he settled in Ravenna at the court of Guido Novello, the ruler of that city and a great admirer of all scholars and learned men by virtue of his own erudition. It was there, at the age of fifty-six, having just returned from a distressing diplomatic mission to Venice on behalf of Novello, that he met his death.

He wrote many books of two kinds: some in the vernacular, 5
others in Latin. As is obvious, he issued some of his vernacular works in the flower of youth, others at an advanced age. In his youth, apart from numerous poems and songs in loose and irregular meters, he composed two important works in the vernacular, of which one is entitled *New Life* and the other *The Banquet*. In both of these opuscula he included explanatory comments on his own poems. At an advanced age, he began to write his poem *The Comedy*, a work more divine than human, in Latin heroic verse beginning "I shall sing the uttermost kingdoms bordering the watery world," and continuing thus through several cantos in a rather elegant style. Then he realized that the rest of his subject would not be appropriate to so noble an exordium, and so he changed the type of diction he was using and started all over again from the beginning and finished the poem in the most felicitous way.

He also wrote some memorable works in Latin. Indeed, in ad- 6
dition to many epistles, he wrote a *Pastoral Poem*. He authored an important work in prose, too, entitled *Monarchy*. This he divided strikingly into three books, each one dedicated to a famous problem. The first book of this work contains a dialectical discussion aimed at assessing whether the rule of one, which in Greek is called *monarchia*, is necessary for the good of the whole world; the second, whether the Roman people justly claimed this monarchical lordship for itself; and the third, finally, whether this rule derives from God alone or from one of His ministers.

7 Sepultus est Ravennae in sacra Minorum aede, egregio quoddam atque eminenti tumulo lapide quadrato examussim[1] constructo ac compluribus quoque sonoris carminibus inciso insignitoque. Epitaphium huiusmodi ab initio quadrato sepulcri lapide incisum fuerat:

Theologus Dantes nullius dogmatis expers
  Quod foveat claro philosophia sinu.

Cum vero postea sex dumtaxat carmina longe prioribus illis elegantiora ab eruditissimo quodam viro ederentur, veteribus e tumulo abolitis, nova haec incisa fuerunt carmina. Apposita ibidem et adhuc extantia haec sunt:

Iura monarchiae, superos, Phlegethonta lacusque
Lustrando cecini, voluerunt fata quousque.
Sed quia pars nostri[2] melioribus edita castris
Auctoremque suum petit felicior astris,
Hic claudor Dantes patriis extorris ab oris
Quem genuit parvi Florentia mater amoris.

8 Franciscus cognomine Petrarcha a Petraco quodam patre florentini populi scriba Arretii natus est, quoniam genitor studio etiam partium e Florentia pulsus erat. Hic vir praestantissimus evasit, cum multis et variis naturae muneribus a primordio suae nativitatis ornaretur. Nam et corpore speciosissimus apparebat et ingenio ac memoria vel maxime valebat. Quocirca magnam quandam et poetarum et historiarum et rhetorum et utriusque philosophiae cognitionem breviter comparavit. Et ne aliquod studiorum genus intentatum relinqueret, ad graecas litteras animum adiecit. Ita enim legendi avidus, itaque librorum helluo erat, ut latina animo suo avidissimo et capacissimo non penitus et omnino satisfacerent. Unde Barlaam monachum quendam constantinopolitanum, illius linguae peritissimum, praeceptorem habuit, quam quidem mirum

He was buried at Ravenna in the church of the Franciscans, in a splendid and imposing tomb built of finely hewn square stones. It was marked with a long and splendid verse inscription. Originally, an epitaph was carved on the square tombstone as follows: 7

Dante the theologian, well-versed in all the principles
that Philosophy may nurture at her noble breast.

Afterwards, a learned man wrote six verses much more elegant than these earlier ones. The earlier ones were then erased from the tomb and these new ones were incised. They were put on the tomb and are still extant, reading as follows:

The rights of monarchy, the gods, the lake of fire
in song did I describe so long as Fate allowed me.
But part of me then left for better campaigns,
To seek its creator happily amid the stars.
Here I, Dante, am enclosed, in exile from my native land,
whom Florence bore, a mother of little love.[6]

Francesco Petrarca, the son of a Florentine notary named Petracco, was born in Arezzo, because his father, too, had been exiled from Florence owing to political partisanship. Francesco became an extraordinary man because nature had loaded him with many different gifts from the day he was born. He was extremely good-looking and had excellent powers of mind and memory. He thus attained in a very short time a deep knowledge of the poets, historians, orators, and both kinds of philosophy.[7] And in order not to leave any form of study untried, he turned to Greek. He was so fond of reading and such a "glutton for books"[8] that Latin literature was not enough to satisfy completely his extraordinarily eager appetite. To this end, he took as his teacher a certain monk from Constantinople, Barlaam, an expert in that language. He would surely have mastered the language in a marvelous way if the 8

in modum didicisset, nisi importuna praeceptoris mors supervenisset, ut ipse quodam librorum suorum loco plane et aperte testatur. Et quod mirabile est et perraro accidit, ad carmina et ad solutam orationem aptissimus fuit et in utroque dicendi genere plurimum potuit atque multa peregregia conscripsit.

9 Nam praeter odas materno sermone compositas, quas 'cantilenas' et 'sonetia' vulgato nomine dicunt, plura quoque latinis litteris mandavit. Eclogas quippe duodecim egregiiis bucolicis versibus edidit; epistulas multas scripsit, numero circiter quadringentas, 'mille aliis,' ut eius verbis utar, non ob aliam causam quam quia locus non caperet praetermissis, easque in duo volumina, instar tullianarum, ipse digessit. Horum alterum *Rerum familiarium*, alterum *Senilium* nuncupavit. Tertium insuper ad Barbatum Sulmonensem versibus dictatum duobus prioribus adiunxit. Invectivas in gallum et in medicum nescio quos eructavit. Scripsit et *De remediis ad utramque fortunam* libros duos, *De vita solitaria* item duos, *De otio religioso* unum, *Rerum memorandarum* quattuor, *De ignorantia sui et aliorum* unum, *De secreto conflictu curarum suarum* et *Contra clericos, De viris illustribus* unum, licet quidam nomine Lombardus, vir apprime doctus, ei singulari amicitia coniunctus, post obitum suum alterum suppleverit. Cunctas denique superioris Africani laudes in uno volumine per novem libros distinctos mirabiliter congessit, quem librum appellavit *Africam* atque inscripsit, licet morte praeventus ei ipsi, iam immature edito, ultimas ut cupiebat manus imponere non potuerit.

10 Cum itaque haec tam multa opera et versibus et soluta oratione cudisset, taedio tandem activae vitae ductus, se in otium et in solitudinem ad patavinum agrum, in villam nomine Arquadam, contulit, ubi in vita quieta, tranquilla et gloriosa feliciter obiit, cum prius multos honores et ingentes pompas a diversis magnis principibus (et ex laurea qua, prisco poetarum imperatorumque more, coronatus fuerit) affluenter et habunde reportasset. Atque ibi in

sudden death of his teacher had not prevented it, as he himself openly admits somewhere in his writings. The most remarkable and truly uncommon thing about him was that he was extremely well fitted both for verse and for prose, and excelled in both forms of writing, composing many outstanding works.

Besides odes in his native tongue, known as *canzoni* and *sonetti* 9
in the vernacular, he also wrote much in Latin. He published twelve eclogues in bucolic verses. He also wrote many epistles, about four hundred in number—putting aside, as he himself says, "a thousand more" simply for lack of space—which he arranged into two volumes, like Cicero's. Of these two, one he called *Letters to His Friends,* the other *Letters of Old Age.* He then added to these two a third volume of letters in verse, dedicating it to Barbato of Sulmona. He fired off invectives against a Frenchman and against a doctor, both unidentified. He also wrote the *Remedies for Good and Bad Fortune,* in two books; *The Life of Solitude,* also in two books; *Religious Retirement* in one book; then the four books of *Things Worth Remembering; On His Own Ignorance and that of Others* in one book; the books *On the Secret Conflict of My Anxieties* and *Against the Clergy;* and the *Illustrious Men,* in one book, though a certain Lombardo, a learned man who was a close friend of his, added another one after his death. Finally, he collected all the great deeds of Scipio Africanus the Elder in a wonderful work consisting of nine books which he entitled *Africa.* However, he died before he could put the final touches he desired on this work, which had been published before it was ready.

Having grown tired of the active life after authoring all these 10
works both in verse and prose, he retired to live in leisure and solitude to a village near Padua by the name of Arquà, where he lived a quiet, tranquil, and glorious life and died happily. Earlier he had amassed numerous honors and great triumphs granted him by various important princes and had even been crowned with the laurel wreath, just like the ancient poets and generals. He was bur-

arca quadam marmorea sepultus est, quam his tribus suis humillimis versibus illustratam extare tradunt:

> Frigida Francisci lapis hic tegit[3] ossa Petrarchae.
> Suscipe, virgo parens, animam; sate virgine, parce,
> Fessaque iam terris caeli requiescat in arce.

11 Ioannes cognomento Boccacius, quod Boccacius ei pater fuerat, apud Certaldum, quoddam florentini agri oppidum, feliciter nascitur. Subtili et acri ingenio praeditus atque ad poeticam praecipue apto accommodatoque, hic tametsi ad studia litterarum, negligentia et incuria patris, tardus lentusque accederet, ob ingenii tamen acrimoniam, postquam se ad studendum contulit, cuncta probe ac celeriter didicit. Unde multarum et magnarum rerum cognitionem adeptus est, quibus peregrina graecorum studia adiungere concupivit et voluit. Itaque Leontium quendam thessalum, Petrarcham in Barlaam constantinopolitano monacho — ut supra diximus — imitatus, illarum litterarum eruditissimum praeceptorem habuit, a quo et prima elementa percepit et utrumque praeclarum Homeri et *Iliadem* et *Odisseam* volumen audivit. Ac magna multarum et diversarum rerum armatus et instructus industria sese ad scribendum conferre non dubitavit. Quocirca plura partim materno, partim latino sermone composuit, quae omnia bifariam scripta apud nos extant. Materna quoque partim carmine, partim soluta oratione bipartita cernuntur. Et quamquam haec omnia ab ipso adulescente descripta fuisse constet, tanto tamen lepore tantaque verborum elegantia condita conspicimus ut latinarum litterarum expertes homines, modo mediocri ingenio praediti, magna quadam sermonis sui lepiditate plurimum capiantur. Proinde fit ut suo[4] illo lepido et ornato dicendi genere imbuti plerumque elegantes appareant.

ied there in a marble vault, adorned with these three humble verses of his (which are reported to be extant):

> This stone covers the cold bones of Francesco Petrarca.
> Virgin mother, receive his soul; seed of the Virgin, have mercy upon it.
> Weary of the world, may his soul now find rest in the vault of heaven.

Giovanni, whose surname "Boccaccio" derives from his father's 11
first name, was happily born in Certaldo, a town in the Florentine territory. He was endowed with a keen and subtle intellect which was particularly suited to poetry. But owing to his father's negligence and indifference, he came late to literary studies. Yet once he turned to study, he learned everything quickly and well, thanks to his keen intellect. Having mastered many important subjects, he longed to add study of a foreign language, Greek. So he studied with Leontius of Thessalonica, a deeply learned teacher of that literature, following the example set by Petrarca with the monk Barlaam of Constantinople, as we said above. Under him he learned the elements of that language and heard lectures on both of Homer's great works, the *Iliad* and the *Odyssey*. Having armed and equipped himself deliberately with this wide and varied knowledge, he did not hesitate to take up writing. He composed many works, some in his native tongue, others in Latin; examples of both kinds survive today. Those in his native tongue may be divided into prose and verse compositions. Although written in his youth, the charm and the elegance of the language gracing all these works are so great that they fascinate even readers ignorant of Latin, as we see, provided they are endowed with an average degree of intelligence. Thus it happens that, imbued as they are with his charming style, they usually have an elegant appearance.

12 Scripta latine item bifariam sunt; alia namque versibus, alia vero prosa oratione dictavit. *Bucolicum* quippe *carmen* per sexdecim eclogas egregie distinxit ac nonnullas etiam epistulas carminibus edidit. Reliqua omnia soluta oratione composuit, siquidem *De casibus virorum illustrium* novem libros condidit; *De montibus et fluminibus et stagnis, lacubus et maribus* nonnulla latinis litteris mandavit; *De mulieribus claris;* postremo praeclarum illud et decantatum *Genealogiarum* opus in quindecim libros optime partitum absolvit.

13 Atque cum haec omnia fecisset, sexagesimo tandem secundo aetatis suae anno Certaldi obiit, ibique in basilica sancti Iacobi lapide quadrato — hoc epigrammate, quod ipse dictaverat, insignito — honorifice sepultus est:

Hac sub mole iacent cineres atque ossa Ioannis.
Mens sedet ante Deum, meritis ornata laborum
Mortalis vitae. Genitor Boccacius illi,
Patria Certaldum, studium fuit alma poesis.

Quae quidem carmina, cum Colucio Salutato viro eruditissimo prae singulari quadam et egregia huius poetae excellentia nimis humilia viderentur, duodecim sua prioribus illis in hunc modum adiecit:

Inclite cur, vates, humili sermone locutus,
De te pertransis? Tu pascua carmine claro
In sublime vehis, tu montium nomina tuque
Silvas et fontes, fluvios ac stagna lacusque
Cum maribus multo digesta labore relinquis,
Illustresque viros infaustis[5] casibus actos
In nostrum aevum a primo colligis Adam.
Tu celebras claras alto dictamine matres,
Tu divos omnes ignota ab origine ducens
Per ter quina refers divina volumina nulli
Cessurus veterum. Te vulgo mille labores
Percelebrem faciunt; aetas te nulla silebit.

His Latin works are also of two kinds: some he wrote in verse, others in prose. He divided his *Bucolic Poem* into sixteen eclogues and also published some verse epistles. He wrote all the rest in prose, namely *The Misfortunes of Illustrious Men* in nine books, a book *On Mountains, Rivers, Lakes, Pools and Seas* and *Famous Women*. Later he finished that famous and widely praised work, the *Genealogies*, well arranged in fifteen books. 12

After all these accomplishments, he died in his sixty-second year in Certaldo, where he was buried honorably in the basilica of Saint James, under a square gravestone upon which is engraved the following epigraph that he himself wrote: 13

Beneath this stone lie the ashes and the bones of Giovanni.
His mind rests before God, embellished by the merits and
labors of his mortal life. Boccaccio was his father,
Certaldo his homeland, poetry his nurse and his passion.

Finding these verses too modest for the unique excellence of such a poet, Coluccio Salutati, a most learned man, added to them twelve of his own, which read as follows:

Distinguished poet, why speak of yourself so humbly,
As though in passing? Your famous verses elevate
pastoral life; the names of mountains,
woods and fountains, rivers, marshes, lakes
and seas you leave behind, most carefully arranged.
Illustrious men and their great misfortunes
you collect together, from Adam to our age.
You celebrate famous mothers in solemn style.
You depict the gods, tracing them all from their obscure
origins in fifteen divine volumes, yielding to none
of the ancients. A thousand labors have made you famous
among the common people, and no age shall remain silent
about you.[9]

14 Lombardus, vir apprime doctus et cum Petrarcha poeta nostro singulari et egregia amicitia coniunctus, unico Petrarchae sui *De viris illustribus* libro post mortem eius alterum adiunxit, quemadmodum paulo superius dixisse meminimus.

15 Barlaam monachus constantinopolitanus, graecae linguae peritissimus, Petrarchae nostri doctissimus praeceptor, nonnulla graecis litteris mandasse perhibetur et traditur.

16 Leontius Thessalus, graecae item linguae doctissimus, Boccaci nostri, ut supra retulimus, magister et doctor, Homeri *Iliadem* in soluta oratione, mirabile dictu, de verbo paene ad verbum traduxisse videtur, quod quidem maximae traductionis opus apud nos extat. [. . .]

17 Ioannes cognomine Villanus, de nobili et generosa Villanorum florentinorum familia oriundus, quamquam materno sermone utile tamen annalium opus composuit, quod ab initio mundi orditus duodecim libris usque ad trecentesimum quadragesimum octavum supra millesimum christianae salutis annum, quo quidem tempore peste correptus e vita decessit, magno cum ordine, nec minori quoque nominis sui gloria, deduxit. Atque hoc eius opus vulgo *Chronica florentina* appellatur. [. . .]

18 Benvenutus Imolensis optimus ac celeberrimus suorum temporum grammaticus erat, et ut vetus et usitatus grammaticorum mos ac consuetudo est, in poetis interpretandis atque historiis cognoscendis multum studii diligentiaeque posuit et ad res caesareas memorandas usque adeo animum adiecit ut ad Nicolaum Estensem, inclitum Ferrariae marchionem, calculantis instar nomina virtutes et vitia omnium caesarum memoria ab ipso C. Iulio, primo a quo cuncti postea successores sui caesares sunt appellati, usque in Vincislaum, praeclarum suorum temporum imperatorem, repetita ex

Lombardo, a very learned man and one of Petrarca's best and closest friends, upon Petrarca's death added a second book to his *Famous Men*, as we said above.[10] 14

Barlaam, a monk from Constantinople and an expert in the Greek language, our Petrarca's most learned teacher, is known to have composed several works in Greek.[11] 15

Leontius of Thessalonica, who was also extremely learned in the Greek language, was our Boccaccio's teacher and tutor, as we reported above; he is the author, remarkably enough, of an almost word-for-word translation of Homer's *Iliad* into prose, of which great work we happen to have a copy.[12] [. . .] 16

Giovanni Villani was born into the noble and distinguished Florentine family of the Villani. He wrote, though in the vernacular, a useful history in twelve books that covers in an orderly way the period from the origin of the world until the year 1348 of Christian salvation (when he died of the plague). This work, which has won great glory for its author's name, is known in the vernacular as the *Cronica fiorentina*.[13] [. . .] 17

Benvenuto da Imola was an excellent and most famous grammarian of his time. In accordance with the inveterate custom and practice of grammarians, he devoted great zeal and effort to interpreting poets and understanding histories. He gave particular attention to the affairs of the Caesars, and dedicated to Niccolò d'Este, the illustrious marquis of Ferrara, a work in which, like a mathematician, he records in chronological order — from Julius Caesar himself, whose successors have all been called "Caesars" after him, down to Wenceslas, the distinguished emperor who ruled in his own time — the virtues and vices of all the Caesars, so that, 18

ordine memoravit, ut quasi dilucido in speculo breviter ac facile diiudicare possit qui boni quive mali fuerant principes Romanorum. Totam praeterea Dantis florentini poetae *Comoediam* latino et non pervulgato ac materno sermone egregie commentatus est. [. . .]

19 Zenobius apud Stratam, vicinum quendam florentini agri vicum, natus est, tantis naturae muneribus ornatus ut, cum inter cetera liberalium artium studia poeticam vel maxime adamasset, multa ac diversa carmina pulcherrime ac suavissime cuderet. Unde sub Carolo inclito Bohemiae rege quarto imperatore Pisis laurea, prisco poetarum more, coronatus est. Cum itaque plures epistulas ac nonnulla egregia opuscula optimis ac pulcherrimis versibus condidisset, quadragesimo demum nono aetatis suae anno Avinione diem suum feliciter obiit. [. . .]

20 Philippus Villanus, civis florentinus, commemorati Ioannis gentilis ac cognatus, praeter singularem quandam multarum rerum cognitionem qua praeditus erat, arte oratoria ac facultate dicendi plurimum valuit atque nonnulla memoratu digna descripsit et librum quendam composuit, cuius titulus est *De viris illustribus florentinis,* dumtaxat civibus, in quo quidem cunctas omnium nostrorum hominum vitas (quicumque vel armis vel scientia vel arte vel aliqua facultate excelluerunt) in unum congessit. Unde et quorundam principum et medicorum et theologorum et iurisconsultorum et poetarum denique ac pictorum simul laudes admiscuit. [. . .]

21 Colucius Pierius, cognomento Linus, ex quodam Stignani florentini agri oppido, antiqua Salutatorum stirpe oriundus, a patre Piero in ipso adulescentiae sinu post prima litterarum elementa artibus libero dignis deditus, excellentia ingenii brevi tempore mirum in modum profecisse videtur. Nam et grammaticam et dialecticam, tenera adhuc aetate, prae ceteris facultatibus prosecutus,

as if looking into a clear mirror, one could see with ease who were the good and who the bad princes of the Romans. Furthermore, he wrote in Latin—not in the vulgar, native tongue—an excellent commentary on the *Commedia* by the Florentine poet Dante.[14] [. . .]

Zenobi was born near Strada, a village close to Florence. Such were his natural gifts that, being fond of poetry more than any other of the liberal arts, he penned many different poems, all of them lovely and pleasant. Hence under Emperor Charles IV of Bohemia he received the laurel crown in Pisa, as was the custom with poets in ancient times. Having issued many epistles and several collections of excellent and most beautiful verses, he died happily at age forty-nine in Avignon.[15] [. . .] 19

Filippo Villani, citizen of Florence, a kinsman and close relative of the above-mentioned Giovanni, had great ability and skill in oratory, quite apart from the remarkably wide knowledge he possessed. He also wrote some works that deserve to be remembered, in particular a book entitled *On the Famous Men of Florence,* in which he collected the lives of all our fellow-citizens who have excelled either in warfare, in science, in the arts or in any other discipline. Hence he mixed together the praises of certain statesmen, doctors, theologians, jurisconsults, and lastly poets and painters. [. . .] 20

Coluccio Pierio Lino was from Stignano, a town in the Florentine territory, and was born from the ancient stock of the Salutati.[16] While still a boy, immediately after learning to read and write, his father Piero sent him to study the arts worthy of a free man, which he soon mastered thanks to his outstanding intelligence. 21

plurima veterum grammaticorum et dialecticorum, assidua et accurata lectione, perlegit. Ad oratoriam vero et poeticam—post parvam quandam iuris civilis cognitionem, cui patri obsecutus aliquamdiu vacavit—penitus se contulit atque in ambabus illis facultatibus, quarum amore flagrabat, tantum valuit ut plura rerum suarum monumenta relinqueret, quae quidem doctrinae atque peritiae suae idonei quidam et accomodati testes esse poterunt. In poetica namque, praeter plurima ac paene infinita carmina hinc inde dispersa nec in volumina redacta, bucolicorum librum in octo eclogas lepidis versibus distinxit, et opusculum quoddam *De questione Phyllidis* hexametris pentametrisque carminibus composuit. At vero in soluta oratione epistulas privatas et publicas paene innumerabiles ita egregie dictavit ut in hoc epistolari genere solus, consensu omnium, temporibus suis regnare diceretur. *De laboribus Herculis* librum edidit, in quo quidquid veteres poetae historicique de Herculibus tradiderunt in unum diligenter accurateque congessit. *De fato et fortuna, De laudibus legum et medicinae, De tyranno, De morte Petrarchae, De saeculo et religione* ac *De verecundia* conscripsit. Haec enim, etsi magnis occupationibus tum publicis tum privatis—utpote florentini populi scriba, quod quidem munus per triginta circiter annos semper exercuit, et ut diligens pater familias in accurata decem liberorum gubernatione—vehementer premeretur, ingenti tamen nominis sui gloria scripsisse reperitur. Atque cum talia vitae suae opera peregisset, septuagesimo tandem sexto aetatis suae anno Florentiae feliciter obiit. [. . .]

22 Antonius cognomine Luscus vicentinus vir elegantissimus atque insignis suorum temporum orator fuit atque in arte dicendi, ad quam non natus sed potius a Deo factus esse videbatur, plurimum valuit. Quippe epistulas multas egregie dictavit et plures quoque orationes elegantissime habuit, quas postea litteris mandavit. Et egregium praeterea opus super plerisque Ciceronis orationibus, explanandi et commentandi causa, composuit.

Having focused above all on grammar and logic already at a very young age, through hard and careful study he eventually attained an excellent knowledge of the ancient grammarians and logicians. He then devoted himself entirely to poetry and rhetoric (after having dedicated some time to studying civil law in obedience to his father's will), and he became so good at both these disciplines, which he loved deeply, that he left numerous literary remains as fit witnesses of his learning and expertise. In verse, apart from the almost countless poems scattered everywhere and never collected into volumes, he wrote a book of bucolic poetry divided into eight delightful eclogues, and also a short work in elegiac couplets entitled *The Complaint of Phyllis*.[17] In prose he dictated an almost infinite number of elegant letters both private and public,[18] so that he was universally regarded as the king of the epistolary genre. He issued a book, *The Labors of Hercules*, in which he carefully and diligently collected whatever the ancient poets and historians had said about Hercules. He also wrote *On Fate and Fortune, In Praise of Law and Medicine, On Tyranny, The Death of Petrarca, On the Worldly and the Religious*, and *On Modesty*. To the great glory of his name, it is known that he wrote all this despite the pressure of numerous public and private cares, for he was at once the chancellor of the Florentine people — in which office he served continuously for thirty years — and a hard-working father who carefully raised ten children. After all these accomplishments he died happily in Florence at the age of seventy-six. [. . .]

Antonio Loschi of Vicenza was a most distinguished man and a 22
leading orator of his time.[19] He excelled in rhetoric, an art for which he was not so much born as divinely fashioned. Thus he wrote many remarkable letters and delivered innumerable orations of the greatest elegance, which he later put down in writing. He also composed an excellent commentary on a good number of Cicero's orations.

23 Matthaeus Villanus Florentiae, ex eadem commemoratorum Villanorum familia oriundus, praedictis duodecim Ioannis cognati ac gentilis sui annalium chronicorum libris undecim alios materno sermone subiunxit atque cuncta quaeque memoratu digna, quae a millesimo trecentesimo quadragesimo octavo (quo quidem tempore Ioannem obiisse diximus) usque ad trecentesimum sexagesimum quartum supra millesimum christianae salutis annum,[6] accuratissime collegit atque in unum volumen congessit. [. . .]

24 Iacobus Angeli filius, in Mucello quodam Florentinorum agro oppido nomine Scarparia natus, ita ingenio ac memoria viguit ut utriusque linguae, graecae scilicet et[7] latinae, notitiam egregie admodum nancisceretur. Nam plura e graeco in latinum idioma traduxit, sed duo prae ceteris in pretio habentur, vita videlicet Magni Pompei a Plutarcho, nobili philosopho, descripta et *Geographia* insuper Ptolemaei, opus profecto ad traducendum asperum, laboriosum ac difficile atque eloquentiae minime capax; et tamen id ipsum ab eo traductum fuisse videmus ut nulla graecae eloquentiae ornamenta et supplementa postulare ac desiderare videatur.

25 Dominicus Arretinus, celebratus ac famosus ludi magister, vir suorum temporum eruditissimus ac doctissimus fuit. Quippe egregiam multarum ac diversarum rerum peritiam habuit, quod in praeclaro illo suo et maximo *Fontis*, sic enim appellavit, volumine, vel potius maximis voluminibus cum plura extent, meridiana ut dicitur luce clarius ostendit. Nam neque in caelo neque in terra, ut his nominibus totius mundi cuncta comprehendam, quicque reliquisse videtur de quo, mirabile dictu, non magna cum diligentia et gravitate tractaret. Quippe de Deo, de angelis, de homine, de arboribus, de montibus, de insulis, de civitatibus et oppidis, de provinciis et regionibus, de populis, de aquis salsis, de dulcibus, de metallis, de lapidibus, de gemmis, de temporibus, de elementis, de impressionibus aeris, de qualitatibus carnium, de piscibus, de qua-

Matteo Villani of Florence, a member of the above-mentioned Villani family, added another eleven books in the vernacular to the aforesaid twelve-book chronicle by his kinsman and close relative Giovanni, and collected most diligently into one single volume all the noteworthy deeds that occurred between the year 1348 (when Giovanni, as we said, passed away) and the year 1364 of Christian salvation.[20] [. . .] 23

Jacopo, son of Angelo, born into a town called Scarperia in the Florentine territory of the Mugello, had such a remarkable intelligence and memory that he mastered both languages, namely Greek and Latin.[21] Indeed, he translated many works from Greek into Latin. Two of these are particularly valuable: the biography of Pompey the Great by the noble philosopher Plutarch and Ptolemy's *Geography*. The latter work — though a harsh, toilsome and difficult work to translate, and one not at all amenable to eloquence — he translated in such a way that it did not lack any ornament and embellishment of Greek eloquence. 24

Domenico of Arezzo, a celebrated teacher, was a most erudite and learned man of his time. He mastered many different subjects, as he showed as clear as the noonday sun (as the saying is) in that renowned and lengthy book of his, the *Fountain* — or, I should rather say, in those lengthy books of his, since it consists of many. In fact, there seems to be nothing either on earth or in the heavens (if I may comprehend the whole world in these two terms) which, marvellous to relate, he has failed to treat with the greatest care and seriousness. He has treated, in fact, of God, angels, man, trees, mountains, islands, cities and towns, provinces and regions, peoples, fresh and salt waters, metals, stones, gems, epochs, elements, the effects of various airs, the properties of meat, fish, quadrupeds, 25

drupedibus, de herbis, de leguminibus magna cum diligentia, ut diximus, graviter eleganterque tractavit.

26 Robertus Russus civis florentinus de generosa et clara Russorum familia oriundus, ceteris omnibus cum civitatis magistratibus tum uxor<e> et liberis tum denique saeculo et pompis suis posthabitis, assiduam quandam et admirabilem diversarum litterarum, et poeticae et oratoriae, historiarum et mathematicorum et philosophiae naturalis ac moralis ac demum metaphysicae graecae ac latinae linguae cognitionem navavit. Quocirca in omnibus praedictorum studiorum generibus usque adeo profecisse creditur ut magnus orator ingensque illius temporis philosophus haberetur atque ob hanc singularem et praecipuam doctrinae et eruditionis suae excellentiam factum est ut eius domus magna quadam generosorum et nobilium discipulorum caterva quotidie frequentaretur. Inter cetera rerum suarum monumenta omnes Aristotelis libri ab eo e graeco in latinum traducti comperiuntur. [. . .]

27 Leonardus, agnomine Iustinianus, e Iustiniana gloriosa familia oriundus, civis venetus, egregiis ingenii ac memoriae muneribus ita ornatus apparuit ut ad sonos et cantus, ad arithmeticam scilicet ac musicam et ad alia similiter mathematica et insuper ad cuncta quaeque liberalium artium studia maxime aptus videretur. Magnam praeterea graecarum et latinarum litterarum peritiam adeptus est, unde plures Plutarchi vitas egregie in latinum sermonem pulchre lepideque traduxit et mores insuper et vitam beati Nicolai ornate simul atque copiose memoriae mandavit.

28 Franciscus, agnomine Barbarus, e Barbara generosa quadam Venetorum familia oriundus, ob singularem et egregiam ingenii sui excellentiam magnam et graecarum et latinarum litterarum cognitionem nactus est. Siquidem nonnullas Plutarchi vitas e graeco in latinum eleganter convertit et de re etiam uxoria plures libros ad

herbs, and legumes, as we have just said, with great care, seriousness and precision.[22]

Roberto de' Rossi was a Florentine citizen from the noble and distinguished Rossi family who set aside public offices, wife and children — in short, the secular world with all its pomps — and attained great and admirable knowledge of various literatures, Greek as well as Latin, including poetry and oratory, history, mathematics, natural and moral philosophy, and finally metaphysics. Eventually, he excelled so much in the aforesaid fields of study that he came to be regarded as a great orator and a leading philosopher of the time. Because of his unique and remarkable learning and the excellence of his erudition his house came to be frequented on a daily basis by a troop of disciples, the sons of distinguished and noble families. Among his literary remains may be found translations from Greek into Latin of all of Aristotle's books. [. . .] 26

Leonardo Giustiniani, a member of the glorious Giustiniani family and a Venetian citizen, was endowed with a remarkable intelligence and memory that seemed most fitted to composing and singing, that is to counting and music and other such mathematical subjects, in addition to every one of the liberal arts. He also attained great knowledge of Greek and Latin, so much so that he translated many of Plutarch's lives beautifully and charmingly into Latin and wrote an elegant and detailed account of the life and mores of Blessed Nicholas.[23] 27

Francesco Barbaro was from the noble Venetian family of the Barbaro, and thanks to his unusual and outstanding intellect he attained great knowledge of both Greek and Latin. He thus translated elegantly some of Plutarch's lives from Greek into Latin and 28

Laurentium Medicem peritissime simul atque eloquentissime scripsit.

29 Marcus, cognomine Lippomanus, ex nobili Lippomanorum progenie, Venetiis natus, tantis ingenii ac memoriae muneribus valuit ut trium linguarum doctissimus evaderet. Nam et in latina et in graeca et in hebraea facultate et familiariter loquebatur et eleganter scribebat. Et cuncta quoque liberalium artium studia mirum in modum assequebatur, quae quidem duo et singularis doctrinae et trium linguarum ornamenta partim in pluribus epistulis, partim in multis orationibus, partim in quibusdam opusculis suis, tribus praedictis linguis conscriptis, facillime demonstrantur.

30 Leonardus Arretinus, Arretii natus, ob admirabilem ingenii magnitudinem vir doctissimus et elegantissimus atque graecarum insuper et latinarum litterarum peritissimus fuit, quod profecto plura et varia opera, partim e graeco in latinum traducta, partim vero ab eo edita, plane et aperte declarant. Haec enim ab eo e graeco in latinum conversa cernuntur: Aristophanis comoedia, ut a levioribus incipiamus, Basilii epistula, Xenophontis *Tyrannus* et haec Plutarchi vitae: M. Antonii, Pauli Aemilii, M. Catonis, T. et C. Gracchorum, Sertorii, Pyrrhi regis Epirotarum; Demosthenis libri singuli orationumque suarum in Philippum libri septem; praeterea Platonis *Phaedon de immortalitate animarum, Gorgias, Phaedrus, Apologia, Crito, Epistulae;* Aristotelis denique *Oeconomicorum* libri duo, *Ethicorum* decem, *Politicorum* octo. Atque haec omnia ita e graeco in latinum convertit ut nulla propriae eloquentiae ornamenta, mirabile dictu, exigere ac desiderare videantur. At vero ipse suopte ingenio suoque, ut dicitur, Marte, haec alia composuit: *De militia* namque, *De interpretatione recta, De laudibus florentinae urbis, Laudationem Ioannis Strozzae, Pro se ipso ad praesides, Vitam Ciceronis,*

dedicated to Lorenzo de' Medici a very learned and polished treatise *On Marriage* in several books.[24]

Marco Lippomano, from the noble stock of the Lippomano, was born in Venice and was so endowed with intelligence and memory that he managed to master three languages. He could speak fluently and write elegantly in Latin, Greek and Hebrew. He also devoted incredible efforts to the study of all the liberal arts. These two attainments of his, namely his unusual learning and his knowledge of three languages, are evidenced with the greatest ease partly by his many letters, partly by his numerous orations, and partly by certain short works written in the three aforementioned languages.[25] 29

Leonardo Aretino, born in Arezzo, thanks to the admirable greatness of his intellect was a most learned and distinguished man, extremely well versed in Greek and Latin, as he shows clearly in many different works, some of which are translations from Greek into Latin while others are his own works.[26] His versions from Greek into Latin include a comedy by Aristophanes (to begin with lighter works), a letter of St. Basil, Xenophon's *Tyrant* and the following lives by Plutarch: Mark Antony, Paulus Aemilius, Marcus Cato, Tiberius and Gaius Gracchus, Sertorius and King Pyrrhus of Epirus. Then seven books of orations by Demosthenes, including his orations against Philip;[27] Plato's *Phaedo on the Immortality of the Soul*, the *Gorgias*, *Phaedrus*, *Apology*, *Crito* and *Letters*. He also translated from Greek into Latin Aristotle's two books on *Economics*, the ten on *Ethics* and the eight on *Politics*, all in such a way that, marvelous to relate, they do not seem to lack any rhetorical ornament of the original. And he himself composed, using his very own genius and prowess, the following: *On Knighthood*, *On Correct Translation*, *In Praise of the City of Florence*, *A Panegyric of Nanni Strozzi*, *In Self-Defense before his Judges*, *The Life of Cicero*, *The Life of* 30

Vitam Aristotelis, *De studiis et litteris*, *Isagogicon moralis philosophiae*, duos explanationum in *Oeconomica* Aristotelis libros, *Dialogorum* totidem, epistularum suarum libros octo. Postremo dictavit *De primo bello punico* libros tres, *Commentarium rerum graecarum* librum unum, *De bello italico adversus Gothos* libros quattuor, *De temporibus suis* libros duos. *Historiarum florentini populi* libros duodecim doctissime simul atque elegantissime conscripsit.

31 Atque haec omnia ipsum in vita semper occupatissima—partim continuis romanae curiae fluctibus agitatum, in qua quidem per multos annos pluribus summis pontificibus in secretariatus officio diligentissime inserviverat, partim florentini populi, cuius scriba diutius fuerat, negotiis hinc inde distractum, partim denique rei familaris molibus oppressum—scripsisse constat. Quod admirabilius ac longe laudabilius fore non iniuria existimatur et creditur quam[8] si in vita quieta et otiosa talia tantaque scripsisset. Cum igitur haec omnia cogitationum suarum monumenta reliquisset atque omnibus florentini populi magistratibus honorifice ac cum magna nominis sui gloria functus fuisset, tandem septuagesimo quarto aetatis suae anno Florentiae feliciter moritur atque ingentibus pompis in aede Minorum, lapide quadrato, sepultus est.

32 Ambrosius monachus de Portico, quoddam florentini agri oppido, oriundus, vir sanctimonia vitae atque ingenii magnitudine et doctrinae excellentia apprime laudandus est. Inter cetera namque magnam quandam et non usitatam graecarum et latinarum litterarum cognitionem liberalibus artibus adiecit atque utramque linguam, et peregrinam et domesticam, ita in promptu habuit ut ex tempore de graeco in latinum absque ulla praemeditatione, mirabile dictu, eleganter et graviter et fideliter cuncta quaeque converteret. Unde multae ac variae interpretationes suae reperiuntur. Nam plures beati Chrysostomi sermones et vita eius ac pleraque Magni Basilii opera, nonnulli insuper aliorum sanctorum virorum dialogi ac

Aristotle, On Literary Study, Introduction to Moral Philosophy, commentaries on the two books of Aristotle's *Ethics, The Dialogues,* also in two books, and eight books of his letters. He also wrote three books *On the First Punic War,* a book of *Commentaries on Greek Affairs,* four books *On the Italian War against the Goths,* and two books *On His Own Times.* He wrote *The History of the Florentine People* in twelve books with the greatest learning and elegance.

And he wrote all this while leading a very busy life, partly agi- 31
tated by the constant instability of the Roman curia, in which he served diligently for many years as papal secretary under various popes, partly distracted hither and yon by the affairs of the Florentine people, whose chancellor he was for a long time, and partly burdened by his own family cares. So his literary achievements should be considered even more admirable and praiseworthy than if he had written so many lengthy works while leading a quiet and leisured life. Having left all these monuments to his genius and served in all the magistracies of the Florentine people in a most honorable and glorious way, he died happily at the age of seventy-four in Florence, and was buried with solemn ceremony in the church of the Franciscans under a square gravestone.

Ambrose, a monk born in Portico, a village in the Florentine terri- 32
tory, was a man whose saintly life, great intelligence, and extraordinary learning made him worthy of high praise. Among his other accomplishments he added to a mastery of the liberal arts a vast and uncommon knowledge of Greek and Latin. Indeed, he was so fluent in both those languages, the foreign and the domestic one, that, marvelous to relate, he could translate extemporaneously anything from Greek into Latin in an elegant, precise, and faithful manner. He has thus left us numerous and varied translations, including many of St. John Chrysostom's sermons and his *Life,* many works by Basil the Great, several dialogues by other saintly men and, above all, the huge volume of Diogenes Laertius *On the Lives*

praeterea[9] ingens illud Laertii Diogenis *De vita et moribus philosophorum* volumen et denique praeclari Dionysii Areopagitae tum *De divinis nominibus* tum *De caelesti et angelica hierarchia* ita apud nos extant, ut cum praedicta Dionysii opera antea traducta partim obscura, partim confusa, partim barbara viderentur, per novam huius praestantissimi viri interpretationem clara, aperta ac latina facta cernantur. [. . .]

33 Carolus Arretinus ob singularia et praecipua raraque ingenii ac memoriae munera quibus suapte natura mirum in modum ornabatur graecae ac latinae linguae notitiam brevi tempore ita nactus est ut graece faciliter ac prompte, quasi Athenis natus esset, eleganter et congrue loqueretur. Et graecos insuper auctores non solum oratores et historicos, attico et communi sermone usos, sed poetas etiam, quos Cicero noster quasi aliena lingua locutos attingere verebatur, ut ipse de se in dialogo *De oratore* his verbis plane et aperte testatur: 'Poetas quasi aliena lingua locutos non cogor attingere,' publice legere et explanare auderet.[10] Quod quidem saepenumero in publicis Florentinorum studiis profiteri non dubitavit.

34 Ad hanc tam singularem ac tam egregiam praedictarum linguarum peritiam admirabilem quandam cunctarum artium, quas liberales vocant, cognitionem adiunxit. Hac itaque eruditione atque ista elegantia instructus, et viva, ut dicitur, voce plura laudabilia doctrinae opera peregit et multa quoque memoratu digna litteris mandavit. Siquidem soluto sermone plures elegantes epistulas multasque pulchras orationes scripsit. Et opusculum insuper Homeri, quod graece *Batrachomyomachia*[11] inscribitur et latine ad verbum 'ranarum ac murium proelium' recte interpretari potest, egregiis carminibus ita in latinum convertit ut nulla homericae eloquentiae, mirabile dictu, exigere ac postulare existimentur — in

and Mores of the Philosophers, and finally the works of the famous Dionysius Areopagite *On the Divine Names* and *On the Celestial and Angelic Hierarchy*. The aforesaid works of Dionysius had been translated before and seemed obscure, confused and barbarous, but thanks to the new translation of this outstanding man they stand revealed as clear and perspicuous—and written in good Latin.[28] [. . .]

Carlo of Arezzo,[29] thanks to the unique, extraordinary and rare gifts of intellect and memory with which he was miraculously endowed by nature, soon attained a knowledge of Greek and Latin so great that he could speak Greek as fluently, tastefully and impeccably as if he had been born in Athens. He did not hesitate to lecture and comment on Greek authors in public, not only the orators and historians, who use Attic and *koiné* Greek, but even the poets—the very ones whom our Cicero did not dare to take up, as though they spoke a foreign language, something he openly admits about himself in the dialogue *De oratore*, where he says: "I prefer not to handle the poets, who speak almost in a different language."[30] But Carlo did not hesitate to teach the poets on many occasions at the University of Florence. 33

To this unique and excellent expertise in the aforesaid languages he also added an admirable knowledge of all those arts that are called liberal. Thus equipped with this erudition and good taste, he accomplished many praiseworthy works of learning with the living voice (as the expression is)[31] and also wrote down much that is worthy of memory. In prose, he wrote numerous elegant epistles and many lovely orations. He also translated into excellent Latin verse a short work by Homer whose title in Greek reads *Batrachomyomachia* (which could be translated as "The Battle between the Frogs and the Mice") in such a way that, marvelous to relate, nothing seems to be lacking of Homeric eloquence—though, again, it is in poetic language, which abhors and distances 34

lingua praesertim poetica, quae a communi et trito ceterorum auctorum loquendi usu longe recedere et abhorrere videtur. Quod de altero celebratissimo praedicti vatis poemate (et *Ilias* graece nuncupatur) iure credere et existimare debemus, nisi acerba morte praeventus inceptum nuper opus reliquisset? Nam et carmina illa bestialis, ut ita dixerim, proelii commemorati elegantia et gravia et duo quoque *Iliadis* libri iam ab eo absoluti id ipsum luce clarius portendere ac significare cernuntur. Hic vir praestantissimus clarus admodum atque famosus fuit atque singularibus quibusdam ingenii ac memoriae dotibus plurimum valebat; et multarum insuper et magnarum rerum cognitionem mirum in modum comparaverat. Quocirca si diutius vixisset admirabiles doctrinae et eloquentiae suae fructus, consensu omnium, peperisset; sed acerba morte, ut diximus, praeventus fructifera arbor illa citius exaruit quod opportunum maturandorum fructuum tempus adventaret. Quinquagesimo enim secundo aetatis suae anno naturae concessit atque in aede Minorum, quadrato lapide, maximis et inusitatis pompis sepultus est.

35 Siccon Polentonius, vir multarum et diversarum rerum doctrina clarus, latinarum litterarum peritissimus atque elegantissimus fuit, quod quidem magnum quoddam eius volumen, cuius titulus est *De viris illustribus*, maxime ostendere et declarare cognoscitur. Nam si quis singulos eius voluminis, quod in decem et octo libros divisum absolvitur, diligenter et accurate legerit, auctorem ipsum tum poetarum tum oratorum tum historiarum tum denique utriusque philosophiae magnam quandam notitiam non iniuria habuisse censebit. In nonnullas quoque Ciceronis orationes commentum, instar Asconii Pediani et Antonii Lusci, eleganter magna cum brevitate perstrinxit.

itself from the commonplace and trite ways of speaking used by other authors. He would have done the same, we must believe and suppose, for that other celebrated poem of Homer, called the *Iliad* in Greek, if bitter death had not forced Carlo to leave unfinished the translation he had only recently begun. This is exactly what those elegant and noble verses commemorating the "Battle of the Beasts" (as I might call it) that we have just mentioned, and the two books of the *Iliad* that he completed, seem to reveal and portend more clearly than light. This most distinguished man was both incredibly renowned and famous and endowed with unique gifts of intellect and memory; he amassed a remarkable knowledge of many important subjects. That is why it is universally believed that if he had lived longer his learning and eloquence would have borne admirable fruit. Yet this, as we said, was prevented by bitter death, and that fruit-tree withered before the time came when its fruits would ripen. For he passed away at the age of fifty-two and was buried in the Franciscan church, under a square gravestone, with great and unusually solemn obsequies.

Sicco Polenton, a man distinguished for his wide and varied learn- 35
ing, had exceptional expertise and good taste in Latin literature, as that lengthy work of his entiled *On Illustrious Men* shows and attests clearly.[32] Anyone who will read with care and diligence all eighteen volumes of that work will correctly conclude that the author had great knowledge of the poets, the orators, the historians and of both kinds of philosophy. He also composed a commentary on some of Cicero's orations, following the example of Asconius Pedianus and Antonio Loschi, in a most felicitous and succinct way.

VITAE SOCRATIS ET SENECAE

Praefatio
Ad Alfonsum Aragonum Regem

1 Illustrem Senecae hispaniensis philosophi vitam, serenissime ac gloriosissime princeps, quondam a me latinis litteris perscriptam, maiestati tuae iampridem misissem, nisi transmissionem indignam tua eximia praestantique excellentia fore existimassem. Sed cum ex litteris Franci, praestantissimi oratoris nostri, hactenus T. Livii historiis annalibusque perlectis et omnibus bellis adversus Christianos principes ac populos non immerito praetermissis, te solum ad optima philosophiae moralis studia animum convertisse nuper intellexerim atque propterea praedictam Senecae vitam (quem latinorum philosophorum principem, pace cunctorum dixerim, fuisse constat) ab eo ipso verbis tuis postulari et exigi plane aperteque cognoverim, eam transmissionem denegare atque ulterius differre non potui, veritus, si tanto et tam eximio ac tam praepotenti regi, praesertim ita benigne et ita humane exigenti, postulata non transmisissem, ne forte serenitati tuae (quam prae ceteris tum ob maximam quandam regalium dignitatum abundantiam, tum etiam ob ingentem plurimorum regnorum excellentiam, nec minus ob admirabilem et paene incredibilem multarum et magnarum virtutum tuarum splendorem, colere, venerari et observare debeo, et cui praecipue obsequi ac gratificari et placere vel maxime cupio) aliquatenus displicuissem.

2 Tu itaque pro singulari quadam ac praecipua in omne genus hominum humanitate ac pro eximia quoque in eruditos et doctos viros benignitate, hoc parvulum munusculum nostrum, quod-

LIVES OF SOCRATES AND SENECA

Preface
To King Alfonso of Aragon

Most Serene and Glorious Prince: The illustrious life of the philosopher Seneca of Spain which I wrote in Latin some time ago I should have already sent to your majesty had I not thought its sending unworthy of your exceptional and outstanding preeminence. But recently, as I understand from the letters of our excellent ambassador Franco,[1] you have, to your credit, abandoned all your wars against Christian princes and peoples, and, having read through the histories and annals of Livy, you have been turning your whole mind towards the finest studies of moral philosophy. I have been informed in clear terms that it is for this reason that you have explicitly requested and required from him the aforementioned life of Seneca—who, if I may say it without offense, is agreed to be the prince of Latin philosophers. So I could no longer delay or refuse to dispatch it, fearing to displease Your Serenity even slightly by not sending something needed by so great and distinguished a prince and so powerful a king, especially when you had asked for it in such a kindly and liberal way. Indeed I should worship, venerate and respect you before all others because of the great abundance of your royal titles, because of the great excellence of your many realms and not least because of the admirable and almost unbelievable splendor of your numerous and great virtues; and I have a powerful and particular desire to serve, gratify and please you. 1

So I beseech and implore you to accept with a joyous and happy heart this little gift of ours, whatever you may think of it, as befits your singular and outstanding humanity towards men of 2

cumque ad te est, hilari laetoque animo accipias quaeso et obsecro, quod equidem nullo umquam tempore tibi mittere ausus essem et de eius parvitate et exiguitate nimirum erubescerem, nisi forte, quemadmodum diximus, abs te exigeretur. At vero ne hoc nostrum opusculum in conspectu regio vilesceret, si solum ac nudum et absque aliqua cuiusdam graeci philosophi comparatione appareret, ipsum socraticae vitae adiunctione cumulare et quodammodo exornare constitui, quoniam neminem Graecorum, cum multa eorum diligenter et accurate legerim, reperire potui qui Socrate sapientior ac Senecae tui similior videretur.

3 Accipe igitur, iterum rogo et obsecro, benigna regalique mente hoc nostrum, quodcumque ad te est, opusculum. In quo duae singularissimorum virorum prolixae et amplae et non breves et intercisae vitae, quemadmodum plerumque fieri consuevit, vel maxime continentur. In qua quidem re Plutarchum prae ceteris imitati sumus, qui quosdam clarissimos viros cum graecos tum latinos in unum comparavit, et egregias quasdam comparatorum hominum vitas graecis litteris mandavit et exinde magnum volumen et celebratum opus absolvit, quod graece *Parallela* appellavit. Ea si latine ad verbum interpretari volumus, *Collationes* non absurde dici posse videntur, quamquam ipse nullum apud Graecos reperire potuisse dicat quem ob singularem quandam et eximiam plurimarum virtutum suarum superabundantiam Senecae compararet. Nos vero, Plutarcho et eius comparationibus omissis, ad nostros philosophos accedamus, si prius pauca quaedam ad exiguam et momentaneam — non omnium condicionum tuarum commentationem, nam id ingens et maximum volumen exigere et postulare videretur — sed potius ad brevem et intercisam nonnullarum virtutum tuarum laudationem et ad humilem et devotam huius admirabilis ac vere divini propositi tui exhortationem brevissime attigerimus.

4 Quanto diligentius quantoque accuratius, serenissime princeps, cum generosum et antiquum genus, a quo originem ducis, tum egregia quoque et admirabilia anteactae vitae tuae gesta mecum

all kinds and your outstanding goodness towards educated and learned men. As I said, if you had not requested it, for my part I should never at any time have dared to send it, and should certainly have blushed at its diminutive size. Indeed, in order that our small book not be cheapened in the royal presence by appearing alone and bare and devoid of comparison with some Greek philosopher, I decided to enlarge and, as it were, embellish it by adding the life of Socrates, since I could find no one among the Greeks, despite a wide and careful reading of their many works, who was wiser than he and more similar to your Seneca.

So once again I pray and implore you to accept with benign and 3
kingly feelings this our small book, whatever you may think of it. In it are contained the lives of two extraordinary men in complete and full form, not reduced and abbreviated as is the usual practice. In writing this work we have imitated Plutarch above all others, the man who in a single book compared certain famous Greek and Latin men and set down in Greek the notable lives of pairs of men so as to complete a voluminous and celebrated book called in Greek the *Parallela*. If we want to turn this literally into our tongue, *Comparisons* does not seem an unreasonable way to say it, even though there is no Greek who compares to Seneca in the unique and exceptional superabundance of his many virtues, as Plutarch himself admits.[2] But we shall leave aside Plutarch and his comparisons and turn to our philosophers, after touching briefly on a few points relative to your marks of distinction — not all of them, for that would require and demand an enormous volume — but rather those pertaining to a short and abridged praise of some of your virtues and to a humble and respectful exhortation that you continue in this admirable and truly sacred resolve.

The more diligently and carefully, most serene prince, I medi- 4
tate upon both the noble and ancient house from which you spring and the outstanding and admirable exploits of your previous life,

ipse considero, et hoc praesens et laudabilem regiae ac profecto regalis mentis de optimis philosophiae moralis studiis et expugnandis barbaris gentibus propositum animadverto, tanto vehementius te laudare et admirari, te venerari et observare cogor. Mihi enim de egregiis condicionibus tuis saepenumero cogitanti talis tantusque videri soles ut et genere et potentia et rerum gestarum gloria et virtutibus et eruditione denique ceteros nostri temporis principes longe superasse ac maiores tuos — non solum antiquissimos illos et clarissimos reges, sed Traianum etiam et Hadrianum, Theodosium et Arcadium, Honorium et alterum Theodosium, quos licet ex hispanis parentibus nascerentur, Romanorum tamen imperatores fuisse non dubitamus — iam pridem adaequasse videaris.

5 Sed ne quis forte hanc nostram de praeclaris condicionibus tuis sententiam in hac praefatiuncula adulandi gratia expressam fuisse existimaret, de praedictis pauca quaedam singillatim commemorabimus. Verum ut ab ipso genere velut ab initio ordiamur, tu ab antiquissimis hispanis regibus, clarissimis celebratissimisque principibus, vetustam et generosam originem ducis, a quibus plura hereditaria et ampla regna per longam et continuatam successionem accepisti, atque ea non modo hactenus conservasti, sed etiam mirabiliter adauxisti. Nam et si fortuna, quae plerumque fortibus et magnanimis viris obstare ac resistere videtur, tibi ad animosam regni Apuliae acquisitionem cum terrestribus copiis et cum maritimis classibus variis temporibus occupato vehementer adversaretur, tu tamen longa patientia atque admirabili quadam ac paene incredibili algoris, aestus, inediae, vigiliarum tolerantia tandem aliquando ita superasti, ut totum praedictum Apuliae regnum in dictionem tuam magna cum gloria redegeris.

6 Latissimus mihi ad pervagandum campus ostenditur, si de virtutibus tuis, quemadmodum dicendi ordo exigere et postulare videbatur, deinceps paulo uberius dicere ac latius tractare voluero. Quod de industria vitavi, praesertim cum ad te scriberem, de quibus omnino silere quam pauca dicere satius esse putavi. Quid vero

and note this present laudable design of your truly regal mind to study the finest kind of moral philosophy and to defeat the barbarous races, the more forcefully am I compelled to praise and admire you, to revere and respect you. For on the many occasions when I consider your exceptional marks of distinction, you generally seem to me to far surpass in lineage, power, glorious deeds, virtue and learning the other princes of our time. And you seem for a long time now to have equalled your ancestors — not only those most ancient and famous kings, but also Trajan and Hadrian, Theodosius and Arcadius, Honorius and the other Theodosius who were undoubtedly Roman emperors, although born of Spanish parents.

But lest anyone think this pronouncement in our little preface 5
about your exceptional marks of distinction has been expressed for the sake of flattery, we shall briefly review some of the aforesaid marks individually. But to begin at the beginning (as it were) with your family, you draw your old and noble origins from the ancient Spanish kings, those famous and celebrated princes, from whom in long and continuous succession you have received many inheritances and many realms, which to this day you have not only preserved, but marvellously extended. For even if Fortune, which generally seems to block and resist brave and high-spirited men, was strenuous in her opposition on different occasions to your valorous acquisition by means of land and naval forces of the realm of Apulia, you nevertheless overcame her by long patience and an almost incredible endurance of cold, heat, starvation and sleeplessness, so that with great glory you brought the whole aforesaid kingdom of Apulia under your sway.

The broadest field lay open for me to wander in if I had wished 6
to describe a little more fully and treat more extensively your virtues as the structure of the speech seemed to require. This I have purposely avoided, thinking it far better to keep silent than say too little, especially when writing to you. But what might I say of your

de tua singulari ac praecipua eruditione dicam, quae profecto talis et tanta est, ut occupatissimum ac potentissimum regem, et in re militari ab infantia hactenus continue ac perpetue educatum, cum litterarum tum eloquentiae tum historiarum cognitionem acquisivisse admirabile simul atque incredibile videatur? Tu enim ad egregiam quandam latinarum litterarum cognitionem magnam historiarum et artis oratoriae notitiam adiunxisti, atque inter ceteros historicos nostros, T. Livium, quem patrem historiae non immerito appellare solemus, diligenti et accurata lectione ita tibi familiarem et domesticum effecisti, ut ne in expeditionibus militaribus ungue, quemadmodum dicitur, latius abs te recedere patereris, ita ut in mediis diversorum bellorum fremitibus quandoque suavi eius lectione fruereris.

7 In quo quidem, ut in ceteris memoratu dignis, praeclara maiorum tuorum vestigia imitari non dubitasti, quos usque adeo universam scriptorum suorum famam admiratos fuisse noveras, ut ipsum eo tempore viventem atque Romae commorantem et per longa maris terrarumque spatia ab illis disiunctum, coram videre concupisse intellexeras. Nam apud Hieronymum de hoc ipso quodam loco scribentem in hunc modum legeras: 'Ad T. Livium, lacteo eloquentiae fonte manantem, de ultimis Hispaniae Galliarumque finibus quosdam venisse nobiles legimus, et quos ad contemplationem sui Roma non traxerat, unius hominis fama perduxit. Habuit illa aetas inauditum omnibus saeculis celebrandumque miraculum, ut urbem tantam ingressi aliud extra urbem quaererent.'

8 Si igitur cum oratoribus et historicis philosophiae moralis studia coniunxeris, quod ut facias te in maiorem modum rogo et obsecro, non modo ceteros nostri temporis principes longe superasse, sed antiquos etiam et celebratos reges adaequasse videberis. Nam et generosissimo et vetustissimo generi et maximae potentiae et plurimis urbanis et domesticis virtutibus et incredibili rerum gestarum gloriae egregiam quandam plurimarum liberalium disci-

singular and excellent erudition, which surely is of such a kind that it seems at once admirable and incredible that a busy and powerful king, instructed continuously since childhood in the military art, has acquired an understanding of literature, eloquence and history? For you have joined a great knowledge of history and the art of rhetoric to a superb understanding of Latin literature, and—to speak of our historians—by diligent and close reading you have made Livy your servant and intimate, whom we are not without reason accustomed to call the father of history, so that even on military campaigns you never let him get more than a finger's breadth away (as the saying is); indeed, sometimes you have enjoyed the pleasure of reading him even amidst the din of battle.

In this, as in many other instances worth recollecting, you did not waver from following in the noble footsteps of your ancestors, who, as you know, felt such deep admiration for Livy's universally famous works that they conceived the desire to see him in person, although he lived in Rome at the time, separated from them by great tracts of land and sea. You may have read about this incident in Jerome, who writes as follows: "We read that certain noblemen from the farthest confines of Spain and Gaul came to see Titus Livy, flowing with the milky font of eloquence. Rome herself had not induced these men to come see her, but the fame of this one man succeeded in attracting them. That epoch experienced the celebrated miracle, unheard of in any age: that men should enter so great a city only to seek out something other than the city."[3] 7

If then you will join the study of moral philosophy to that of rhetoric and history, which I pray mightily and beg that you may do, you shall be seen to have far surpassed not only the other rulers of our time, but even equalled the ancient and celebrated kings. For you shall have contributed exceptional learning and erudition in numerous liberal arts to your noble and ancient lineage, your splendid power, your many private and civic virtues and the in- 8

plinarum eruditionem doctrinamque adhibebis. Quod una cum tanto cunctorum bonorum cumulo nemini antiquorum et nostrorum regum hactenus contigisse videmus.

9 Quapropter dicendi libertate atque ipsa veritate armati, ea ipsa impraesentiarum repetere et affirmare non dubitamus quae iam pridem, dum florentini populi nomine apud te tunc forte Neapoli commorantem oratoris munere fungeremur, dixisse meminimus. Condiciones namque tuas, quemadmodum decebat, egregie digneque pro tempore laudantes, in hunc modum locuti sumus: 'Tu enim, virtutibus tuis praetermissis, ab antiquis regibus ortus, plura et ampla regna gubernas. Tu fratres, tu cognatos magnos et illustres reges habes. Tu liberos, servatis tibi pluribus regnis, regiis insignibus condecorare et illustrare potes.

10 'Si praeclaram igitur sobolem ex hoc tanto et tam admirabili unici filii coniugio tibi nasci contigerit, et tu nepotes illos quorundam aliorum hereditariorum regnorum reges constitueris, quale apud priscos illos et claros principes exemplum tui simile reperiretur non sane intellegimus. Nullum enim neque in hebraeis neque in graecis neque in latinis codicibus legentes et pervolutantes et usque a creatione orbis repetentes fuisse regem reperire potuimus qui fratres, qui cognatos, qui liberos, qui nepotes simul reges haberet.' Quibus quidem tam egregiis et tam inusitatis condicionibus, quoniam iam illa per novam quandam felicis et clarae subolis susceptionem tibi evenisse vel ventura esse conspicimus, duo admirabilia et vix credibilia <adiunxisti>,[1] praecipuam scilicet multarum disciplinarum cognitionem et certam animi tui adversus immanes et barbaras gentes conversionem, quemadmodum speramus et credimus, postquam te una cum cunctis christianis principibus ac populis pacem et concordiam iniisse et contraxisse videmus.

11 Si<c> itaque tunc maiestatem tuam magnopere laudantes, in calce orationis nostrae ad Deum conversi nonnullas humiles et devotas preces his verbis effudimus: 'Quas ob res, ut haec tempora

credible glory of your deeds. And as we see, such an accumulation of all good qualities has never yet chanced to grace any king of ancient or modern times.

Thus fortified with both the freedom to speak and with the truth itself, we do not hesitate at this point in time to reiterate and affirm the things which we remember saying to you in Naples some time ago, while we were serving in the office of ambassador of the Florentine people.[4] In bestowing extraordinary and due praise upon your marks of distinction as befitted that occasion, we spoke as follows: "For to say nothing of your virtues, you are descended from ancient kings and rule many great kingdoms. You have great and illustrious kings as your brothers and cousins. You have preserved many realms for yourself and thus may grace and embellish your sons with signs of royalty. 9

"If distinguished offspring shall happen to be born from this great and wonderful marriage of your only son, you shall also establish those grandsons as kings in other hereditary realms, an outcome unexampled, I truly believe, among those famous princes of old. For in reading and paging through Hebrew, Greek and Latin books we could find no king from the creation of the world who had brothers, cousins, sons and grandsons as kings simultaneously."[5] To these extraordinary and uncommon distinctions, seeing that they have already happened or are about to happen, thanks to this blessed and famous offspring you have newly received into your family,[6] you have added two wonderful and almost unbelievable ones, namely, your exceptional knowledge of many disciplines, and your fixed intention to turn against the inhuman and barbarous races — as we hope and believe you will do, given that you have made peace and concord with all Christian princes and peoples. 10

Thus did we bestow earnest praise upon Your Majesty. At the end of our oration, addressing God, we poured forth some humble and devout prayers in these words: "Wherefore, that our times 11

nostra admirabili quodam maiestatis tuae privilegio fulgere videantur, quo quidem prisca illa a dignis auctoribus tantopere laudata caruisse conspicimus, omnipotentem Deum piis precibus obsecramus, ut nepotes tibi ex hoc tam fausto et tam felici coniugio largiri et condonare dignetur.' Nunc, postquam exauditi sumus, multo magis rogare multoque vehementius obsecrare debemus, ut mentem tuam ad optima philosophiae moralis studia et ad gloriosam barbararum et immanium gentium expugnationem conversam conservare, conservatamque adaugere, et adauctam secundare et prosperare dignetur, ut tu in hac vita mortali cum maximis cunctorum Christianorum emolumentis atque cum ingentibus fidei nostrae honoribus omnes non modo nostri temporis reges, sed antiquos illos etiam maiores tuos incredibili tantorum bonorum accumulatione vicisse et superasse videaris, et post mortem celestia gloriosissimorum laborum tuorum praemia nanciscaris.

12 Quod tibi contingere et evenire speramus et credimus, si ceteris posthabitis te totum partim ad optima philosophiae moralis studia, partim ad gloriosam barbararum gentium victoriam penitus omninoque converteris. Quod ut facias, totis animi et corporis viribus, quantum possum, ad Iesum Christum Dominum nostrum devota et pura mente conversus oro et obsecro, quatenus tibi, pro certa quadam Christianorum populorum conservatione et pro insigni catholicae fidei amplificatione, gratiam suam largiri et condonare dignetur; teque in maiorem modum rogo ut eam gratiam, iam per huiusmodi animi tui praeventionem preparatam, humiliter devoteque suscipias, susceptamque venerari, colere et exaequi concupiscas, ut commemorata mortalis et eternae vitae praemia consequaris. Vale diu felix, et Iannotii, fidelissimi maiestatis tuae famuli, quandoque recordari et meminisse digneris, rogo et obsecro.

may seem to glow with the wondrous prerogatives of Your Majesty—prerogatives that we see were lacking in those early times so much praised by trustworthy authorities—we call upon Omnipotent God with pious prayers that he may deign to grant and bestow grandsons upon you from this auspicious and blessed marriage."[7] Now that our wish has been granted, we ought to call upon him all the more earnestly that he may deign to preserve, increase, and cause to prosper your resolve to turn to the excellent study of moral philosophy and to defeat gloriously the barbarous and cruel races, so that in this mortal life you shall be seen to have overcome and surpassed in the incredible accumulation of good deeds—to the greatest benefit of all Christians and to the honor of our faith—not only the rulers of our time, but also those ancient ancestors of yours; and so that in the next life you may meet with the heavenly prizes your most glorious labors deserve.

This, we hope and believe, shall come to pass and happen if 12
you leave aside other tasks and dedicate yourself entirely to the excellent study of moral philosophy and to the glorious defeat of the barbarous races. I beg and pray that you do this with the whole strength of my body and soul, turning as much as I can with pure and devoted heart to our Lord Jesus Christ, that he might deign to grant and bestow His grace upon you for the sure preservation of Christian peoples and the conspicuous increase of the Catholic faith. And I pray earnestly that you will receive this prevenient grace, made ready for a soul like yours, with humility and devotion, and having received it will desire to venerate, respect and cooperate with it, so that you may attain the aforesaid prizes of mortal and eternal life. Farewell in prolonged happiness; and I pray and beg that you will deign sometimes to call to mind and remember Giannozzo, Your Majesty's most faithful servant.

13 Socrates philosophus patria atheniensis, pago alopecensis, fuisse traditur; Sophronisco lapidario vel, ut expressius dixerim, marmorario patre, Phaenareta vero obstetrice matre. Huiusmodi parentibus ortus, quarto septuagesimae septimae Olympiadis anno Athenis, in summo omnis prosperitatis illius urbis culmine, ea die nascitur, qua Athenienses urbem lustrabant. 'Huic enim urbi primum non advenae neque passim collecta populi illuvies,' ut brevis inquit historicus, 'originem dedit; sed eodem innati solo quod incolebant oppidum condidere, proinde quae illis sedes eadem origo est. Primi deinde lanificii et olei usum et vini docuere; arare quoque ac frumenta serere glandem vescentibus ostenderunt. Graecae insuper litterae atque facundia et omnis civilis disciplinae ordo veluti templum Athenas habent,' et quae sequuntur.

14 Eo praeterea tempore natus est quo Athenae et rerum gestarum gloria et sapientia ac bonarum artium studiis apprime florebant. Et ipse admirabili ingenio et praecipua memoria, singularibus naturae donis, ornatus, quamquam ignobili genere nasceretur, in lucem editur, ibique prima aetate educatur. Sed ubi adolescere coepit, litterarum studiis operam dedit. At vero ut prima illa puerilia litterarum studia transegit (quamvis secundum quosdam et ligna interdum ministraverit et lapides quandoque sculpserit), in dialecticis tamen egregie eruditus, adulescentiae suae flore Anaxagoram Clazomenium, summum eius temporis philosophum, in physicis una cum Euripide audivit; ac usque adeo in eius disciplina, siquidem mira quadam discendi cupiditate flagrabat, adolescens perseveravit quoad vel exilio vel morte ob varias calumniae causas dam-

Life of Socrates

According to tradition the philosopher Socrates was from the city 13
of Athens and the deme of Alopece. His father was Sophroniscus, a stonecutter or rather sculptor, and his mother was Phaenarete, a midwife.[8] He was born to these parents in Athens in the fourth year of the seventy-seventh Olympiad in the period of that city's greatest prosperity, on the very day when its citizens were ceremonially purifying the city.[9] "This city was founded neither by immigrants nor by the dregs of a populace randomly assembled," as an historian states concisely, "but rather by autochthonous peoples; hence their place of residence is the same as their place of origin. They were the first to learn the use of wool, oil and wine; and they were also the ones who made known ploughing and sowing grain to men who still ate acorns. Moreover, Greek literature and eloquence and all the arts of civilization have Athens as their temple,"[10] and so forth.

Socrates was born, moreover, at a time when Athens was flour- 14
ishing in glorious deeds, wisdom and the study of the liberal arts. And he himself was brought into the light adorned with a remarkable intellect and an exceptional memory, singular gifts of nature, even though he was born of humble stock and received his first training in that milieu.[11] But on entering boyhood he gave himself over to the study of letters. Once he had finished basic literary studies (although some say that he had in the meantime worked as a woodcarver and sometimes as a stonemason), he obtained instruction in logic, and in the flower of his youth, together with Euripides, he studied natural philosophy with Anaxagoras of Clazomene, the greatest philosopher of the time.[12] Burning with an amazing desire to learn, the youth continued under his teaching until Anaxagoras was condemned to death or exile owing to some calumnious accusation or other. Among other charges he was ac-

naretur. Inter cetera namque insimulabatur quod solem, quem Athenienses pro deo colentes venerabantur, nihil esse aliud quam lapidem ardentem diffiniverit. Quod Socrati postea, dum in iudicium capitis ab accusatoribus vocaretur, obiectum fuisse tradunt. Inter plurima enim obiectum est quod solem lapidem, lunam vero terram esse existimarit et dixerit.

15 Damnato igitur Anaxagora, ad Archelaum physicum, illius discipulum, se contulisse dicitur, ut ab eo veras naturalium rerum causas perscrutaretur. Cicero enim quodam loco 'Socrates,' inquit, 'Archelaum, Anaxagorae discipulum, audierat.' Verum enim vero cum diutius ipsum viva, ut aiunt, voce audisset atque propterea secum sive in Samum sive in Pythonem sive in Isthmum (ut sunt variae philosophorum de hac eius cum Archelao profectione sententiae) pervenisset, posteaquam defuncti Anaxagorae libros assidua et accurata lectione perlegisset et in quoddam Heracliti opusculum discendi cupidus incidisset, ut ex quibus singula fiant atque intereant cuncta perciperet, longa tandem magnarum et altissimarum rerum perscrutatione defessus, ethicae operam navavit, sive quod nihil certi verive sciri posse arbitraretur (ut est vetus quaedam Academicorum, quae ab eo tamquam a capite et fonte emanavit et fluxit, opinio), sive potius quod nullum naturalis historiae fructum ad bene beateque vivendum fore existimaret et crederet (ut Laertius Diogenes in libro *De vita et moribus philosophorum* plane et aperte sensisse videtur), sive ut mente ob haec ipsa verae philosophiae studia omni vitiorum labe purgata in cognitionem altissimarum ac divinarum rerum facilius deveniret (quemadmodum beatus Augustinus octavo *De civitate Dei* libro testatus est).

16 Quocirca huiusmodi rebus tamquam obscuris, frivolis et inanibus penitus praetermissis ac pro nihilo habitis quando exinde

cused of asserting that the sun, which the Athenians worshipped as a god, was nothing but a burning stone. The same charge is said to have been brought against Socrates when his accusers summonsed him before a capital trial, for one of the many accusations was that he believed and stated that the sun was a stone and the moon was made of earth.[13]

After the condemnation of Anaxagoras, it is said that Socrates 15
went to study with Archelaus the natural philosopher, Anaxagoras's pupil, in order to investigate with him the true causes of natural phenomena.[14] Thus, as Cicero writes somewhere: "Socrates studied with Archelaus, a disciple of Anaxagoras."[15] And indeed he did listen to his lectures for quite some time, and for that purpose went with him either to Samos, Delphi or Corinth (the statements of the philosophers about this voyage of Socrates with Archelaus differ).[16] Later, he read closely and assiduously the writings of the late Anaxagoras, and came upon a brief work of Heraclitus in his thirst to learn how all things came into being and passed away. At last, worn out with his scrutiny of these large and profound questions, he devoted his energies to ethics.[17] He did this either because he thought it impossible to reach true and certain understanding (this being an ancient belief of the Academics, who have in Socrates their head and source); or because he thought and believed that the study of natural history was fruitless with regard to the good and blessed life (such being plainly the view of Diogenes Laertius in his book *On the Lives and Mores of the Philosophers*); or else (as St. Augustine declares in the eighth book of his *City of God*) he used this very study of true philosophy to purge his mind of the corruption of vice, so that he might arrive more easily at an understanding of the most profound and divine subjects.[18]

Thus he set aside such studies as obscure, frivolous and empty, 16
holding them for naught since nothing useful for human life could come of them,[19] and gave himself up to the study of morals after

nulla ad humanam vitam proventura esset utilitas, posteaquam aliquotiens militavit, moralibus, ut diximus, studiis operam dedit. Quippe et in Amphipolim armatam militiam secutus est proelioque circa Delium commisso Xenophontem, equo lapsum, apprehendit atque servavit, quando fugientibus ceteris Atheniensibus e proelio superatus abibat ac saepe clam retro ulciscendi gratia respiciebat, si quis se a tergo invadere tentasset. Per mare quoque usque in Potidaeam militavit (nam pedibus fremente et obsistente bello eo nequaquam accedere licebat) ibique cum nocte tota uno habitu permansisset et in ea expeditione fortissime pugnasset ad extremumque vicisset, victoriam Alcibiadi, quem plurimum diligebat, sponte sua concessisse dicitur. Atque his et eiusmodi egregiis rei militaris facinoribus magna cum nominis sui gloria peractis, animum ad moralia, ut praediximus, studia convertit; quibus ita se dedit, ut non multo post eius philosophiae primus inventor et summus princeps haberetur. Primus quippe ob excellentiam suam, quamquam antea Pythagoras de moribus et virtutibus nonnulla reliquisset, philosophiam tamen e caelo evocasse et in urbibus collocasse perhibetur.

17 Cicero enim de eo loquens quodam loco verba haec ponit: 'Sed ab antiqua philosophia usque ad Socratem, qui Archelaum, Anaxagorae discipulum, audierat, numeri motusque tractabantur et unde omnia orirentur quove recederent, studioseque ab iis siderum magnitudines, intervalla, cursus requirebantur et cuncta caelestia. Socrates autem primus philosophiam evocavit e caelo et in urbibus collocavit et in domos etiam introduxit et coegit de vita et moribus rebusque bonis et malis quaerere. Cuius multiplex ratio disserendi rerumque varietas et ingenii magnitudo, memoria et lit-

having served in the military for some time. Indeed, he accompanied a military force to Amphipolis and in a pitched battle near Delos he picked up and saved Xenophon, who had fallen off his horse. Overwhelmed, he retreated from battle with the rest of the fleeing Athenians, and if someone tried to attack him from behind, he would often, unnoticed, turn round to face them and take his revenge. He also went by sea all the way to Potidaea to fight (since under wartime conditions it could not be reached by land); there he remained a whole night without moving. And in that expedition he fought valiantly, winning in the end, and it is said that of his own accord he conceded the merit of the victory to Alcibiades, whom he loved dearly.[20] Having accomplished these and similar distinguished military feats to the great glory of his name, he turned his mind, as we said, to moral philosophy, so dedicating himself to it that soon thereafter he was regarded as the first inventor and greatest exponent of this kind of philosophy. Thanks to his excellence he was reputed the first to have called philosophy down from the skies and to have placed it in cities, even though Pythagoras had previously left some writings on morality and virtue.[21]

Cicero, in speaking about him, writes somewhere as follows: 17
"But from antiquity down to the time of Socrates, who studied with Archelaus, the pupil of Anaxagoras, philosophy dealt with numbers and movements and sought zealously to discover whence all things came or whither they returned, inquiring into the size of the stars, the spaces that divide them, their courses and all celestial phenomena. Socrates, on the other hand, was the first to call philosophy down from the heavens and set her in the cities of men and even to bring her into their homes, compelling her to ask questions about life and morality and things good and evil. His many-sided method of discussion, the variety of subjects he discussed and the greatness of his genius, which have been immortalized in books and in memory, have produced many warring philo-

teris consecrata, plura genera efficit disserentium philosophorum.' Et in eodem libro his verbis usus est: 'Non mihi quidem soli sed, id quod admirari saepe soleo, maioribus quoque nostris hoc ita visum intellego multis saeculis ante Socratem, a quo haec omnis quae est de vita et moribus philosophia manavit.' Et alibi in *Officiorum* libris, cum de honesto et utili loqueretur, sic inquit: 'Itaque accepimus Socratem exsecrari solitum eos qui primum haec natura cohaerentia, opinione distraxissent. Cui quidem ita sunt Stoici assensi, ut et quicquid honestum esset et utile esse censerent; nec utile quicquam quod non honestum.' Et in secundo *De finibus* verba haec ponit: 'Quando enim Socrates, qui parens philosophiae iure dici potest, quicquam tale fecit?'

18 Tantumque ingenio et diligentia valuit, ut tametsi bis in longinqua, quemadmodum ostendimus, loca militaverit et duas quoque uxores habuerit et plures exinde filios susceperit et nonnullos denique Athenis magistratus gesserit, poeticam tamen, ut a levioribus incipiam, non ignoravit. Acer etiam et promptus ad dicendum fuit, praedicareque solebat omnes in eo, quod scirent, satis esse eloquentes. Disserendi insuper artem, quam Graeci 'dialecticen' appellant, ita intellexit ut de ea publice docere ac praecepta tradere non dubitaverit. Quod ne cui mirum esse videatur, Apuleium audiat, qui de Platone in libro de eius dogmate loquens, ita ferme inquit: 'Plato naturalem philosophiam a Pythagoreis, dialecticam vero, hoc est rationalem ac moralem, ex ipso Socratis fonte suscepit.' Et ne musicae omnino expers haberetur, fidibus canere instituit, cui quidem rei cum provecta aetate operam dare non erubesceret, an requiescendi animi an discendi gratia fecerit, ut apud

sophic sects."[22] And in the same book he uses these words: "I understand that this has seemed true not just to me, but also, remarkably, to our ancestors many centuries before Socrates, the fountain-head of all modern philosophy that deals with life and conduct."[23] And elsewhere, in his book *On Duties,* discussing the good and the expedient, he speaks as follows: "Thus we take it that Socrates used to curse those who first drew a conceptual distinction between things naturally inseparable. With this doctrine the Stoics are in agreement, insofar as they maintain that if anything is morally right, it is expedient, and if anything is not morally right, it is not expedient."[24] And in the second book of *On Final Causes,* he posits this: "When did Socrates, who may rightly be called the father of philosophy, do anything of the sort?"[25]

Such was his intelligence and application that, even after twice 18
performing military service in distant lands, as we said, and also maintaining two wives and raising numerous children, and even after holding several magistracies in Athens, he still did not neglect poetry (to start with lighter subjects).[26] He was keen and ready of speech, and used to say that everyone was eloquent enough when speaking of what he knew.[27] Furthermore, he knew the art of discussion (which the Greeks call "dialectic") so well that he did not hesitate to teach it publicly and pass on teachings about it. If anyone is surprised at this, let him listen to Apuleius, who, speaking about Plato in a book on his teachings, says something like this: "Plato drew his natural philosophy from the Pythagoreans, but dialectic—that is, epistemology and moral philosophy—he received from the very fountain-head, Socrates."[28] Socrates did not want to be considered ignorant of music, so he learned to sing to the lyre, something he didn't blush to devote effort to even though he was advanced in years.[29] Whether he did this to refresh his spirit or (as some authors have written) for the sake of learning is uncertain. For some say that he took up singing to the lyre because he did not believe it was shameful for anyone

nonnullos auctores scriptum videmus, incertum est. Quidam enim ipsum propterea fidibus cecinisse aiunt, quoniam ea discere turpe esse non putaret quae quisque ignoraret. In qua quidem opinione et Cicero noster esse videtur, qui in libro *De senectute* verba haec ponit: 'Quod cum fecisse Socratem in fidibus audirem, vellem etiam illud (discebant enim fidibus antiqui),' et quae sequuntur. Et alibi: 'Summam,' inquit, 'eruditionem Graeci sitam censebant in nervorum vocumque cantibus. Igitur et Epaminondas, princeps meo iudicio Graeciae, fidibus praeclare cecinisse dicitur, Themistoclesque aliquot ante annos cum in epulis recusaret lyram est habitus indoctior.' Quidam vero idcirco eam psallendi artem didicisse autumant, ut quandocumque crebris altissimarum rerum meditationibus defatigaretur, exinde aliquatenus relaxaretur. Qui ita putant eo vel maxime argumento ducuntur, quod, arundine cruribus supposita, relaxandi animi causa interdum cum parvulis ludebat; quod dum Alcibiades, amicus et familiaris eius, conspicaretur, risisse dicitur.

19 Physicae praeterea non ignarus extitit, tametsi se aliosve homines atque quoscumque philosophos quicquam scire posse inficiaretur. Hoc enim unum et solum se scire quod nesciebat tantummodo extrema fere aetate profitebatur, atque eo solo a ceteris sapientibus sese differre dicebat: quod ceteri ea, quae ignorarent, se scire asseverabant, ipse vero, quemadmodum nesciebat, ita se nescire praedicabat. Postremo ethicen, abstrusam prius et incognitam, solus ex ignorantiae tenebris, ubi a constitutione mundi per multa saecula hactenus demersa iacuerat, in lucem evocavit. Nam et si Pythagoras nonnulla de virtutibus et moribus, ut diximus, primitus tradidisset, ita tamen obscura et falsa erant, cum ad numerum omnia referret, ut traditionibus suis vel parum vel nihil et

to learn something he didn't know.[30] This seems to be the opinion of our Cicero, who in his book *On Old Age* wrote as follows: "And when I read what Socrates did in the case of the lyre, an instrument much cultivated by the ancients, I should have liked to have done it, too," etc.[31] And elsewhere: "The Greeks held that instrumental and vocal music were of the highest educational value; thus it was that Epaminondas, to my mind the leading man of Greece, is said to have been an accomplished singer to the lyre, whereas Themistocles, some years before that, was held to have shown a lack of culture by refusing to play the lyre at banquets."[32] Some, on the other hand, suppose that he learnt the art of the lyre in order to relax whenever he was exhausted from intense meditation on profound subjects. Those taking this view are led to it chiefly by the argument that he used to play with little children from time to time for relaxation, propping his shepherd's pipes on his legs—a sight which his friend and intimate Alcibiades is said to have laughed at.[33]

Moreover, he was not ignorant of natural philosophy, although he would deny that either he or other men or any philosopher could have any certain knowledge about it.[34] For almost to the end of his life he used to maintain that he knew only one thing, namely, that he knew nothing, and he would say that this alone distinguished him from other wise men: that the rest would assert that they knew something they didn't know, whereas he himself, being without knowledge, would proclaim that he had no knowledge.[35] Finally, he alone summoned into the light from the shadows of ignorance the study of ethics, which had earlier been hidden and unknown, having lain buried for many centuries from the foundation of the world. For even if Pythagoras originally handed down a few sayings about virtues and mores, as we have said, these were so obscure and false, since he related everything to number, that his tradition seems to have contributed little or nothing to a 19

ad veram virtutum cognitionem et ad bene beateque vivendum profecisse videretur.

20 Hunc Socrates postea secutus, de virtutibus ipsis planius ac verius disputavit. In quo licet ab Aristotele (philosophorum, Platonem semper excipio, magistro et principe) redarguatur, irrideatur et, si Ciceroni credimus, contemnatur, quoniam virtutes scientias esse diffiniverit, a Platone tamen, nobilitato eius discipulo (cuius ego iudicium, quamvis aristotelico non anteponam, inferius tamen illius censura existimandum esse non arbitror) simul atque a ceteris egregiis sapientibus ita laudatur, ut solus et primus philosophiam, ut aiunt, e caelo evocasse et in urbibus collocasse videatur. Sed, ut Aristoteles hoc loco de ipsa Socratis obiurgatione tandem aliquando refellatur, ob hanc solam, ut arbitror, moralium rerum cognitionem, summa quadam morum et probitate vitae conditam, Socratem non modo uno cunctorum hominum consensu, sed divino quoque Apollinis oraculo sapientissimum omnium iudicatum memoriae prodiderunt (cum antea 'philosophi', quod primus Pythagoras nomen invenit, non 'sapientes' appellarentur). Et quamvis Apollo vera proferret, propterea tamen ipsum contra inveteratam respondendi consuetudinem palam et aperte enuntiasse creditur, ut perinde viro omnium iustissimo atque integerrimo, populari invidia conflata, mortem machinaretur. Atque, ita moriens, multiplices humanae vitae molestias evitaret. Idque propterea adducor ut credam, quoniam ipse anceps et obscurus erat ac semper per quaedam involucra atque aenigmata respondere solebat.

21 Cum igitur memorato Apollinis oraculo sapientissimus omnium, ut diximus, iudicatus esset, satis admirari non poterat, propterea quod nec se sapientem esse intellegebat, nec oraculum mentiri ac falsa proferre existimabat. Hac itaque admiratione ductus, cum Apollinis responsum, inveterata respondendi consuetudine, per aenigmata traditum atque ambiguum esse arbitraretur, unumquodque genus hominum eorum, qui consensu omnium sa-

true understanding of the virtues and to the good and blessed life.[36]

Though Socrates came after Pythagoras, he analyzed the vir- 20
tues themselves with greater clarity and truth. In this regard he was contradicted, mocked and (if we are to believe Cicero) despised by Aristotle, the master and prince of philosophers (always excepting Plato), for having defined virtue as knowledge.[37] Nevertheless, Socrates was praised by Plato, his renowned disciple (whose judgement I should not prefer to Aristotle's, though I do not think it should be subject to Aristotle's censure). Plato and other eminent wise men praised Socrates as unique and as the first to have brought philosophy down from the skies and to have located it in cities. But Aristotle's objections to Socrates may here, I believe, be rebutted on the sole grounds of Socrates' understanding of morality, based as it was on the high probity of his own life and character. It was on these grounds, according to tradition, that the consensus of all mankind and the divine oracle of Apollo judged him to be the wisest of men[38] (although before that time such men were not called "wise men" but "philosophers," a word introduced by Pythagoras). And although Apollo spoke the truth, it is believed that, by departing from his ancient custom of answering—by speaking in clear and open language—he stirred up popular envy against this most just and upright of men and so engineered his death.[39] By dying in this way Socrates avoided the innumerable sufferings of human life. I am inclined to accept this story because Apollo had ever been ambiguous and obscure and used to respond to inquiries with veiled words and enigmas.

So after being judged the wisest of all by the oracle of Apollo, 21
Socrates could not stop wondering about this, since he did not think of himself as wise, but neither did he think the oracle capable of lying and falsehood. Thus he concluded that the oracle must be following its ancient custom of speaking ambiguously and in riddles, and drawn by curiosity he decided to test every category of

pientes habebantur, experiri statuit an se sapientiores essent. Unde et rerum publicarum gubernatores et opifices et poetas et philosophos denique tentandi et experiendi gratia percontatus, neminem illorum sapientem esse plane et aperte et sensit et vidit. Sed se a memoratis omnibus eo solo differre animadvertit, quod illi ea, quae nesciebant, se scire profitebantur; ipse vero, quemadmodum ignorabat, ita se ignorare asseverabat. Ac per hunc modum ambiguam et obscuram oraculi sententiam interpretabatur, quasi ita dictum esset: 'Ex vobis, o homines, is sapientissimus foret, si quis ceu Socrates se nihil scire intelligeret.'

22 Insuper, licet Aristoteles de definiendis atque inter se distinguendis animi virtutibus probe egregieque tractaverit, nihil tamen accurate legentibus attulisse videbatur quo virtutes ardentius appeterentur, vitia enixius evitarentur. Quod Socrates et Plato praecipue apud Graecos, apud nostros vero Cicero et Seneca prae ceteris fecisse laudantur, ut suasionibus suis ad incredibilem quendam virtutum amorem simul atque vitiorum detestationem et dormientes homines et aliud agentes vehementius excitarentur, quemadmodum de Ciceronis *Hortensio* a beato Augustino scriptum esse videmus; in quem librum cum forte incidisset, tantum philosophiae ardorem, cuius exhortationem continebat, inter legendum sibi iniecisse dicit ut, mirabile dictu, mentem suam repente mutaverit et vota ac desideria sua longe alia fecerit.

23 Tanta ergo huius singularissimi viri atque optimi philosophi fama et opinio per universam praecipue Graeciam iam dudum increbuerat, ut ideo plures illustres reges atque clarissimi principes ipsum per epistulas ac legatos, per munerum oblationem, ad sese advocare et arcessere conarentur. Nam et Archelaum Macedonem et Scopam Crannonium Eurylochumque Larisseum illum ad sese evocasse ingentesque pecunias, ut libentius accederet, dono dandas misisse legimus. At Socrates, pretiosa memoratorum regum mu-

those men who were generally held to be wise, to see whether they were indeed wiser than he. Hence, having interrogated statesmen, artists, poets and finally philosophers with this end in view, he came to the clear realization that none of them were wise, because they claimed to know what they didn't know, whereas when he himself didn't know something, he confessed his own ignorance. And that was how he interpreted the oracle's dark and ambiguous utterance: it was as though he had said, "He shall be the wisest among you, O men, who like Socrates understands that he does not know anything."[40]

Furthermore, although Aristotle gave an excellent treatment of 22
the definitions and distinctions among the soul's virtues, he seems to have offered careful readers nothing to make them desire the virtues more ardently and avoid the vices more earnestly. That is something for which Socrates and Plato among the Greeks, and Cicero and Seneca among our authors, have won praise. Their exhortations have awakened men who were asleep or distracted to an incredible love of virtue and detestation of vice. What St. Augustine writes about Cicero's *Hortensius* is a case in point. Coming by chance upon that book, which contained an exhortation to philosophy, he was possessed of so powerful an enthusiasm for philosophy while reading it that, marvelous to relate, he immediately had a change of heart and experienced a radical transformation of his wishes and desires.[41]

Thus the fame and reputation of this unique man and best of 23
philosophers in due course grew and spread, especially through all of Greece, so that many celebrated kings and distinguished princes strove through letters, embassies and gifts to summon him to their courts. Thus we read that Archelaus of Macedonia, Scopas of Cranon, and Eurylochus of Larissa summoned him to themselves, sending him large sums of money as inducements.[42] Yet Socrates magnanimously spurned these rulers' valuable gifts and the money that was sent him, having no wish to travel to their

nera magnanimiter aspernatus, neque missas pecunias accepit neque ad eos proficisci ipse voluit. Tantaque Athenis eius auctoritas erat, ut nonnunquam contra civium morem agere auderet. Id sibi ob singularem quandam hominis auctoritatem iure permitti videbatur. Cicero enim in libro *De officiis* ita dicit: 'Nec quemquam hoc errore duci oportet ut, si quid Socrates aut Aristippus contra morem civilemque consuetudinem fecerint locutive sint, idem sibi arbitretur licere. Magnis enim illi et divinis bonis hanc licentiam assequebantur.'

24 Quid plura de studiis suis loquar? Tanta denique ipsius scientiae et virtutis opinio hinc inde ferebatur, ut cum Athenis bonarum artium studia doceret, ad eum audiendum discipuli undique confluebant. Unde tanta ac tam magna discentium multitudo quotidie concurrebat, ut eius ludus praecipuis et egregiis adulescentibus frequentaretur, qui discendi gratia certatim accedebant. Neque id mercede aliqua ductus, sed gratuito faciebat; cuius rei testis erat ingens hominis paupertas, qua graviter premebatur. Qui vero divites atque opulenti videbantur, nonnulla munera magistro et praeceptori suo donare consuerant. Unde Aeschines, unus ex discipulis, cum ita pauper esset ut ob paupertatem neque pecuniam neque munera dare posset, 'Nihil,' inquit, 'te dignum invenio quod tibi donare valeam, in quo uno me pauperem et inopem esse recognosco. Itaque me ipsum, quo nihil carius habeo, tibi do.' Cui Socrates humanissime simul atque liberalissime respondisse fertur: 'Magnum mihi munus dedisti. Conabor igitur ut meliorem te tibi reddam quam acceperim.' At cum Alcibiadi persuasisset eum nihil hominis esse nec quicquam inter Alcibiadem, summo loco natum summaque corporis pulchritudine ceteris omnibus praestantem, et quemvis baiulum interesse, ita se adulescens afflictabat ut lacrimis non parceret. Ideoque Socrati supplex fuit ac etiam atque etiam rogavit ut sibi virtutem traderet turpitudinemque depelleret. Ac per hunc modum Alcibiades in Socraticam disciplinam se contulit.

courts.[43] So great was his authority in Athens that he sometimes dared to challenge the mores of his fellow citizens. This practice seems to have been allowed him by right, on account of the man's unique authority. For Cicero in his book *On Duties* says: "And no one ought to make the mistake of supposing that, because Socrates or Aristippus did or said something contrary to the mores and established customs of their city, he has a right to do the same; it was by reason of their great and superhuman virtues that those famous men acquired this special privilege."[44]

To sum up our discussion of his learning, his reputation for learning and virtue spread everywhere, so that when he taught the liberal arts in Athens, disciples poured in from everywhere to hear him. Hence so large a multitude of students used to flock to him every day that his school was mobbed with outstanding and distinguished youths who competed to learn from him.[45] In his teaching he was not motivated by gain, but taught gratis, the proof of this being the extreme and oppressive poverty in which he lived.[46] Nevertheless, it seems that his wealthy and opulent students used to give occasional gifts to their master and teacher. Hence Aeschines, one of his disciples, being poor and unable to furnish either money or gifts, said: "I find I have no worthy gift to give you, and I recognize that in this one respect I am poor and resourceless. So I give you myself, having nothing more valuable." To this Socrates answered with great kindness and liberality: "You give me a great gift indeed. I shall try to give you back to yourself in a better state than I received you."[47] On the other hand, he persuaded Alcibiades that he was worthless, and that there was no difference between him, a high-born youth of exceptional physical beauty, and an ordinary porter. Alcibiades was so hurt by this that he wept ceaselessly and begged Socrates on bended knee to make him virtuous and to expel his shameful vices. That is how Alcibiades became Socrates' disciple.[48] 24

25 Inter multos autem nobilitatos eius discipulos, qui post mortem suam 'Socratici' sunt appellati, Xenophontem et Platonem prae ceteris omnibus floruisse accepimus. Platonicorum vero discipulorum praestantissimus Aristoteles fuit. Unde cum alter academicae, alter autem peripateticae opinionis auctores et principes fuerint qui a Socrate profluxerunt, dubitari non potest quin quicquid ab his duabus excellentibus et praecipuis philosophorum haeresibus bonarum artium provenerit, ab eo ipso tamquam a capite et fonte acceptum referre debeamus. Quod Cicero his verbis palam et aperte expressisse videtur: 'Itaque illius verae elegantisque philosophiae — quae ducta a Socrate in Peripateticis adhuc permansit et idem alio modo dicentibus Stoicis, cum Academici eorum controversias disceptarent — nulla fere sunt aut pauca admodum latina monumenta.' Et alibi: 'Urgerent praeterea,' inquit, 'philosophorum greges iam ab illo fonte et capite Socrate, nihil te de bonis rebus in vita, nihil de malis, nihil de animi permotionibus, nihil de hominum moribus, nihil de ratione vitae didicisse, nihil omnino quaesisse, nihil scire convincerent.' Et alio loco, de eo ipso loquens, verba haec posuit: '. . . cuius ingenium variosque sermones immortalitati scriptis suis Plato tradidit, cum ipse Socrates nullam litteram reliquisset. Hinc discidium illud extitit quasi linguae atque cordis, absurdum sane et inutile ac reprehendendum, ut alii nos sapere, alii dicere docerent. Nam cum essent plures orti fere a Socrate, quod ex illius variis et diversis et in omnem partem diffusis disputationibus alius aliud apprehenderat, proseminatae sunt quasi familiae dissentientes inter se et multum disiuncte et dispares, cum tamen omnes se philosophos et dici vellent et esse arbitrarentur. Ac primo ab ipso Platone Aristoteles et Xenocrates,

25 Among his many famous pupils, known as the Socratics after his death, we are told that Xenophon and Plato were exceptionally eminent.[49] The most outstanding disciple of Plato was Aristotle. Since these men were, respectively, the founders and leaders of the Academic and Peripatetic schools of thought and were derived from Socrates, there can be no doubt that whatever of value the liberal arts took from these two excellent and eminent philosophical sects we ought to trace back to Socrates himself as their fountainhead. Cicero appears to have expressed this idea in the plainest possible language: "Thus there are few or no records in Latin of that true and refined philosophy which, derived from Socrates, still survives among the Peripatetics and the Stoics (who say the same things using different terminology), while the Academics debate their points of disagreement."[50] And elsewhere: "Moreover, the herds of philosophers, deriving from their fountainhead, Socrates, would beset you, convincing you that you had neither learned nor investigated nor knew anything about what is good and evil in life, nothing about the passions, human behavior, or the purpose of life."[51] Elsewhere he writes as follows of the very same man: "The genius and various discourses of Socrates have been immortalized in the writings of Plato, since Socrates himself did not leave behind a single scrap of writing. This is the source from which has sprung the absurd and unprofitable and reprehensible severance between the tongue and the brain, as a result of which we have one set of professors to teach us to think and another to teach us to speak. For a number of schools practically took their origin from Socrates, because from his varied and wide-ranging discussions every disciple took something different. Thus were engendered what might be called family quarrels, splitting off in every direction, although all of them wanted to be called and believed themselves to be philosophers. First, from Plato sprang Aristotle and Xenocrates, the former's disciples being named Peripatetics, the latter's Academics. Then from Antisthenes, who was

quorum alter Peripateticorum, alter Academiae nomen obtinuit. Deinde ab Antisthene, qui et patientiam et duritiam in socratico sermone maxime adamarat, Cynici primum, deinde Stoici. Tum ab Aristippo, quem illae magis voluptariae disputationes delectarant, cyrenaica disputatio manavit, quam ille et eius posteri simpliciter defenderunt. Hi qui nunc voluptate omnia metiuntur, dum verecundius id agunt, nec dignitati satisfaciunt quam non aspernantur, nec voluptatem tuentur quam amplexari volunt. Fuerunt etiam alia genera philosophorum, qui se omnes fere socraticos esse dicebant: Eretricorum, Herilliorum, Megaricorum, Pyrrhoneorum.'

26 Quapropter Socratem ipsum totius philosophiae atque eloquentiae principem non immerito dicere et praedicare debemus. Cum paulo post Cicero noster in hunc modum subiunxerit: 'Haec autem, ut ex Apennino fluminum, sic ex communi sapientium iugo sunt doctrinarum facta divortia, ut philosophi tamquam in superum mare Ionium defluerent, gratum quoddam et portuosum, oratores autem in inferum, hoc Tuscum et barbarum, scopulosum atque infestum, laberentur.' Et ut id quod dicimus clarius appareat, Cicero etiam quodam loco, cum de Socrate loqueretur, ita dicit: 'Sic enim princeps ille philosophiae disserebat.'

27 Ceterum ne quis forte ipsum tantarum et tam magnarum rerum cognitionem habuisse suspicaretur, praeter acre ingenium singularemque memoriam, quibus maxime pollebat, in percontando ac perdiscendo admirabili quadam et paene incredibili diligentia utebatur. Quippe, ut ex libris Platonis atque ex sententia Aristotelis plane aperteque deprehenditur, mira discendi cupiditate flagrabat. Nam et Plato in libris suis, in quibus fere omnibus Socrates loquens exprimitur, ipsum plerumque et Gorgiam Leontinum et Prodicum Chium et Hippiam Eleum aliosque celebratos eius temporis sophistas — qui, de qua quisque re audire vellet, ut mos tunc in universa Graecia erat, se dicere paratos esse denuntiarent — interrogantem inducit. Et Aristoteles quodam loco scribit quod So-

attracted chiefly by the Socratic themes of endurance and toughness, came first the Cynics, then the Stoics. Then from Aristippus, who took greater delight in the discussions of pleasure, came the Cyrenaic line of argument which he and his progeny defended single-mindedly — whereas contemporary thinkers who make pleasure the sole standard of value,[52] while they do so with a greater sense of shame, neither achieve the dignity they have not abandoned nor defend the pleasure they would like to embrace. There have also been other kinds of philosophers who almost all professed to be followers of Socrates: the Eretrians, the pupils of Herillus, the Megareans, and the school of Pyrrho."[53]

Thus we may with perfect justice proclaim Socrates to be the founder of all philosophy and eloquence. As our Cicero adds shortly thereafter: "However, the streams of learning flowing from this common watershed of wisdom, as rivers do from the Apennines, divided in two, the philosophers flowing down into the calm waters of the Adriatic Sea with its plentiful supply of harbors, while the orators tumbled into the rocky and inhospitable Tyrrhenian Sea."[54] And to make my contention clearer still, Cicero also described Socrates somewhere as follows: "This is how the founder of philosophy treated the matter."[55] 26

No one should doubt his understanding of many important subjects. In addition to his penetrating intelligence and unusual memory, which were of the greatest potency, he practiced a wonderful and almost unbelievable diligence in his questioning and in the acquisition of knowledge. Indeed, as may be learned with perfect clarity from the books of Plato and the testimony of Aristotle, he was on fire with a wondrous desire to learn. For Plato, who in his works almost always depicts Socrates speaking, has him interrogate Gorgias of Leontini and Prodicus of Chios and Hippias of Elis and other celebrated sophists of the time — the men who used to announce that they were ready to speak about any given subject, as was the custom in all of Greece at the time. And Aristotle 27

crates semper interrogabat nec aliquando respondebat, quia se nescire fatebatur.

28 Cicero insuper id ipsum his verbis manifeste testatur: 'Haec est enim, ut scis, vetus et socratica ratio contra alterius opinionem disserendi. Nam ita facillime quod veri simillimum esset inveniri posse Socrates arbitrabatur.' Quamvis autem se nihil scire praedicaret, ita tamen plerumque disputabat, ut ea quae ab ipso disputata essent philosophis et sapientibus viris admirabilia et praeter communem hominum opinionem viderentur. Ex quo 'paradoxa' graece appellabant, atque divinitus dicta fuisse existimabant. Tantam itaque et tam ingentem curam in crebris magnarum rerum cogitationibus adhibebat, ut nonnunquam firmus et immobilis—a summo lucis ortu usque ad alterum solem orientem—statu quodam pertinaci eisdemque vestigiis atque oculis directis, tamquam in stupore mentis attonitus, ceu in libro *Noctium Atticarum* testatur A. Gellius, persistere reperiretur.

29 Si quantum igitur primum ingenio valuerit, si quanta deinde diligentia plures egregios philosophos audiverit, si quantum denique et quam multos doctos homines discendi gratia interrogaverit ac per se ipsum perpetuo cogitaverit vel saltem parumper considerabitur, omnis illa de virtutibus suis admiratio cessabit. Et quamquam tanta ac tam multa cognoverit, semper tamen nihil se scire fatebatur, vel potius tamquam maximus quidam ironicus, ut expressius dixerim, cuncta nisi hoc solum, quod nihil sciebat, se ignorare praedicabat. Id unum a Socrate scitum Arcesilaus ita postea moleste tulit, ut tamquam professorem nimis audacem reprehendere ausus sit. In hac tam humili nihil sciendi professione naturam suam sequebatur. Nam in omnibus rebus suis, agente et impellente eius natura, ironia vel maxime utebatur, in quo longe secus quam magnus quidam eius temporis sophistarum numerus agebat. Illi enim, cum nihil vel pauca quaedam cognoscerent, de quacumque tamen re—ita audaces et impudentes erant—se dicturos in conventu hominum profitebantur. Hic vero, cum multa sci-

writes somewhere that Socrates always asked questions and never answered, professing that he knew nothing.[56]

This is further attested clearly by Cicero in the following words: "This, as you know, is the old Socratic method of arguing against your adversary's position; for Socrates believed that probable truths were most readily discovered in this way."[57] And although he would claim that he knew nothing, he generally argued in such a way that philosophers and wise men found the things he argued about to be wonderful and counterintuitional. Hence they called them "paradoxes" in Greek, believing them to have been said under divine inspiration. Thus he displayed such enormous concentration in thinking intensely about profound subjects that he would be found standing stiff and immobile from one dawn to the next, in a certain fixed stance, his eyes and feet in the same alignment as though stunned, as Aulus Gellius attests in his *Attic Nights*.[58] 28

If we then consider even for a little while his formidable intelligence, his great dedication in studying with many eminent philosophers, the many learned men he interrogated with a view to learning, and how he was always himself lost in thought, his virtues will cease to generate any wonder. And although his knowledge was great and varied, he always nevertheless professed that he knew nothing, or rather (to speak more precisely) he would proclaim, like the great ironist he was, that he was ignorant of everything except that he knew nothing. Arcesilaus later took umbrage at Socrates' claim to know even this one thing, daring to criticize him as presumptuous.[59] Socrates was following his own nature in this humble claim to know nothing, for in all his affairs his nature drove and impelled him to employ a great deal of irony; in this respect he acted far otherwise than did a great number of the sophists of his time.[60] The latter, knowing little or nothing, had the audacity and presumption to claim they could speak before an assembly on any subject. Socrates, on the other hand, despite his 29

ret, se nihil intellegere prae se ferebat, quoniam vel maxime gloriosa, instar ironicorum, ab eo longe abesse praedicabat. 'Ironici enim,' ut inquit Aristoteles, 'maxime gloriosa negant, ceu Socrates faciebat, qui, etsi plura cognosceret, cuncta tamen sese ignorare dictitabat.'

30 Hanc ergo ironiae opinionem omni vitae suae tempore secutus, numquam adduci potuit ut aliquid scriberet nisi pridie quam moreretur. Tunc enim aesopiam fabulam et laudes Apollinis carminibus descripsit, ut paulo post, cum de morte eius loquemur, latius dicemus. Nullum igitur doctrinae suae apud nos monumentum extat, nisi si quis forte Platonis libros Socratis, magistri sui, monumenta appellare vellet. In quibus fere omnibus, cum Socrates loquens exprimatur, eas Socratis sententias fuisse vere simul atque eleganter dici potest quae in Platonis dialogis illius verbis efferuntur; et versa vice eas Platonis opiniones extitisse dicemus, quae ex ore Socratis pronuntiantur. In hac sive ironia, ut Graeci, sive dissimulatione, ut Latini tradunt, ipsum longe lepore et humanitate ceteris omnibus praestitisse fertur. Inventi sunt qui hanc sophisticam dicendi exercitationem, 'cum ipsi doctrina et ingeniis abundarent,' ut ait Cicero, 'exagitarent atque contemnerent. Quorum princeps Socrates fuit. Is qui, omnium eruditorum testimonio totiusque iudicio Graeciae, cum prudentia et acumine, venustate ac subtilitate, tum vero eloquentia, varietate, copia, quam se cumque in partem dedisset, omnium fuit facile princeps.' Hunc igitur sapientissimum virum libri, quos non scripsit, non tam bene dixisse quam discipuli, quos ab eo profluxisse diximus, probe docuisse testantur.

31 Ad comparandam autem hanc tantam et tam singularem eius sapientiam ob ingenii acrimoniam et incredibilem investigandi diligentiam sibi peregrinationibus uti, quemadmodum ceteris philosophantibus, opus non fuit, nisi in quantum militavit et in quantum cum Archelao physico, eius magistro, ut supradiximus, peraegre profectus est. Sed semper in eodem loco manens, conten-

great knowlege, would parade his ignorance, and like all ironists distance himself as much as possible from boastful claims. For as Aristotles states, "It is the ironist who boasts the least, as Socrates used to do, who insisted on his total ignorance despite his vast knowledge."[61]

He adopted this ironic stance throughout his life, and could 30
never be induced to write anything except on the day before his death. At that point, to be sure, he turned a fable of Aesop into song and wrote a hymn to Apollo, and of this we shall speak shortly while discussing his death. Thus no written records of his teaching have come down to us, unless one wishes to call Plato's books records of his master Socrates. For in almost all of them, when he represents Socrates speaking, one may say with precise truth that the ideas attributed to Socrates in the dialogues of Plato were his and, vice versa, that Plato's views are those spoken by the mouth of Socrates. In that irony of his, as the Greeks call it (or *dissimulatio*, to use the Latin expression),[62] Socrates is said to have excelled all others in kindness and wit. There were those who, "though rich in learning and talent," as Cicero says, "criticized and condemned" this sophistical practice of speaking. "The chief of these was Socrates, the person who, by the testimony of all men of learning and the verdict of the whole of Greece, thanks not only to his wisdom and penetration, charm and subtlety, but also to his rich and varied eloquence, easily took the lead, no matter what side in a debate he took up."[63] Hence this wisest of men was not so much a great speaker, as is attested by the books he did not write, as he was a fine teacher, as is attested by the students he did teach.

Thanks to the sharpness of his mind and his incredible curios- 31
ity, it was not necessary for him, as it was for other philosophers, to travel in order to obtain such great and remarkable wisdom—aside from the aforesaid military expeditions and his difficult journey with Archelaus, his master in natural philosophy. Instead, he

tius cum familiaribus ac studiosis hominibus disputabat; summoque ingenii sui acumine non tam illos ex sententia refellere quam ipse quid verum esset invenire nitebatur. Per hunc igitur modum tantam humanarum et divinarum rerum cognitionem adeptus est, ut humanae sapientiae quasi quoddam terrestre oraculum videri et appellari meruerit. Quid plura? In omnibus denique disputationibus suis ea locutus est quae ipsi philosophi, nedum homines quos tulit vita communis, ut supradiximus, divinitus ferunt esse dicta. Verum haec pauca ex multis de studiis suis hactenus dixisse sufficiat.

32 Nunc vero de forma corporis et domesticis moribus eius deinceps breviter dicemus. Pusillo corpore fuisse ac simas nares frontemque recalvam habuisse perhibetur et, ut uno verbo cunctas corporis sui deformitates ineptiasque complectar, deformis et foedus erat, ceu Hieronymus in libro primo *Contra Iovinianum* palam et aperte sensisse videtur. Et quamquam summus, ut diximus, philosophus fuerit, civilem tamen vitam, ceterorum civium more, Athenis degebat, siquidem et cum Atheniensibus conversabatur et matrimonio iungebatur et civitatis magistratus gerebat, et nihil denique omittebat quod ad civilem consuetudinem vel maxime pertinere arbitraretur.

33 Duas enim, non unam dumtaxat, uxores ipsum suscepisse fertur. Nam quidam Xanthippem, morosam illam et iurgiosam, et Myrtonem, Aristidis illius iusti hominis filiam, eisdem (quidam vero diversis) temporibus utramque habuisse tradunt. Qui autem variis eum temporibus duas uxores accepisse dicunt, Xanthippem prius, Mirthonem posterius duxisse scribunt, cuius opinionis Aristoteles auctor est. Qui vero simul ambas accepisse putant, hanc eiusmodi acceptionis causam fuisse aiunt. Athenienses enim diuturnis bellis et assiduis pestibus inanem civibus et paene exhaustam civitatem conspicientes, eam, quoad poterant, reparare subolemque propagare contendebant. Quocirca decrevisse inquiunt ut quibuscumque Athenarum cultoribus duas uxores simul

remained always in the same place, debating contentedly with friends and learned men, and he aimed with his supreme intellectual penetration less to refute their views than to discover the truth for himself.[64] In this way he arrived at such a knowledge of things human and divine as to earn the title and reputation of a kind of earthly oracle of human wisdom.[65] In short, he delivered utterances in all his disputations which the philosophers themselves, to say nothing of men leading ordinary lives, thought were divinely inspired, as we noted above. But though much more might be said, let these few remarks about his studies suffice.

Let us now speak briefly of his phyical appearance and domes- 32
tic habits. He is said to have been small of build with a broad nose and a forehead which was quite bald; to sum up all his physical deformities and follies in a word, he was ugly and unkempt, as St. Jerome seems frankly to recognize in the first book of *Against Jovinianus*.[66] And although he was a great philosopher, as we said, he still led a civic life like any other Athenian citizen, conversing with his fellow citizens, marrying, and holding civic magistracies—in short, omitting nothing he considered pertinent to citizenship.

Indeed, he is said to have taken not just one, but two wives. 33
Some say that he had Xanthippe, the shrewish and contentious one, and Myrto, daughter of Aristides the Just, at the same time, while others say he had them at different times. Those who say he had his wives at different times write that he married Xanthippe first and Myrto second, a view which comes from Aristotle. Those who believe he was married to both at the same time adduce the following explanation. The Athenians after long wars and continual plagues saw that their city was destitute of citizens and almost empty, and were trying to restore the city as far as they could and propagate offspring. On this account, they say, it was decreed that

habere ac ducere liceret; atque huiusmodi Atheniensium decreto Socratem paruisse commemoratasque uxores habuisse referunt. Sed sive diversis, ut aiunt, temporibus sive simul habuerit, ex utrisque tamen liberos consensu omnium suscepisse constat, siquidem ex Xanthippe masculum filium genuit, nomine Lamproclem; Mirthonem vero, quam sine dote acceperat, Sophroniscum et Menexenum, duos sibi natos, peperit.

34 Pluribus deinde in re publica magistratibus functus est. Singulari insuper et egregia domi ac foris patientia utebatur. Nam erga uxores, maxime vero erga Xanthippem — morosam illam et iurgiosam ac domesticis contentionibus die noctuque scatentem, atque propterea universam domum pervertentem — et erga liberos, etiam uxoris potius quam sui similes, sibi praecipua uti tolerantia opus erat. Huius singularis patientiae suae plura cum domestica tum forensia extant exempla, sed pauca e multis brevitatis causa retulisse sat erit. Haec enim duae contentiosae mulieres ob virum suum, quamquam deformis esset, ut diximus, quasi dividi posset, mira inter se contentione certabant. Unde cum quadam die ad invicem iurgarentur atque idcirco a Socrate irriderentur, iurgationibus suis omissis, ita furiosum in eum impetum converterunt, ut fuga saluti suae consulere cogeretur. Xanthippe quoque ipsum aspere nimis redarguere non desistebat. Proinde quadam die factum est ut incredibili iracundiae rabie concitata et efferata, post multas contumelias sibi illatas, aqua tandem immunda e fenestra quadam de industria super ipsum proiciens, totum hominem aspergeret.

35 Atque haec et his similia (sive convicia et maledicta sive iniurias et improbe facta) ita aequo animo tolerabat, ut iocis et facetiis patientiam suam conditam non sine singulari omnium admiratione prae se ferret. Ad aquae enim immundae vel turpem aspersionem se minime mirari respondebat, quoniam post tonitrua pluere consuesse sciebat, vel sic potius: 'Nonne dicebam Xanthippem tonantem quandoque pluituram?' Cum pallium deinde suum illa sibi semel in platea sustulisset monereturque a familiaribus ut eam

any inhabitant of Athens could marry and maintain two wives at the same time, and it is reported that Socrates complied with a decree of this kind and had the aforementioned wives. But whether at different times or at the same time, all agree that he had children by both wives, a male child, Lamprocles, by Xanthippe, and Sophroniscus and Menexenus by Myrto, whom he married without a dowry.[67]

He held many magistracies in the state, and in addition he be- 34
haved with rare and exceptional patience at home and outside it. Indeed, towards his wives—above all the petulant and contentious Xanthippe, whose fractiousness was on the boil night and day, upsetting the entire household—and towards his children, more like her than him, he was obliged to act with extraordinary tolerance. There are numerous examples of his unusual patience, both domestic and public, but for brevity's sake a few instances among many will suffice. These two quarrelsome wives used to fight over him mightily, ugly though he was, as though they might cut him in two. So when one day they were scolding each other and Socrates laughed at this, they left off their mutual hostility to attack him with such violence that to save himself he had to take to his heels.[68] Xanthippe would never stop criticizing him with indescribable harshness, and thus it happened one day that she flew into an incredible mad rage, and after dealing him many insults leant out of a window and gave him a thorough soaking with dirty water.[69]

This and similar uproars, foul language, insults and misdeeds 35
he withstood with so calm a spirit that he used to make a show of seasoning his patience with jests and witty stories to the great admiration of everyone. After that shameful dousing with dirty water he responded that he wasn't surprised, because he knew that rain usually followed thunder. Or rather, he put it this way: "Didn't I say that with Xanthippe thundering there was going to be rain at some point?" Once when Xanthippe tore away his man-

iniuriam publice illatam palam ulcisceretur, 'Praeclara,' inquit, 'res esset si nobis corrixantibus atque invicem contendentibus hinc inde acclamaretur: "Eia Socrates! Eia, Xanthippe!"'

36 Ob haec igitur pluraque alia iniuriarum genera, dicenti Alcibiadi non esse tolerandam Xanthippem, adeo morosam adeoque perversam, se iam pridem hisce domesticis contumeliis atque uxoriis petulantiis assuesse ac per hoc quemadmodum foris agendum esset domi didicisse respondebat. A. Gellius enim in libro *Noctium Atticarum* verba haec ponit: 'Xanthippe, Socratis philosophi uxor, morosa admodum fuisse dicitur et iurgiosa, irarumque et molestiarum muliebrium per diem perque noctem scatebat. Ob has eius intemperies in maritum, Alcibiades iratus interrogavit Socratem quaenam ratio esset cur mulierem tam acerbam domo non exigeret. "Quoniam," inquit Socrates, "cum illam domi talem perpetior, insuesco et exerceor ut ceterarum quoque foris petulantiam et iniuriam facilius feram." Idque dictum urbanitate quadam prosequebatur: "An vero tu," inquit, "non toleras clamore perstrepentes anseres?" Illo dicente "At mihi ova pullosque parient," — "Et mihi," aiebat, "Xanthippe filios generat."' Lamproclem praeterea eius natum, in matrem nimis ferum et immitem, persuasionibus suis ita molliebat itaque coercebat ut ad maternam tandem reverentiam reduceretur, quemadmodum vel maxime decere videbatur. Atque haec domestica.

37 Forensia vero plura huiusmodi sunt. Dum enim loqueretur, ob vehementiam orationis saepenumero iactare digitos et crines vellere solebat. (Id Graeci 'chironomiam,' ab heroicis usque temporibus ortam, quasi 'legem gestus' appellant.) Qua de re, cum a plerisque rideretur, aequanimiter ferebat neque solum iurgiosa verba, sed illatas etiam iniurias patienter tolerabat. Unde cum fuisset a quodam calce percussus, cunctis eius tolerantiam admirantibus, 'Quid enim,' inquit, 'si me asinus calcibus impetisset, num illi

tle in a public square, he was urged by his friends to take revenge for that injury in public. "It would be a fine thing indeed," he rejoined, "for us to be brawling and fighting each other, surrounded by cries of 'Go Socrates!' and 'Go Xanthippe!'"[70]

36 To Alcibiades, who said that Xanthippe was a shrewish and perverse woman and not to be endured, Socrates replied that he had long been used to these domestic outrages and wifely bickerings, and that they had taught him at home how to behave in public.[71] Aulus Gellius writes in the *Attic Nights* as follows: "Xanthippe, the wife of the philosopher Socrates, is said to have been ill-tempered and quarrelsome to a degree, with a constant flood of feminine tantrums and annoyances day and night. Alcibiades, angered at this unruly conduct of hers towards her husband, asked Socrates what earthly reason he had for not driving so shrewish a woman out of his house. 'Because,' replied Socrates, 'it is by enduring such a person at home that I accustom and train myself to bear more easily away from home the impudence and injustice of other persons.' And he followed this dictum with a jest: 'Don't you yourself put up with the noise of geese?' he asked.—'Well, they provide me with eggs and chicks,' Alcibiades replied. To which Socrates said, 'And Xanthippe has borne me sons.'"[72] Moreover, he persuaded his son Lamprocles, who was overly rude and harsh towards his mother, to calm down and restrain himself, thus leading him back to a proper respect for her.[73] So much for his home life.

37 To be sure, there are many incidents of this kind from his public life, too. When speaking agitatedly he was wont to throw his hands about and pull his hair. (The Greeks call this *cheironomia*, or "the rules of gesture," an art that arose in the heroic age.) He tolerated with equanimity being laughed at for these gestures and bore with patience not only insulting words but even injuries. Hence when someone kicked him and everyone expressed surprised at his tolerance, Socrates rejoined: "If a donkey had kicked me, should I

diem dixissem?' Colapho etiam semel verberatus, nihil aliud dixisse fertur nisi ob id molestum esse quod nescirent homines quando cum galea vel sine galea prodirent. Ab homine quoque petulante manibus ita vehementer pulsatus est ut in faciem eius petulantissime cederetur. Socrates vero non modo non repugnavit, sed illius irae ac petulantiae se tractandum eo usque permisit, quoad ei vultus undique tuber fieret. Verum ubi Socrates illius iram diutius satiatam tandem efferbuisse cognovit, nihil aliud egit nisi quod fronti suae percussoris nomen inscripsit, quemadmodum statuis fieri consuevit: 'Ille,' inquit, 'hoc opus effecit.' Nec ulterius ulcisci perrexit.

38 Pro iustitia insuper servanda iniuriaque propulsanda, quandocumque contingeret, graves et capitales inimicitias subire ac suscipere non formidabat. Quod tum vel ex eo maxime declaravit, cum solus adversus triginta potentissimos viros, occupata iam civitatis libertate, pro Leonte Salaminio, homine illustri et opulento, sententiam ferre ausus est, quem illi iniuste ac certatim perimere contendebant. Nec minus ex hoc altero praeclarissimo ac iustissimo eius facinore magnitudinem animi sui demonstravit. Cum universa enim Atheniensium civitas, iniquissimo ac truculentissimo errore ducta, de capite decem praetorum, qui apud Arginusas lacedaemoniam[2] classem deleverant, tristem sententiam tulisset, forte tunc tantae auctoritatis Socrates erat, ut eius arbitrio plebiscita ordinarentur, indignum simul et iniquum fore ratus ut tot cives et de patria bene meriti ex iniusta causa impetu invidiae abriperentur. Unde temeritati multitudinis constantiam suam obiecit, maximoque contionis fragore ac ferocibus minis numquam compelli potuit ut se publicae dementiae auctorem ascriberet. Ex hac Socratis repugnantia, plebs, legitima grassari[3] via prohibita, iniusto et innocentium praetorum cruore manus suas contaminare

have taken it to court?"[74] Once, when somebody punched him, it is reported that he said only what a nuisance it was that you didn't know when to put your helmet on and when to leave it off.[75] On another occasion, some aggressive fellow attacked him with such violence that, with the greatest impudence, he struck him on the face. Socrates not only did not fight back, but he allowed the man to take out his anger and aggression on him until his face became completely swollen. When Socrates saw that the man's rage had finally spent itself, his only response was to write his attacker's name on his forehead, as used to be done on statues: "So-and-so made this work." And that was the extent of his revenge.[76]

To uphold justice and fend off wrongdoing whenever it hap- 38
pened, he was not afraid to undergo and take upon himself grave and mortal enmities. This courage he showed in the highest degree when alone against thirty powerful men who had taken control of the city[77] he dared to pass sentence in favor of Leon of Salamis, an eminent and wealthy man, whom they were competing with each other to destroy.[78] He showed no less greatness of soul in another great and famous act of justice. At the time when the whole city of Athens, misled by a wicked and cruel error, had passed a dire sentence of death against ten magistrates who had destroyed the Spartan fleet at Arginusae,[79] Socrates by chance was in charge of the voting procedure. He concluded that it was unworthy and unfair that so many citizens who had deserved well of their country were being done away with on an unjust charge in a burst of ill-will. Hence he faced down the recklessness of the mob with his own resolution, and neither the uproar in the assembly nor ferocious threats could compel him to subscribe to this act of public madness.[80] In the face of Socrates' resistance, the mob found the legitimate outlet for their rage blocked, but went on to stain their hands unjustly with the blood of the innocent magistrates. In this incident that great-souled man seemed to have no

perseveravit. In quo minime vir magnanimus timuisse videtur ne mors eius consternatae patriae undecimus furor existeret.

39 Quid plura de eximia eius iustitia loquar, cum iniuriam pati quam inferre satius esse putaret? Unde peius esse iniuriam facere quam pati vulgo 'socraticum decretum' appellabatur. Frugi erat et continens. Saepe enim, dum variam venalium rerum multitudinem intueretur, secum hilaris dicere solebat: 'Quam multis ipse non egeo!' Ac semper habebat in ore iambos illos quibus 'argentum et purpura ceteraque id genus tragoedis potius quam usui vitae necessaria' ostendebantur. Cicero enim 'nisi cupiditatibus,' inquit, 'pecuniae adhibeatur continuo ratio, quasi quaedam socratica medicina, quae omnino sanaret, permanare in venas et in visceribus inhaerere' testatur. Archelai insuper et Scopae Eurylochique pecunias, ut supra diximus, mirum in modum sprevit atque contempsit, et cum in pompa magna vis auri argentique ferretur: 'Quam multa non desidero!' inquit. Unde si aurum et argentum et pecuniam omnem, quemadmodum diximus, aspernabatur, de extrema eius paupertate minime mirari debemus, sed potius mirandum esset si, cunctas pecunias floccipendens, dives evasisset.

40 Idque totum, quanti divitias et honores fecerit, unico eius responso declaravit. Nam cum interrogaretur memoratum Archelaum, Perdiccae filium, qui tum fortunatissimus habebatur, nonne beatum diceret, 'Haud scio;' inquit, 'numquam enim cum eo collocutus sum.' Et cum iterum ex eo quaereretur an aliter scire non posset, 'Nullo modo' respondere non dubitavit. Et cum tertio rogaretur de Persarum rege beatusne esset, 'An ego possum,' inquit,

fear that his death might provide an eleventh example of his country's mad frenzy.[81]

Regarding his extraordinary sense of justice one need only mention his belief that it is preferable to suffer than to commit injustice.[82] Hence the principle that it is worse to injure someone than to suffer injury is commonly known as the "Socratic Principle." Socrates was also thrifty and temperate. Often when he would gaze at a varied multitude of wares exposed for sale, he would say cheerfully to himself, "Look at all the things I don't need!" Always on his lips were those verses: 39

> The purple robe and silver's shine
> More fits an actor's need than mine.[83]

Cicero indeed states "Unless reason is continuously applied to the desire for money as a kind of Socratic remedy (which cures it entirely), the evil circulates in the veins and sticks to the vital organs."[84] Besides, as noted, he had a marvellous disdain for the money of Archelaus, Scopas and Eurylochus; and when a great quantity of gold and silver was being carried in a procession, Socrates said: "How many things there are that I don't want !"[85] Since he spurned gold, silver and money of any kind, we should not be surprised at his extreme poverty; with his neglect of money, it would have been remarkable if he had turned out to be a rich man.

All that — his estimate of wealth and honors — he made known in a single response. Asked if he thought the aforesaid Archelaus, Perdiccas's son, was blessed — a man who at that time was thought the most fortunate of men — he replied: "I have no idea, I've never spoken with him." And when he was asked again whether he might not find out in some other way, he instantly responded, "There *is* no other way." And when he was asked a third time whether the king of the Persians was blessed or not, he said, "How can I know, since I don't know how wise or good he is?"[86] 40

'cum ignorem quam sit doctus, quam vir bonus?' Quid plura? Beatam vitam una virtute contineri prorsus existimabat. Quocirca bonos beatos, improbos miseros esse putabat, et ad extremum, si iniustus foret, miserum Archelaum, tam magnum ac tam praepotentem regem, palam et aperte predicabat.

41 Adeo etiam parce ac temperate vixit, ut cum Athenarum civitas crebris, ut fit, pestibus vastaretur, ipse numquam aegrotaverit. A. Gellius namque, in memorato *Noctium Atticarum* libro, de Socrate loquens, verba haec ponit: 'Temperantia eum fuisse tanta traditum est, ut omnia fere vitae suae tempora valitudine inoffensa vixerit. In illius etiam pestilentiae vastitate, quae in bello peloponnesiaco Atheniensium civitatem internecivo genere morbi depopulata est, his parcendi moderandique rationibus dicitur et a voluptatum labe cavisse et salubritates corporis retinuisse, ut nequaquam fuerit communi omnium cladi obnoxius.' Facilibus et communibus cibariis vescebatur atque in eo maxime gloriabatur; ac illos qui suavissime comederent minime obsoniis et splendidis epulis indigere dicebat et eos qui cum voluptate biberent pretiosa pocula non curare. Cibi quoque condimentum famem, potionis sitim esse aiebat; plerosque etiam homines vivere ut essent, se vero esse ut viveret dictitare solebat, illosque diis maxime propinquos videri, qui parvis minimisque egerent. Nec verbis solum tenuem victum laudabat, ut Epicurus faciebat, sed id ipsum re vera, ut ait Cicero, exequebatur.

42 Ad haec omnia virtutum suarum exempla singularis quaedam et inusitata mitissimi hominis mansuetudo accedebat. Cuius rei evidens et apertum testimonium illud afferri potest quod, cum adversus eius servum verberonem (vel ancillam, ut nonnulli putaverunt; ipsum enim unius ancillae ministerio contentum fuisse apud idoneos auctores scriptum legimus), non immerito irasceretur: 'Te,' inquit, 'caederem, nisi iratus essem!' Ab hac ergo integra et

In short, he thought the blessed life consisted in virtue alone. That is why he thought that the good were blessed and the wicked miserable, and why he frankly declared that Archelaus, for all his great and overweening power, must exist at an extreme of misery if he were unjust.

He lived with such parsimony and temperance that, despite the 41
pestilences that were liable to devastate Athens, he never had an illness. Indeed, Aulus Gellius in the aforementioned *Attic Nights* says of Socrates: "His temperance also is said to have been so great that he lived almost his entire lifetime with unimpaired health. Even during the havoc of that plague which at the beginning of the Peloponnesian war devastated Athens with a deadly species of disease, he is said to have avoided, thanks to his temperate and abstemious habits, the ill-effects of indulgence and to have kept his physical vigor so completely that he was quite unaffected by the common calamity."[87] He ate plain and easily obtainable fare and took great pride in this. He would say that those who did not have need of elaborate condiments and dishes ate with the most pleasure, and that men who enjoy drinking do not care about precious goblets. He called hunger the condiment of food and thirst of drink, and he used to repeat that many men lived to eat but that he ate to live; and he would say that the men who needed the least were the closest to the gods.[88] Nor did he praise slender fare with words only like Epicurus, but, as Cicero says, he put his sayings into practice.[89]

In addition to all these examples of his virtues there was the 42
singular and unusual kindness of this gentlest of men. A clear and obvious proof of this quality is afforded by the following incident. Once, when he had become justifiably angry with a rascally slave of his (others think it was a maid-servant, since reliable authors tell us that he was content to be served by a single maid-servant), he said to him, "I would beat you if I weren't angry."[90] This upright and admirable mental disposition was the source of that un-

admirabili mentis suae dispositione ille idem semper vultus procedebat, cum quo Xanthippe, altera eius uxor, eodem semper se vidisse ipsum exeuntem domo et revertentem praedicabat. Unde nemo mirari debet qui eandem perpetuo eius mentem fuisse consideraverit, a qua eius vultus fingebatur. Nec vero ea frons erat quae M. Crassi illius divitis, quem semel ait in omni vita risisse Lucilius, sed tranquilla et serena. Iure autem erat idem vultus, cum mentis, a qua is fingebatur, nulla fieret mutatio.

43 Cura illi fuit corporeae exercitationis. Proinde interdum usque ad vesperam contentius ambulabat, ut illinc obsonaret ambulando famem ac per hoc melius cenaret. Quandoque etiam saltabat, quod id exercitii genus plurimum ad tuendam bonam valitudinem conducere existimabat. Hoc ipsum veteribus Romanis dedecori non fuisse in *Institutionibus oratoriis* Quintilianus auctor est. Interdum vero per totam diem firmus immobilisque stabat, ut his verbis in libro *Noctium Atticarum,* quemadmodum supradiximus, testatur A. Gellius: 'Stare solitus Socrates dicitur pertinaci statu perdius atque pernox, a summo lucis ortu ad solem alterum orientem inconnivens, immobilis, iisdem in vestigiis, et ore atque oculis eundem in locum directis cogitabundus, tamquam quodam secessu mentis atque animi facto a corpore.' Et quando a meditatione altissimarum rerum se parumper averterat, cum parvulis, arundine cruribus supposita, requiescendi animi gratia ludebat.

44 Inculto pallio, philosophorum more, plerumque utebatur. Cicero namque de paupertate quodam loco loquens, 'Hic,' inquit, 'Socrates commemoratur, hic Diogenes, hic Caecilianum illud:

Saepe enim est sub sordido palliolo sapientia.'

Cumque hoc instituto vitae degeret, interdum tamen tempori et civium moribus congruens venustiori habitu amiciebatur. Tanta praeterea paupertate et rerum inopia opprimebatur ut nisi discipulorum ope adiutus fuisset (qui non ex conventione, sed sponte sua,

changing expression which his second wife Xanthippe used to say she always saw on him when he left and returned home. Anyone who considers how his expression was molded by his constancy of mind should not be surprised at this. We are talking about a quiet and serene countenance, not the face of some Marcus Crassus, the wealthy man whom Lucilius says laughed but once in his whole life.[91] It was right that Socrates' face showed constancy, for his mind, which shapes the face, was constant.

He took care to exercise the body. That is why he liked to take a walk around sunset, so that he could work up an appetite by walking and so dine better.[92] Sometimes, too, he used to dance, believing that this type of activity was conducive to maintaining good health.[93] This activity was not considered undignified by the old Romans, according to Quintilian's *Institutes*.[94] From time to time he would stand still all day long, as we said before and as Aulus Gellius attests in the *Attic Nights* as follows: "It is said that Socrates used to stand still in one position all day and all night, from dawn until the next sunrise, open-eyed, frozen in his very tracks and with face and eyes riveted to the same spot in deep meditation, as though his mind and soul had been withdrawn from his body."[95] And when he turned his thoughts awhile from meditation on the highest things, he would prop a flute on his knees for relaxation and play with children.[96] 43

Usually he wore a rough mantle after the fashion of philosophers. For Cicero in a passage about poverty says: "Now Socrates is cited, now Diogenes, now Caecilius' well-known line: 44

Even beneath the tattered mantle wisdom oft doth hide."[97]

But despite following this plan of life, from time to time, as befitted the occasion or civic custom, he would don more attractive garb.[98] Moreover, such was the burden of his poverty and lack of resources that he would surely have undergone the varied trials of human life had he not been helped out by his disciples, who

necessitatis admoniti, tribuebant), multa profecto ac varia humanae vitae incommoda sustinuisset.

45 His igitur moribus et hac integritate vitae usus, daemonem suum sibi a nativitate, secundum veram illam Platonis sententiam, pro custode datum recognovit; cuius monitis cuncta, quaecumque agenda essent, agi oportere censeret. Quapropter nemo mirari debet si hic vir optimus ac probatissimus testimonio Apollinis, ut supra dicebamus, sapientissimus omnium iudicatus est. Rursus nullus admirabitur si vir, divina oraculi sententia cunctis hominibus in sapientia praelatus, memoratum custodem suum non ignoraverit. Ex parte namque, non ex toto, vera est illa Platonis nostri opinio, qua putat singulis a nativitate hominibus singulos daemones datos. Nos autem binos angelos (alterum bonum, alterum malum) non modo actorum, sed cogitatorum etiam arbitros humano generi, ut quisque in lucem editur, traditos tradendosque praedicamus et dicimus; probum scilicet ut ad virtutes diligendas, improbum vero ut ad vitia capessenda hominem suum exhortetur.

46 Sed quoniam Socrates probitate vitae et singularitate morum vir conspicuus fuit, non nisi bonum suasorem sentiebat, quamquam nonnulli ipsum in libidines suapte natura proniorem fuisse adulescentiae suae fervore memoriae prodiderunt, idque ex certo Zopiri cuiusdam physionomi nescio cuius iudicio probare et attestari nituntur. Hic enim ex habitu corporis et liniamentis oris et vultus se intrinsecos hominum mores et, ut breviter dixerim, ex forma cuiusque naturam procul dubio cognoscere ac perspicere profitebatur. Cum ergo Athenas per id temporis forte accessisset atque ad Socratem, ceterorum omnium sapientissimum modestissimumque tandem adductus esset, post multam corporis intuitionem, ipsum suapte natura, interrogantibus qui aderant discipulis quid sibi videretur, libidinosum esse respondit. Unde cum ab eis qui illa in Socrate vitia non cognoscerent vehementer irrideretur crebrisque cachinnationibus illius sententiam floccipenderent, Socrates dixisse fertur eius physionomi de se iudicium verum fuisse.

used to give him gifts of their own free will—not by prior agreement—when informed of his needs.[99]

The practice of upright conduct like this led him to recognize 45
that he had been given a tutelary daimon at his birth (according to Plato's truthful statement), and he believed that whatever he did should be done in accordance with its warnings.[100] Thus no one should be surprised that this excellent man of extreme probity was, as we said before, judged the wisest of all men by the oracle of Apollo. And again, no one should wonder if this man, who was declared first in wisdom by the sentence of a holy oracle, did not neglect his aforementioned guardian. For the view of our Plato, that to each man is given a single daimon at birth, is only partially true. We say and declare, on the contrary, that each person is given two angels at birth, one good and one bad, to act as the arbiters of mankind's thoughts and deeds. The good one exhorts his man to love the virtues, the bad one to seize upon the vices.[101]

But Socrates, owing to his unique and conspicuous moral excel- 46
lence, heeded only the good counselor, although some sources record that in the fervor of his youth he had been naturally inclined to lust. This they try to certify from the dubious judgement of a certain Zopyrus, a physiognomist. This man claimed he could beyond doubt learn the inherent nature of a man from the attitude of his body and the lineaments of his face and features—in short, that he could tell each man's nature from his outward form. Thus when he happened to come to Athens around this time and was introduced to Socrates, the wisest and most temperate of men, after inspecting his body at length, he was asked by Socrates' disciples what he made of the philosopher's nature. He replied that Socrates was inclined to sensuality. At this he was roundly mocked by the disciples, who knew of no such vices in Socrates, and they dismissed his pronouncement with gales of laughter. But Socrates is said to have replied that the physiognomist's judgment

Nam sese in libidines suapte natura proniorem extitisse dicebat, sed singulari animi modestia eiusmodi naturae vel condicionem vel inclinationem repressisse atque conculcasse.

47 Quod etsi ita esset, ut a physionomo dicebatur, modestia tamen sua usque adeo illos naturales impetus ab initio temperasse, ut numquam posterius apparerent. Quod Plato in *Symposio* eo loco testari videtur, ubi Alcibiadem inducit confitentem de se quid a Socrate pati voluerit; non enim ut illum culparet haec scripsisse existimandum est, sed potius ut incredibilem quandam et invictam Socratis continentiam ostenderet, quae corrumpi tanta ac tam obvia speciosissimi hominis voluntate non posset. Utrum vero hic Zopirus fuerit ille magus, quem Aristoteles e Syria Athenas usque profectum Socratem pluribus rebus reprehendisse eique violentam mortem futuram praedixisse refert, incertum est.

48 Hunc ergo bonum sive angelum sive daemonem sive deum (sic enim varie, ut tradit Augustinus, a plerisque appellatur), Socratem cognovisse Plato auctor est, cuius probis monitis cuncta agenda esse censebat. De hoc Socratis daemone Apuleius Madaurensis, platonicus nobilis, in quodam eius libro loquens (qui *De deo* potius quam *De daemone* propterea, ut inquit Augustinus, inscribitur, ne titulum praelegentes, novitate rei perterriti, antequam ad eam disputationem progrederentur, 'nequaquam illum hominem sanum fuisse sentirent') hunc sibi in tota vita virtutes suscipiendas, vitia vero execranda illum plane et aperte monuisse testatur. Hunc etenim eius daemonem Socrates (ut ait ille, 'vir apprime perfectus et Apollinis quoque testimonio sapiens' iudicatus) mirum in modum cognoscebat colebatque. Unde ille eius custos et contubernio familiaris cuncta quae arcenda erant diligenter arguebat.

49 At vero Socrates, cum sapiens esset, non consilio sed praesagio potius indigere videbatur, quippe multa quondam accidisse legi-

was correct: he *had* been naturally prone to lust, but he had repressed and stamped out this condition or inclination thanks to the unusual restraint of his rational soul.[102]

In fact, although things stood as the physiognomist said, he 47 had from the start tempered those natural impulses through his habit of restraint so that they never afterwards came to light. The same thing is attested by Plato in that passage of the *Symposium* where Alcibiades is represented as confessing what he would like to get from Socrates. It is unthinkable that this was written to inculpate Socrates; rather, it was intended to show that his incredible and invincible temperance could not be corrupted even by the obvious desire of the most comely of youths.[103] Whether this Zopyrus was the wizard said by Aristotle to have travelled to Athens from Syria, and who found fault with Socrates on numerous subjects and who predicted his violent death, is uncertain.[104]

As Plato attests, Socrates recognized this good angel or daimon 48 or god—for it is thus variously referred to by many writers, as Augustine states—and he deemed he ought to follow its good counsel in all that he did. Of Socrates' daimon the noble Platonist Apuleius of Madaura speaks in a book of his (called *On the God [of Socrates]* rather than *On the Demon* lest—as Augustine states—the reader, noting the title, should take fright at the novelty of the subject before reaching the discussion and "suppose the man was totally insane").[105] Here he attests that the aforesaid daimon warned him in the plainest terms throughout his life to take up the virtues and spurn the vices. Indeed, Socrates, who (as Apuleius says) was "foremost in perfection and adjudged a wise man by the very testimony of Apollo," had a wondrous knowledge of and reverence for this daimon of his.[106] Hence that guardian and close companion of his would carefully inform him of everything that was to be avoided.

As a wise man Socrates had need not so much of counsel as of 49 prophecy. Indeed, we read that many times it happened that men,

mus de quibus homines, quamvis sapientes viros secum haberent, ad hariolos tamen et oracula, hauriendae veritatis gratia, nonnumquam confugiebant, siquidem haec duo divinationis et sapientiae officia ab invicem distincta ac seorsum separata fuisse cernuntur. Nam, cum duo totius achivi exercitus summa cacumina, Agamemnon et Achilles, inter se dissiderent, vir quidam sapientia et eloquentia clarus desiderabatur, qui virtutibus suis Atridae superbiam et Pelidae ferociam compesceret. Delectus est Phylides, vir sapientia conspicuus et summus eius temporis orator. Ulixes vero et Diomedes, utpote ceteris Grais callidiores, sortiti sunt ut in tempesta nocte, speculandi gratia, castra hostium ingrederentur. Et quamquam memorati Phylides et Ulixes Graecorum omnium sapientissimi viderentur, cum tamen ad difficultatem gerendi belli et facultatem itineris et tranquillitatem maris remedia quaererentur, Calcantem vatem consuluerunt, qui sua divinatione et tempestates diremit et classem deduxit et longam decem annorum obsidionem futuram esse praedixit. Non secus in troiano exercitu contingebat cum divinatione res indigeret. Nam ille sapiens senatus tacebat, nec aliquid pronuntiare audebat, sed omnes, silentio facto, aut ingrata Helenae auguria aut non credita Cassandrae vaticinia auscultabant. Eodem modo Socrates agebat; nam ubi consilio, propria sapientia; ubi vero praesagio, vi daemonis utebatur.

Quid plura? Cunctis eius monitis sedulo oboediebat. Sed forte, dicet quispiam, quonam modo Socrates suadentis vel dissuadentis daemonis sui signa deprehendebat? Platonis sententia est quod vox sibi nescio quae divinitus exoriebatur, quae a nullo alio audiebatur. Apuleius vero non modo auribus eum, verum etiam oculis signa daemonis sui usurpasse ac percepisse testatur. Id signum poterat ipsius daemonis spiritus fuisse quem Socrates solus cerneret, non secus quam homericus Achilles suam Minervam conspicabatur; sed sive ex auditu, sive ex visu, sive quavis alia via signa huius daemonis hauriret, eius ut aiunt monitis ad unguem obtemperabat. Hic est denique ille daemon qui sibi persuasit ne ad rei pu-

despite having wise counsellors with them, turned to fortune tellers and oracles in order to have their fill of truth, since these two offices, divination and wisdom, were kept distinct and separate. For when the two heads of the Achaean army, Agamemnon and Achilles, were at variance, some man of outstanding wisdom and eloquence was sought whose virtues could mitigate the pride of the son of Atreus and the fierceness of the son of Peleus. The man chosen was Nestor of Pylos, a man notable for wisdom and a leading orator of his times.[107] Ulysses and Diomedes, being cleverer than the other Greeks, were chosen to enter the enemy camp in the dark of night to spy; and although Nestor and Ulysses were seen to be the wisest of the Greeks, yet at times when they sought solutions for the difficulties of warfare or means of navigation or a calm sea, they consulted the soothsayer Calchas, whose divinations calmed tempests and directed the fleet and predicted that the siege to come would last ten years. The same happened in the Trojan army when there was need of divination. Their wise senate kept silent and did not dare to say anything, but they all listened in silence to the unwelcome auguries about Helen or to the distrusted predictions of Cassandra.[108] Socrates acted in the same way: when he needed counsel, he applied his own wisdom; when he needed foresight, he used the power of the daimon.

In short, he keenly obeyed all its warnings. But one may ask, in 50
what way did Socrates apprehend the signs of his approving or disapproving daimon? It is the view of Plato that some divine voice would arise, heard by no one else. Apuleius instead holds that he appropriated and perceived the daimon's signs not just with his ears, but also with his eyes.[109] That sign could have been the spirit of the daimon, discerned by Socrates alone, just as Homer's Achilles used to see his Minerva.[110] But whether he imbibed the signs of his daimon by hearing, sight or otherwise, Socrates obeyed its warnings, they say, to the letter. It was this daimon that persuaded him not to attempt a career in politics;

blicae gubernationem accederet, unde et timide accessit et paucos gerens magistratus praetermisit, neve mortiferam iniquorum iudicum sententiam evitaret aufugiretque, cum ob invidiam procerum civitatis quibusdam capitalibus criminibus accusaretur, ac propterea morti ad extremum damnaretur. De quo quidem pauca quaedam, brevitatis causa, referemus.

51 Socrates, ob admirabilem eius sapientiam atque praecipuam vitae integritatem, vir ceteris Atheniensibus sapientior ac melior communi consensu omnium habebatur. Quocirca principes civitatis optimatesque ei plurimum invidebant. Hanc eorum invidiam celebratum illud Apollinis de sapientia sua testimonium multum admodum adauxit, cuius quidem oraculo sapientissimum mortalium omnium iudicatum, ut supra dicebamus, fuisse ferebatur. Huiusmodi igitur invidiam aliquot principes civitatis, post celebratum illud Apollinis iudicium, diutius non ferentes, accusatores quosdam subornarunt qui hominem quibusdam capitalibus criminibus falso apud iudices accusarent. Ad hanc optimatum simultatem accedebat etiam quod Socrates ipse oratores poetasque et opifices apprime contemnere atque irridere solebat. Unde magna et quasi popularis istorum omnium in illum invidia conflata est.

52 Quamobrem, dedita opera tres accusatores in eum (Anytus, Lycon et Melitus) invicem coniurarunt; et Anytus quidem opificum, Lycon autem oratorum, Melitus vero poetarum partes tuebatur, quod eos omnes carperet Socrates. Melitus autem ipse pro reliquis coniuratis partes accusationis suscepit, ac per hunc modum accusatoris officio fungens duobus criminibus innocentem hominem accusavit. Primum quod publica civitatis iura violaret, deinde quod iuventutem corrumperet, siquidem deos esse non putaret quos ex maiorum instituto civitas ante susceperat, et alias quoque novas quasdam daemonum species superstitionesque contra inveteratam Atheniensium consuetudinem induceret. Per hunc igitur modum Socrates de his duobus criminibus ab invidis accusatus, in carcerem truditur, ob eam profecto quam ex sententia Apollinis

hence his steps were cautious and he held few offices. The daimon also advised him not to avoid or flee the mortal sentence of unjust judges when the ill-will of the city's leaders caused capital charges to be made against him, thanks to which he was sentenced to die.[111] For the sake of brevity we shall say only a few words about this case.

Socrates, because of his wonderful wisdom and remarkable integrity, was commonly agreed to be wiser and better than the other Athenians. That is why the city's leaders and ruling class hated him so much. The famous pronouncement of the oracle of Apollo greatly increased this envy; for the oracle, as we said, judged him to be the wisest of all mortals.[112] Thus several of the city's leaders, unable to control their malice any longer, suborned certain complainants to accuse him falsely of capital charges before judges. In addition to arousing the animosity of the ruling class, Socrates himself tended to despise and ridicule orators, poets and artisans. So the great and almost popular ill-will of all these persons was stirred up against him.[113] 51

Thus it was that three accusers deliberately conspired against him, Anytus, Lycon and Meletus, with Anytus protecting the interests of the artists, Lycon the orators and Meletus the poets—Socrates having criticized each group. Meletus in particular took up the role of plaintiff for the other conspirators, and charged the innocent Socrates with two crimes. The first was that he had violated the public law of the city, the other that he had corrupted youth, since he did not believe that the beings the city had accepted as gods by ancestral usage were in fact gods. He had also introduced certain other new kinds of daimons and superstitions contrary to the long-standing customs of the Athenians.[114] Thus accused in this way of two crimes by his enemies, Socrates was thrown into prison. The reason was the envy he had provoked 52

invidiam contraxerat, cum exinde ceteris hominibus in sapientia praeferretur.

53 At Lysias, eximius eius temporis orator, sive quod nimiam innocentis hominis pertinaciam ac superbiam fore adversus iudices conspicaretur, sive quod ipsum parum idoneum satisque ineptum ad se defendendum adversus tam praepotentes aemulos arbitraretur, sive utrumque potius incommodum illi <non> deesse suspicaretur, ei utcumque fuerit scriptam orationem attulisse dicitur, qua pro se, si sibi placeret, in iudicio uteretur. Ille vero, etsi elegans et oratoria eiusmodi oratio videretur, propterea tamen quod fortis et virilis non videbatur ita ut viro philosopho conveniret, ea se uti nolle respondit. De quo *Memorabilium* scriptor loquens, quodam loco verba haec posuit: 'Socrates, graecae doctrinae clarissimum columen, cum Athenis causam diceret defensionemque ei Lysias a se compositam, qua in iudicio uteretur, recitasset demissam et supplicem imminentique procellae accommodatam: "Aufer," inquit, "quaeso istam. Nam ego, si adduci possem ut eam in ultima Scytharum solitudine perorarem, tum me ipse morte multandum concederem." Spiritum contempsit ne careret gravitate, Socratesque extingui quam Lysias superesse maluit.' Deinde subiunxit: 'Quantus hic in sapientia, tantus in armis Alexander fuit.'

54 Et Cicero de hoc ipso verba faciens in libro *De oratore*, 'Socrates', inquit, 'cum omnium sapientissimus esset sanctissimeque vixisset, ita in iudicio capitis pro se ipse dixit, ut non supplex aut reus, sed magister aut dominus videretur esse iudicum. Quin etiam, cum ei scriptam orationem disertissimus orator Lysias attulisset quam, si ei videretur, edisceret, ut ea pro se in iudicio uteretur, non invitus legit et commode scriptam dixit. "Sed ut," inquit, "si mihi calceos sicyonios attulisses non uterer, quamvis essent habiles atque apti ad pedem, quia non essent viriles," sic illam oratio-

thanks to the utterance of Apollo, according to which he surpassed all other men in wisdom.

Now Lysias, an illustrious orator of the time, either because he saw that the obstinacy and pride of an innocent man would disfavor him with the judges, or because he considered Socrates to be quite unable to defend himself against such powerful rivals, or for both reasons, is said to have offered him a written speech which he might use at the trial if he wished. The oration seemed elegant and rhetorically effective, but to Socrates it did not seem to be strong and manly as befitted a wisdom-loving man, and he declined to use it. Of this the author of the *Memorabilia* writes somewhere as follows: "But when Socrates, the most illustrious pillar of Greek learning, was pleading his case in Athens, Lysias read him a defence, composed by himself for use at the trial, that was humble and pleading and suitable to the threatening storm. 'Pray take this away,' said Socrates. 'If I could be persuaded to deliver it even in the farthest wilderness of Scythia, I'd admit myself that I deserve the death penalty.' He despised any life that lacked seriousness and preferred extinction as Socrates to survival as Lysias."[115] Then he added: "He was as great in wisdom as Alexander was in arms."[116] 53

Cicero too writes about this in *On the Orator* as follows: "Socrates, since he was the wisest of men and had lived a life of the utmost piety, defended himself on a capital charge in such a way that he seemed to be the teacher and master of his judges, rather than a suppliant or defendant. Indeed when Lysias, a most accomplished orator, brought him a written speech which he might commit to memory, if he saw fit, for use at his trial, he was willing to read it and said it was aptly phrased: 'But,' said he, 'just as I wouldn't use a pair of Sicyonian shoes if you brought them to me, however well they fitted, because they are effeminate,' in the same way that speech seems skilful and rhetorically effective, but it doesn't seem brave and manly. Thus he too was condemned not only on the first vote, when the tribunal merely determined the issue of con- 54

nem disertam sibi et oratoriam videri, fortem et virilem non videri. Ergo ille quoque damnatus est; neque solum primis sententiis, quibus tantum statuebant iudices damnarent an absolverent, sed etiam illis, quas iterum legibus ferre debebant. Erat enim reo damnato, si fraus capitalis non esset, quasi poenae ea existimatio ex sententia. Nam cum iudicibus daretur, interrogabatur reus quam existimationem commeruisse se maxime confiteretur. Quod cum interrogatus Socrates esset, respondit sese meruisse ut amplissimis honoribus et praemiis decoraretur et ut ei victus cotidianus in Prytaneo publice praeberetur, qui honor apud Graecos vel maximus haberetur. Cuius responso sic iudices exarserunt, ut capitis hominem innocentissimum condemnarent. Qui quidem si absolutus esset (quod mehercule, etiam si nihil ad nos pertinet, tamen prae eius ingenii magnitudine vellem), quonam modo istos philosophos ferre possemus qui, cum ille damnatus esset nullam aliam ob culpam nisi propter dicendi inscientiam, tamen a se peti oportere dicunt praecepta dicendi?'

55 Quin immo, ut haec ipsa apertius expresserim, cum iudices ipsum, iuxta veterem Atheniensium de percontandis reis consuetudinem, percontarentur quam poenam mereretur, libera contumacia (non ut humilis et reus, sed ut princeps et dominus iudicum esse videretur) tantum abesse inquit ut poenam meruisset, quod victu cottidiano publice, quemadmodum diximus, in Prytaneo dignus ali crederetur, qui honor apud Graecos maximus habebatur. Hoc eius tam acerbo ac tam aspero importunoque responso ita iudices exarserunt, ut hominem innocentem capite condemnarent, quem prius pecunia mulctare contendebant, dum inter se tractarent quid illum pati conveniret. Itaque 'nec patronum ad iudicium capitis quaesivit, nec iudicibus supplex fuit; adhibuitque liberam contumaciam a magnitudine animi ductam,' ut ait Cicero, 'non a superbia.' Cum vero iudicium ageretur, Platonem, celebratum eius discipulum, in suggestum contionandi gratia ascendisse dicunt; or-

viction or acquittal, but also on the further vote which they were bound by law to give. For it was the practice when a defendant was convicted, if it was not a capital crime, for the punishment to be assigned by vote of the jury. In fact, when he was handed over to the judges, the defendant was asked to declare what he thought the maximum penalty should be. When this question was put to Socrates he replied that he deserved to be awarded the most splendid honors and prizes and that he should receive daily sustenance in the town hall at public expense, this being rated among the Greeks as the highest of honors. His answer so incensed his judges that they condemned a perfectly blameless man to death. Even had he been acquitted, as I devoutly wish he had been—not that it is any business of ours, but for the sake of his vast genius—how could we bear these philosophers of yours who tell us that it is from themselves that the rules of eloquence should be learnt, when [their master] Socrates was condemned for the sole fault of rhetorical ignorance?"[117]

Now to clarify this point: when the judges, following the an- 55
cient Athenian custom of examining the accused, questioned him as to what sentence he merited, he replied, with a bold frankness more like a prince and lord of his judges than like a humble accused man, that, far from being punished, he deserved to be maintained at public expense, as we said, in the town hall, this being rated among the Greeks as the highest of honors. At this reply, so acerbic, harsh and impolitic, the judges exploded with rage and condemned to death an innocent man whom, up to that point, while negotiating his punishment among themselves, they had merely sought to fine. Thus Cicero states, "Socrates sought out no advocate when on trial for his life, and was not humble before his judges, but showed a noble obstinacy derived from greatness of soul, not from pride."[118] And when the trial was going on, his celebrated pupil Plato is said to have taken the rostrum to make a speech; but no sooner had he started to speak than all the judges

sus autem dicere, cunctis iudicibus ut descenderet reclamantibus, non peroravit. Sic enim inceperat: 'Minor natu cum sim, viri Athenienses, his omnibus qui tribunal ascenderunt. . . .' Nec ulterius dicere permissus, descendit et se consessum recepit.

56 Per hunc igitur modum Socrates morte damnatur, primusque philosophorum damnatus moritur atque continuo in vincula et in carcerem conicitur. Ac post paucos dies venenum, ex sententia iudicum exhibitum, intrepide atque magnanimiter hausit, cum multa prius de immortalitate animorum ac praeclara disseruisset. Qua re vero non statim post eius damnationem supplicium sumpserunt, paucis aperiam. Vetus quoddam Athenis institutum erat ut de nullo reo supplicium ante sumeretur quam navis ex Delo Athenas solemni pompa reverteretur, quae quotannis inde eo usque ab Atheniensibus mittebatur. Haec enim erat ea navis in qua Theseus olim bis septem illos tulerat in Cretam, servaveratque eos et ipse servatus erat. Itaque Athenienses Apollini voverant, si illi servarentur, spectaculum quotannis mittere in Delum, quod quidem ex illo tempore singulis annis continue servaverunt.

57 Damnato igitur Socrate et in carcerem truso, nondum forte, ut fit, memorata navis Athenas remigraverat. Unde de illo supplicium eo usque dilatum est, quoad navis missa rediret. In hoc itaque paucorum dierum intervallo variis amicorum et discipulorum suasionibus hinc inde agebatur, ut quando innocens damnatus esset e carcere exiret ac per hunc modum fuga saluti suae consuleret. Quod cum adduci non posset, ut faceret, saltem suadebant ut se ab illis educi permitteret. Cum enim educi facile posset, noluit. Commemorati enim amici atque discipuli hunc educendi sui modum invenerant, quod quidem ob pecuniam id se facturos pollicerentur, quam postulabant hi qui ipsum servare atque educere promittebant; atque ad hoc ipsum paratum argentum attulerant. Quod cum Socrates postea rescisset, id factum velut turpe quoddam et scelestum facinus improbavit atque exire renuit.

cried to him to step down, so he did not finish his harangue. His opening words were: "Though I am younger, O men of Athens, than all those who have addressed you so far . . ."[119] Prevented from speaking further, he stepped down and regained his seat.

In this manner Socrates was condemned to death, the first phi- 56
losopher to die condemned, and he was at once put into prison in chains. A few days later he followed the judges' sentence and took poison, fearlessly and with magnaminity, having first said many notable things about the immortality of souls.[120] Why he was not put to death immediately after the sentencing I shall explain briefly. It was the ancient custom in Athens to put no sentenced man to death before a ship that the Athenians sent with solemn pomp to Delos each year had returned. This was the ship in which Theseus had taken twice seven youths to Crete, saving them and himself. The Athenians had therefore vowed to Apollo that if these men were saved they would send an annual spectacle to Delos, a usage they kept each year from that time onwards.[121]

It so happened that the ship had not yet returned to Athens 57
when Socrates was condemned and thrown into prison. His execution was therefore delayed until the ship came back. In this brief interval of a few days various friends and pupils on every side sought to persuade and convince him to escape from prison and save himself by flight, since though condemned he was after all innocent; and when he refused to act, they tried to persuade him at least to let them rescue him. But although rescue would have been easy he did not wish it. Those friends and students had in fact found the following means of taking him away. They had arranged for it to be done in exchange for a bribe that was being demanded by certain persons who were prepared to rescue him, and they had gathered money for this purpose. But when Socrates came to know of it he thought it a bad and wicked action and refused to be rescued.[122]

58 Cum illi eius utpote ineptum et absurdum consilium reprobarent atque ne illud facere vellet, quoad poterant, dissuaderent, tandem vero, adventante navi, iam parata mors esse videbatur. Quocirca Crito, necessarius eius, ante lucem ad illum venit suasurus ut servari se patetetur, ac multas hinc inde rationes colligebat quas plurimum valere arbitrabatur. Nam et de infamia populi et de proditione propriae salutis et ad extremum de filiorum orbitate plurimam mentionem habuit, atque in huiusmodi rebus admodum versatus est. Ad haec vero ita Socrates respondebat ut cuncta facile dilueret atque in firmo quodam moriendi proposito magnanimiter permaneret, inter cetera deum suum id sibi suasisse testatus. Postremo, mortiferum illud paene in manibus tenens poculum, ita locutus est, ut non ad mortem trudi, verum in caelum videretur ascendere, quemadmodum ex oratione eius manifeste deprehenditur, qua ipsum Plato usum fuisse dicit apud iudices iam morte multatum: 'Magna enim me,' inquit, 'spes tenet, iudices, mihi evenire quod mittar ad mortem. Necesse enim sit alterum de duobus, ut aut sensus omnis omnino mors auferat, aut in alium quendam locum morte migretur' et cetera huiusmodi ita prosecutus est, ut non modo mortem non fugere, sed eam vel maxime cupere et appetere videretur.

59 In hoc itaque paucorum dierum intervallo (antequam de ipso post damnationem, ut diximus, supplicium sumeretur) pluribus eius familiaribus, et in primis Critoni, necessario et amico, suadentibus ut e carcere tandem aliquando educi pateretur, plurimis rationibus refragatus est. Et de immortalitate quoque animorum ita disseruit, ut non imperitia sermonis, sed contemptu mortis se mori cupere palam et aperte demonstraverit. Quod quam optime fecerit, satis dici non potest. Vir enim sapientissimus quod superesset ex vita sibi perire maluit quam quod praeterisset; et quando ab hominibus sui temporis parum intelligebatur, posterorum se iudiciis reservavit, brevi detrimento iam ultimae senectutis aevum saeculorum omnium consecutus. Atque ea ipsa Plato in libro, qui

They were condemning his resolve as silly and absurd and seeking as far as possible to dissuade him from carrying it out, when the ship at last arrived and death seemed to be in the offing. Then Crito, his close friend, came before dawn to persuade him to let himself be saved and marshalled many arguments which he thought of great validity. He repeatedly cited and focused upon subjects like the infamy he would suffer in the eyes of the people, the betrayal of his own life, and lastly the orphaning of his sons. But Socrates easily rebutted all these arguments and high-mindedly held fast to his resolve to die, noting among other things that this was the advice of his god.[123] And afterwards, with the fatal cup almost in his hands, he spoke in such a way that made him seem, not one cast out to die, but one ascending to heaven, as we learn clearly from the speech Plato says he made before the judges after the death sentence. "'I entertain, gentlemen of the jury, high hopes,' said he, 'that it is for my good that I am sent to death; for there must follow one of two consequences, either that death takes away all sensation altogether, or that by death a passage is secured to another place,'"[124] and he went on to say other things which showed that not only did he not flee death, but greatly wanted and desired it. 58

In this span of a few days, then, (after his condemnation but before the sentence was carried out, as we said), he used many arguments to refute his many friends and especially Crito, who sought to persuade him to let himself be rescued from prison. He spoke of the immortality of the soul, making it plain that he wished to die not because of his inability to speak, but because of his contempt for death. No words are equal to the excellence of his conduct. For this wisest of men preferred to lose the rest of his life rather than the life he had already lived;[125] and while he may have been little understood by the men of his own day, he kept himself intact for the judgement of posterity, gaining immortality 59

inscribitur *Phaedon*, optime eleganterque digessit. Huiusmodi Socratis de aeternitate animorum disputatio, in memorato *Phaedonis* libro a Platone introducta, quondam tantas vires habebat ut nonnulli, propterea quod Platoni crederent, mortem sibi ipsi consciscerent, ceu de Cleombroto[4] quodam apud idoneos auctores scriptum legimus.

60 Paeana denique, hoc est laudes Apollinis, et aesopiam fabulam in extremo mortis articulo constitutus tantummodo descripsit. Quod ut tunc faceret, cum numquam in tota vita antea fecisset, porro ea de causa adductus fuisse dicitur, quippe et navis rediturae mora et Apollinis festivitas mortem inhibebant. Unde, in somniis nescio quibus crebro monebatur ut, priusquam e vita decederet, musicam operaretur atque exerceret et religione quadam animum expiaret faceretque poemata aliqua. Proinde primum illud fecit in ipsum deum, cuius sacra celebrabantur; deinde, ut visis in somnis cumulatius satisfaceret, poeta esse nolens, quasdam Aesopi fabulas, quas promptius sciebat, modulatus est. Apollineae laudis initium huiusmodi ferebatur:

> Delie Apollo, salve, simulque Diana!

Principium vero fabulae hoc fuisse traditur: 'Aesopus haec retulit,' et quae sequuntur.

61 His igitur atque huiusmodi sapienter magnanimiterque peractis, tandem, cum iam moriendi tempus urgeret, rogatus a Critone, eius discipulo, quemadmodum sepeliri vellet, respondens '"Multam," inquit, "operam, amice, frustra consumpsi. Critoni enim nostro non persuasi me hinc advolaturum neque mei quicquam relicturum." Verum tamen ad eum postea conversus, "Si me," inquit, "Crito, assequi potueris aut sicubi nactus eris, ut videbitur, sepelito,"' et cetera huiusmodi. Paulo deinde post, septuagesimo aetatis suae anno, ex sententia iudicum venenum bibit ac per hunc modum, superstitibus filiis, e vita decessit. Nullum rerum suarum

at the price of a small deduction from his already advanced age. This is finely laid out by Plato in his book entitled *Phaedo*. Socrates' discussion of the eternity of souls, as put forth by Plato in this book, is of such force that in former times some men, because they believed Plato, took their own lives, as we read of a certain Cleombrotus in respected authors.[126]

At last, on the point of death, he wrote a simple paean, that is, 60
a song in praise of Apollo, and an Aesopian fable. It is said that he who had never in his entire life written anything before did this because the delay in the ship's return and the feast of Apollo had postponed his death. He had received a number of warnings in dreams to write and perform some musical work before he died, to purify his soul by some religious act and to write some poetry. So he wrote verses in honor of the god whose festivities were being celebrated, and then, to satisfy more fully the nightly visions, and having no wish to be a poet, he set to music some fables of Aesop which he knew by heart. The song to Apollo is reported to have begun like this:

Hail, Delian Apollo, in company with Diana!

and this was the start of the fable: "Aesop narrates this" and so on.[127]

Having finished compositions like these with wisdom and 61
greatness of soul, the moment of death now came upon him, and, asked by his disciple Crito how he wished to be buried, he replied: "'My friends,' said he, 'I have indeed spent a deal of labor to no purpose, for I have not convinced our friend Crito that I shall fly hence and leave nothing of me behind.' Then turning towards him he said: 'But if, Crito, you can catch me or light upon me anywhere, bury me [as you think fit],'"[128] et cetera. Soon thereafter, in the seventieth year of his life, he drank the poison as his judges had willed and in this way he departed this life, survived by his

monumentum nisi tantummodo prooemium Apollinis et Aesopi fabulam reliquit, ut diximus.

62 Quantum vero paenitentiae ex hac Socratis morte Atheniensibus incesserit, exinde deprehendi vel facile potest quod mox palaestras et gymnasia clauserunt, velut in quibuscumque civitatis luctibus fieri consuerat. Deinde accusatores quidem eius alios exilio, alios vero morte damnarunt. Nam Anytum ipsa die revertentem Heracleotae exterminaverunt; Melitum autem summo supplicio condemnarunt. Nec his contenti, Socratem insuper aerea statua publice honoraverunt, quam a Lysippo, optimo eius temporis statuario, perfectam in urbis celeberrimo loco statuerunt. Mortuus est primo nonagesimae quintae Olympiadis anno, ex quo ipsum septuagenarium mortem obisse manifestum est, cum septuagesimae septimae anno quarto, ut supradiximus, nasceretur.

63 Fuit et alius Socrates historicus, qui de Argonautis nonnulla memoriae mandavit. Alius item peripateticus Bithynius, atque alius poeta epigrammatum. Ultimus Cous, qui deorum imprecationes invocationesque descripsit.

sons. He left no piece of writing, as we said, save the proem to Apollo and the fable of Aesop.

How repentant the Athenians were for the death of Socrates can easily be grasped from their closing of the exercise grounds and gymnasia, as was customary in cases of civic mourning. Afterwards his accusers were condemned, some to exile, others to death. Anytus was cast out by the people of Heraclea the very day he came back to them and Meletus was given the severest sentence. Not content with this, the Athenians publicly honored Socrates with a bronze statue finished by Lysippus, an excellent sculptor of the time, which was set up in a much frequented spot in the city. He died in the first year of the ninety-fifth Olympiad, so it is clear that he died at the age of seventy, since, as we said, he was born in the fourth year of the seventy-seventh.[129] 62

There was another Socrates, an historian, who wrote something about the Argonauts. Another was a Peripatetic from Bithynia, and there was a poet who wrote epigrams. Lastly, there was Socrates of Cos, who wrote prayers and invocations to the gods.[130] 63

Vita Senecae

1 Lucius Annaeus Seneca, quemadmodum ipse in libro *De beneficiis* sese appellat ('nam si quid,' inquit, 'a Seneca accepisses, an Annaeo te debere an Lucio diceres, cum non creditorem, sed nomen tantummodo mutares'), Cordubae in Hispania natus est, quae quidem nullis eius provinciae urbibus vel vetustate vel magnitudine oppidi vel multitudine populi cedere videatur. De hoc toto eius nomine, quoniam varia hinc inde traduntur, quid sentiam breviter explicabo. Cum Romani Sabinos finitimos suos in societatem regni atque in communionem civitatis ascivissent, ut maioribus caritatis vinculis invicem iungerentur utrique, aliorum nomina suis nominibus praeponebant, quod postea Romae usque adeo servaverunt ut nullus Romanorum absque praenomine reperiretur. Quin immo variae etiam orbis terrarum gentes, quae in dicionem populi Romani in dies redigebantur, hanc victorum suorum consuetudinem imitari videbantur; filiis enim qui nascebantur, postquam subacti erant, iuxta veterem Romanorum ritum plura nomina imponebant.

2 Cordubam vero, celebrem quandam Hispaniae urbem, ubi Senecam natum fuisse diximus, a C. Iulio Caesare, antequam ille nasceretur, in populi Romani potestatem redactam fuisse tradunt. Unde parentes eius Senecae postea nato, ut Romanorum victorum consuetudinem imitarentur, proprio nomini praenomen cognomenque praeponentes non immerito adiunxerunt. Ac propterea L. Annaeum Senecam appellarunt, quemadmodum ipse in memorato *De beneficiis* libro his verbis innuere videtur. Ubi enim totius nominis sui mentionem fecit, statim in hunc ferme modum subiunxit: 'Quoniam sive praenomen eius sive nomen sive cognomen dixeris, idem tamen ipse est.' Ex quibus quidem verbis Lucium eius praenomen, Annaeum autem cognomen, Senecam nomen suum fuisse plane aperteque deprehenditur.

Life of Seneca

Lucius Annaeus Seneca, as he calls himself in his book *On Benefits* ("For if you had received a benefit from Seneca," he writes, "whether you said you were indebted to Annaeus or to Lucius, you would be changing not your creditor but his name only")[1] was born at Cordova in Spain, a city seemingly second to none of that province in its antiquity, size, or population. I shall briefly explain my views about his complete name, since different versions of it have been handed down from various sources. When the Romans adopted their neighbors, the Sabines, as allies in their kingdom and sharers in their city, they prefixed to their own names other [Sabine] names, so that both peoples would be joined together by greater ties of love. This custom was henceforth preserved in Rome, so that after that time one may find no Roman who lacked a praenomen. Later, the various nations of the world that in due course were brought under the sway of the Roman people seem to have imitated this custom of their conquerors, for after their subjection they started to give children several names according to the old Roman style. 1

Cordova, the celebrated city of Spain where (as we said) Seneca was born, is known to have been brought under the rule of the Roman people before his birth by Julius Caesar. Hence it was that his parents, after Seneca's birth, imitated the custom of the Roman victors and correctly added a praenomen and a cognomen to his name. That is why they named him Lucius Annaeus Seneca, as he himself seems to suggest in his aforementioned book *On Benefits*. There he mentions his entire name, adding at once approximately the following: "When you say the praenomen, the name or the cognomen, you are always talking about the same person."[2] We can thus say with certainty that Lucius was his praenomen, Annaeus his cognomen, and Seneca his name. 2

3 Seneca igitur Cordubae in Hispania, quemadmodum diximus, natus est patre nobili ex familia Annaeorum, matre vero Helbia, ad quam extat egregia quaedam de obitu filii sui consolatio. Huius nativitatis suae imprimis testis est inveteratus Hispaniorum omnium consensus, qui certam quandam habitationis suae domum digito, ut aiunt, ostendentes, Cordubae usque ad haec nostra tempora extare et apparere testantur, aedesque illas et vicum insuper 'Senecae' nomine, veteri ac vulgata consuetudine, nuncuparunt. Atque non aliter vicum illum totum, in quo habitasse dicitur, 'Senecae' cognomine illustrarunt quam Romae 'Appia' via cognominaretur quod ab Appio Claudio, viro clarissimo, strata esset. Testis est etiam indubitata quaedam scriptorum omnium sententia, qui aliquam vel paulo maiorem huius singularissimi atque optimi viri mentionem facientes ipsum cordubensem civem fuisse scribunt. Nam et Eusebius Caesariensis et Hieronymus noster et Sidonius Apollinaris pluresque alii nobiles scriptores hoc idem, ut paulo post manifestius apparebit, palam et aperte testantur.

4 Sed cum non multo post Corduba a Romanorum imperio descivisset atque a Cn. Domitio Ahenobarbo, qui cum Romanorum exercitu ad expugnationem eius missus erat, iterum imperio populi Romani subigeretur, forte evenit ut Seneca, una cum duobus fratribus suis <Iunio> Annaeo Gallione et L. Annaeo Mela, Lucani poetae patre, in illius urbis direptione caperetur. Libertati vero postea donatus, una cum memoratis fratribus ac nepote parvulo Romam contendit, quae quidem cum omnis prosperitatis culmine tum omni doctrinarum genere eo tempore vel maxime pollebat, ut ipse quodam loco palam et aperte his ferme verbis innuere videtur: 'Quicquid,' inquit, 'habet romana facundia quod insolenti Graeciae aut opponat aut praeferat circa Ciceronem effloruit; omnia ingenia, quae aliquam nostris studiis lucem attulerunt, tunc nata sunt.' Et paulo post subdit: 'Omnes magnos in eloquentia viros praeter Ciceronem videor audisse, nec eum quidem aetas mihi eripuerat, sed bellorum civilium furor, qui iam totum terrarum or-

Seneca, then, as we said, was born in the Spanish city of Cordova. His father was a member of the noble family of the Annaei; his mother was Helbia, to whom he addressed an excellent consolation upon the death of her son. A principal testimony to the circumstances of his birth comes from the ancient and universal consensus of the Spaniards, who, they say, point out a certain house at Cordoba as his dwelling, asserting that it has been in continuous existence down to our times. By an ancient and popular tradition they call "Seneca" both the house and that part of town. To distinguish that whole part of town where he is said to have lived with the name "Seneca" is exactly what was done at Rome when the Appian Way was named after the famous Appius Claudius, who had laid it out. A further unquestionable proof is the opinion of all writers who have mentioned either slightly or at somewhat greater length this extraordinary and excellent man; they all refer to him as a citizen of Cordova. Eusebius of Caesarea, our Jerome, Sidonius Apollinaris and many other noble authors explicitly attest to this, as will shortly become clearer. 3

Not long after his birth, Cordova rebelled against the Roman empire and Ahenobarbus was sent with an army to subdue it. Thus it happened that Seneca and his two brothers—Junius Annaeus Gallio and Lucius Annaeus Mela, father of the poet Lucan—were taken prisoner when the city was reconquered. On being granted his liberty, he set out together with the aforesaid brothers and his young nephew for Rome, a city then at the height of its prosperity and vigorous in every field of study, as Seneca himself in a certain passage comes close to indicating explicitly: "All the rhetorical skills with which Rome challenged and excelled haughty Greece reached their peak in Cicero's day: all the minds which have shed light on our studies were born then." And he adds a little later: "I think I have heard every orator of great repute with the exception of Cicero; and even Cicero I was deprived of not by my age, but by the raging civil wars which at that time 4

bem pervagabatur,' et cetera huiusmodi prosecutus est. Ex quibus quidem verbis et tunc studia doctrinae Romae vel maxime floruisse et ipsum extrema Ciceronis aetate non modo natum sed adultum etiam fuisse manifestum est.

Ubi igitur litterarum ludo deditus prima illa poetarum studia transegit, sub Marullo rhetore una cum pluribus aliis condiscipulis rhetoricae praeceptis eruditur; qua in arte et Cestium Smyrnaeum celebrem rhetorem et Asinium Pollionem praeclarum oratorem inter ceteros praecipue audivit. Itaque in eloquentia usque adeo profecit ut omnibus praeter quam Caligulae, tunc forte imperanti, summopere placeret, cum ingenio et memoria plurimum valeret et assiduam quandam huiusmodi humanitatis studiis operam navaret. Suetonius enim de Caligula in eius vita loquens ita scribit: 'Caligula lentius et comptius scribendi genus ita spernere ac contemnere solebat ut Senecam tunc' (et nunc etiam, ut Petrarcha ait) 'vel maxime placentem commissiones meras,' sic enim inquit, 'componere et arenam esse sine calce diceret.' De quo minime mirabimur, si ipsum, ut scriptum est, de abolendis Homeri carminibus cogitasse meminerimus, idem sibi licere testatus quod Platoni homini privato, quamvis docto et erudito, iam antea licuisset, qui illum e civitate quam constituebat eiciendum esse existimabat. Sed et cuncta Maronis et Livii scripta parum abfuit quin ex omnibus bibliothecis amoveret, quorum alterum ut nullius ingenii minimeque eloquentiae, alterum ut verbosum in historia negligentemque carpebat. Sotionem deinde Alexandrinum, celebratum illorum temporum ex Stoicorum opinione philosophum, secutus, sub eo in ipsa philosophia quae ad mores et ad institutionem vitae pertinet apprime claruit, tantaque doctrinae et eloquentiae suae fama increbuerat ut propterea Claudio, Caligulae successori, singulari amicitia iungeretur. Unde ex cordubensi romanus civis effectus et in senatorum quoque numero susceptus est.

were criss-crossing the entire world," and he continues along these lines.[3] From this passage it is plain that learning was flourishing at the time and that towards the end of Cicero's life Seneca was not only alive, but an adult.

5 So when he had taken the course in literature and finished those initial studies of the poets, he was educated in the precepts of rhetoric under the rhetorician Marullus along with many fellow students. While studying this art he heard, among others, the celebrated rhetorician Cestius Smyrnaeus and the famous orator Asinius Pollio. He made so much progress in eloquence that he delighted everyone but Caligula, who happened to be emperor at the time. For not only was Seneca endowed with a keen intellect and a strong memory but he also devoted great effort to humanistic studies. In his life of Caligula, Suetonius writes as follows: "Caligula used to spurn and have contempt for that measured and refined kind of writing, and would call Seneca, then much in vogue," (as he is now, too, as Petrarca says) "a composer of mere entertainments, like sand without quicklime."[4] This statement will excite no surprise if we remember what is written about his plan to ban Homer's poetry; how he swore he had the right to do what it had been licit long ago for Plato to do as a private individual, however wise and learned—the man who thought that Homer should be banned from the state he was founding. He came very close to removing all the works of Vergil and Livy from all the libraries, complaining that the former lacked genius and eloquence, while the latter was verbose and careless.[5] Seneca then became a follower of Sotio of Alexandria, a celebrated Stoic philosopher of the time, and under his guidance attained great distinction in the branch of philosophy that pertains to moral conduct and education. The fame of his learning and eloquence grew to such an extent that he entered into a unique friendship with Claudius, Caligula's successor. Thus it was that the Cordovan was made a Roman citizen and a member of the senate.

6 Claudio deinde postea causis nescio quibus infensus, ab eo in Corsicam insulam relegatur, quamquam non defuerint qui ipsum sponte sua, studiorum gratia, eo usque se contulisse scripserint, quo liberius, ut cupiebat, romanarum ac civilium rerum strepitibus velut quibusdam arbitris atque interpellatoribus remotis, sapientiae operam navare posset. Ubi vero Claudius, post mortem Messalinae uxoris suae, Agrippinam, Neronis matrem, ex Cn. Domitio eius viro matrimonio sibi copulavit, suis persuasionibus obsecutus Senecam e Corsica insula (nam ibi aliquamdiu commoratus in ea solitudine philosophiae operam dederat) ab exilio revocavit, simul atque ei praeturam concessit. Ac demum Flavium Neronem — undecimo aetatis suae anno iam pridem ab eo adoptatum, deinde generum sibi ex sponsione Octaviae filiae factum ac propterea denique ad imperatoriam dignitatem designatum — in disciplinam tradidit. Cornelius enim Tacitus in duodecimo *Historiarum* suarum libro verba haec ponit: 'Agrippina, ne malis tantum facinoribus notesceret, veniam exilii pro Annaeo Seneca simul et praeturam impetrat, fore rata ut ob claritudinem studiorum eius Domitii pueritia tali magistro adolesceret et consiliis eiusdem hominis ad spem dominationis uteretur, quia Seneca fidus in Agrippinam memoria beneficii et infensus Claudio dolore iniuriae credebatur.'

7 Ferunt Senecam inter cetera, ut scribit Suetonius, 'proxima nocte sibi per quietem visum Caesari praecipere,' cui quidem somnio Nero paulo post fidem fecit, 'prodita,' ut eius verbis utar, 'immanitate naturae quibus primum potuit experimentis,' quod Petrarca poeta in libro *Rerum memorandarum* aliter in hunc modum expressisse videtur. Inquit enim: 'Proxima nocte somniasse dicitur Seneca C. Caligulam, cuius iam pridem famosissima crudelitas dignum exitum invenerat, se discipulum habere; potuit experrectus

Then at a later point he alienated Claudius for unknown reasons and was exiled by him to the island of Corsica, although some writers say that he left of his own free will, in the desire to devote himself with greater freedom to philosophy, far from the din of Roman life and civil affairs, free from surveillance and interruptions. At this point Claudius—who after the death of his wife Messalina had married Agrippina, the mother of Nero and Gnaeus Domitius' former wife—was persuaded by her to call Seneca back from his exile on the island of Corsica, where he had spent quite some time in solitude absorbed in the study of philosophy, and at the same time gave him a praetorship. In due course Claudius entrusted him with the schooling of Flavius Nero, whom Claudius had previously adopted at the age of eleven, and who later became his son-in-law through marriage to his daughter Octavia and hence destined for the imperial title. These are the words of Cornelius Tacitus from the twelfth book of his *Histories*: "Agrippina, to avoid being tainted only with crimes, pleaded for a remission of banishment and a praetorship for Seneca, believing that Domitius would have greatly profited, in his transit from boyhood to adolescence, from the tutorship of so famous a scholar, whose advice would prove useful in their designs upon the throne. She also thought that Seneca would be faithful to her by the memory of her kindness and embittered against Claudius by resentment of his injury."[6] 6

As Suetonius writes, one story was that "on the following night Seneca dreamt that he was schooling the emperor," a dream that Nero soon justified (to use Suetonius' words again) "by betraying the cruelty of his disposition at the earliest possible opportunity." The poet Petrarca seems to have expressed this differently in his book *Things Worth Remembering*. He says, "On the next night Seneca is said to have dreamt that Gaius Caligula, whose notorious cruelty had already come to a worthy end, was his pupil. He woke up in a state of shock, but Nero's behavior and his spirit, bereft of 7

admirari, sed mores et omnis humanitatis expers animus admirationem sustulerunt, quoniam tam Caligulae similis evasit Nero ut non alter, sed ille idem quodammodo ab inferis resurrexisse videretur.'

8 Non multo post, mortuo Claudio atque Nerone ad imperium sublimato, tantam praeceptor eius potentiam tantasque etiam opes et divitias comparavit ut, quoad ipse pietatem coleret atque probi principis muneribus fungeretur, nihil fere sine consilio Senecae ab imperatore agi crederetur. Per hunc itaque modum Nero in eius disciplinam puer traditus, sub illo uno et solo magistro et praeceptore per decem et novem annos, ceteris dicendi aut docendi professoribus omissis, ita attente perseveravit ut doctissimus simul atque eloquentissimus evaderet. Nam et carmina scripsit et tragoedias edidit ac multa alia memoriae mandavit. Quod autem ipse solum Senecam, ceteris rhetoribus ac philosophis omissis, audierit, testis est Suetonius, qui ait ipsum a cognitione veterum oratorum ideo Neronem avertisse 'quo diutius illum in admiratione eius detineret.' Proinde cum apud imperatorem potentissimus esset et ita potentissimus haberetur ut et magnos honores et incredibiles opes nancisceretur, ei tamen postea, causis nescio quibus, adeo infensus fuit ut ipsum morte damnaret, de qua ad extremum paulo latius dicemus, si prius pauca quaedam de studiis et moribus ac progressibus vitae suae, ab origine repetita, in medium adduxerimus.

9 Senecam igitur Cordubae in Hispania natum, in recuperatione eius urbis quae a romano imperio defecerat una cum duobus fratribus captum ac postea libertati donatum, Romam studiorum gratia contendisse diximus. Ubi cunctis liberalibus artibus apprime eruditus, in tanto ac tam magno honore propterea habitus est ut ex cordubensi romanus civis effectus, senatus ac quaesturae praeturaeque et consulatus etiam, ut ex iure civili plane aperteque deprehenditur, insignia meruerit, atque apud Neronem, forte tunc

all humanity, eventually dispelled his amazement. Indeed, Nero turned out to be so similar to Caligula that he seemed to be not a different person, but the very same one, resurrected somehow from the dead."[7]

Soon thereafter Claudius died and Nero was raised to power. 8
As Nero's teacher, Seneca grew so powerful and wealthy that, as long as his pupil behaved piously and discharged with probity the duties of a prince, it was believed that the emperor did nothing without his advice. Nero in fact had been put to study under him as a boy, and Seneca was his only master and teacher for no less than nineteen years, all his other teachers of rhetoric and other subjects having been dismissed. The boy applied himself with such concentration that he became an erudite and well-spoken man. He wrote poems, composed tragedies, and set down many other things in writing. That he studied only with Seneca and not with other rhetoricians and philosophers is attested by Suetonius, who states that Seneca deflected Nero from the study of the old orators, "that he might keep the boy in awe of him the longer."[8] Thereafter, although he had great influence over the emperor and so was considered very powerful, obtaining great honors and incredible riches, the emperor later, for mysterious reasons, became so hostile to him that he condemned him to death. I shall speak of this in somewhat greater detail at the end, but first let us bring under consideration a few things about his studies, behavior, and development, starting over from the beginning.

Born in the Spanish city of Cordova, he and his two brothers, 9
as we said, were taken prisoner in the Roman reconquest of the city after its rebellion against the empire. Shortly thereafter, he was freed and set out for Rome to study. There he mastered all the liberal arts, and on that account acquired such great honor that the Cordovan was made a Roman citizen, earning also the distinctions of senator, quaestor, praetor and consul, as may be discovered explicitly from a perusal of the civil law, and he obtained a

temporis Romae imperantem, primum locum obtinuerit. Haec enim verba quodam *Digestorum* suorum libro scripta esse cernuntur: 'Explicito tractatu, qui ad fidei commissa singularum rerum pertinet, transeamus nunc ad interpretationem senatus consulti Trebelliani. Factum est enim senatus consultum temporibus Neronis octavo kalendas Septembres, Annaeo Seneca et Trebellio Maximo consulibus,' et quae sequuntur.

10 Et ut de singulari ac praecipua doctrina et eruditione eius, probitate morum et sanctimonia vitae condita, nonnulla breviter attingamus, poetas imprimis non ignoravit. Nam poeticis allegationibus omnes fere eius libros refertos esse conspicimus. Rhetoricam deinde ita percepit ut omnes egregios eius artis professores, qui eo tempore vel maxime florebant ac ceteris longe praestabant, summa attentione audierit, quemadmodum de se ipse, ut supra diximus, testatus est. Nec solum maximos dicendi magistros audisse sed etiam intellexisse eorumque vestigia imitatus fuisse traditur; unde, inter cetera, nonnullos declamationum libros conscripsit. Magnarum tum rerum cognitionem nancisci cupiens, in physicis ita profecit ut egregios quosdam *De quaestionibus naturalibus* libros scribere non dubitaret.

11 Postremo eam partem philosophiae quae ad mores et ad institutionem vitae pertinet totis animi et corporis viribus <tractavit>, velut ipse in epistula quadam ad Lucilium eius familiarem scribens testatur. Ita cum docendo tum scribendo atque modeste insuper temperateque vivendo descriptionibus suis humano generi usque adeo profuisse perhibetur ut solus in hac morali philosophia excellere ac ceteris omnibus harum rerum scriptoribus, consensu omnium, praestare videatur. Quocirca solus moralis philosophus, hoc est, cunctis excellens, vulgo apud Latinos non immerito appellari consuevit. Atque sicut de Vergilio, si poetam, aut de Cicerone, si oratorem apud nos, si vero apud Graecos de Homero ac Demos-

position of primary importance with Nero, then emperor in Rome. For the following words are found written in a certain book of the *Digests of Roman Law*: "Having discussed all aspects pertaining to trusts, let us now pass to the interpretation of the 'Senatus Consultum Trebellianum,' which was issued under Emperor Nero, on 25 August, during the consulate of Annaeus Seneca and Trebellio Maximus," and so on.[9]

10 Let us now touch briefly upon his remarkable learning and erudition, which was salted by upright moral conduct and a saintly life. First of all, he was acquainted with poetry. Indeed, we see that all of his books are filled with citations from the poets. Furthermore, he mastered rhetoric, having studied with the utmost concentration, as we noted before, under the greatest exponents of this art, who at that time flourished exceedingly, far excelling all others, as he himself bears witness. Nor, we are told, did he simply hear lectures of the greatest masters of rhetoric, but he also understood them and imitated them. Hence he wrote, among other compositions, several books of declamations.[10] Desirous of obtaining an understanding of important subjects, he also made so much progress in natural philosophy that he was bold enough to write some excellent books called *On Natural Questions*.

11 In due course he took up with all his might, as he writes in an epistle to his friend Lucilius, that branch of philosophy dealing with moral behavior and education.[11] Thus by his teaching and writing—and also by giving an example of modest and temperate living—his representations of morality were of such profit to the human race that he stands at the forefront of moral philosophy, excelling by common consent all other writers on these subjects. Hence it is not without justice that he alone among Latin authors is commonly referred to as "the moral philosopher," that is, the one who excels the rest. And just as when we ask for "the poet" or "the orator," we normally understand and answer "Vergil" and "Cicero" among Latin authors and "Homer" and "Demosthenes"

thene eadem quaerimus, sic etiam de Seneca, si moralem dicimus, intelligere et respondere solemus.

12 De hac igitur tam singulari ac tam excellenti doctrina sua minime mirabimur, si quantum ingenio ac memoria valuerit, si quantum insuper huiusmodi humanitatis studiis operae laborisque impenderit vel paulisper considerabimus. Memoria siquidem tanta ac tam singulari fuit ut duo milia nominum eo ordine quo erant dicta et ultra ducentos quoque versus fideliter redderet; nec ad complectendum modo quae audiebat, sed ad retinendum etiam valebat, quorum alterum ex celeri apprehensione facile oblivionem, alterum vero ex multarum rerum complexione plerumque tarditatem parere consuevit. Quid plura? Ipse in memorato *Declamationum* libro de se loquens tantum memoria valuisse testatur ut in miraculum usque procederet. Haec enim eius verba sunt: 'Memoriam in me floruisse aliquando, ut non modo ad usum sufficeret, sed in miraculum usque procederet non nego. Nam duo milia nominum recitata quo erant ordine dicta reddebam, et ab ipsis qui ad audiendum praeceptorem nostrum convenerant singulos versus a singulis datos, cum plus quam ducenti efficerentur, ab ultimo incipiens usque ad primum recitabam. Nec ad complectendum tantum quae vellem velox mihi erat memoria, sed ad continenda quae acceperat.' Ad haec tam singularia ac tam praecipua dona naturae maximam atque paene incredibilem quandam diligentiam adhibebat. Nam et lectionem et meditationem et magnarum quoque rerum descriptionem ceteris omnibus praeferebat, licet multiplicibus cum privatarum tum magnarum rerum curis iugiter angeretur.

13 Itaque de magnis et paene incredibilibus laborum suorum fructibus, quos posteris dimisit, mirari desinemus, vel potius minime mirabimur, si ipsum his tantis ac tam singularibus naturae et industriae donis mirum in modum adiutum fuisse meminerimus. Nam haec ipsa litteris mandavit: etenim ad Paulum apostolum, cui amicita iungebatur, praeter complures epistulas, librum *De verborum copia* conscripsit, *De septem liberalibus artibus, De quattuor vir-*

among the Greeks, so when we talk about "the moralist," we generally mean Seneca.

We shall not be surprised at all about the extraordinary excellence of his learning if we consider how powerful were his mind and memory, and how much effort he devoted, moreover, to humanistic studies. His memory was so extraordinary that he could repeat correctly two thousand words or two hundred verses in the same order they had been spoken. And he was able not only to repeat what he had heard, but to retain it, whereas normally a quick study forgets easily and a summary grasp of many subjects leads to slowness of wit. In short, he himself, in the aforesaid book of *Declamations*, writes that his own memory was so powerful as to border on the miraculous. These are his words: "I do not deny that my own memory was at one time so flourishing that it not only sufficed for the purposes [of rhetoric], but bordered on the prodigious. Indeed, I could repeat two thousand words in the order in which they had been spoken and recite backwards every single verse composition produced by the students who had come to study with my teacher, even when they had composed more than two hundred of them."[12] And he joined to these unique and outstanding gifts of nature an enormous and almost unbelievable diligence. For he preferred reading, meditation and learned disquisitions on important subjects to all other activities, even though he was continually vexed by his manifold involvements in great as well as private affairs. 12

Thus we should cease to marvel — or rather we shouldn't marvel at all — at the great and almost incredible fruits of the labors he left to posterity, once we take into account the wonderful help he derived from these many extraordinary gifts of heredity and application. He wrote the following works. In addition to the many epistles he wrote to his friend, the Apostle Paul, he also wrote *How to Have a Large Vocabulary*, *On the Seven Liberal Arts*, and *On the Four Virtues*. Our Petrarca, in a letter to Boccaccio, denies Seneca's 13

tutibus; quem librum Petrarcha noster in quadam epistula ad Boccacium scribens, licet plerumque eius nomine inscribatur, Senecae tamen fuisse negat. Cui equidem assentior; nam paulo diligentius intuentibus et singula quoque, ut decet, accuratius considerantibus, pleraque in eo libro contineri videbuntur quae Senecae gravitati haudquaquam convenire dignoscentur. *De proverbiis, De moribus* libros singulos composuit; *De beneficiis* ad Eburtium Lugdunensem libros septem, *De ira* ad Novatum tres, iterum ad eundem *Declamationum* libros novem, *De beata vita* ad Gallionem eius fratrem librum unum, ad eundem *De remediis fortuitorum* librum unum, *De brevitate vitae* ad Paulinum unum, *Quod iniuria et contumelia non cadant in sapientem* ad Serenum unum, *Proverbiorum* diversorum a praedictis librum unum, *De quaestionibus naturalibus* ad Lucilium, familiarem suum, sex libros edidit (ad quem etiam, insulae Siciliae forte populi romani nomine tunc praesidentem, viginti duos epistularum libros transmiserat), *De ludis Claudii* librum unum, de quo quidem libro Boccacius quodam loco an Senecae fuerit dubitare videtur.

14 Extant insuper duae egregiae de obitu liberorum consolationes, altera *Ad Marciam,* Seiani cuiusdam praepotentis hominis filiam, altera *Ad Helbiam matrem.* Scripsit praeterea quaedam alia, quorum apud nos nulla penitus vestigia remanserunt, quippe et *Contra superstitiones deorum gentilium* et *De immatura morte* et *De exhortationibus* nescio quibus, ut Lactantius pluribus *Divinarum Institutionum* libris plane et aperte testatur, et *De motu* insuper *terrae* nonnulla memoratu digna et *De consolatione ad Pollionem* nescio quem librum unum edidisse perhibetur. Scripsit praeterea, ut Quintilianus tradit, orationes, poemata ac dialogos, et, si Hieronymo credimus, *De matrimonio* libros quosdam composuit. Ex quibus quidem nihil aliud quam memoratorum codicum allegationes reperire potuimus, nisi si quis forte per poemata tragoedias intelligere voluerit ac Quintilianum ita sensisse existimarit.

authorship of this last book, although it generally circulates under his name.[13] I agree, personally, for those who take the effort to look into the case and consider every particular carefully, as is proper, will find many things in that book which hardly accord with Seneca's gravity. Seneca also wrote *On Proverbs* and *On Moral Behavior,* both in one book;[14] *On Benefits* in seven books, dedicated to Eburtius of Lyon; *On Anger* in three books, dedicated to Novatus; and nine books of *Declamations,* also to Novatus;[15] *On the Blessed Life* in one book to his brother Gallio; *Cures for Misfortunes* in one book to the same man; *On the Brevity of Life* in one book to Paulinus; *That Injury and Insult do not Befall the Wise Man* in one book to Serenus; one book of *Proverbs* (different from the one mentioned above); and the six books entitled *Natural Questions,* which he dedicated to his friend Lucilius. The latter is also the addressee of the twenty-two books of letters which Seneca sent him while his friend happened to be serving as the Roman governor of Sicily. As for the one book entitled *Making Fun of Claudius,* Boccaccio seems to doubt Seneca's authorship.[16]

There are extant, in addition, two fine consolatory epistles on the death of children: one *To Marcia,* who was the daughter of a certain powerful man named Sejanus, and the other *To His Mother Helbia.* He wrote several other works that have vanished without a trace, such as the works explicitly cited by Lactantius in many books of his *Divine Institutes,* namely, *Against the Superstitions Regarding the Gentile Gods, On Premature Death,* and something or other *On Exhortations.*[17] He is, moreover, said to have written a memorable work *On Earthquakes* and something or other *On Consolation to Pollio.* Quintilian further reports that he wrote orations, poems, and dialogues, and if we believe Jerome he composed certain books *On Marriage.*[18] We have been able to find nothing but citations of the aforesaid books, unless someone wants to understand "poems" here to mean "tragedies," and thinks Quintilian held the same view.[19] 14

15 Atque haec omnia rerum suarum monumenta reliquit quamquam multis ac variis cum privatis tum publicis curis multum admodum impediretur ac etiam perpetuis quibusdam, ut ita dixerim, valitudinibus iugiter angeretur. Nam et re familiari, quae sibi ampla erat, et uxore ac liberis et publicis insuper negotiis plerumque ita distrahebatur ut contemplationi magnarum et altissimarum rerum, quemadmodum cupiebat, vacare non posset; ex quo ipsum singularibus ac praecipuis naturae donis ornatum fuisse manifestum est. Opulentissimus namque simul ac ditissimus fuit, siquidem et amplos et pulcherrimos Romae hortos habuit, ut quidam non ignobilis poeta his verbis expressit:

> et magni Senecae praedivitis hortos
> clausit.

Et Cornelius Tacitus, historiarum scriptor, de memoratis eius hortis mentionem faciens, Senecae hortos sicut Sallustianos hortos et dixit et sensit. Pluribus quoque suburbanis ornabatur; etenim Nomentanum et Albanum et plura insuper alia eiusmodi suburbana, ut ex epistulis eius ad Lucilium scriptis manifestissime apparet, simul atque eodem tempore possidebat. Praeterea apud Neronem imperatorem tunc vel ubique imperantem plurimum poterat, cuius eruditionem vel maxime curabat.

16 Uxorem denique habuit nomine Pompeiam Paulinam, ex qua plures filios suscepit. Eam, ut ipse quodam loco refert, unice ac supra humanum modum diligebat. Quae etsi ab eo scripta esse videamus, ob incredibilem tamen hominis severitatem dubitare nec possumus nec debemus quod illa de se ipso intelligeret quae in libro *De matrimonio* scripsisse perhibetur. 'Refert' enim 'se cognovisse quendam ornatum hominem qui exiturus in publicum fascia uxoris pectus alligabat et neque puncto quidem horae praesentia eius carere poterat; potionemque nullam, nisi alternis tactam labris, vir et uxor hauriebant.' Haec, cum gravitati hominis minime convenire videantur, de se sensisse stultum est credere. Ad haec

He left behind all these writings despite being troubled by a 15
great deal of public and private business of various kinds, and despite also being continually vexed with health problems. For he was so distracted by the cares of a large estate, his wife and children, as well as public duties that he was unable to free himself as he would have liked for contemplation of great and profound issues and for which his unique and remarkable gifts of nature had manifestly fitted him. He was extraordinarily wealthy and opulent, having large and beautiful gardens in Rome, which a certain noteworthy poet mentions as follows:

> and he closed off the opulent gardens of great Seneca.[20]

The historian Cornelius Tacitus also mentions the same gardens, putting them in the same class as the gardens of Sallust.[21] Seneca was also provided with several pleasure-grounds near the city, and indeed, as is perfectly clear from his letters to Lucilius, he possessed at one and the same time properties at Nomentum and Albanum and many other places like this near the city. Besides, he had great responsibilities as the emperor Nero's tutor, and had great influence with him while the latter was exercising his imperial power throughout the world.

He had a wife called Pompeia Paulina by whom he had many 16
children. As he tells us somewhere in his works, his love for her was unique and above the measure of human kind.[22] Yet even if he did write it, we neither can nor ought to call into question, given the man's incredible severity of conduct, whether he meant to refer to himself in what he is reported to have written in his book *On Matrimony*: "He says he knew a certain distinguished man who, when venturing out in public, pinned his wife's hairband to his breast and could not survive an hour away from her presence; and the man and his wife used to swallow no drink unless both their lips had touched it."[23] Since such behavior ill comports with the man's gravity, it is foolish to believe that he entertained such an

omnia tam multiplicia ac tam varia impedimentorum genera ingens valitudinis suae cura accedebat. Nam pluribus morborum generibus simul die noctuque angebatur, siquidem et stomacho et morbo destillationis et *dyspnoia*[1] eodem tempore laborabat et podagra quoque ac chiragra interdum vexabatur. Et 'omnia denique corporis incommoda atque pericula,' ut eius verbis utar, expertus erat; sed id ceteris omnibus maius ac molestius sibi fuisse testatur quo respirandi difficultatem patiebatur, quem morbum Graeci *dyspnoia*,[2] nos 'asthma' appellare solemus.

17 Quamquam ergo his tantis ac tam multiplicibus curis incommodisque impeditus esset atque, ut diximus, doctissimus evaderet pluraque doctrinae et eruditionis suae monumenta memoratu digna reliquerit ac satis eloquentiae, mea quidem sententia, habuerit, non defuerunt tamen qui et doctrinam suam et genus dicendi aspernarentur ac contemnerent. A. Gellius enim, vir apprime eruditus, in libris *Noctium Atticarum* de Seneca loquens verba haec posuit: 'De Annaeo Seneca partim existimant ut de scriptore minime utili, cuius libros attingere nullum pretium operae sit, quia oratio eius vulgaris videatur et pertrita, res atque sententiae aut inepto inanique impetu sint aut levi et quasi dicaci argutia; eruditio autem vernacula et plebeia nihilque ex veterum scriptis habens neque gratiae neque dignitatis. Alii vero elegantiae quidem in verbis parum esse non inficias eunt, sed et rerum, quas dicat, scientiam doctrinamque eius non deesse dicunt et in vitiis morum obiurgandis severitatem gravitatemque non invenustam. Mihi de omni eius ingenio deque omni scripto iudicium censuramque facere non necessum est. Sed quod de M. Cicerone et Q. Ennio et P. Virgilio iudicavit, ea res, cuiusmodi sit, ad considerandum ponemus.' Et cum deinde causas subiecisset, quibus memoratos auctores redarguere adductus esset, sic inquit: 'Sed iam verborum Senecae me piget. Haec tamen inepti et insipidi insulsique hominis ioca non praeteribo'; et cum postea versus Q. Ennii de Cethego a Seneca re-

opinion of himself. His immense concern for his own health only added to all these numerous and varied sorts of impediment. He was troubled night and day by many kinds of illness, as he had a weak stomach and suffered at the same time from catarrh and asthma and was from time to time attacked by gout and arthritis. To use his own words, he was acquainted with "all the discomforts and dangers of the body;"[24] but he affirmed that the greatest and most trying of his ills was the difficulty he had in breathing, a malady the Greeks call *dyspnoia* and we call 'asthma.'

Although hindered by so many great cares and problems, he 17
still became, as we said, a very wise man, leaving behind many memorable proofs of his learning and erudition; nor in my opinion did he lack eloquence. Nevertheless, there was no lack of people who spurned and had contempt for his learning and his rhetorical style. Thus Aulus Gellius, a highly learned man, put down the following opinion about Seneca in his *Attic Nights:* "Some think of Annaeus Seneca as a writer of little value, whose works are not worth taking up, since his style seems commonplace and ordinary, while the matter and the thought are characterized, now by a foolish and empty vehemence, now by a vain and affected cleverness. His learning, besides, is common and plebeian, lacking the charm and distinction of earlier writers. Others, on the contrary, while not denying that his diction lacks elegance, declare that he is not without learning and knowledge of the subjects of which he treats, and that he censures vices with a seriousness and dignity which are not wanting in charm. I myself do not feel called upon to criticize and pass judgement upon all of his writings; but I shall select for consideration the nature of the opinions which he has expressed about Cicero, Ennius and Vergil." And after giving the reasons why he had been led to reprove those authors, he added: "But I am already weary of quoting Seneca; yet I shall not pass by these jokes of that foolish, mediocre and tasteless man"; and when afterwards he turns to verses of Ennius on Cethegus

prehensos subdidisset, 'dignus sane,' inquit, 'Seneca videbatur lectione ac studio adulescentium,' et quae sequuntur.

18 Quintilianus vero, licet severus et gravis auctor haberetur, leviter tamen ac varie de Seneca et sensit et dixit; nam et genus dicendi eius minime probavit et tamen plerumque ex eo artis oratoriae exempla sumpsit, siquidem pluribus *Institutionum* suarum locis ab eo exempla ponit. Nam et octavo memorati operis libro 'sola,' inquit, 'geminatio quasdam sententias efficit. Qualis est Senecae in eo scripto quod Nero ad senatum misit, occisa matre, cum se periclitatum videri vellet: "Salvum me esse adhuc nec credo nec gaudeo."' Et in nono etiam ita ait: 'ut Seneca in controversia cuius summa est quod pater filium et novercam, inducente et insimulante altero filio, in adulterio deprehensos occidit.' Et alibi eodem libro 'a Seneca' quoque 'eleganter dictum' fuisse refert: 'Non patronorum hoc esse, sed testium.'

19 Doctrinam autem ac sententias suas satis superque satis laudasse videtur. Et tamen in philosophia parum diligentem extitisse testantur. Haec ipsa et alia huiusmodi quantum inter se cohaereant quantumque scriptoris gravitati conveniant ita manifestum est ut simultatem quandam inter eos intercessisse cunctis legentibus innotescat, quod dum ille vitare cupit, in id vitium scribens maxime incidit. Decimo enim *Institutionum* suarum libro verba haec ponit: 'Senecam in omni genere eloquentiae distuli propter vulgatam falso de me opinionem qua damnare eum <et> invisum quoque habere sum creditus. Quod accidit mihi dum corruptum et omnibus vitiis fractum dicendi genus revocare ad severiora iudicia contendo.' Et paulo post, cum solum 'in manibus adulescentium' fuisse asseruerit, 'ingenium,' inquit, 'facile et copiosum; plurimi studii, multa rerum cognitio. In philosophia parum dili-

that were criticized by Seneca, he states: "Worthy indeed would Seneca appear of the reading and study of the young!" and so on.[25]

Quintilian, now, although considered a strict and grave author, made various superficial criticisms of Seneca. He disapproved of his style, and yet took many examples of oratorical art from him, citing them in numerous places in the *Institutes*. Thus in the eighth book: "Some sentences consist of mere doublings. Take, for instance, the letter composed by Seneca that Nero sent to the senate when his mother was killed, when he wanted it to seem that he had been in danger. 'As yet I can neither believe nor rejoice that I am safe.'" And in the ninth book he says: "As Seneca writes in a controversial theme whose burden is that a father, led on by the allegation of one son, finds another son committing adultery with his stepmother and kills both." And elsewhere in the same book: "Seneca made a neat comment to this effect when he said that such things were the business of the witness, not the advocate."[26] 18

It seems he praised abundantly the learning and the opinions of Seneca. And yet he asserts that his philosophy lacked rigor. These and other such remarks are so contradictory and so manifestly unsuited to the gravity of the writer that every reader notices the animosity that existed between them—a vice to which Quintilian often succumbs in his writing, even as he strives to avoid it. Look what he writes in book ten of his *Institutes:* "I have deliberately quoted Seneca for each kind of rhetorical style owing to the fact that there is a general, though false, impression that I condemn and even detest him. This happened to me when I tried to summon back to a stricter standard a corrupt style of speech, exhausted by every vice." And shortly thereafter, when he had asserted that Seneca was "only in the hands of adolescents," he says, "He had a ready and fertile intelligence, showing a great deal of study and vast knowledge. In philosophy he displayed a lack of rigor, but was nonetheless admirable for his denunciations of vice. His works contain many penetrating insights and much that is 19

gens, egregius tamen vitiorum insectator fuit. Multae tamen in eo claraeque sententiae, multa etiam — morum gratia — legenda, sed in eloquendo corrupta pleraque atque eo perniciosissima, quod abundant dulcibus vitiis.' Et cetera huiusmodi ita varie prosecutus est ut clarum ac celebratum scriptorem varia atque inter se diversa, eodem praesertim contextu orationis, posuisse mirandum sit; quibus nimirum si causam Senecae suscipere voluissem, satis abundeque respondere potuissem atque in huiusmodi tanti viri defensione mihi profecto orationem non defuisse arbitrarer. Unum est tamen de quo quidem prae ceteris omnibus admirari cogor, quonam scilicet modo A. Gellius ipse sanam ac perutilem Senecae nostri doctrinam iure vituperare potuerit, quae ab omnibus prope scriptoribus summopere ac non immerito laudatur.

Sed ut A. Gellius de hac ipsa doctrinae et eruditionis suae vana et temeraria damnatione tandem aliquando convincatur, omissis multiplicibus ac variis scriptorum suorum traditionibus omni humanitate atque magna quadam sapientia refertis, non indignas quorundam clarorum virorum auctoritates in medium adducamus, ut — quando auctoritatibus agendum est — memoratos auctores cum A. Gellii grammatici, licet elegantissimi hominis, auctoritate conferamus. Plutarchus, natione graecus ac litterarum graecarum peritissimus vir, gravissimus severusque philosophus, in illis suis praeclaris et celebratis Graecorum et Latinorum hominum comparationibus, quae graece *Parallela* dicuntur, cum Platoni Varronem, Homero Vergilium, Demostheni Ciceronem comparasset, se neminem reperire potuisse quem ex Graecis Senecae in moralibus institutionibus conferret confiteri non dubitavit. Magna immo vel maxima laus, ex ore praesertim philosophi et peregrini et animosi hominis et multarum rerum scientia praepollentis, 'qui nostro Iulio Caesari,' ut ait quidam non ignobilis auctor, 'suum Alexandrum Macedonem antea comparasset,' vel, quod longe maius est, gesta populi romani cum Alexandri Magni fortuna in quodam proprio et peculiari eius libro conferre non dubitasset, quem idcirco *De for-*

worth reading for the sake of edification; but his style is for the most part corrupt and exceedingly pernicious, because it abounds in attractive vices."[27] And he goes on to make sundry other remarks in this vein, so that one has to wonder how a distinguished and celebrated writer could have put down so many different and conflicting views, especially in the very same discourse. If I wished to take Seneca's side, I could of course reply to these comments in more than sufficient detail, and I would certainly not lack for things to say in defense of this great man. Yet the one thing that I am compelled to wonder at the most is how Aulus Gellius could in justice blame the sound and extremely useful teaching of our Seneca, which is deservedly praised to the skies by almost all writers.

But in order that Aulus Gellius's rash and empty criticisms of 20
Seneca's learning and erudition may be refuted, I shall leave aside the innumerable and varied teachings of wisdom and humanity that fill his writings. Instead, I shall bring forward authoritative statements by certain distinguished men so that — since we are debating about authorities — we may compare the authority of these men with that of Aulus Gellius, a man of refined taste, but still a grammarian. Plutarch, a Greek and an expert in Greek literature as well as a grave and severe philosopher, in his famous and celebrated comparisons of Greeks and Romans, called in Greek the *Parallela*, after comparing Varro to Plato, Vergil to Homer, and Cicero to Demosthenes, did not hesitate to confess that he had been able to find no one among the Greeks whom he might compare to Seneca as a moralist.[28] Great praise indeed, or rather the greatest praise of all, especially coming from the mouth of a philosopher, a foreigner and a haughty and highly learned man who, as an author of some weight put it, "had compared our Julius Caesar to his Alexander the Great," and even more remarkably, had not held back from comparing the deeds of the Roman people with the fortune of Alexander the Great in a separate book of his

tuna populi romani et Alexandri praenotasse atque inscripsisse manifestum est.

21 Plinius quoque, vir doctissimus, in decimo quarto *Naturalis historiae* libro de Seneca loquens, honorificam et laudabilem eius mentionem habuit. Nam et de singulari et praecipua eius sapientia, quam 'nimiam' vocat, scientia et virtutibus comparatam, palam et aperte et sensit et dixit. Cornelius etiam Tacitus, vetus et celebratus historicus, in duodecimo *Historiarum* suarum libro Agrippinam, Claudii uxorem et Neronis matrem, veniam exilii, quod Senecam in Corsica insula pertulisse supra diximus, simul atque pro eo a viro suo praeturam impetrasse testatur, atque ut id postularet 'ob claritudinem studiorum' suorum adductam fuisse scribit. Suetonius insuper in libro *De duodecim Caesaribus* ipsum ob excellentiam doctrinae Neroni, tunc puero ac paulo post imperaturo, praeceptorem datum refert. Quintilianus praeterea, quem ei infensum ob studiorum aemulationem fuisse diximus, se continere non potuit quin — vi veritatis, quae maxima est, victus — doctrinam suam summopere laudaret; siquidem de eo loquens quodam loco 'Optandum,' inquit, 'fore pares ac saltem proximos illi viro fieri.' Nam et orationes et poemata et epistulas et dialogos scripsisse et magnam insuper rerum cognitionem habuisse commemorat.

22 Et ne plures ethnicorum virorum auctoritates complectamur, ad doctos et sanctos homines accedamus. Lactantius, vir doctissimus simul atque eloquentissimus ac probitate vitae sanctimoniaque morum apprime conspicuus, pluribus suarum *Divinarum institutionum* locis Senecam miris quibusdam in caelum laudibus effert. Nam quodam loco ita dicit: 'Si quis autem volet scire planius cur malos et iniustos Deus potentes, beatos, divites fieri sinat, sumat eum Senecae librum cui titulus est *Qua re bonis viris mala accidant*

which for that reason, as is well known, he entitled *On the Fortune of the Roman People and of Alexander.*[29]

Pliny, too, the most learned of men, speaking of Seneca in the fourteenth book of his *Natural History,* mentions him in honorable and praiseworthy terms. For he felt and explicitly acknowledged his singular and exceptional wisdom, which he calls "superabundant," coupling it with his knowledge and virtues.[30] Cornelius Tacitus, an old and famous historian, asserts in the twelfth book of his *Histories* that Agrippina, wife of Claudius and mother of Nero, pleaded with her husband, as we said above, to permit Seneca's return from his exile in Corsica and to grant him a praetorship; and she was moved to ask for this, Tacitus writes, by Seneca's fame as a scholar.[31] Suetonius, furthermore, in his book *On the Twelve Caesars,* attests that he was made the tutor of Nero, who at that time was a boy and was shortly to become emperor, because of the excellence of his learning.[32] Quintilian, who (as we said) was hostile to him as a scholarly rival, could not keep himself—conquered by the greatest power of all, the truth—from praising his learning to the skies, and so speaks of him somewhere, saying: "For I only wish they had equalled or at least had approached his level," and then recording that he had written orations, poems, epistles and dialogues and that he had possessed great knowledge.[33] 21

And so as not to embrace further pagan authorities, let us turn to wise and holy men. Lactantius, a very wise as well as an eloquent man, conspicuous for his upright and saintly life, praises Seneca to the skies in many passages of his *Divine Institutes.* In one place, for instance, he writes: "If anyone wants to know clearly why God makes bad and unjust men strong, happy and rich, let him take Seneca's books entitled *Why Providence Lets Bad Things Happen to Good People,* where he utters numerous ideas, not with the ignorance of the world, but in a wise and holy way." And elsewhere: "Seneca's maxim in his books of moral philosophy is true: 22

cum sit providentia, in quo ille multa, non plane imperitia saeculari, sed sapienter ac divinitus elocutus est.' Et alibi: 'Vera est,' inquit, 'illa Senecae sententia in libris moralis philosophiae dicentis: "Hic est ille homo honestus, non apice purpurave, non lictorum insignis ministerio."' Et alio loco verba haec ponit: 'Exhortationes suas Seneca mirabili sententia terminavit: "Magnum," inquit, "nescio quid maiusque quam cogitari potest numen est, cui vivendo operam damus. Huic nos approbemus. Nihil prodest inclusam esse conscientiam; patemus Deo." Quid verius dici potest ab eo, qui Deum nosset, quam dictum est ab homine verae religionis ignaro? Nam et maiestatem Dei expressit, maiorem esse dicendo quam ut eam cogitatio mentis humanae capere posset, et ipsum veritatis attigit fontem sentiendo vitam hominum supervacuam non esse, ut Epicurei volunt, sed Deo ab his operam vivendo dari, siquidem iuste ac pie vixerint. Potuit esse verus Dei cultor, si quis illi monstrasset aut contempsisset Zenonem aut magistrum suum Socionem, si verae sapientiae ducem nactus esset. "Huic nos," inquit, "approbemus;" caelestis prorsus oratio,' et quae sequuntur. Et paulo post, cum de quibusdam gentilium sacrificiis loqueretur, 'Quanto,' ait, 'melius et verius Seneca quam Plato: "Vultisne vos," inquit, "deum cogitare magnum et placidum et maiestate leni verendum, amicum et semper in proximo, non immolationibus et sanguine multo colendum (quae enim ex trucidatione immolantium voluptas est?), sed mente pura, bono honestoque proposito? Non templa illi congestis in altitudine saxis exstruenda sunt; in suo cuique consecrandum est pectore."'

23 Quid plura? Vir iste eloquentissimus et ob sanctitatem suam sincerus veritatis amator tantum Senecae suis allegationibus plerumque tribuit ut ipsum ceteris omnibus veteribus et claris philosophis praeferre voluerit. Hieronymus quoque, vir sanctissimus simul atque eruditissimus, usque adeo Senecam laudasse visus est ut in libro *De viris illustribus* ipsum in catalogo sanctorum ponere et collocare non dubitarit. Cuius verba haec sunt: 'L. Annaeus Se-

'What gives a man honor is not a crown or rich garments or the attendance of lictors.'"[34] In yet another passage he writes: "Seneca ended his exhortations with the following splendid maxim: 'There is a great deity, something greater than can be imagined, whom we serve by living. Let us commend ourselves to him. A hardened conscience is of no value; let us open ourselves to God.' Could a man who knows God have said anything truer than was said by this man who was ignorant of true religion? For he expressed the majesty of God by calling it something greater than human thought could grasp, and he touched the very font of truth by realizing that human life is not vain, as the Epicureans hold, but that men serve God by their living, provided they live justly and piously. He could have been a true worshipper of God if someone had shown him the way, and he would have despised Zeno and his own master, Sotio, if he had found a guide to true wisdom. 'Let us commend ourselves to him,' he says; a truly divine prayer," and so forth.[35] And a bit further on, when speaking of certain pagan sacrifices: "How much better and more truly Seneca put it than Plato when he said 'Would you imagine a God great and calm, awe-inspiring in his gentle majesty, amicable and always approachable, not to be worshipped with immolations or great spillings of blood (for what pleasure is there in slaughtering victims?) but with a pure mind, with good and honorable intentions? Temples in his honor are not to be built by piling up stones to great heights; they must be consecrated by each man in his own heart.'"[36]

In short, that most eloquent man, who owing to his sanctity 23
was a sincere lover of truth, reveals so much regard for Seneca in his citations from his works that he was willing to prefer him to all other famous ancient philosphers. Jerome, too, a most saintly and learned man, praised Seneca so much in his *Famous Men* that he did not hesitate to include him in his catalogue of saints. His words are as follows: "Lucius Annaeus Seneca of Cordova, pupil

neca cordubensis, Socionis stoici discipulus et patruus Lucani poetae, continentissimae vitae fuit. Quem non ponerem in catalogo sanctorum nisi me illae epistolae provocarent quae leguntur a pluribus, Pauli ad Senecam et Senecae ad Paulum. In quibus, cum esset Neronis magister et illius temporis potentissimus, optare se dicit eiusdem esse loci apud suos cuius sit Paulus apud Christianos.' Ex quibus quidem verbis dubitari non potest quin Hieronymus ipsum eruditissimum ac doctissimum virum fuisse consenserit, quando ipsum Paulum apostolum nova quaedam et obscura et praeter inveteratam omnium paene hominum opinionem praedicantem intellexisse ac percepisse dicit.

24 Augustinus etiam in sexto *De civitate Dei* libro Senecam ipsum summopere commendasse visus est, quandoquidem eum Varroni suo, viro doctissimo simul atque eloquentissimo, praetulisse deprehenditur, quem prae magnitudine scientiae suae satis laudari non posse putat. Nam cum inter cetera duo theologiae genera, secundum Varronis sententiam, apud veteres illos fuisse retulisset, poeticam scilicet et civilem, 'Hanc,' inquit, 'Varro libertatem non habuit; tantummodo poeticam theologiam reprehendere ausus est; civilem vero ne attingere quidem ausus est,' quod Seneca in libro contra superstitiones deorum gentilium acerrime ac vehementissime insectatus est. In quo quidem 'multo copiosius atque vehementius reprehendit ipse civilem istam et urbanam theologiam, quam Varro theatricam atque fabulosam,' et reliqua. Et paulo superius, Annaeum inquit Senecam 'nonnullis indiciis invenimus apostolorum nostrorum claruisse temporibus.' Quid? Paulus apostolus, ut ait quidam, 'vas electionis et magister gentium,' nonne in epistulis quas ad Senecam scripsit ipsum admirari et eius doctrinam divinam potius quam humanam venerari videtur?

25 Atque haec pauca ex multis Plutarchi, Plinii, Cornelii, Suetonii, Quintiliani, Lactantii insuper et Hieronymi, Augustini ac denique Pauli apostoli, tantorum ac tam excellentium virorum, ad A.

of Sotio the Stoic and uncle of the poet Lucan, was a man of the most temperate life. I would not have included him in the catalogue of saints had I not been encouraged by those widely-read letters exchanged between Paul and Seneca. In these letters, despite being Nero's teacher and a most powerful person at the time, he says he wishes he had the same position among his people that Paul had among the Christians."[37] From these words we can have no doubt that Jerome agreed he was a most learned and wise man, for he says that Seneca understood and saw that Paul the Apostle was preaching something new, difficult, and higher than the long-standing beliefs of nearly all mankind.

Augustine, too, in the sixth book of his *City of God* seems to have commended Seneca in the highest terms, seeing how he can be caught preferring him to his Varro, a most learned and eloquent man, whom he thinks beyond praise on account of his immense knowledge. Varro attests, for example, that there were two kinds of theology among the ancients: poetical and civic. "Varro," Augustine writes, "lacked complete liberty. He dared criticize only the poetic theology, and drew back from even mentioning the civic." But Seneca, on the contrary, in his book against superstitions concerning the pagan gods, attacked it in the sharpest and most vigorous way. There "he censured that civic and urban theology in greater detail and more forcefully than Varro had criticized the theatrical and mythical theology," and so on. And just before this he says that Annaeus Seneca, "as some evidence shows, flourished in the time of our apostles."[38] And did not Paul the Apostle, the "vessel of election and teacher of the gentiles," as someone calls him,[39] seem to admire Seneca in the letters that he wrote to him, and to venerate his teachings as divine rather than human?[40] 24

These few citations, drawn from a number of great and excellent men like Plutarch, Pliny, Tacitus, Suetonius, and Quintilian, as well as Lactantius, Jerome, Augustine and even Paul the Apostle, should suffice as a reply to Aulus Gellius. For if we were to 25

Gellii auctoritatem respondisse sufficiat. Nam si graves illas severasque memoratorum tam sanctorum ac tam clarorum hominum auctoritates cum A. Gellio grammatico unico et solo contulerimus, illum quam primum eis ipsis <non> concessurum nemo sanae mentis ne suspicari quidem poterit. Ad genus autem dicendi illud idem non iniuria respondere possem, quod ille in primo *De finibus* ad Epicurum respondisse dicitur. Sic enim inquit: 'Oratio me istius philosophi non offendit; nam et complectitur verbis quod vult et dicit plane quod intelligam; et tamen a philosopho, si afferat eloquentiam, non asperner, si non habeat, non admodum flagitem.' Sic ego ad illaudatam, ut ita dixerim, Senecae nostri eloquentiam non immerito respondere posse videbor. Etenim quamquam artis oratoriae praeceptis imbutus esset, ut diximus, philosophiae tamen munus prae se ferebat, ac se philosophum prae ceteris profitebatur. Unde si forte vel Ciceronis vel Lactantii eloquentiam, quos Latinorum omnium eloquentissimos fuisse constat, praeter singularem quandam eius doctrinam, miro dicendi lepore tamquam sale quodam conditam et aspersam attulisset, profecto dubitare non possumus quin multo magis laudandus esset; sin minus, non tamen propterea vituperandus quia eo caruisset quod ad eius professionem minime pertineret.

26 Sua insuper scripta accurate legentibus et singula quaeque paulo diligentius, ut decet, considerantibus et, ut ita dixerim, olfacientibus, et id quod voluit verbis expressisse et aperte ea quae senserit explicasse videbitur. Sed alio genere dicendi oratores, alio vero philosophi uti debent; quippe oratores ea quae dicunt cum illustribus verbis exornare tum quoque amplificare solent, philosophorum autem proprium et peculiare munus est sensa sua plane dilucideque enarrare. Ad Quintilianum illud etiam accedebat, quod cum ambo hispani essent doctrinaque excellerent, ita se invicem aemulabantur ut alter alteri detrahere conaretur. Praeterea hoc idem Platoni atque Varroni (ut de nobilioribus utriusque linguae auctoribus loquar), Homero et Virgilio, Thucydidi et Li-

compare the grave and severe authority of such holy and distinguished men with the single, isolated authority of the grammarian Aulus Gellius, no one in his right mind would even begin to think that the latter should not, with the utmost speed, give way before the former. As for his style, I can with perfect justice cite what was said about Epicurus in the first book of [Cicero's] *On Final Causes:* "With this philosopher's style I have no fault to find. He expresses his meaning adequately, and gives me a plain intelligible statement. Not that I despise eloquence in a philosopher if he has it to offer, but I should not greatly insist on it if he has not."[41] Thus could I see myself defending with some justice what I might call the "unappreciated eloquence" of our Seneca. After all, though imbued with the precepts of the oratorical art, as we have described, he dedicated his greatest efforts to philosophy and considered himself above all to be a philosopher. Hence if he had happened to possess, in addition to his remarkable knowledge, the spicy wit that salted the eloquence of Cicero and Lactantius, who are agreed to have been the most eloquent of all Latin writers, we can surely have no doubt that he would have deserved even more praise. Nevertheless, he is not to be criticized for lacking something that has little to do with his profession.

Besides, those who read his writings closely and carefully from 26
beginning to end, as is fitting, weighing them and, as it were, sniffing them out, can see that he expressed well in words what he wanted to say and that he explained his views with clarity. But the orator has one way of speaking, the philosopher must use another. Orators commonly amplify and embellish with fine words what they have to say, while the proper and particular task of philosophers is to set out their meaning in plain and lucid speech. As for Quintilian's remark, it may be added that both he and Seneca were Spaniards and excelled in learning, and being thus in rivalry with each other they each tried to detract from the other. Moreover, let us not forget that Plato and Varro (to speak of the nobler authors

vio, Demostheni et Ciceroni et, ne de sanctis hominibus taceam, Eusebio et Hieronymo ceterisque omnibus optimis ac probatissimis tam graecis quam latinis quarumcumque rerum scriptoribus evenisse non ignoramus, ut a quibusdam detractoribus suis indignissime simul atque iniquissime carperentur. Quod vitare nullo modo potuissent, ut de se ipso refert Cicero, nisi nihil omnino scribere voluissent. Quod nisi doctissimus eruditissimusque fuisset Seneca noster, Neroni puero iam adoptato a Claudio et ad imperium quoque orbis terrarum designato nequaquam praeceptor traderetur.

27 Atque haec idcirco interposui, non quia res ipsas approbatione indigere existimarem, sed ut potius A. Gellio grammatico, tam acerrimo ac tam temerario eius reprehensori, exinde satis abundeque responderetur. Fuit igitur, ut diximus, vir doctissimus, omnibus liberalibus artibus apprime eruditus, sed praecipue in philosophia claruit. Masculam namque et virilem Stoicorum sententiam ceteris aliorum philosophorum, velut muliebribus et enervatis opinionibus, praetulit. Cuius quidem sectae quasi magister et princeps omnium acerrimus habebatur.

28 Corpus eius deforme, imbecillum multisque morborum generibus obnoxium ac valetudinarium erat, quae omnia aequo animo tolerabat; modico insuper somnio utebatur, unde et varias villarum amoenitates assidue quaerebat et nonnullas peregrinatiunculas spatiandi gratia plerumque sumebat. Uxorem suam Paulinam, ex qua eum plures filios suscepisse diximus, ita unice diligebat ut ipse quodam loco supra humanum modum adamasse fateatur. Duos fratres habuit, Gallionem et Melam, quorum unus egregius declamator, alter Lucani poetae pater fuisse scribitur. Haec enim Eusebii, de germanis Senecae loquentis, verba sunt: 'Iunius Annaeus Gallio, frater Senecae, egregius declamator, propria se manu interfecit, Nerone in sua praesentia deferente.' Et de Mela ita dicit: 'L.

in the two languages), Homer and Vergil, Thucydides and Livy, Demosthenes and Cicero and, not to omit holy men, Eusebius, Jerome and all the other great and esteemed Greek and Roman writers on every subject, were all unworthily and unjustly attacked by certain detractors. As Cicero wrote concerning his own case, detractors are unavoidable, unless one wishes to write nothing at all.[42] And if Seneca had not been a extremely wise and erudite man, he would never have been chosen as tutor to the boy Nero when the latter had already been adopted by Claudius and marked out to be the emperor of the world.

I have inserted this discussion, not because I thought the sub- 27
ject itself required approval, but rather so that a full and complete reply be given to Aulus Gellius the grammarian, his sharpest and most reckless critic. Thus, as we have stated, Seneca was a very wise man, highly schooled in all the liberal arts, though he was most famous as a philosopher. He preferred the manly and virile beliefs of the Stoics to those of other philosophers, as though the beliefs of the latter were weak and womanish. Indeed, he was considered practically the most acute master and leader in that whole sect.

His body was ugly, weak and subject to many kinds of illnesses, 28
and he was a valetudinarian, suffering all his trials with a steady spirit. He slept little, so he regularly sought out the varied amenities of his villas, often taking short trips there to go walking. For his wife Paulina—who, as we said, bore him many children—he had so special a love that he himself confesses somewhere that he loved her above the usual measure of humankind.[43] He had two brothers, Gallio and Mela, of whom the former is known to have been an outstanding orator, while the latter was the father of the poet Lucan. These are Eusebius's words about Seneca's brothers: "Iunius Annaeus Gallio, Seneca's brother, was an exceptional public speaker who died by his own hand in the presence of Nero who had denounced him." And of Mela he says: "Lucius Annaeus

Annaeus Mela, Senecae frater et Gallionis, bona Lucani poetae filii sui a Nerone promeretur.' Et ne singula eius gesta complectar sed brevissime simul ac verissime dixerim, in omnibus totius vitae suae moribus, uno dumtaxat excepto, summopere a cunctis scriptoribus laudatus est; paupertatem enim pluribus verbis ab eo commendatam fuisse dicunt, cum divitias atque opes plus quam viro philosopho convenire videretur re, non nomine, complexus esset.

29 Illud vero quod Petrarcha noster sibi obicit in epistula quadam, quam ad eum apud inferos degentem misisse fingit, leve quiddam videri debet, ubi ipsi tamquam probrum quoddam ac viro philosopho minime conveniens obiecisse videtur: quod Neroni, in libris quos ad eum *De clementia* conscripsit, nimis adulatus esset. Quod ad singularem quandam hominis prudentiam meo quidem iudicio adscribendum est, ita apud imperatorem in regia se gerere ut paene solus, peregrinus et alienigena in urbe iam totius orbis dominatrice et regina, regnare videretur. Nam 'fuit illi viro,' ut scribit Cornelius Tacitus, 'ingenium amoenum et temporis eius auribus accommodatum.' Quippe in morte Claudii funebrem laudationem composuerat, qua Nero in funere uteretur, ubi defunctum imperatorem pluribus quam oportebat in caelum laudibus extulerat. Ipse enim Petrarcha pluribus librorum suorum locis Senecam tantis ac tam praecipuis in caelum laudibus extollit ut satis hominem laudare non posse credat. Nam et in epistula quadam ipsum 'incomparabilem,' ut eius verbis utar, 'morum praeceptorem' appellat et alibi, in libro quodam *Rerum memorandarum*, verba haec ponit: 'L. Annaeus Seneca, cordubensis originis sed romanae virtutis, hanc divinam memoriae ubertatem sibi usque in miraculum contigisse testatur,' et reliqua huiusmodi, variis laudibus et commendationibus refertissima, egregie admodum prosecutus est.

30 Ad divitias autem suas — in quibus inter ceteros a beato Augustino propterea redargutum fuisse constat, quod, licet paupertatem

Mela, brother to Seneca and Gallio, obtained from Nero the possessions of his son Lucan the poet."[44] And, lest we mention every single action of his life, I may say briefly but truly that the moral conduct of his entire life has been highly lauded by all writers, except in one particular: that he many times commended poverty, while he himself embraced riches and property more than seems appropriate for a philosopher.

This criticism, thrown up against him by Petrarca in the letter 29
he pretends to send him in Hades, should not be taken too seriously. Here he objects that it was a shameful thing and little in keeping with his character as a philosopher that Seneca flattered Nero so excessively in those books dedicated to him *On Clemency*.[45] In my opinion, however, it should be set down to the man's unusual prudence that he acted towards the emperor in his own palace in such a way that he alone appeared to reign — a foreign-born alien, in a city that was then the mistress and queen of the entire world. For, as Tacitus wrote, "That man possessed a genial wit, suitable to the fashion of the time."[46] To be sure, he did compose an oration upon the death of Claudius, used by Nero at the funeral ceremony, which extolls the dead emperor to the skies with more praise than was necessary. After all, Petrarca himself extolls Seneca to the skies in many passages in his books with such exceptional titles of praise that you would think he couldn't praise the man enough. In one letter, for instance, he calls him "an incomparable teacher of morals," and elsewhere, in *Things Worth Remembering*, he writes: "Lucius Annaeus Seneca, Cordovan by birth but Roman in virtue, is said to have attained that divinely rich kind of memory to a miraculous degree," etc., continuing on in this remarkable fashion with various titles of praise and commendation.[47]

As for his riches — for which St. Augustine (among others) 30
censured him, in that he was always extremely wealthy himself while praising poverty[48] — one may answer with some justice as

laudasset, semper tamen opulentissimus fuisset—illud non iniuria responderi potest: divitias omnium philosophorum consensu vel bona esse, ut Peripatetici, vel commoda, ut Stoici putaverunt. Unde cum nulla philosophorum sententia divitiae in malis recenseantur, illis affluentem vituperare non licet. Quod beatus Augustinus non fecisset, nisi sibi in laudanda paupertate nimius, ut arbitror, visus esset is qui ceterorum opulentissimus ac ditissimus fuisset. Sed quid pluribus opus est verbis? Ipsum namque continentissimae ac modestissimae vitae fuisse nemo negat, et quidam non ignobilis poeta palam et aperte his verbis expressit:

ore suo Seneca mores Romae monebat,
optimus sculptor morum mentisque colonus,

et quae sequuntur.

31 Cum itaque Seneca ob singulares et incredibiles virtutes suas ex cordubensi non solum romanus civis effectus, sed dignioribus etiam romanae civitatis magistratibus functus esset, ut diximus, et insuper magister Neronis et apud eum potentissimus haberetur et ad extremum opulentissimus ac ditissimus evaderet, latentem quorundam praepotentium hominum invidiam, solam regnorum labem ac perniciem (haec enim diutius latuisse videbatur), adversus se ipsum, splendoribus suis quasi dormientem, usque adeo excitavit ut invidorum et obtrectatorum hominum machinamentis nescio quibus postea ab imperatore necaretur. Sed ut res tota clarius appareat, paulo altius ob origine repetemus.

32 Afranium Burrum et Annaeum Senecam, multarum 'rerum experientia cognitos,' Neronem sibi prae ceteris delegisse ut eorum consiliis uteretur Cornelius Tacitus auctor est. 'Hi' enim 'rectores imperatoriae iuventutis erant ac diversis artibus ex aequo pollebant. Burrus namque militaribus curis et severitate morum, Seneca praeceptis eloquentiae et honesta comit<at>e' iuvabant. His igitur duobus singularissimis et clarissimis viris usque adeo credebat confidebatque ut, eorum exhortationibus monitus, a variis ho-

follows: by the universal consensus of philosophers, riches are either goods, as the Peripatetics hold, or things advantageous,[49] as the Stoics believe. Therefore, since in the judgement of no philosopher are riches to be included among evil things, they have no business criticizing a rich man. St. Augustine would not have done so, I think, if it had not seemed to him that this extremely wealthy and opulent man had gone to excess in his praise of poverty. But there is no need to discuss the matter further. No one denies that he led a most temperate and restrained style of life, as one noteworthy poet stated explicitly in these words:

> Seneca's lips gave warning to Rome about her behavior,
> that excellent sculptor of mores and cultivator of the mind,

and so forth.[50]

In recognition of his unique and incredible virtues, as we said, 31
the Cordovan was not only made a Roman citizen, but held the highest offices in the Roman state, served as tutor to Nero, was thought to have ascendancy over him and became extraordinarily rich and wealthy. All this aroused the latent envy (the scourge and plague of kingdoms) of some very important men. These envious and slanderous persons in due course schemed somehow against him—who had been resting on his laurels, as it were—and had Nero put him to death. But to clarify the whole matter, we need to trace it back to its beginnings.

"Given their experience of affairs," as Tacitus writes, Nero re- 32
solved that the counsel of Afranius Burrus and Annaeus Seneca was to be preferred to that of others. "Both guardians of the imperial youth, they exercised equal influence by different methods: Burrus, with his military teachings and strict discipline, Seneca, with his lessons in eloquence and his honorable companionship."[51] He trusted and relied upon these two exceptional and very famous men to the point that he would heed their urgings and refrain from committing various murders. Thus Tacitus: "The affair

minum caedibus abstinuerit. Cornelius enim sic inquit: 'Ibatur in caedes, nisi Afranius Burrus et Annaeus Seneca obviam euntes restitissent.' 'Legatis' quoque 'Armeniorum, causam gentis suae apud Neronem agentibus, ascendere suggestum imperatoris ac respondere parabat, nisi ceteris omnibus pavore defixis Seneca admonuisset ut venienti matri occurreret. Ita per hunc modum, specie pietatis, obviam itum dedecori' idem Cornelius tradit.

33 Sed cum Burrus postea, veneno pro antidoto ad faucium aegrotarum remedium dato, exinde periisset, eius mors Senecae potentiam multum admodum infregisse videbatur, quod Nero Tigellinum quendam (crebris Pompeiae Sabinae suasionibus monitus, quam ipse antea unice dilectam, post mortem Octaviae sororis et coniugis uxorem acceperat) eius loco substituerat. Haec mulier Senecae propterea infensa esse credebatur quia ipsum ab amoribus suis avocare et avellere voluisse cognoverat. Quamvis enim Seneca Pompeiam antea sibi infensam fuisse rescisset, violentam tamen Burri illius familiaris sui mortem atque memorati Tigellini inimici eius substitutionem postea conspicatus, non ulterius cunctandum ratus, exinde recedere statuit, ut per hunc modum, quando aliter fieri non posset, saluti suae consuleret.

34 Unde a Nerone summis precibus postulavit ut valetudini simul ac senectuti suae a publicis curis et occupationibus vacare liceret; quod ut facilius impetraret, omnibus bonis suis, quae maxima erant, cedere et se in otium et solitudinem conferre promittebat. Nero autem postulata sua palam et aperte sibi negasse dicitur, et ut ab eo omnem suspicionem amoveret, iureiurando adhibito pollicebatur ne sibi aliqua ex parte noceret. Et ut verbis suis maiorem atque indubitatam quandam et certam fidem adhiberet, 'se potius,' ut Suetonius ait, 'moriturum quam nociturum sibi' crebro iuraverat. Hac igitur imperatoria necessitate astrictus, Seneca libere, ut cupiebat, abire non potuit, sed pollicitis et iuramentis discipuli sui, licet imperatoris (nam intus et in cute eum, ut dicitur, cognoscebat), nequaquam confisus, excusatione adversae valitudinis simul

would have issued in murder, had not Afranius Burrus and Seneca intervened." The same Tacitus tells us, "When an Armenian deputation was pleading the national cause before Nero, she [Agrippina] was preparing to ascend the emperor's tribunal and reply to them, had not Seneca, while all the others stood aghast, admonished the sovereign to step down and meet his mother: a simulation of filial piety which averted a scandal."[52]

Later, however, after Burrus died by taking a poison given him 33
as medicine for a sore throat, his death seems to have damaged Seneca's ascendancy to the point where Nero replaced him by one Tigellinus, thus yielding to the frequent entreaties of Pompeia Sabina. Nero had formerly loved her above all others and eventually married her upon the death of Octavia, who was both his sister and his wife. This woman was believed to be hostile to Seneca because she understood that he wanted to wrest Nero away from the influence of her love. Although previously aware of her hostility, it was only after seeing the violent death of his friend Burrus and the latter's replacement by his own enemy Tigellinus that Seneca resolved to leave without further delay in order to save his own life, as no other way was possible.

Hence he addressed urgent pleas to Nero to let him abandon 34
his public duties and activities in view both of his age and the state of his health; and to obtain this the more easily, he promised to rid himself of all his possessions, which were extremely numerous, and retire to a life of leisure and solitude. But Nero is said to have denied the request in the frankest terms, and in order to allay suspicion swore an oath promising that the philosopher would not be harmed in any way. And to further enhance the credibility of his words, he swore up and down, as Suetonius says, "that he would rather die than harm him."[53] Bound by the emperor's will, Seneca could not depart freely, as he wanted; but having little trust in his disciple's promises and oaths, however imperial they might be (for he knew him inside out, as it were), he employed the excuse of ill

atque senectutis suae utebatur. Ac propterea non modo a regia, sed ab urbe etiam paulatim abstinebat, atque in dies magis magisque omnes civiles et publicas curas abiciebat ac per rura Campaniae dedita opera hinc inde vagabatur infectumque urbis aerem et naturae suae minime consentaneum accusabat.

35 Patefacta deinde post coniuratione Pisonis cuiusdam nobilissimi hominis, in qua multi cives romani cuiuscumque ordinis deprehensi occubuere, per hunc modum, quasi eius coniurationis conscius esset, Seneca crimine laesae maiestatis insimulabatur. Nam ab Antonio quodam Natali in memorata coniuratione forte deprehenso, cum eculeo torqueretur, confessionibus suis Senecam coniurationis conscium fuisse proditum est. Hic enim a Nerone in illa coniuratione deprehensus, cum ab eo interrogaretur quinam essent hi qui adversum maiestatem suam coniurassent, post horrenda et parata vincula primo Pisonem confessus est. Adiecit deinde Annaeum Senecam, sive quia amicus Pisonis fuisset sive potius ut per illam Senecae commemorationem Neronis gratiam iniret, quem Senecae iam pridem infensum fuisse intellexerat. In hac igitur coniuratione, praeter Pisonem et Antonium—quasi illius seditionis auctores et principes—multosque alios romanos cives capitali poena propterea damnatos, Lucanus etiam poeta, nepos Senecae, ob eandem causam morte damnatur.

36 Quippe ut Eusebii verbis utar, 'M. Annaeus cordubensis poeta, in pisoniana coniuratione deprehensus brachium ad secandas venas medico praebuit,' cuius bona L. Annaeus Mela, eius pater, iam fisco damnata, ut supra diximus, a Nerone promeretur. Per id tempus forte Seneca de Campania in Nomentanum, villam suam, reverterat, quae ab urbe per quattuor circiter milia passuum distabat. Nero igitur, ubi de eius reversione certior factus est, confestim Sillanum quendam, praetoriae cohortis praefectum, ad eum cum huiusmodi mandatis misit, quod videlicet sibi moriendum esset, quoniam per absentiam suam scrupulum suspicionis iniecerat quod pisonianae coniurationis conscius ac particeps fuisset; Piso-

health and old age. On this account he avoided little by little the palace and even the city, and each day cast aside more and more of his civic and and public concerns, and intentionally began to wander about the countryside of Campania, blaming the infected air of the city as little suited to his constitution.

Then, after the discovery of the conspiracy of Piso, a member 35
of the high nobility, in which many Roman citizens of every class were arrested and put to death, Seneca was charged with the crime of treason as an accessory before the fact. A certain Antonius Natalis who happened to have been arrested in the said conspiracy was tortured on the rack and confessed that Seneca had known about the plot. The man had been arrested by Nero in the course of the conspiracy and was interrogated by him as to who the conspirators against his majesty were; finally, after being threatened with the noose, he first produced the name of Piso. He then added that of Annaeus Seneca, either because he was a friend of Piso or else in order to ingratiate himself with Nero by naming Seneca, having previously learned of the emperor's enmity towards the philosopher. In this conspiracy, besides Piso and Antonius, who were the authors and leaders of the uprising, many other Roman citizens incurred the death penalty; among them was the poet Lucan, Seneca's nephew, who was sentenced to death for the same reason.

To quote Eusebius: "Marcus Annaeus [Lucan], the poet of 36
Cordova, having been arrested in the conspiracy of Piso, presented his arm to a doctor for his veins to be cut."[54] His father, Lucius Annaeus Mela, was awarded his property by Nero after it had been confiscated, as we said above. About that time, Seneca had left Campania to return to his villa near Nomentum, some four miles from Rome. Nero, having ascertained that Seneca had returned, immediately sent one Sillanus, prefect of the praetorian guard, to transmit to him the order that he must die, since his ab-

nis namque amicus et familiaris erat. Hanc deinde suspicionem Natalem illum, coniurationis eius auctorem, confessione sua confirmasse adiungebat. Sillanus itaque, ut imperatori pareret, domum eius ingressus, Senecam forte una cum Paulina paucisque amicis ad mensam sedentem ac cenantem offendit. Cui cum Neronis mandata exposuisset, eum ad voluntariae mortis coegit arbitrium. Unde Seneca, quando aliter fieri non poterat, Paulinam uxorem primo consolari adortus, paulo post forti ac virili animo mori non dubitavit.

37 Cum ergo per edictum Caesaris, cui refragari non poterat, sibi moriendum esset, per incisionem venarum, instar Lucani poetae nepotis sui, perire maluit. Sed cum eiusmodi mortis genus lentius ageret ac diutius quam cupiebat vitam protraheret, Statium Annaeum medicum, cognatum et familiarem suum, forte ibi assistentem, impensius rogavit ut, quando sibi quoquo modo moriendum esset, venenum exhibere non dubitaret. At medicus eius precibus obsecutus, ut petebat, venenum praebuit, ac per hunc modum in quodam calidae aquae stagno incisione venarum ac veneno hausto periit, ut Eusebius his verbis expressit: 'L. Annaeus Seneca cordubensis, praeceptor Neronis et patruus Lucani poetae, incisione venarum ac veneno hausto periit.'

38 Mortuus est autem Seneca biennio, ut inquit Hieronymus, 'ante quam Petrus et Paulum,' apostolorum principes, 'martyrio coronarentur,' iam prope senio confectus; ultra enim centum aetatis annos tempore mortis suae natus erat. Si enim, ut ipse in libro *Declamationum* palam et aperte testatur, 'illud ingenium cognoscere potuisset,' de Cicerone haud dubie sentiens, 'quod solum populus romanus par imperio suo habuit,' nisi 'bellorum civilium furore' impeditus esset, ipsum ultra centum aetatis annos tempore mortis suae natum fuisse manifestum est. Ab illo enim nefario scelestoque Octavii, Lepidi et Antonii triumviratu, quo Ciceronem necatum fuisse constat, usque ad undecimum Neronis annum, quo Senecam interiisse diximus, plus quam centum anni intercessere.

sence had created the suspicion that he had known about and participated in the conspiracy of his intimate friend Piso. He then added that the man Natalis, an instigator of the conspiracy, had confirmed this suspicion in his confession. Sillanus, in obedience to the emperor, went to Seneca's house and found him sitting at dinner with Paulina and a few friends. He then reported Nero's command by which he was required to take his own life. Seeing he had no choice, he first tried to comfort his wife Paulina, then did not hesitate to die with a courageous and manly spirit.

Since by the emperor's irrefragable edict he was required to die, 37
Seneca resolved to do so by cutting his veins, exactly like his nephew Lucan, the poet. But since this way of dying was slow to take effect and he had no wish to further protract his life, he insisted that his kinsman and intimate, the doctor Statius Annaeus, who happened to be sitting there, not hesitate to give him poison, as he would have to die in some way or other. The physician heeded his prayers and gave him poison as requested. And it was in this way, in a pool of warm water, that he died, having cut his veins open and drunk poison. In the words of Eusebius, "Lucius Annaeus Seneca, tutor to Nero and uncle of Lucan the poet, perished by cutting his veins and drinking poison."[55]

Jerome says that Seneca died two years "before Peter and Paul," 38
the princes of the apostles, "were crowned with martyrdom,"[56] having already entered extreme old age; at the time of his death, in fact, he was more than one hundred years old. For if, as he himself explicitly attests in his *Declamations,* he "could have known that genius which the Roman people valued equally with their empire" (by which he undoubtedly meant Cicero) "had the fury of civil war not prevented it," it is obvious that he was more than a hundred years old at the time of his death.[57] For from the time of that wicked and criminal triumvirate of Octavian, Lepidus and Antony, under which Cicero is known to have been killed, down to the

Octavianus namque solus, victo Antonio, ultra quadraginta annos imperium tenuit. Quibus quidem, si duodecimum triumviratus atque vigesimum tertium Tiberii ac quartum fere C. Caligulae, quattuor decimumque Claudii atque demum Neronis undecimum, qui invicem per mutuam successionem tantundem regnaverunt, annum adieceris, illud tempus simul connumeratum unum saeculum, ut diximus, vel circiter adaequasse vel potius excessisse videbitur.

39 Mortis suae causam fuisse dicunt quod in coniuratione illa pisoniana, ut supra breviter enarravimus, adversus Neronem inita deprehensus esset; sed nihil certi compertum est. Sunt enim qui odio et simultate Agrippinae insimulatum periisse dicant. Fuerunt etiam qui invidia praepotentium civium id sibi accidisse putaverunt, cum ad magnos et altissimos dignitatis gradus peregrinus atque alienigena et ignobilis ascendisset, ac romanos cives et nobiles insuper viros honoribus et gloria praecessisset. Nec defuerunt qui inhumanam Neronis crudelitatem et nimiam in omne genus hominum saevitiam accusarent. De quo, si quis forte se mirari diceret quod quisquam ab eo frustra et sine causa interfectus esset, ponat sibi ante oculos crudelia quaedam ac nefaria saevi et truculenti regis facinora, atque imprimis Britannicum veneno necatum recognoscat, matrem deinde mactatam recordetur, parricidio parentis et amitae necem adhibuisse meminerit, Octaviam insuper sororem eius simul atque coniugem interemptam animadvertat.

40 Et quando haec omnia pluraque alia huiusmodi scelesta et inhumana facinora ab eo ipso perpetrata fuisse iterum atque iterum consideraverit ac memoriae mandaverit, profecto mirari desinet si is — qui fratris ac matris, amitae, sororis atque denique coniugis interemptor fuerit — ut totam fabulam perageret praeceptorem suum, doctissimum simul ac sapientissimum virum, sine causa iniustissime interemerit. Cuius etiam opinionis, quia Seneca inno-

eleventh year of Nero's rule, when we said Seneca died, there passed more than one hundred years. Indeed, after the defeat of Antony, Octavian controlled the empire for over forty years. If you add to this period the twelve years of the triumvirate, the twenty-three years of Tiberius's reign, the nearly four years of Caligula, the fourteen of Claudius, and finally eleven years of Nero, the sum total of all these years, as we said, is around a century, or even greater.[58]

As we related briefly above, his death was said to have been a result of his having been implicated in the Pisonian conspiracy, but nothing was ever established with certainty. There are those who say he perished owing to the hatred and malice of Agrippina. And there were also those who thought this occurred through the envy of over-mighty citizens, when as a foreign-born alien and a commoner he rose to the highest dignities, taking precedence over Roman citizens and noblemen in honor and glory. Nor were there lacking persons who pointed to the bestial cruelty and exceeding ferocity of Nero against the whole human race. If anyone finds it hard to believe that Nero may have killed a man needlessly and without just cause, let him contemplate the cruel and nefarious crimes of this savage and bloodthirsty ruler; let him consider the murder of Britannicus by poison, let him remember the slaying of his mother, the parricide of his father, the killing of his aunt, and finally the assassination of Octavia, who was both his wife and his sister. 39

When one calls to mind and considers these and many similar heinous and bestial crimes perpetrated by Nero, one can surely no longer wonder that, after murdering his own brother and mother, his aunt and his sister-wife, this same man, as if to bring the whole play to a conclusion, killed his own tutor, an extremely learned and wise man, without any shred of justification whatsoever. Certain highly learned and exceptional men are thought to have been of this opinion, too: that Seneca died innocent and 40

cens et insons perierit, quidam eruditissimi atque singularissimi viri fuisse creduntur. Cornelius quippe Tacitus pluribus *Historiarum* suarum locis hoc idem sensisse videtur, quando nihil certi de coniuratione compertum fuisse scribit, praesertim cum Neronem usque adeo immanem fuisse dicat ut eius immanitas omnium hominum questus et querelas anteiret. Boethius etiam id ipsum sentiens in libro *De consolatione* verba haec ponit: 'Quod si nec Anaxagorae fugam nec Socratis venenum nec Zenonis tormenta (quoniam sunt peregrina) novisti, at Canios, at Senecas, at Soranos, quorum nec pervetusta nec incelebris memoria est, scire potuisti. Quos nihil aliud in cladem detraxit, nisi quod nostris' (id est philosophicis) 'moribus' (quoniam ibidem in illo consolatorio dialogo Philosophia loquens inducitur) 'instituti studiis improborum dissimillimi videbantur.'

41 Ad haec accedit communis quaedam scriptorum paene omnium opinio, qui de immani Neronis crudelitate loquentes inter saeva et inhumana regis eius multiplicia et varia facinora impiam praeceptoris sui necem connumerare non dubitant. Ceterum si Seneca noster memoratae coniurationis conscius fuisset idque propterea tacuisset, ut tanta ac tam singularis imperatoris immanitas exinde forte periret, praecipuis magnanimi viri virtutibus adscribendum — mea quidem sententia — putarem, tantumque abesset ut ex illa taciturnitate fortem et constantem hominem vituperarem, ut summis propterea laudibus dignum esse censerem. Corpus eius, quemadmodum supra diximus necati, sine ulla funeris solemnitate crematum ferunt.

42 Cum igitur de studiis, moribus atque progressibus vitae Senecae tui, vel potius nostri (nam eius memoriam, ob singulares et innumeras virtutes suas, summa caritate et veneratione toto animo et mente complector) haec pauca scripserimus, reliquum est ut quot Senecae fuerint breviter summatimque expediamus. Duos Senecas Cordubam genuisse, cum omnes hispanienses homines tum etiam Apollinaris Sidonius, non ignobilis scriptor, testes sunt.

guiltless. Certainly Cornelius Tacitus seems to believe this in many passages of his *Histories,* for instance when he writes that nothing certain had been established about the conspiracy and states that Nero was so inhuman that his cruelty had already gone far beyond the outcries and protests of all men.[59] Boethius agrees, and in his *Consolation of Philosophy* writes: "You may not happen to know of the flight of Anaxagoras, of the poison administered to Socrates and of Zeno's torture, since these are foreign events. Yet you must have heard what befell Canius, Seneca, and Soranus, the memory of which is neither ancient nor obscure. The sole reason why their lives ended in disaster is that they were imbued with our teachings" (that is, philosophical ones, since in this consolatory dialogue it is Philosophy who speaks) "and so became persons whose motivations appeared utterly unlike those of evil men."[60]

To this may be added the common opinion of almost all writers, who in speaking of Nero's bestial cruelty do not hesitate to include the impious murder of his tutor among the innumerable crimes of this king. Besides, if our Seneca *had* known about the conspiracy and kept quiet about it so as to abet the death of such an extraordinarily cruel emperor, I would put this down to the outstanding virtues of that noble-hearted man. Far from blaming that brave and steadfast man for his silence, I would esteem him worthy of the highest praise on that very account. His body was cremated without any funeral ceremony, as he died in the way we have described. 41

Now that we have written this short account of the studies, moral character and career of your Seneca — or rather our Seneca, for I love and venerate his memory with all my heart and mind in recognition of his unique and innumerable virtues — it remains for us briefly to clear up the issue of how many Senecas there have been. As all Spaniards bear witness, as well as the notable writer Sidonius Apollinaris,[61] Cordova gave birth to two Senecas, of 42

Quorum alter is fuit de quo haec ipsa perscripsimus, alter vero tragoediarum auctor fuisse creditur. Sed cum de tragoediis a quo Seneca compilatae fuerint communiter dubitari soleat, eius dubitationis rationes in medium adducere placuit, ut id quod verisimilius videretur clarius appareret.

43 Nobile et decantatum tragoediarum opus elegantibus carminibus scriptum atque ex pluribus graecis auctoribus a Seneca in latinum traductum fuisse constat. Sed a quo Seneca id factum fuerit, non iniuria dubitatur. Nam a nostro philosopho et quidem severissimo Stoico eiusmodi poema compositum fuisse absurdum videri aiunt ac naturae hominis minime consentaneum, quem severissimum philosophum atque Stoicorum omnium acerrimum extitisse manifestum et aliquod poema scripsisse incertum est. Sunt qui Senecam nostrum harum tragoediarum auctorem fuisse credant, forte ea de causa adducti, quia ipse poetis adulescentiae suae tempore apprime delectaretur, Cornelii insuper Taciti, Quintiliani quoque ac forsitan beati Augustini auctoritatibus moti. Horum alter in *Historiarum* suarum codicibus inter cetera sibi obiectum fuisse scribit quod carmina factitarit; alter vero ab eo poemata facta fuisse tradit. Augustinus autem quinto *De civitate Dei* libro ita inquit: 'Annaei Senecae, ni fallor, sunt hi versus:

Duc, summe pater altique dominator poli,
quocumque placuit; nulla parendi mora est.
Adsum impiger; fac nolle, comitabor gemens
malusque patiar facere quod licuit bono.
Ducunt volentem fata, nolentem trahunt,'

ex tragoediis haud dubie eiusmodi carmina sumens. Et paulo post, in sexto eiusdem operis libro, 'Annaeus,' inquit, 'Seneca in libro contra superstitiones,' et quae sequuntur, quasi eundem moralem

whom one is he of whom we have been writing, while the other is believed to have been an author of tragedies. But since it is often doubted which of the two Senecas wrote the tragedies, I would like to adduce the reasons for this doubt in the hope of showing what is more likely to be true.[62]

It is evident that there was an *oeuvre* consisting of noble and be- 43
witching tragedies written in elegant verse and translated by Seneca into Latin from the writings of a number of Greek authors. But *which* Seneca did this is rightly a matter for conjecture. For they say that it seems preposterous and out of character for our philosopher, strict Stoic that he was, to have composed this kind of poem—he who is obviously the strictest of philosophers and keenest of Stoics—and that it is uncertain whether he wrote any poems at all. There are some who believe that our Seneca was the author of these tragedies; such persons are perhaps influenced by the great delight he took in poetry as a youth, as well as by the authority of Cornelius Tacitus, Quintilian and perhaps St. Augustine too. The first of them wrote in his *Histories* that Seneca was criticized, among other things, for engaging in the writing of poetry; the next records that he did indeed write poems.[63] And Augustine says in the fifth book of his *City of God*, "If I am not mistaken, the following verses are by Annaeus Seneca:

Father Supreme, Thou ruler of lofty heaven
Lead me wherever is Thy pleasure; I shall give
prompt obedience, making no delay. Should I refuse,
Then with groans shall I accompany You,
Suffering in sin what I might have done in virtue.
Fates lead the willing soul, the unwilling one they drag."[64]

There is no doubt he took these verses from some tragedy. And a little later, in the sixth book of the same work, he writes: "Annaeus Seneca, in his book against superstitions," etc., as though he

et tragoediarum illarum auctorem fuisse senserit. Cui quidem opinioni et Petrarca noster in quadam eius epistula assentitur.

44 Quidam autem alii non ignobiles et eruditi viri hoc idem opus alteri Senecae attribuunt, forsan eam tragoediam quae inscribitur *Octavia* id ipsum attestari posse rati, in qua palam et aperte ab Agrippina matre mors Neronis praedicta ac praenuntiata est, cum post interfectionem Senecae subsecuta fuerit. Nam et memoratus Sidonius hoc ipsum his versibus palam et aperte confirmat:

Non quod Corduba praepotens alumnis
facundum ciet, hic putes legendum,
quorum unus colit hispidum Platona
incassumque suum monet Neronem;
orchestram quatit alter Euripidis,
pictum faucibus[3] Aeschylon secutus
aut plectris[4] solitus sonare Thespin,
qui post pulpita trita sub cothurno
ducebant olidae marem[5] capellae.

Et Boccacius et Coluccius, egregii ac novi paulo ante nostra tempora poetae, huius sententiae astipulatores sunt.

45 Ceterum nos hanc veterem et antiquam ac sane futilem controversiam multiplicibus causis et variis auctoritatibus hinc inde munitam esse animadvertentes, ambiguam et non solutam relinquere quam ancipitibus et incertis rationibus solvere maluimus, ac demum satis esse duximus frivola haec et inutilia grammaticis perquirenda dimittere, quam tempus, cuiuscumque suppellectilis pretiosissimum, in parvarum et minimarum rerum investigatione frustra conterere. Itaque haec, qualiacumque sint, grammaticis ac litterarum dumtaxat professoribus solvenda dimittimus, atque hoc eis leviuscularum controversiarum opus iniungimus, ut diligentius et accuratius hinc inde librentur qui puerilia haec et frivola usque

thought the moralist and the tragedian to be the same author.[65] Petrarca agrees with this view in one of his epistles.[66]

Certain other notable and erudite men ascribe this same *oeuvre* to another Seneca, perhaps believing that the tragedy *Octavia* is proof of this, since in it the death of Nero is clearly and publicly predicted and foreseen by his mother Agrippina, an event which came to pass after the death of Seneca. The aforementioned Sidonius explicitly confirms this in the following verses: 44

Nor must you expect to find here the eloquence
called forth by Cordova, great in her sons,
of whom one is devoted to shaggy Plato
and vainly admonishes his pupil Nero;
another treads the stage of Euripides
and follows painted Aeschylus with his jaws
or Thespis, wont to sing to the lyre,
who after treading the stage with their buskins
would bring on the mare of a stinking she-goat.[67]

Both Boccaccio and Coluccio, distinguished recent poets who flourished a little before our day, subscribe to this view as well.[68]

However, seeing that this old, ancient and rather futile controversy has been sustained with numerous arguments and various authorities from every angle, we have preferred to leave it ambiguous and unresolved, rather than providing solutions based on dubious and uncertain grounds. We believe it is much better in the end to leave it to the grammarians to investigate such frivolous and idle things rather than waste time, the most precious possession of all, by investigating minute and trivial matters in vain. So we leave it to the grammarians and mere professors of literature to resolve the issue in some fashion or other, adding this task to their foolish little controversies. Let the men who think these childish and frivolous investigations, which it is shameful even for boys to study, should be pursued into old age, weigh these matters with diligence 45

ad senectutem putant esse discenda quae ne pueris didicisse turpe erat. Sed ipsi inter se certant et adhuc sub iudice lis est et, ut arbitror, semper erit; et si optata fierent, nullo umquam tempore cessaturam etiam atque etiam cuperem, quandoquidem has et huiusmodi nugas omni quidem tempore, ceteris posthabitis, perscrutari consueverunt. Sed si forte quadam paulo graviori vel publica vel privata cura tenerentur, profecto ab huiusmodi tam parvarum et tam minimarum ac tam denique frivolarum rerum cogitationibus longe abhorrerent. Fuit praeter hos duos tertius Seneca, celebratus Hierosolymorum episcopus.

46 Si itaque, serenissime ac gloriosissime princeps, ut ad te tandem aliquando quasi longo quodam postliminio revertamur, haec omnia quae de his duobus singularissimis ac sapientissimis viris superius a nobis descripta sunt etiam atque etiam consideraveris, hanc nostram, ut arbitror, comparationem non imparem fuisse censebis. Nam utrumque primo corpore deformem, animo vero et mente formosum; utrumque deinde longaevum extitisse, utrumque etiam uxorem ac liberos habuisse, utrumque insuper civitatis suae magistratus gessisse et in ampla et gloriosa re publica variis temporibus floruisse. Utrumque praeterea sapientiae studiosissimum ac singularem suorum temporum philosophum, utrumque denique modestissimum et iustissimum virum atque ad extremum quorundam praepotentium hominum invidia et simultate iniquissime interemptum fuisse constat. Cum in paucis, vel in uno potius dissimiles extitisse viderentur. Nam alter pauperrimus, alter ditissimus fuit, quamquam uterque amplas sibi divitias atque opes, ut supra diximus, parare potuerit.

and accuracy from every angle. But still they dispute among themselves and the case is far from being solved (as I believe it always will be). And if wishes are granted, I would wish over and over that the controversy will never come to an end, since they have grown used to devoting all their time to examining trifles of this sort, putting everything else aside. But if perchance they were burdened with somewhat greater cares, either public or private, they would surely never give the least thought to such small, unimportant and ultimately frivolous matters. Besides these two Senecas there was a third one, a celebrated bishop of Jerusalem.

Finally, most serene and glorious Prince—to return to you as 46
though returning from exile—if you consider carefully all that I have written above about these two most remarkable and learned men, I believe you will not find the following comparison of ours unjust. First of all, both men were ugly in body, yet beautiful in soul and mind. Secondly, they both lived to a ripe age, both had a wife and children, both served in the government of their cities and flourished in wealthy, glorious states at different times. Furthermore, it is known that both were men most zealous for wisdom, the most extraordinary philosophers of their times; both were extremely temperate and just; and both eventually suffered utterly unjust deaths because of the envy and enmity of some extremely powerful men. They were alike in most respects, but in one way they were unlike. For one of them was extremely poor and the other extremely rich, although, as we said above, either one of them could have garnered for himself great riches and power.

Note on the Text and Translation

Giannozzo Manetti's *Vitae trium illustrium poetarum florentinorum* ("Lives of Three Illustrious Florentine Poets") survive in the following manuscripts:

El Escorial, Biblioteca del Monastero de San Lorenzo El Real, MS O.I.10
Florence, Biblioteca Laurenziana, MS Plut. LXIII, 30
Florence, Biblioteca Nazionale Centrale, MS Naz. II.VIII.40 (*olim* Magl. VII.1143)
—— MS Naz. II.VIII.47 (*olim* Magl. XI.133)
Livorno, Biblioteca Labronica, MS CXII.3.5
Oxford, Lincoln College, University of Oxford, MS Latin 111
Paris, Bibliothèque Nationale de France, MS Par. lat. 5828
Rome, Biblioteca Casanatense, MS 325 (*olim* B.IV.31)
Vatican City, Biblioteca Apostolica Vaticana, MS Barb. lat. 2323
—— MS Pal. lat. 1601
—— MS Pal. lat. 1602
—— MS Regin. lat. 768
—— MS Urb. lat. 448

The size of the textual tradition (to which should be added one witness from Cassino used by Granata in 1838 for his edition, now lost) proves that Manetti's biographies of the so-called "three crowns of Florence" enjoyed a certain success. A tentative *stemma codicum* has been proposed by Daniela Fedi in a *tesi di laurea* supervised by Prof. Giuliano Tanturli (Università degli Studi di Firenze, 1993). Fedi's work has provided a useful starting point for a new full recension. My survey of the whole textual tradition confirms Fedi's opinion that MSS. Pal. lat. 1601 and 1602 (respectively *V* and *V1* in the present edition) are the most reliable witnesses and

the closest to the archetype. Here is a brief description of these two manuscripts:

V Mbr., sec. XV med., fols. I + 135 + I. It contains the following works, all by Manetti: *Dialogus consolatorius, Vitae trium illustrium poetarum florentinorum,* and *Apologia Nunnii.* The first two texts are written in "littera antiqua," the third in humanist cursive by Agnolo Manetti (as already noted by Albinia C. de la Mare). See M. Vattasso, *Codici petrarcheschi della Biblioteca Vaticana* (Rome: Tipografia Poliglotta Vaticana, 1908), pp. 170–171, n.186; G. M. Cagni, "I codici Vaticani Palatino-Latini appartenuti alla Biblioteca di Giannozzo Manetti," *La Bibliofilia,* 62 (1960), p. 35, n. 120; G. Manetti, *Apologeticus,* ed. A. De Petris (Rome: Edizioni di storia e letteratura, 1983), pp. LIII–LV, and J. N. H. Lawrance, *Un episodio del proto-humanismo español: Tres opúsculos de Nuño de Guzmán y Giannozzo Manetti* (Salamanca: Biblioteca Española del Siglo XV, 1989), pp. 61–62, especially p. 61, note 2, for de la Mare's identification of Agnolo's hand for the text of the *Apologia Nunnii.*

V1 Mbr., sec. XV med., fols. II + 91 + I. Florentine miniatures. It contains the following works, both by Manetti: *Dialogus consolatorius* and *Vitae trium illustrium poetarum florentinorum.* See Vattasso, *Codici petrarcheschi,* p. 168, n. 187; Cagni, "I codici," p. 35, n. 119, and De Petris' edition of the *Dialogus consolatorius,* op. cit., pp. LVI–LVII.

Both *V* and *V1* belonged to Giannozzo's personal library. It is important to note that, while the author himself wrote annotations in the margin of *V,* his son Agnolo (and in one case Giannozzo himself) inserted corrections in the text of the *Vitae* in *V1*. As is well known, Agnolo often served as his father's main assistant in transcribing his works and preparing the dedication copies. It is thus highly probable that *V1* represents the final stage in the redac-

tion of the *Vitae*. As such, I have followed its version except for a handful of cases illustrated in the philological apparatus.

The author's archetype contained a few errors, which are pointed out in the notes. As is typical of humanist works circulating during the author's life, the present text of the *Vitae* is to be considered a work in progress. Like most humanists, Manetti had the habit of endlessly revising his works. Such a continuous polishing, however, inevitably caused new mistakes in the transcription of the text. Also, Manetti's redundant style at times led the author himself astray (not to mention the scribe), as is shown by the omission of prepositions and conjunctions in long, convoluted periods. I have pointed out such cases by adding the missing terms in angle brackets. Finally, as with most of his works, the astonishingly fast pace of Manetti's literary production accounts for a series of errors and oversights concerning the life and works of Dante, Petrarca, and Boccaccio. The most important inaccuracies of this kind are discussed in the notes to the text and the translation. For a more detailed discussion, see my forthcoming Italian translation of these biographies in *Testo a Fronte*, 29 (2003).

The textual tradition of the *Contra Iudaeos et Gentes* and the *De illustribus longaevis* is less complicated. The former work is preserved in a single manuscript (Vatican City, Biblioteca Apostolica Vaticana, Urb. lat. 154, produced by Vespasiano da Bisticci's workshop for Duke Federigo of Urbino). The latter survives in the following witnesses:

Bruxelles, Bibliothèque Royale Albert Ier, MS 11466–11478 (containing only Petrarch's life)

—— MS IV 957 (also limited to Petrarch's life)

Madrid, Biblioteca Particular de Francisco Zabalbury y Basabe, MS 11–139 (dedication copy for Ludovico de Guzmán prepared by Vespasiano da Bisticci's workshop, dated 1440)

Vatican City, Biblioteca Apostolica Vaticana, MS Barb. lat. 2299.
—— MS Pal. lat. 43
—— MS Pal. lat. 1603
—— MS Pal. lat. 1605
—— MS Urb. lat. 387

I have based my partial edition of Book VI on MS Pal. lat. 1605, collating it with MSS Barb. lat. 2299, Pal. lat. 1603, and the excerpts in Bibliothèque Royale MSS IV.957 and 11466–11478 (seen on microfilm at the Istituto Nazionale di Studi sul Rinascimento in Florence). A first sketch of the textual tradition of the *De illustribus longaevis* has been attempted by A. Campana, "Giannozzo Manetti, Ciriaco e l'Arco di Traiano ad Ancona," *Italia medioevale e umanistica,* 2 (1959), 483–504. According to Campana, MS Pal. lat. 1605 is to be considered the most reliable witness, from which Pal. lat. 1603 derives. Both Pal. lat. 1605 and 1603 belonged to Manetti, who inserted some corrections in the former's text of the *De illustribus longaevis*.

In the case of the *Vitae Socratis et Senecae,* I have simply reproduced (by permission) the text of Alfonso De Petris's excellent critical edition. A few minor changes have been indicated in the notes and some punctuation has been adjusted. We refer the reader to De Petris's volume for fuller information on the textual tradition and the sources. The notes to the *Life of Socrates* are indebted to those printed in the 1995 edition of Montuori's text (see Bibliography), as well as to those in De Petris's edition.

In editing all the texts in this volume capitalization and punctuation have been modernized, as well as Manetti's orthography. As regards proper names, the classical spelling is kept in the Latin text but the modern English or Italian forms are given in the translation (e.g. "Ancisa" in the Latin text and "Incisa" in the translation of Petrarca's life). Proper names in the index are keyed to the English text.

Finally, a few words on the translation. As noted above, Manetti's style is highly ornate and rich in figures of speech (especially dittologies) to the point of redundancy. As such, it is far distant from what would be considered good prose today. This, however, is true of much humanist literature, and particularly true of the epideictic genre to which most of Manetti's writings belong. First and foremost, Manetti was an orator, and this certainly shows in his style, regardless of the topic being discussed. Two other characteristics to be mentioned concern the vocabulary and the syntax. First, Manetti does not shrink from mixing purely classical and medieval Latin; sometimes rare classical expressions and terms are to be found in the same paragraph together with samples of scholastic terminology. Second, it is not uncommon in his prose to have concise and colloquial phrases immediately after long and complex periods composed in a highly elaborate language. In our English translations Rolf Bagemihl (who translated the lives of Socrates and Seneca) and I have tried, of course, to preserve these features. We are fully aware that the result may sometimes strike the reader as odd and, again, foreign to the literary taste now prevalent.

In translating some longer quotations from classical authors, we have sometimes simply adapted the versions found in the Loeb Classical Library.

S. U. B.

Notes to the Text

LIFE OF DANTE

1. nostrum propositum *V*
2. *om. V1*
3. cum ipse . . . vixerit *om. V*
4. Circuli *om. V1*
5. *scil.* menses *(possibly an authorial error)*
6. annis *V1*
7. *scil.* decenti. *All MSS read* decente *except Urb. lat. 387, a descendant of V.*
8. *Probably Manettian usage for the more usual* dicunt
9. loquendi *V*
10. *scil.* ipse . . . obnoxius iudicatus esset *(possibly an authorial error)*
11. *scil.* Herrici *(possibly an authorial error)*
12. poeta postea *V*
13. eiusmodi *V*

LIFE OF FRANCESCO PETRARCA

1. in quamdam parvam eius provinciae urbem *V*
2. peregregiis *V*
3. tam *added in V1 by Agnolo's hand*
4. *All the witnesses erroneously report these words in the nominative instead of reading* 'barbam candidiorem . . . comam senescentem . . . festinam . . . intempestivam canitiem.'
5. simul atque *V*
6. conarentur *V*
7. episcopum libros duos *V1*
8. *The entire manuscript tradition erroneously reads* 'cuiusve' *instead of* 'cuiusque.'

LIFE OF GIOVANNI BOCCACCIO

1. ex *om. V*
2. sola poetica *V*
3. avide *V*
4. adductus *V1*
5. eo *added in V1 in what seems to be Giannozzo's hand. The reading* ab eo adulescente *is*

also in MS Barb lat. 2323, a direct descendant of V1.

6. libros duos *V1*
7. *corrected to* infaustis *in V (impossible to identify the hand). Also in Villani, De origine, cit., p. 377, the text of this poem reads* infaustis.
8. igitur *V*
9. ob divinam tamen quamdam *V*
10. Petrarcha *added in V1 by Agnolo*

ON FAMOUS MEN OF GREAT AGE

1. *All MSS checked read erroneously* inepte.
2. *All MSS checked read erroneously* nomine.
3. *It is unlikely (though not to be altogether rejected) that Manetti meant to repeat* ad unguem *for rhetorical purposes. It is probably an erroneous repetition by a very early scribe and, as such, it should be eliminated.*

AGAINST THE JEWS AND THE GENTILES

1. *The MS erroneously reads* examussum *instead of* examussim, *an adverb Manetti uses often in describing works of art.*
2. *The MS erroneously reads* nostris *instead of either* nostri *or* cessit *(the latter variant being contained in the best MSS reporting this epitaph). Note also that here the MS reads* edita *instead of* hospita *(a better reading transmitted by the best MSS containing the epitaph on Dante's tomb). In our translation we have followed the most reliable version.*
3. *The MS erroneously reads* tetigit.
4. *The MS erroneously reads* sub.
5. Infaustis *is 'lectio facilior' for* infestis, *the reading preserved in the best MSS.*
6. *A word (possibly* acciderunt *or* evenerunt*) is missing.*
7. *The MS reports together in the text the following variants:* et ac.
8. *The MS erroneously reads* quem *instead of* quam.
9. Propterea *MS*
10. *See Cicero,* De orat. *2.14.61, where the text reads:* Poetas

omnino quasi alia quadam lingua locutos non conor attingere.

11. *In the MS the title of this Greek work is erroneously reported as* Vactromymachia.

LIFE OF SOCRATES

1. *Emendation added by the present editors*
2. lacedaemoniam *Val. Max.;* -monicam *MSS*
3. crassari *MSS; emended by the present editors to* grassari, *following Val. Max.*
4. Teombroto *or* Tembroto *MSS*

LIFE OF SENECA

1. disnia *MSS*
2. disnia *MSS*
3. faecibus *MSS*
4. plaustris *MSS*
5. patrem *MSS*

Notes to the Translation

LIFE OF DANTE

1. See, respectively, Boccaccio's *Trattatello*, ed. L. Sasso (Milan: Garzanti, 1995) and Bruni's *Le vite di Dante e del Petrarca*, ed. A. Lanza (Rome: Archivio Guido Izzi, 1987). For an English translation of Bruni's *Lives of Dante and Petrarch* see *Images of Quattrocento Florence: Selected Writings in Literature, History, and Art*, ed. and trans. S. U. Baldassarri and A. Saiber (New Haven: Yale University Press, 2000), pp. 125–138, and the bibliography on p. 334.

2. Filippo Villani, *De origine civitatis Florentie et eiusdem famosis civibus*, ed. G. Tanturli (Padua: Antenore, 1997).

3. Cicero, *Tusc.* 4.31 and *Fam.* 5.12.7.

4. See *Inf.* 15.61–78.

5. Leonardo Bruni, *History of the Florentine People*, ed. J. Hankins (Cambridge, Mass.: Harvard University Press, 2001), p. 95 (1.76). Bruni, Manetti's teacher, has no doubt that the culprit was Totila.

6. Charlemagne being derived from *Carolus Magnus*, Charles the Great. Bruni, by contrast, had sought to minimize the role of Charlemagne in the refoundation of Florence.

7. *Par.* 15, esp. vv. 136–138.

8. *Trattatello*, cit. p. 12 and pp. 76–83.

9. See, respectively, Valerius Maximus 1.7, ext. 7, and Petrarca, *Rer. mem.* 4.64 for Dionysus, and Donatus, *Vita Verg.* 3 (ed. C. Hardie) for Vergil. The dream of Dionysus' mother was particularly famous, as it was also reported in Cicero, *Tusc.* 2.31 and *De div.* 1.20.39.

10. This epistle, now lost, is mentioned by Bruni, *Le vite*, pp. 33–34. See also his *History*, pp. 340–341 (4.10).

11. A powerful, semi-secret patriotic society in late medieval Florence.

12. Private discussions of politics were considered seditious in medieval and Renaissance Florence. This whole section on Dante's exile is paraphrased from Bruni's *History*, p. 398 (4.55–56).

13. Charles of Valois, brother of the King of France.

14. The classicizing term used here by Manetti (*praetor urbanus* instead of the medieval Latin *potestas*, from the vernacular *podestà*) reveals his desire to underscore Florence's Roman origins.

15. Bruni, *History*, pp. 409–410 (4.66–67).

16. Manetti is probably thinking of Plautus, *Men.* 253 or *Capt.* 592. The whole invective against Florence is modeled on Boccaccio's *Trattatello*, cit., pp. 37–43. See also Cicero, *Pro Mil.* 93–98 and 104–105.

17. Cicero, *Pro Ar.* 8.19.

18. Plato, *Rep.* 10, 605B.

19. The most common source for this famous anecdote is Valerius Maximus 5.3.2b. Manetti certainly also read Petrarca's portrait of Scipio in the *Africa* and the *De viris illustribus*; see the edition by G. Martellotti (Florence: Sansoni, 1964), vol. I, 12.45–46.

20. The reading *annos* in all the MSS. is certainly a mistake either by the author or by a very early scribe. In the translation we have changed it into a much more likely *menses*.

21. This is one of the mistakes Manetti makes through following Boccaccio's *Trattatello*. Actually, Dante stayed with Bartolomeo della Scala, not with Alberto.

22. This epistle too, now lost, is mentioned by Bruni, *Le vite*, p. 43.

23. Cicero, *Fam.* 9.1.2.

24. Bruni, *History*, p. 461 (4.116).

25. It is the sixth epistle among the ones by Dante that have come down to us. See Bruni, *History*, p. 469 (4.123), whom Manetti follows here.

26. Terence, *Pho.* 1.68.

27. Now the Bargello.

28. This saying is attributed to Socrates in Diogenes Laertius 2.5.34 and Aulus Gellius 19.2.7. Manetti mentions it also in his *Vita Socratis*, §41.

29. The Latin is ambiguous and could also mean that Dante composed songs or lyrics for songs. On the question of Dante and music, see John Freccero, "Casella's Song, Purgatorio II.12," in idem, *Dante: The Poetics of Conversion* (Cambridge, Mass.: Harvard University Press, 1986), pp. 186–194, and the article on "Music" by Maria Ann Roglieri in *The Dante Encyclopedia,* ed. Richard Lansing (New York: Garland Publishing, 2000), pp. 631–634.

30. I.e., the *dolce stil novo.*

31. For this anecdote, see Cicero, *Tusc.* 4.37.80, and Manetti's *Vita Socratis,* §46.

32. Cicero, *De fin.* 3.2.7.

33. As also pointed out in the notes to the text, this is a controversial passage. All the witnesses read *Federici.* We consider it a mistake in the author's archetype for *Herrici* and have translated accordingly.

34. Manetti describes the procedure of a formal university debate on disputed questions: a theologian offers to defend some position, objections are raised, the theologian answers the objections seriatim, then offers his own solution to the problem.

35. Cicero, *Pro Archia* 11.26.

36. Cicero, *De orat.* 1.3.11–12.

37. In the margin of MS Barb. lat. 2323 (f. 55), a sixteenth-century hand has written the well-known formula: "S'io vo, chi sta? S'io sto, chi va?" ("If I go, who stays? If I stay, who goes?"). See Dante's biography in Villani, *De origine,* p. 352.

38. "I shall sing the uttermost kingdoms bordering the watery world."

39. "Io dico seguitando" (*Inf.* 8.1). For the discovery of the first seven cantos of the *Comedy,* see Boccaccio, *Trattatello,* cit., pp. 66–68.

40. In calculating the years Dante spent working on the *Comedy,* Manetti follows Villani, *De origine,* pp. 354 and 357. For Jacopo's dream and the discovery of the last cantos, see Boccaccio, *Trattatello,* cit., pp. 69–71.

41. As for the translation of Giovanni del Virgilio's first two verses in praise of Dante, it is worth quoting Curtius's warning: "But 'theologus'

means 'theologian' as little as 'dogma' means 'dogma' and 'philosophia' 'philosophy'—or, we might add, as 'commedia' in Dante means 'comedy.' We must understand Giovanni del Virgilio's verbal usages in the light of his historical situation." See E. R. Curtius, *European Literature and the Latin Middle Ages,* tr. W. R. Trask (Princeton: Princeton University Press, 1990), p. 215.

42. On the epitaphs composed for Dante's tomb, see the article by A. Campana in *Enciclopedia Dantesca* (Rome: Istituto della Enciclopedia Italiana, 1970), vol. II, pp. 710–713.

LIFE OF FRANCESCO PETRARCA

1. *Sen.* 8.1.

2. I.e., the notary in charge of registering the acts of Florentine legislative bodies.

3. Actually, Gherardo was Petrarca's younger brother. He was born in 1307.

4. Petrarca's teacher in Carpentras was Convenevole da Prato. On him, see the article by E. Pasquini in *Dizionario Biografico degli Italiani* (Rome: Istituto della Enciclopedia Italiana, 1983), vol. XXVIII, pp. 563–568.

5. *Fam.* 20.4.3–4. See also *Fam.* 4.16.14; *Rer. mem.* 3.99.3; *Sen.* 16.1 and the famous *Letter to Posterity,* pp. 4–5 of the English translation by Mark Musa (Oxford: Oxford University Press, 1985). A recent excellent edition of the Latin original of the *Epistula posteritati* is the one by G. Villani (Rome: Salerno, 1990), who also publishes *Sen.* 10.2 to Guido Sette, archbishop of Genoa, both with facing Italian translation.

6. *Sen.* 10.2.42.

7. I.e., Northern Italy above the Apennines.

8. Manetti's judgement about the causes of Roman cultural decline follows that of Bruni in his *History of Florence;* see especially 1.38–40 and 1.64–68 (and 1.68 for the figure of 204 years for the duration of the Lombard Kingdom).

9. For this laudatory comparison between Petrarca and the greatest glories of classical literature see C. Salutati, *Epistolario,* ed. F. Novati (Rome:

Istituto Storico Italiano, 1891), vol. I, ep. 3.15, pp. 180–182. The judgement was repeated ironically in Bruni's *Dialogi ad Petrum Paulum Histrum*, ed. S. U. Baldassarri (Florence: Olschki, 1994), p. 272; English version in G. Griffiths, J. Hankins, and D. Thompson, eds., *The Humanism of Leonardo Bruni* (Binghamton, N.Y.: Center for Medieval and Early Renaissance Studies, 1987), p. 83. The comparison with Homer and Vergil is something of an "inside joke," since no prose works, not even pseudonymous prose works, were ever attributed to these writers either in antiquity or the Middle Ages.

10. *Sen.* 13.3.

11. *Fam.* 11.5.

12. I.e., so that he could receive minor ecclesiastical benefices, which were often if not usually sinecures.

13. *Sen.* 17.2.

14. *Sen.* 16.7.

15. Jerome, *Epist.* 53.1.

16. Florentines of the later middle ages and Renaissance believed, incorrectly, that the ancient poet Claudian was of Florentine extraction.

17. Both Pythagoras and Plato were traditionally supposed to have travelled widely in the ancient world in search of wisdom. Manetti would have been familiar with these traditions from his reading of Cicero, Diogenes Laertius and Jerome's *De viris illustribus*, among other sources.

18. Vergil, *Aen.* 6.809; see Petrarca, *De viris illustribus* 2.1.

19. *Secret.*, book 3, in *Francesco Petrarca: Prose*, ed. G. Martellotti et al. (Milan: Ricciardi, 1955), p. 178.

20. *Sen.* 12.1 and 16.3; the allusion is to Juvenal 10.218.

21. *Fam.* 3.18.2–3.

22. *Sen.* 16.1.

23. *Fam.* 18.2.7–8.

24. See in particular the following epistles: *Letter to Posterity*, cit., p. 6 and *Fam.* 5.10.3; 8.3.9; 12.6.1; 12.8.1; 13.8.14; 17.5.7; 21.13.8.

25. *Sen.* 16.3.

26. Donato Albanzani, on whom see the article by G. Martellotti in *Dizionario*, cit., vol. I, pp. 611–613.

27. See Villani, *De origine*, p. 96.

28. See Salutati, *Epistolario*, ed. Novati, vol. I, ep. 3.18, p. 201, and ep. 3.25, pp. 223–228.

LIFE OF GIOVANNI BOCCACCIO

1. The close succession of the three crowns is already celebrated by Villani, *De origine*, ed. Tanturli, p. 374, where he adds Zenobi da Strada to Dante, Petrarca, and Boccaccio.

2. I.e., Zenobi da Strada; see *Against the Jews and the Gentiles*, below, cap. 15.

3. I.e., an "abacus school," a kind of elementary business school where boys were taught to keep accounts, calculate and write business correspondence.

4. Manetti's main source of information on Boccaccio's life is *Genealogiae*, 15.10.

5. I.e., the law of the church, as distinct from civil law, the law of the state.

6. *Genealogiae*, 15.10.8.

7. Andalò dal Negro. See ibid., 15.6.4.

8. Ibid., 15.6.9 and 15.7.5–6.

9. Manetti is referring to the revival of Greek studies in Florence following the teaching of Manuel Chrysoloras there in 1397–1399; see below. Compare this simile with Leonardo Bruni, *Dialogi ad Petrum Paulum Histrum*, ed. Baldassarri, 1.9–12, p. 235; English translation in Griffiths, Hankins and Thompson, *The Humanism of Leonardo Bruni*, p. 63.

10. Petrarca, *Fam.* 18.2.7–8.

11. *Genealogiae*, 15.7.6.

12. Boccaccio was criticized by some for his use of Greek in this work; see *Genealogiae*, 15.7.5.

13. Manetti is thinking of the papal curia in Rome and of Lombardy, where Chrysoloras taught members of the Visconti court.

14. The *De casibus* is actually dedicated to Mainardo Cavalcanti.

15. Juvenal, *Sat.* 3.164–165.

16. This poem by Salutati was already in Villani's life of Boccaccio; see Villani, *De origine*, ed. Tanturli, p. 339.

ON FAMOUS MEN OF GREAT AGE

1. I.e., the notary in charge of registering the acts of Florentine legislative bodies.

2. An inside joke. No prose works, even pseudonymous works, were ever attributed to Vergil in antiquity or the Middle Ages.

3. Respectively, the Camaldulensian monk Gerolamo da Uzzano and the doctor Antonio Baruffaldi.

4. Coluccio Salutati, *Epistolario*, ed. F. Novati (Rome: Istituto Storico Italiano per il Medio Evo, 1911), vol. III, epp. 11.17, pp. 392–396 (esp. pp. 393–395) and ep. 11.23, pp. 408–422 (esp. pp. 416–422).

5. The *honestum* or the morally correct is a technical term in Roman moral philosophy, used to translate the Greek *to kalon*; it is explicitly distinguished from the *utile* or the profitable. See Cicero, *Off.* 1.79, *Leg.* 1.41, *Fin.* 1.61.

6. See Poggio Bracciolini, *Oratio in funere Nicolai Nicoli civis florentini*, in idem, *Opera omnia*, ed. R. Fubini (Turin: Bottega d'Erasmo 1964), vol. I, p. 272. Similarities and differences between Poggio's oration and Manetti's sketch of Niccoli are noted by H. Baron, *The Crisis of the Early Italian Renaissance* (Princeton: Princeton University Press, 1966), pp. 322–323. The view that the study of Greek was primarily useful as an aid to Latin culture was commonplace among the students of Salutati and Chrysoloras; see J. Hankins, "Lo studio del greco in occidente fra medioevo ed età moderna," in *I Greci: Storia Cultura Arte Società*, vol. 3: *I Greci oltre la Grecia*, ed. Salvatore Settis (Turin: Einaudi, 2001), pp. 1252–53.

7. Bracciolini, *Oratio in funere Nicolai Nicoli*, p. 272.

8. Ibid., p. 273. Similarities can also be found, immediately before this passage, with Bracciolini's praise of Niccoli's knowledge of history.

9. Ibid., p. 274.

10. For this expression, see Cicero, *De fin.* 3.2.7, where it is attributed to Cato.

11. Diogenes Laertius 3.41–43.

12. Ibid., 5.12–16; see also Leonardo Bruni's *Life of Aristotle,* in *Leonardo Bruni: Opere letterarie e politiche,* ed. P. Viti (Turin: U.T.E.T., 1996), pp. 516–18.

13. Diogenes Laertius 5.51–57.

AGAINST THE JEWS AND THE GENTILES

1. Guido Cavalcanti (?1259–1300), Florentine love poet and a close friend of Dante.

2. The poem, *Donna me prega,* is a virtuoso *canzone* describing the physiological origins of amorous passion using Aristotelian terminology. The commentary by Dino del Garbo (1280–1327) was a major influence on Boccaccio. The commentary by Giles of Rome does not survive.

3. Brunetto Latini (?1220–1294) composed his encyclopedic work, *Li livres dou Trésor,* in the mid 1260s; it is the first scientific work in a vernacular language, and was later translated into Italian and Castilian.

4. See *Inf.* 15.118–120.

5. Pierre Bersuire (?1290–1362), whose *Dictionarium morale utriusque Testamenti* ["Moral Dictionary of Both Testaments"] Manetti mentions here, is today most famous for his *Ovidius moralizatus* ["Ovid Moralized"]; he is sometimes considered a representative of early French humanism.

6. On the epitaphs composed for Dante's tomb, see the article by A. Campana in *Enciclopedia Dantesca* (Rome: Istituto della Enciclopedia Italiana, 1970), vol. II, pp. 710–713.

7. I.e., theoretical and practical (an Aristotelian division).

8. See *On Famous Men of Great Age*, note 10.

9. This poem by Salutati was already in Villani's life of Boccaccio; see Villani, *De origine*, ed. Tanturli, p. 339.

10. Lombardo della Seta, a disciple of Petrarca's last years who edited some of his unfinished works. On his additions to the *De viris illustribus* see G. Billanovich, *Petrarca letterato: Lo scrittoio del Petrarca* (Rome: Storia e letteratura, 1947), p. 319.

11. See R. Weiss, "Petrarca e il mondo greco," in his *Medieval and Humanist Greek* (Padua: Antenore, 1977), pp. 166–192. Barlaam died of plague in 1348. On his writings see R. E. Sinkewicz, "The Solutions Addressed to George Lapithes by Barlaam the Calabrian and Their Philosophical Context," *Mediaeval Studies*, 43 (1981), pp. 151–201.

12. On Pilatus's works and teaching in Florence see A. Pertusi, *Leonzio Pilato fra Petrarca e Boccaccio* (Venice: Fondazione Giorgio Cini, 1979); N. G. Wilson, *From Byzantium to Italy: Greek Studies in the Italian Renaissance* (Baltimore: Johns Hopkins University Press, 1992), pp. 2–6.

13. *Giovanni Villani: Nuova cronica*, ed. G. Porta (Parma: Fondazione Pietro Bembo, 1990).

14. On Benvenuto da Imola (?after 1320–1387/88) see the brief biography by D. M. Schullian in *Catalogus Translationum et Commentariorum*, F. E. Cranz and P. O. Kristeller, eds. vol. V (Washington, D.C.: The Catholic University of America Press, 1984), p. 350. Manetti refers to his *Libellus Augustalis*, a compendium of Roman history from Julius Caesar to Wenceslas, and to his commentary on the *Divine Comedy*. Benvenuto also composed commentaries on Lucan, Vergil and Petrarca's *Bucolicum Carmen*.

15. Villani, *De origine*, ed. Tanturli, pp. 371–373.

16. Coluccio Salutati (1331–1406), Florentine humanist and chancellor. See R. G. Witt, *Hercules at the Crossroads: The Life, Work and Thought of Coluccio Salutati* (Durham, North Carolina: Duke University Press, 1983).

17. This long-neglected poem can now be read in *Coluccio Salutati. Index*, eds. C. Zinten, U. Ecker, and P. Riemer (Tübingen: Narr, 1992), pp. 253–260.

18. I.e., personal or familiar letters and state letters written on behalf of Florence in his capacity as chancellor.

19. The word "orator" in fifteenth-century Latin can also mean "ambassador." Loschi (1368–1441) was the chancellor of the Duke of Milan, a papal official, a diplomat and a friend of Salutati and Leonardo Bruni.

20. Matteo Villani (d. 1364) was the brother of Giovanni; see §17, above.

21. On Jacopo Angeli da Scarperia (c. 1360–1410/11), see Weiss, *Medieval and Humanist Greek*, pp. 255–277.

22. Domenico Bandini of Arezzo, a friend and younger contemporary of Salutati, was the author of an encyclopedic work, the *Fons rerum memorabilium*, which is still unpublished. On his life and work see A. T. Hankey, "The Successive Revisions and Surviving Codices of the *Fons Memorabilium Universi* of Domenico di Bandino," *Rinascimento*, 11 (1960), pp. 3–49.

23. The *Vita beati Nicolai Myrensis episcopi*. On Giustiniani (c. 1389–1446), see M. L. King, *Venetian Humanism in an Age of Patrician Dominance* (Princeton: Princeton University Press, 1986), pp. 383–385.

24. On Barbaro (1390–1454) see King, *Venetian Humanism*, pp. 323–325.

25. On Lippomano (c. 1390–after 1446) see King, *Venetian Humanism*, pp. 389–390.

26. Leonardo Bruni of Arezzo (1370–1444), Florentine humanist and chancellor, on whom see Griffiths, Hankins and Thompson, *The Humanism of Leonardo Bruni*.

27. Namely his orations *Pro Diopithe* and *Pro Ctesiphonte* (*De corona*) against Philip of Macedon.

28. On Traversari see C. L. Stinger, *Humanism and the Church Fathers: Ambrogio Traversari (1386–1439) and Christian Antiquity in the Italian Renaissance* (Albany, N.Y.: State University of New York Press, 1977).

29. Now better known as Carlo Marsuppini (1398–1453). On his life and works, especially his translations, see A. Rocco, *Carlo Marsuppini traduttore d'Omero: La prima traduzione umanistica in versi dell'Iliade (primo e nono libro)* (Padua: Il Poligrafo, 2000)

30. See Cicero, *De orat.* 2.14.61.

31. I.e., in his teaching.

32. Manetti is speaking of Polenton's *Scriptorum illustrium latinae linguae libri XVIII*. See the edition by B. L. Ullman (Rome: American Academy in Rome, 1928).

LIFE OF SOCRATES

1. Franco Sacchetti, grandson and namesake of the famous storyteller, served as Florentine ambassador in Naples in 1450, the same year that Manetti wrote this preface to his lives of Socrates and Seneca.

2. Petrarca attributes this statement to Plutarch in his *Familiares*, 24.5.3–4.

3. Jerome, *Ep. LIII ad Paulinum* (*Patrologiae cursus completus, series latina*, ed. J.-P. Migne [Paris: Migne, 1844–64], hereafter *PL*, 22.541).

4. Manetti, together with Noferi Parenti, served as Florentine ambassador at the marriage of Alfonso's son, Ferdinand I, with Isabella Chiaromonte in 1445. On that occasion he delivered the oration quoted below.

5. *Iannotii Manetti et Honofrii Parenti Florentinorum legatorum oratio ad Alfonsum clarissimum Aragonum Regem in nuptiali unici filii inclyti Calabriae Ducis celebritate*, in Felino Sandeo, *De regibus Siciliae et Apuliae* (Hannover, 1611), p. 174, lines 6–17. After his conquest of the Neapolitan kingdom in the summer of 1442, Alfonso repeatedly advertised the intention of launching a crusade against the Turks. In 1455 he would send Manetti himself as ambassador to Pope Callixtus III to gain papal support for this enterprise.

6. I.e., through Ferdinand's marraige to Isabella Chiaromonte.

7. Ibid., p. 174, lines 18–22.

8. Diogenes Laertius 2.18; Manetti's wording is indebted here as elsewhere to the Latin translation of this text by Ambrogio Traversari, completed in 1433.

9. Ibid., 2.44.

10. Justin, *Epitome Hist. Phil.* 2.6.1–5.

11. Valerius Maximus 3.4, ext. 1.

12. Diogenes Laertius 2.19.

13. I.e., one of the four sublunary elements. The impiety consisted in having maintained that "divine" and therefore immutable beings were composed of mutable and therefore imperfect substances.

14. Diogenes Laertius 2.19.

15. Cicero, *Tusc.* 5.4.10.

16. Diogenes Laertius 2.23.

17. Cicero, *Tusc.* 3.4.8; Seneca, *Ad Luc.* 71.7; Lactantius, *Inst.* 3.12.6, 3.21.1; Petrarca, *Rer. Mem.* 1, ext. 27.

18. Diogenes Laertius 2.21 and Augustine, *Civ. Dei* 8.3, respectively.

19. Diogenes Laertius 2.20; Xenophon, *Mem.* 1.2.17, 4.7.6; Cicero, *Acad.* 1.4.15; *Tusc.* 5.4.10; Valerius Maximus 3.4, ext. 1; Augustine, *Civ. Dei* 8.3.

20. Diogenes Laertius 2.23; Plato, *Symp.* 219E–221B.

21. Jerome, *Apol. adv. Ruf.* 2 (= *PL* 23.487); Eusebius, *Praep. evang.* 14.5 (= *PG* 21.1197).

22. Cicero, *Tusc.* 5.4.10–11.

23. Ibid., 3.4.7–8.

24. Cicero, *De off.* 3.3.11.

25. Cicero, *De fin.* 2.1.1.

26. Diogenes Laertius 2.22–23.

27. Cicero, *De orat.* 1.14.63; Diogenes Laertius 2.19; Xenophon, *Mem.* 1.2.31.

28. Apuleius, *De Plat.* 1.3.187.

29. Valerius Maximus 8.7, ext. 8.

30. Diogenes Laertius 2.32.

31. Cicero, *De sen.* 8.26.

32. Cicero, *Tusc.* 1.2.3–4.

33. Valerius Maximus 8.8, ext. 1.

34. Diogenes Laertius 2.45.

35. Ibid., 2.32; Plato, *Ap.* 21C–22E, 29B; Cicero, *Acad.* 1.4.16, 1.12.44, 2.23.74.

36. Diogenes Laertius 2.20–21; Cicero, *De orat.* 3.19.72; idem, *Brutus* 8.32.

37. Cicero, *Tusc.* 1.42.100.

38. Valerius Maximus 3.4, ext. 1

39. Diogenes Laertius 2.38.

40. Plato, *Ap.* 23B.

41. Augustine, *Conf.* 3.4.7.

42. Diogenes Laertius 2.25.

43. Boccaccio, *Espos. sopra la Commedia, Inf.* 4.267.

44. Cicero, *De off.* 1.41.148.

45. Aulus Gellius 7.10.5.

46. Diogenes Laertius 2.27.

47. Ibid., 2.34; Seneca, *De beneficiis* 1.8.1

48. Cicero, *Tusc.* 3.32.77.

49. Diogenes Laertius 2.47.

50. Cicero, *Tusc.* 4.3.5–6.

51. Cicero, *De orat.* 1.10. 42.

52. The Epicureans.

53. Cicero, *De orat.*, 3.16.60–62.

54. Ibid., 3.19.69.

55. Cicero, *Tusc.*, 3.16.60.

56. Aristotle, *Soph. elenc.* 183B, 6–8.

57. Cicero, *Tusc.* 1.4.7–8.

58. Aulus Gellius 2.1.2.

59. Arcesilaus of Pitane (316/5–242/1 BC), scholarch of the Academy. For his critique of Socrates see Cicero, *Acad.* 1.16.4–45, *De fin.* 2.1–2, Diogenes Laertius 6.28–45.

60. Cicero, *Off.* 1.30.108; *De orat.* 2.68.270.

61. Aristotle, *Eth. Nic.* 4.13, 1127B.

62. Cicero, *Acad.* 2.5.15.

63. Cicero, *De orat.* 3.16.59–60.

64. Diogenes Laertius 2.22.

65. The phrase is from Valerius Maximus 7.2, ext 1a.

66. Jerome, *Adv. Jovin.* 1 (= *PL* 23.278–279).

67. Diogenes Laertius 2.26.

68. Jerome, *Adv. Jovin.* 1; Aulus Gellius 1.17–1–3.

69. Diogenes Laertius 2.36.

70. Ibid., 2.36–37.

71. Ibid.

72. Aulus Gellius, *Noct. Att* 1.7.1–3 and Diogenes Laertius 2.37.

73. Diogenes Laertius 2.29.

74. Ibid., 2.21.

75. Seneca, *De ira* 3.11.2.

76. Diogenes Laertius 2.24.

77. Manetti refers to the oligarchy of the Thirty, which ruled Athens in 404/3 BC.

78. Diogenes Laertius 2.24.

79. The last great battle of the Peloponnesian War, in 406 BC.

80. Socrates had been chosen by lot to be President of the Assembly, the sovereign body of the Athenian democracy, in which capacity he had refused to put this illegal motion to a vote.

81. Valerius Maximus 3.8, ext. 3.

82. Plato's *Gorg.* 469B.

83. Diogenes Laertius 2.25. The verse translation follows that of R. D. Hicks in the Loeb Classical Library.

84. Cicero, *Tusc.* 4.10.24.

85. Ibid., 5.32.93; Diogenes Laertius 2.25.

86. Cicero, *Tusc.* 5.12.34–35, based on Plato, *Gorg.* 470D–E.

87. Aulus Gellius, *Noct. Att.* 2.1.4–5.

88. Diogenes Laertius 2.27.

89. Cicero, *De fin.* 2.28.90.

90. Seneca, *De const. sap.* 15.3.

91. Cicero, *Tusc.* 3.15.31.

92. Ibid. 5.34.97.

93. Diogenes Laertius 2.22.

94. Quintilian, *Inst. orat.* 1.11.17.

95. Aulus Gellius, *Noct. Att.* 2.1.2.

96. See above, §18.

97. Cicero, *Tusc.* 3.23.56.

98. Diogenes Laertius 2.28.

99. Ibid., 2.27.

100. Ibid., 2.29; Plato, *Ap.* 30A–31D; Xenophon, *Mem.* 1.1.3.4, 4.8.1.11; Xenophon, *Ap.* 4, 5, 8, 13; Cicero, *De divin.* 1.54.122.

101. Augustine, *Civ. Dei* 9.2 et passim. Manetti is implicitly rejecting Augustine's position on demons.

102. Cicero, *De fato* 5.10 and *Tusc.* 4.37.80. This anecdote is also used in the *Vita Dantis*, §43.

103. Plato, *Symp.* 216E–219E.

104. Diogenes Laertius 2.45.

105. Augustine, *De civ. Dei* 8.14 and Plato, *Ap.* 31D.

106. Apuleius, *De deo Socr.* 17.157.

107. Here Manetti seems to have misunderstood Apuleius, *De deo Socr.* 17.158, mistaking Nestor of Pylos for Meges, son of Phyleus, a minor figure of the *Iliad*. For the Homeric episode referred to by Apuleius, see *Iliad*, 10.72 ff.

108. Apuleius, *De deo Socr.* 18.159–161.

109. Plato, *Ap.* 31D; Apuleius, *De deo Socr.* 20.166.

110. *Iliad* 1.188.

111. Plato, *Ap.* 29D, 30A, 40A; Xenophon, *Ap.* 32.

112. Diogenes Laertius 2.38.

113. Ibid., 2.39.

114. Ibid., 2.40; Plato, *Ap.* 19C, 24B, 25D; Xenophon, *Ap.* 10; Quintilian, *Inst.* 4.4.5.

115. Valerius Maximus 6.4, ext. 2.

116. Ibid., 6.4, ext. 3.

117. Cicero, *De orat.* 1.54.231–233.

118. Cicero, *Tusc.* 1.29.71.

119. Diogenes Laertius 2.41.

120. Ibid., 2.20, 2.42.

121. Plato, *Phd.* 58A–B.

122. Ibid. Some of the wording comes from the argument to Leonardo Bruni's Latin translation of the *Crito,* in *Il Critone latino di Leonardo Bruni e di Rinuccio Aretino,* ed. E. Berti and A. Carosini (Florence: Olschki, 1983), p. 205, which is also based on the *Phaedo.*

123. Plato, *Crito,* passim.

124. Cicero, *Tusc.* 1.41.97–98, based on Plato, *Ap.* 40C.

125. I.e., he preferred to die rather than make his previous life meaningless by betraying his principles.

126. Cicero, *Tusc.* 1.34.84.

127. Diogenes Laertius 2.42.

128. Cicero, *Tusc.* 1.43.103. See also Plato, *Phd.* 115D–E and *Crito* 45C–D.

129. Diogenes Laertius 2.43.

130. Ibid., 2.47. Manetti, misled by Traversari's translation, misreads Diogenes' description of Socrates Historicus, whom Diogenes in fact describes as the author of a geographical work on Argos.

LIFE OF SENECA

1. Seneca, *De ben.* 4.8.3.

2. Ibid. 4.8.3.

3. Seneca Rhetor, *Controv.* I, Praef. 6–7. In Manetti's time Lucius Annaeus Seneca, the moral philosopher and tragedian, had not yet been distinguished from his father, Lucius Annaeus Seneca the Rhetorician; hence Manetti cites the latter's works as evidence for the former's life. Since the time of Petrarca, however, humanists like Coluccio Salutati, Lorenzo Valla and Petrarca himself had explored the separate issue of whether Seneca the moral philosopher should be distinguished from Seneca the tragedian; see below, §42.

4. Suetonius, *Cal.* 53.2; Petrarca, *Rer. mem.* 1.18.3.

5. Suetonius, *Cal.* 34.2.

6. Tacitus, *Ann.* 12.8.2.

7. Suetonius, *Nero* 7.1. For Petrarca, see *Rer. mem.* 4.52.1–2.

8. Suetonius, *Nero* 5.2, 7.1.

9. *Dig.* 36.1. Manetti infers from Seneca's consulship that he must have received the prerequisite honors of a quaestorship and a praetorship (the latter office being also attested by Tacitus in a passage previously cited).

10. These declamations are now attributed to his father, Lucius Annaeus Seneca the Rhetorician (d. 37/41 CE).

11. Seneca, *Ad Luc.* 106.1–2.

12. Seneca Rhetor, *Controv.* I, Praef. 2.

13. Petrarca, *Sen.* 2.4. In fact, none of the four works just named are now ascribed to Seneca.

14. Neither work is now attributed to Seneca.

15. Now attributed to Seneca Rhetor.

16. Boccaccio, *Espos. sopra la Commedia, Inf.* 4.338. The work is now known as the *Apocolocyntosis* or "The Pumpkinification of Claudius."

17. Lactantius, *Div. inst.* 1.5.26.

18. Quintilian, *Inst. orat.* 10.1.128 and Jerome, *Adv. Jovin.* 2 (= *PL*, 23.280).

19. There are in fact several epigrams attributed to Seneca in the *Anthologia Latina*.

20. Juvenal 10.16.

21. Tacitus, *Ann.* 14.52.2.

22. Seneca, *Ad Luc.* 104.1–3.

23. Jerome, *Adv. Jovin.* 2 (= *PL*, 23.281).

24. Seneca, *Ad Luc.* 54.2.

25. For these quotations, see Aulus Gellius, *Noct. Att.* 13.2, 1–2 and 11–12.

26. Quintilian, *Inst. orat.* 8.5.18; 9.2.42 and 9.2.98.

27. Quintilian, *Inst. orat.* 10.1.125 and 10.1.128–129.

28. It is Petrarca who attributes this statement to Plutarch; see Petrarca, *Fam.* 24.5.3–4.

29. Ibid., 24.5.3–4.

30. Pliny the Elder, *Nat. hist.* 14.4.51.

31. See Tacitus, *Ann.* 12.7.2; 12.8.2.

32. Suetonius, *Nero* 7.1.

33. Quintilian, *Inst. orat.* 10.1.127–128.

34. Lactantius, *Div. inst.* 6.22.11 and 6.17.28, respectively.

35. Lactantius, *Div. inst.* 6.25.1–2.

36. Ibid., 6.25.3.

37. Jerome, *De vir. ill.* 12 (= *PL*, 23.629–630).

38. Augustine, *Civ. Dei* 6.5–10.

39. Acts 9:15.

40. Manetti, like most of his contemporaries, believed the correspondence between St. Paul and Seneca to be genuine. On this, see De Petris's introduction to his edition, pp. 90 and 98–99.

41. Cicero, *De fin.* 1.5.15.

42. Cicero, *Tusc.* 2.1.3.

43. Seneca, *Ad Luc.* 104.1–3 and 5.

44. Jerome, *Interp. Chron. Eus.* (=*PL*, 27.587–590).

45. Petrarca, *Fam.* 24.5.18–19.

46. Tacitus, *Ann.* 13.3.1–2.

47. Petrarca, *Fam.* 24.5.5 and *Rer. mem.* 2, ext. 6.1–3, respectively.

48. Augustine, *Civ. Dei* 6.10.1–3.

49. "Things advantageous" *(commoda)* is a technical term in Stoic philosophy; only the honorable *(honestum)* is truly good, but there are other "things advantageous" (like wealth) which have no absolute moral value, although it is rational to prefer them to "things disadvantageous" *(incommoda)*.

50. Alanus de Insulis, *Anticlaudianus* 1.135–136 (= *PL*, 210.491).

51. Tacitus, *Ann.* 13.2.1.

52. Ibid., 13.5.2.

53. Suetonius, *Nero* 35.5.

54. Jerome, *Interp. Chron. Eus.* (= *PL*, 27.586).

55. Ibid. (= *PL*, 27.587–588).

56. Jerome, *De vir. ill.* 12 (= *PL*, 23.629–630).

57. Seneca Rhetor, *Controv.* I, Praef. 11.

58. Oddly, the one-time merchant Manetti stops short of concluding that if Seneca was an adult during Cicero's lifetime he in fact would have been over 120 years old at his death.

59. See Tacitus, *Ann.* 14.65.2; 14.45.3; 15.56.2 and 15.60.2.

60. Boethius, *Philos. Cons.* 1.3.9–10.

61. Sidonius Apollinaris, *Carm.* 23 *(Ad Consentium)* vv. 162–168.

62. See note 3. On the question of the two Senecas in the early Renaissance, see G. Martellotti, "La questione dei due Seneca da Petrarca a Benvenuto," *Italia medioevale e umanistica* 15 (1972), pp. 149–169, and (for

Valla) R. Sabbadini, *Storia e critica di testi latini* (Padua: Antenore, 1971), pp. 295–298.

63. See Tacitus, *Ann.* 14.52.3 and Quintilian, *Inst. orat.* 10.1.128, respectively.

64. Augustine, *Civ. Dei* 5.8.

65. Ibid. 6.10.

66. See Petrarca, *Fam.* 4.16.9.

67. Sidonius Apollinaris, *Carm.* 9 (*Ad Felicem*) vv. 230–238.

68. See Boccaccio, *Esp. sopra la Commedia, Inf.* 4.333 and Coluccio Salutati, *Epist.* I, ed. F. Novati (Rome: Istituto Storico Italiano per il Medio Evo, 1891), pp. 150–155.

Bibliography

EDITIONS OF LATIN TEXTS AND TRANSLATIONS

Lives of Dante, Petrarch, and Boccaccio

Specimen historiae litterariae florentinae saeculi decimiterti ac decimiquarti sive vitae Dantis, Petrarchae et Boccacci a celebri Jannotio Manetto saeculo XV scriptae, ed. Lorenzo Mehus. Florence: Giovannelli, 1746. Mehus's edition is based on Florence, Biblioteca Medicea Laurenziana, MS. Plut. LXIII, 30.

Un antico manoscritto latino che contiene le vite di Dante, del Petrarca e del Boccaccio, ed. Mauro Granata. Messina: Capra, 1838. Edition based on a manuscript from Cassino now lost.

Philippi Villani 'Liber de origine civitatis Florentiae famosis civibus,' ed. Gustavo C. Galletti. Florence: Mazzoni, 1847. Pp. 58–93 reproduce Mehus's edition.

Le vite di Dante, Petrarca e Boccaccio scritte fino al secolo decimosesto, ed. Angelo Solerti. Milano: Vallardi, 1904. Pp. 108–151, 303–319, and 680–693 contain Granata's edition and an Italian translation. Solerti also puts in the apparatus variants from Florence, Biblioteca Medicea Laurenziana, MS. Plut. LXIII, 30 and Florence, Biblioteca Nazionale Centrale, MS Naz. II.VIII.47.

Le vite di Dante scritte da Giovanni e Filippo Villani, da Giovanni Boccaccio, Leonardo Aretino e Giannozzo Manetti, ora novamente pubblicate, con introduzione e con note, ed. Giuseppe L. Passerini. Florence: Sansoni, 1917. Pp. 235–278 contain Solerti's edition of the *Vita Dantis*.

Lives of Socrates and Seneca

For editions of the *Vitae Socratis et Senecae* prior to 1979 see Alfonso De Petris's introduction to his critical edition of these texts (Florence: Olschki, 1979) and the appendix on pp. 217–221, commenting on Montuori's 1974 edition of the *Vita Socratis* (see below).

Iannotius Manetti: Vita Socratis, ed. Mario Montuori. Biblioteca di "De homine," 6. Florence: Sansoni, 1974.

"La *Vita Socratis* di Giannozzo Manetti," Latin text edited by Mario Montuori. In *Socrate, un problema storico*, pp. 235–273. Naples: Società editrice napoletana, 1984. Reproduces Montuori's 1974 edition.

Giannozzo Manetti: Vita di Socrate, ed. Mario Montuori. Palermo: Sellerio, 1995. Latin text with a facing Italian translation by Michele Bandini. The Latin text is that of Montuori's 1974 edition "con vari ritocchi."

On Famous Men of Great Age

Hans Baron, *The Crisis of the Early Italian Renaissance: Civic Humanism and Republican Liberty in an Age of Classicism and Tyranny* (Princeton: Princeton University Press, 1955). Vol. I, pp. 289–290, contains a partial English translation of Niccoli's life; for the original Latin text of this excerpt (taken from Vatican City, Biblioteca Apostolica Vaticana, MSS. Urb. lat. 387 and Pal. lat. 1605) see vol. II, pp. 571–572.

On pp. 210–216 of Giannozzo Manetti, *Vita Socratis et Senecae*, cited above, De Petris excerpts the lives of Socrates and Seneca from Vatican City, Biblioteca Apostolica Vaticana, MS. Pal. lat. 1605.

Ambrogio Traversari, *Latinae Epistolae*, ed. Lorenzo Mehus. Florence: Ex Typographio Caesareo, 1759 (anastatic reprint, Bologna: Forni, 1968). Vol. I, pp. LXXVI–LXXVIII, contains the life of Niccoli based on Vatican City, Biblioteca Apostolica Vaticana, MS. Urb. lat. 387.

Against the Jews and the Gentiles

Hans Baron, *The Crisis* (1955), vol. I, p. 289, contains a partial English translation of the sketch of Roberto de' Rossi. For the Latin original see vol. II, p. 570.

Ferdinand-Marie Delorme, "Vie de S. François par l'humaniste florentin Giannozzo Manetti," *Archivum Franciscanum Historicum*, 31.1–2 (1938), pp. 210–218. On pp. 213–218 Delorme excerpts the life of St. Francis.

Dionisio Pacetti, "Breve vita inedita di S. Bernardino da Siena scritta da Giannozzo Manetti," *Bollettino di Studi Bernardiniani*, 1 (1935), pp. 182–190. Pp. 186–190 excerpt Manetti's life of the Sienese saint.

SELECTED MODERN STUDIES

Badaloni, Nicola, "Filosofia della mente e filosofia delle arti in Giannozzo Manetti," *Critica Storica*, 2.4 (1963), pp. 395–450.

Baldassarri, Stefano U., "Clichés and Myth-Making in Giannozzo Manetti's Biographies," *Italian History and Culture*, 8 (2002), pp. 15–33.

Bigi, Emilio, "Dante e la cultura fiorentina del Quattrocento," in idem, *Forme e significati della 'Divina Commedia'* (Bologna: Cappelli, 1981), pp. 145–172.

Connell, William J., "The Humanist Citizen as Provincial Governor," in *Florentine Tuscany: Structures and Practices of Power*, eds. William J. Connell and Andrea Zorzi (Cambridge: Cambridge University Press, 2000), pp. 144–164.

De Petris, Alfonso, "L'*Adversus Judaeos et Gentes* di Giannozzo Manetti," *Rinascimento*, ser. 2, 16 (1976), pp. 193–205.

Dröge, Christoph, *Giannozzo Manetti als Denker und Hebraist* (Frankfurt am Main: Lang, 1987).

Fioravanti, Gianfranco, "L'apologetica anti-giudaica di Giannozzo Manetti," *Rinascimento*, ser. 2, 23 (1983), pp. 3–32.

Fubini, Riccardo, "Leonardo Bruni e la discussa recezione dell'opera: Giannozzo Manetti e il *Dialogus* di Benedetto Accolti," in idem, *L'umanesimo italiano e i suoi storici* (Milan: Franco Angeli, 2001), pp. 104–129.

Glaap, Oliver, *Untersuchungen zu Giannozzo Manetti. 'De Dignitate et excellentia hominis': Ein Renaissance-Humanist und sein Menschenbild* (Stuttgart-Leipzig: Teubner, 1994).

Madrignani, Carlo Alberto, "Di alcune biografie umanistiche di Dante e Petrarca," *Belfagor*, 18 (1963), pp. 29–48.

Martelli, Mario, "Profilo ideologico di Giannozzo Manetti," *Studi Italiani*, 1 (1989), pp. 5–41.

Martines, Lauro, *The Social World of the Florentine Humanists 1390–1460* (Princeton: Princeton University Press, 1963).

Trinkaus, Charles, *In Our Image and Likeness: Humanity and Divinity in Italian Humanist Thought* (Chicago: University of Chicago Press, 1970).

Trivellato, Francesca, "La missione diplomatica a Venezia del fiorentino Giannozzo Manetti a metà Quattrocento," *Studi veneziani*, n.s., 28 (1994), pp. 203–235.

Wittschier, Heinz Willi, "Vespasiano da Bisticci und Giannozzo Manetti," *Romanische Forschungen*, 79.3 (1967), pp. 271–287.

Index

References are by work and paragraph number. A = *Against the Jews and the Gentiles;* B = *Life of Boccaccio;* D = *Life of Dante;* F = *On Famous Men of Great Age;* P = *Life of Petrarca;* Pr = Preface to the *Lives of Three Illustrious Florentine Poets;* Pr2 = Preface to the *Lives of Socrates and Seneca;* Sen = *Life of Seneca;* Soc = *Life of Socrates.*

Publication of this volume has been made possible by

The Myron and Sheila Gilmore Publication Fund at I Tatti

The Robert Lehman Endowment Fund

The Jean-François Malle Scholarly Programs and Publications Fund

The Andrew W. Mellon Scholarly Publications Fund

The Craig and Barbara Smyth Fund
for Scholarly Programs and Publications

The Lila Wallace–Reader's Digest Endowment Fund

The Malcolm Wiener Fund for Scholarly Programs and Publications